SECURED TRANSACTIONS

PROBLEMS AND MATERIALS

SECURED TRANSACTIONS

PROBLEMS AND MATERIALS

NEWLY REVISED FIRST EDITION

Edited by Larry Bates
Professor of Law
Baylor University

Bassim Hamadeh, CEO and Publisher
Carrie Montoya, Manager, Revisions and Author Care
Kaela Martin, Project Editor
Chelsey Schmid, Production Editor
Jess Estrella, Senior Graphic Designer
Alexa Lucido, Licensing Supervisor
Natalie Piccotti, Director of Marketing
Kassie Graves, Vice President of Editorial
Jamie Giganti, Director of Academic Publishing

Cover image copyright © 2010 Depositphotos/Andriy Dykun.
All court cases are in the public domain.

Printed in the United States of America.

ISBN: 978-1-5165-4451-6 (pbk) / 978-1-5165-4452-3 (br)

Dedicated to
Vern Countryman
&
Stan Lehmberg

CONTENTS

PREFACE

This book provides the materials I believe necessary to develop in students a basic understanding of secured financing under Article 9 of the Uniform Commercial Code. My goal in the secured transactions course I teach is to overcome the fear and anxiety with which many students approach codes and statutes by exposing the Code as a system of inter-related and intuitive rules working together to guide the participants in a secured transaction to their desired objectives and to resolve disputes that arise along the way. I'm not trying to turn out a class of experts in secured financing. But, if I'm doing my job, I can instill in them a level of comfort and confidence when it comes to working with Article 9 and the Code that enables them to effectively address the needs of their clients once in practice. And maybe, just maybe, I can also convince them that Article 9 is actually fun.

The book is built around a series of problems that connect the cases and the original material back to the text of Article 9. The objective is to get students to see the Code as the primary source of commercial law rather than as a source that is secondary to judicial interpretation of its provisions. The snapshots of specific provisions provided by the cases can animate the Code for students, but they can also leave students with the false impression that, without the cases, the Code itself is lifeless. That was not Llewellyn's vision for his Code.

I've always preferred textbooks that did not get in the way of how I wanted to teach my classes—that provided me with the materials I needed to teach the course, but that ultimately left the teaching to me. I've tried to be true to that ideal with this book. The cases, problems, and limited text, are intended to provide the materials needed to teach secured transactions—your way.

As are all who teach Article 9, I am indebted to the works of Grant Gilmore, and his two-volume treatise Security Interests in Personal Property (Little,

Brown and Company, 1965) is referenced throughout the text as "Gilmore at" the designated page. Most footnotes have been edited out of the cases, but the numbering of those I thought necessary has been incorporated into the footnote numbering of the text as a whole.

The team at Cognella, Jessica Knott, Jess Busch, and Chelsey Rogers, has been exceptionally helpful and accommodating, and have made putting this book together enjoyable.

Finally, this project would still be only piles of cases and notes on my desk without the dedicated and enthusiastic help of my two research assistants, Saba Syed and Anna Williams. I will miss you both.

CHAPTER 1

SECURED TRANSACTIONS: INTRODUCTION

Our principal focus in this course is on Article 9 of the Uniform Commercial Code. Article 9 is concerned with the creation, priority, and enforcement of security interests in personal property. Although the term "secured transactions" may seem foreign to you at this point, you may have already, at some moment in your life, engaged in such a transaction. When you purchased your car, you probably did so on "credit"—that is you did not pay cash for the car, but rather, you promised to make periodic payments for some defined period of time until the purchase price of the car (plus any interest charged) was paid in full. In return for its agreement to let you have the car today on the basis of your promise to pay for it over time, the dealer most likely took a "security interest" in the car; that is, you gave the dealer the right to take the car—to "repossess" the car—if at any time you failed to make a promised payment. The car became "collateral" and as such "secured" your promise to make payments to the dealer.

As we shall see, secured transactions existed long before Article 9 came about. Article 9 evolved from a drafting process that lasted more than a decade and was intended to bring uniformity to the process of taking, protecting, and enforcing security interests in personal property. Fifty years and one major revision later, it remains a vital component of commercial life in the United States, thanks in part to its drafters' understanding that commercial legislation is more effective when it reflects commercial realities than when it attempts to transform or remake commercial practices. As Grant Gilmore, one of Article 9's principal architects, explained:

> The principal objects of draftsmen of general commercial legislation—by which I mean legislation that is designed to clarify the law about business transaction rather than to change the habits of the business community—are to be accurate and not to be original.

Their intention is to assure that if a given transaction involving commercial paper is initiated, it shall have a specified result; they attempt to state as a matter of law the conclusion which the business community apart from statute and as a matter of fact gives to the transaction in any case. But achievement of these modest goals is a task of considerable difficulty. The draftsman is called upon to build a coherent pattern out of an infinite variety of business customs and practices in an unstable and rapidly changing economy. The more detail and color he loads into his statute, the sooner it will begin to wither on the vine; if, on the other hand, he proceeds from generalization to abstraction, his statute will never be of much use or interest to anyone. The process demands a nice eye, a steady hand, and a sure judgement.[1]

A. SECURED VS. UNSECURED FINANCING

Secured transactions are one form of credit transaction. To understand secured financing, it helps to understand the main alternative to secured financing—unsecured financing. Much of your credit experience to date is likely to have been of the unsecured variety: most credit card transactions are not secured transactions. But credit cards are only one form of unsecured financing. Generally, in unsecured financing, goods are sold or services provided in return for a promise to pay on defined terms. The promise to pay may be memorialized in the form of a promissory note, and the note will set the terms of repayment and detail the promisee's other obligations. But the promise doesn't have to be put in writing—in which case the transaction gives rise to what we call an account receivable. We will develop these variations of the unsecured transaction as we work through the materials in this book. In so doing, we will discover that the rights created in an unsecured transaction themselves can be used as the collateral for a secured transaction.

The distinctive feature of all unsecured financing is that the party providing the goods or services on credit relies exclusively on the other party's promise to pay for them in the future. Consider the journey of a common appliance from manufacturer to you, the consumer:

Maytag builds a wash machine which it sells to a regional distributor. The distributor sells it to a local appliance shop—let's call it Ray's Appliances. Ray then sells the washer to you.

It's the last sale in this series that you and I are familiar with, but that sale is not really any different from the transactions that took the washer from Maytag to Ray. The payment terms between you and Ray are probably different than the terms between Ray and the distributor, but the essence of the transactions is the same. In each transaction, the seller gave up any interest it had in the washer prior to the sale. As a result, if the buyer does not pay—does

---

1   Gilmore, *On the Differences of Codifying Commercial Law*, 57 Yale L. J. 1341 (1948).

not keep its promise—the seller will have to sue the buyer on the buyer's promise, obtain a judgment against the buyer, and then attempt to collect its judgment from the buyer personally. The seller may also be able to enforce that judgment against the buyer's personal property—but the seller will not have an exclusive claim to any particular property of the buyer.

If instead, each of the transactions in the washer's journey were secured, the seller would have retained an interest in the washer and that interest would have entitled the seller to take back—repossess—the washer without resort to judicial process if the buyer stopped making the promised payments. In each transaction, the buyer owned the washer, but subject to the right of the seller to repossess on default. The interest retained by the seller is what the Uniform Commercial Code calls a "security interest" and it's these security interests that are the subject of Article 9.

Much of Article 9 is intended to deal with the transactions in our washer's journey that precede the sale to you, the consumer. But Article 9 does govern transactions involving consumers, sometimes applying special rules to those transactions. So, some of the transactions we discuss will seem quite familiar to you. But others, because they take place upstream from the sale to a consumer or because they do not actually involve the purchase of goods like wash machines, may seem very foreign to you. Sometimes just trying to figure out what it is that the parties are using as the collateral for a loan can be a challenge. If the parties to a transaction can identify an attribute of personal property and agree to assign a value to it—they can build a credit transaction around that attribute—that attribute (whatever they call it) can serve as collateral for a loan. If, for example, Lady Gaga turned a song you wrote and copyrighted during your first year of law school into her next hit record, you could use your copyright interest as collateral for a loan. Copyrights are personal property even though they are not tangible property like a wash machine. The royalty payments you would be entitled to based on the millions of records she sells give your copyright value—thanks to Lady Gaga it's become income-generating property and a most desirable form of collateral for many lenders.

Alternatively, you could use the right to royalty payments attribute of your copyright by itself as collateral. Upon your default, the lender would be entitled to the stream of payments from Lady Gaga but not the copyright itself. And if your lender had been taking as collateral the rights to royalty payments of other songwriters, the lender could bundle together all of its security interests in songwriters' rights to royalty payments and use that bundle as collateral for a loan of its own. The lender's rights to all of the songwriters' rights has a value, just like the wash machine you bought from Ray. And as we will soon see, almost anything that has value—no matter how abstract that value—can support a secured transaction.

B. A BRIEF HISTORY OF SECURITY INTERESTS IN PERSONAL PROPERTY BEFORE THE CODE

In today's world, it's hard for most of us to imagine life without credit—credit cards, car loans, school loans, home loans; but credit—especially unsecured credit—has not always been so ubiquitous or so cheap. And certainly not for individuals—for consumers. The road to plentiful credit was a long and arduous road, with many battles along the way. One of the most protracted of these battles was the battle to liberate personal property financing from the perception of fraud that had claimed it for centuries. Why was a transaction so common place today universally portrayed as fraudulent at the inception of our country? What was the evil perpetrated when a borrower put up her personal property as collateral to secure a loan or some other advance of credit? As the *Barlow* case reveals, the answer is really rather simple.

BARLOW v. FOX
Supreme Court of Pennsylvania
52 A. 57 (Pa.1902)

FELL, *Justice.*

When by the action of the parties there has been a separation of the title and possession of personal property, courts will scrutinize the transaction to determine the real intention, and but little regard will be given to the form which it has taken or the name by which it is called. The law is liberal in not requiring an actual change of possession when it will defeat the lawful purpose of the parties. But there has been no deviation from the general rule that delivery of possession is indispensable to transfer a title, by the act of the owner, that shall be valid against creditors. In *Clow v. Woods*, 5 S. & R. 275, which is said by Judge SHARSWOOD in *McKibbin v. Martin*, 64 Pa. 352, to be "the magna charta of our law on the subject," it was decided that there is no difference in the application of the rule between absolute sales and contingent sales or mortgages, and that as to both the retention of possession when actual delivery is practicable, is a fraud in law. In *Jenkins v. Eichelberger*, 4 Watts, 121, GIBSON, C.J., said: "To tolerate a lien severed from the possession by any device whatever, would be pregnant with all the mischiefs of colorable owner-ship; and to sanction it at the expense of the community could be justified but by the accomplishment of more important objects than individual accom-modation." These decisions have been followed in numerous cases which it is needless to cite. In a review of the cases in this state by the American editors of 1 Smith's Leading Cases, p. 78, it is said: "That mortgages are within the rule has been expressly decided; and it is now established in Pennsylvania, as a general principle of law, that by no device whatever, whether of sale and agreement of resale, or by the title at the time of the purchase being vested in one who is a surety for the purchaser who takes possession, can a lien be created on personal property separate from the possession of it. The delivery must be actual and not merely symbolical where actual delivery is practicable, and if it is not practicable the parties should leave nothing undone to secure the public from deception."

The facts on which a verdict for the defendant was directed were these: Edwards sold the personal property in a hotel to Oliver Brothers for $10,000. They paid $4,000 and went into possession, agreeing to pay the balance in four equal annual installments. They paid the first three annual installments as they became due. Before the fourth was due, Edwards wanted the money, and to oblige him an arrangement was made to obtain it from the Citizens' National Bank of Corry. The parties gave the bank their joint note for $1,500. Oliver Brothers executed a written cancelation of their contract of purchase so as to place the title to the furniture in Edwards, who sold it to Barlow, trustee for the bank, and he leased it to Oliver Brothers for one year for $1,500 with interest. There was no delivery, actual or symbolical, and Barlow never had possession of the furniture in any manner or form. The cancelation of the first contract, the sale to the trustee, and the lease by him were all one transaction, intended to secure the payment of the note. The note was renewed from time to time until the firm of Oliver Brothers was dissolved by the withdrawal of one of its members, and a new firm of Oliver & English was formed. This firm took up the note of Oliver Brothers and gave the bank its note in place thereof, and a new lease was made by the trustee to it. This new arrangement was continued by renewals of the note and lease for over two years, when Oliver & English were adjudged bankrupt, and their interest in the furniture was sold by the trustee in bankruptcy to the defendant, against whom this action was brought by Barlow, trustee for the bank.

There was not a sale to Barlow and a bailment for use by him except in form merely. It was not intended that he should become the real owner of the furniture and that Oliver Brothers should pay him rent for its use. The rent reserved by the so-called lease was the exact amount of the note, and what was paid was interest for the use of the money, not rent for the use of the furniture. The apparent, in fact the avowed, purpose of the whole arrangement was to secure the bank by the pledge of the goods. This pledge was invalid against the creditors of the last firm as well as those of the first. Oliver & English came into possession of the property as owners, and there was a novation. They assumed the debt, took up the note of Oliver Brothers, gave their note in place of it, and pledged their own goods to secure its payment.

The judgment is affirmed.

The *Barlow* opinion reflects the early Anglo-American view that there was something inherently dishonest about separating title from possession—many courts proclaimed simply that when title is separated from possession fraud results. This was the ostensible ownership problem the court referenced in *Barlow*. Courts early on had equated possession with ownership and required anyone claiming an interest in personal property to do something that would put others on notice of that claim. The fear was that a debtor with possession of and control over the collateral would be in a position to mislead others with whom she dealt—creditors could be induced to extend credit on the basis that her property was unencumbered. See Gilmore, at 438-39. As the court in *Clow*, which the Barlow court referred to as "the Magna Carta" of the anti-security interest movement, admonished:

> The law will not and ought not to permit the owner of personal property to create an interest in another, either by mortgage or absolute sale, and still to continue to be the ostensible owner; and where the creating of such an interest is the sole object, the conveyance will be fraudulent. ...
>
> 5 Serg. & Rawle 279.

In *Barlow*, anyone contemplating extending credit to the Oliver brothers would have presumed that because the hotel furniture was in their possession, there were no other claims to it—and would have learned otherwise only if the brothers had revealed their arrangement with Barlow. As a result, the court struck down the arrangement without remorse.

But the Barlows of the world never lost their faith in the cause. Gilmore likened their movement to legitimize security interests in personal property to guerrilla warfare:

> For over a hundred and fifty years ... the forces of the establishment, led by the judiciary, black robes flying and pens at the ready, have campaigned against the guerrilla bands of the personal property security people. The judicial literature is a long paean of denunciation in which the constructive fraud inherent in superficially innocent transactions is astutely detected and relentlessly laid bare. But the guerillas, worsted at each encounter, always fled to fight another day. And from time to time the guerrillas managed to establish a beachhead, to occupy an enclave, to settle down on some bit of unwanted territory—either because the Establishment was momentarily distracted by affairs of greater moment or because the guerrillas had cleverly disguised themselves in the armor of the righteous, or because, in the long run, even the most gallant defender of the faith will have his moment of weakness.[2]

Parties seeking to use personal property as collateral did have an alternative to the *Barlow*-type arrangement—it was called a pledge. The pledge alternative solved the ostensible ownership problem because the creditor—the secured party—took possession of the collateral. If Barlow had taken possession of the hotel furniture, no one dealing with the Oliver brothers could have been misled because no one would have believed the brothers owned furniture not in their possession. Of course for most debtors, the pledge was not practical. Imagine the reaction of customers booking rooms at the brothers' hotel when they were

---

2 Gilmore, *Security Law, Formalism and Article 9*, 47 Neb. L. Rev. 659, 659 (1968).

told that the bed they were expecting to be in their room was up the street and around the corner at a place called Barlow's. How useful would the washer you bought on credit from Ray be to you if you had to take your laundry to Ray's store to use the washer? And imagine how happy Ray would be to see you each week as you dragged your bags of dirty clothes across his showroom floor.

As we will see later, the solution to the ostensible ownership problem was relatively simple: create a filing system open to the public where secured creditors could record their non-possessory security interests. Subsequent creditors dealing with the Oliver Brothers would check the filing system and discover Barlow's interest in the hotel furniture. But there were more battles to be fought before we get to that filing system.

In many businesses, the primary assets available to use as collateral are not tangible property like hotel furniture, but are intangibles—property we recognize as existing even though we can't see it, hold it, or pass it around the room. The right of a business to be paid for services or goods it has provided to customers—its account receivables—are often the most valuable asset of a business. Since an account receivable has no tangible form, there would appear to be no ostensible ownership problem if a creditor accepted it as collateral for a loan. If there is no potential for fraud, then the courts would have no basis for invalidating such arrangements. But as Justice Brandeis explains in the next case, ostensible ownership is not the only means of perpetrating fraud on third parties.

BENEDICT v. RATNER
Supreme Court of the United States
268 U.S. 353 (1925)

BRANDEIS, *Justice.*

B = RECEIVER + TRUSTEE

The Hub Carpet Company was adjudicated bankrupt by the federal court for southern New York in involuntary proceedings commenced September 26, 1921. Benedict, who was appointed receiver and later trustee, collected the book accounts of the company. Ratner filed in that court a petition in equity praying that the amounts so collected be paid over to him. He claimed them under a writing given May 23, 1921—four months and three days before the commencement of the bankruptcy proceedings. By it the company purported to assign to him, as collateral for certain loans, all accounts present and future. Those collected by the receiver were, so far as appears, all accounts which had arisen after the date of the assignment, and were enumerated in the monthly list of accounts outstanding which was delivered to Ratner September 23. Benedict resisted the petition on the ground that the original assignment was void under the law of New York as a fraudulent conveyance; that, for this reason, the delivery of the September list of accounts was inoperative to perfect a lien in Ratner; and that it was a preference under the Bankruptcy Act. He also filed a cross-petition in which he asked that Ratner be ordered to pay to the estate the proceeds of certain collections which had been made by the company after September 17 and turned over to Ratner pursuant to his request made on that day. The company was then insolvent and Ratner had reason to believe it to be so. These accounts also had apparently been acquired by the company after the date of the original assignment.

The District Judge decided both petitions in Ratner's favor. He ruled that the assignment executed in May was not fraudulent in law; that it created an equity in the future acquired accounts; that because of this equity, Ratner was entitled to retain, as against the bankrupt's estate, the proceeds of the accounts which had been collected by the company in September and turned over to him; that by delivery of the list of the accounts outstanding on September 23, this equity in them had ripened into a perfect title to the remaining accounts; and that the title so perfected was good as against the supervening bankruptcy. Accordingly, the District Court ordered that, to the extent of the balance remaining unpaid on his loans, there be paid Ratner all collections made from accounts enumerated in any of the lists delivered to Ratner; and that the cross-petition of Benedict be denied. There was no finding of fraud in fact. On appeal, the Circuit Court of Appeals affirmed the order. *282 Fed. 12.* A writ of certiorari was granted by this Court. *259 U.S. 579.*

The rights of the parties depend primarily upon the law of New York. *Hiscock v. Varick Bank of N. Y., 206 U.S. 28.* It may be assumed that, unless the arrangement of May 23 was void because fraudulent in law, the original assignment of the future acquired accounts became operative under the state law, both as to those paid over to Ratner before the bankruptcy proceedings and as to those collected by the receiver; and that the assignment will be deemed to have taken effect as of May 23. *Sexton v. Kessler, 225 U.S. 90, 99.* That being so, it is clear that, if the original assignment was a valid one under the law of New York, the Bankruptcy Act did not invalidate the subsequent dealings of the parties. *Thompson v. Fairbanks, 196 U.S. 516.* The sole question for decision is, therefore, whether on the following undisputed facts the assignment of May 23 was in law fraudulent.

The Hub Carpet Company was, on May 23, a mercantile concern doing business in New York City and proposing to continue to do so. The assignment was made there to secure an existing loan of $15,000, and further advances not exceeding $15,000 which were in fact made July 1, 1921. It included all accounts receivable then outstanding and all which should thereafter accrue in the ordinary course of business. A list of the existing accounts was delivered at the time. Similar lists were to be delivered to Ratner on or about the 23d day of each succeeding month containing the accounts outstanding at such future dates. Those enumerated in each of the lists delivered prior to September, aggregated between $100,000 and $120,000. The receivables were to be collected by the company. Ratner was given the right, at any time, to demand a full disclosure of the business and financial conditions; to require that all amounts collected be applied in payment of his loans; and to enforce the assignment although no loan had matured. But until he did so, the company was not required to apply any of the collections to the repayment of Ratner's loan. It was not required to replace accounts collected by other collateral of equal value. It was not required to account in any way to Ratner. It was at liberty to use the proceeds of all accounts collected as it might see fit. The existence of the assignment was to be kept secret. The business was to be conducted as theretofore. Indebtedness was to be incurred, as usual, for the purchase of merchandise and otherwise in the ordinary course of business. The amount of such indebtedness unpaid at the time of the commencement of the bankruptcy proceedings was large. Prior to September 17, the company collected from accounts so assigned about $150,000, all of which it applied to purposes other than the payment of Ratner's loan. The outstanding accounts enumerated in the list delivered September 23 aggregated $ 90,000.

Under the law of New York a transfer of property as security which reserves to the transferor the right to dispose of the same, or to apply the proceeds thereof, for his own uses is, as to creditors, fraudulent in law and void. This is true whether the right of disposition for the transferor's use be reserved in the instrument or by agreement *in pais*, oral or written; whether the right of disposition reserved be unlimited in time or be expressly terminable by the happening of an event; whether the transfer cover [sic] all the property of the debtor or only a part; whether the right of disposition extends to all the property transferred or only to a part thereof; and whether the instrument of transfer be recorded or not.

If this rule applies to the assignment of book accounts, the arrangement of May 23 was clearly void; and the equity in the future acquired accounts, which it would otherwise have created, did not arise. Whether the rule applies to accounts does not appear to have been passed upon by the Court of Appeals of New York. But it would seem clear that whether the collateral consist of chattels or of accounts, reservation of dominion inconsistent with the effective disposition of title must render the transaction void. Ratner asserts that the rule stated above rests upon ostensible ownership, and argues that the doctrine of ostensible ownership is not applicable to book accounts. That doctrine raises a presumption of fraud where chattels are mortgaged (or sold) and possession of the property is not delivered to the mortgagee (or vendee). The presumption may be avoided by recording the mortgage (or sale). It may be assumed, as Ratner contends, that the doctrine does not apply to the assignment of accounts. In their transfer there is nothing which corresponds to the delivery of possession of chattels. The statutes which embody the doctrine and provide for recording as a substitute for delivery do not include accounts. A title to an account good against creditors may be transferred without notice to the debtor or record of any kind. But it is not true that the rule stated above and invoked by the receiver is either based upon or delimited by the doctrine of ostensible ownership. It rests not upon seeming ownership because of possession retained, but upon a lack of ownership because of dominion reserved. It does not raise a presumption of fraud. It imputes fraud conclusively because of the reservation of dominion inconsistent with the effective disposition of title and creation of a lien.

The nature of the rule is made clear by its limitations. Where the mortgagor of chattels agrees to apply the proceeds of their sale to the payment of the mortgage debt or to the purchase of other chattels which shall become subject to the lien, the mortgage is good as against creditors, if recorded. The mortgage is sustained in such cases "upon the ground that such sale and application of proceeds is the normal and proper purpose of a chattel mortgage, and within the precise boundaries of its lawful operation and effect. It does no more than to substitute the mortgagor as the agent of the mortgagee to do exactly what the latter had the right to do, and what it was his privilege and his duty to accomplish. It devotes, as it should, the mortgaged property to the payment of the mortgage debt." The permission to use the proceeds to furnish substitute collateral "provides only for a shifting of the lien from one piece of property to another taken in exchange." *Brackett v. Harvey, 91 N. Y. 214, 221, 223.* On the other hand, if the agreement is that the mortgagor may sell and use the proceeds for his own benefit, the mortgage is of no effect although recorded. Seeming ownership exists in both classes of cases because the mortgagor is permitted to remain in possession of the stock in trade and to sell it freely. But it is only where the unrestricted dominion over the proceeds is reserved to the mortgagor that the mortgage is void. This dominion is the differentiating and deciding element. The distinction was recognized in *Sexton v. Kessler, 225 U.S. 90, 98,* where a transfer of securities was sustained. It was pointed out that a reservation of full control by the mortgagor might well prevent the effective creation of a lien in the mortgagee and that the New York cases holding such a mortgage void rest upon that doctrine.

The results which flow from reserving dominion inconsistent with the effective disposition of title must be the same whatever the nature of the property transferred. The doctrine which imputes fraud where full dominion is reserved must apply to assignments of accounts although the doctrine of ostensible ownership does not. There must also be the same distinction as to degrees of dominion. Thus, although an agreement that the assignor of accounts shall collect them and pay the proceeds to the assignee will not invalidate the assignment which it accompanies, the assignment must be deemed fraudulent in law if it is agreed that the assignor may use the proceeds as he sees fit.

In the case at bar, the arrangement for the unfettered use by the company of the proceeds of the accounts precluded the effective creation of a lien and rendered the original assignment fraudulent in law. Consequently the payments to Ratner and the delivery of the September list of accounts were inoperative to perfect a lien in him, and were unlawful preferences. On this ground, and also because the payment was fraudulent under the law of the State, the trustee was entitled to recover the amount.

Reversed.

Although *Barlow's* ostensible ownership and *Benedict's* unfettered dominion would seem to be the classic opposite sides of the same coin situation, the response to each of these problems was markedly different. There appeared to be, short of legislative action, no solution for the ostensible ownership problem. But within Justice Brandeis's opinion, Gilmore's guerrillas found an opening they could exploit. *Benedict* stops short of declaring all such arrangements invalid. It was simply a matter of degree—something less than unfettered dominion over the accounts that were to serve as collateral was required. And as Gilmore noted, those seeking to liberate accounts receivables from the chains of fraud moved quickly:

> After having read Justice Brandeis's stern and uncompromising opinion, a student, ignorant of the history of this peculiar field, might reasonably have assumed that *Benedict* had dealt such arrangements their death blow. The truth of the matter is that, within ten years after *Benedict* and indeed as the direct result of *Benedict*, there had been a sensational increase in the volume of receivables financing arrangements under which the account debtors were not notified of the assignment and the assignor made collections he then used on the ordinary course of his business.[3]

C. COUNTERING [NEUTRALIZING] THE OSTENSIBLE OWNERSHIP PROBLEM

Although Gilmore's guerrillas may have lost the day in cases like *Barlow* and *Benedict*, their wills were never completely broken. Each defeat only sent them back to their workshops more determined than ever to recast their non-possessory security interest as a new form that would neutralize the ostensible ownership problem and find a modicum of acceptance. Usually, a successful reformulation required legislative assistance. Thus, for example, by the time Article 9 was ready, most states had enacted some form of what came to be known as a chattel mortgage act, which validated under specified circumstances non-possessory security interests in personal property. The chattel mortgage acts solved the ostensible ownership problem by creating a recording system for security interests in personal property that made such interests discoverable to subsequent creditors dealing with the debtor. Courts were bound to follow these acts, but often did so begrudgingly, at least initially, by interpreting the acts as doing nothing more than rebutting the presumption that such arrangements were fraudulent. *See* Gilmore, at 27. And deficiencies in the chattel mortgage acts often limited their utility. For example, because the early chattel mortgage acts invalidated a security interest if the debtor was authorized to sell the collateral, inventory financing was still a problem. Most dealers in goods can't afford to pay cash for the inventory they stock. If Maytag could not take an enforceable security interest in the wash machines it sold to Ray to secure Ray's promise to pay for the washers because Ray

---

3   Gilmore, 47 Neb. L. Rev. 664.

planned on selling the washers to customers like you, Ray might not have any washers—or other appliances—to sell.

So, Gilmore's guerillas opened up a new front. By the time of the court's decision in *Benedict*, field warehousing, in essence a modified form of pledge, had established its validity as a way to take inventory as collateral even though the secured party itself did not have actual possession of the inventory. In a field warehouse arrangement, the debtor would lease space to a field warehouse company which would then take control of the space by sealing it off from the rest of the debtor's premises. Signs would be posted on the perimeter alerting all that the segregated space and the goods within it were under the custody and control of the warehouse company—as opposed to the debtor who otherwise appeared to occupy the premises – in theory solving the ostensible ownership problem. The company would then issue a warehouse receipt covering the sequestered goods to the bank which provided the loan to be secured by the inventory. The bank could claim possession of the goods through the warehouse company as its agent—so no ostensible ownership issue—and the goods could be made available to the debtor on the terms pro-vided by the loan agreement. Over time, lenders were allowed to release the collateral to the debtor for temporary and limited purposes—e.g., to process for sale or for repairs—without risk of invalidating their claim to the goods.

Other deficiencies in the chattel mortgage acts were attacked and counter-attacked. And there were other triumphs along the way, but at the end of the day these triumphs were overshadowed by what Gilmore called the "intolerable complexity" by which such progress was marked. The more complex things became the greater the need for professionals who specialized in performing the rituals necessary to create a valid security interest in personal property, all of which drove up the costs of secured financing. As Gilmore later explained:

> Eventually, of course, the personal property people had their way—but the point of enduring consequence is that they had their way in a complicated, devious, and even underground fashion. In time it became possible, throughout the country, to finance on the security of inventory and receivable, to cover after-acquired property and to provide for future advances. What did not become possible—we are still talking about pre-Code law—was to do any of these things simply.[4]

Article 9 was an attempt to return secured financing to a level of simplicity that reflected what Gilmore called the relative simplicity of a secured transaction.

D. ADVANTAGES OF SECURED FINANCING

What was so special about the non-possessory security interest in personal property that drove Gilmore's guerrillas to fight on so long for their cause?

4   Gilmore, 47 Neb. L. Rev. 660

What made it so important that it was one of the eight areas of commercial law that a uniform commercial code could not live without? Secured financing has several distinct advantages for creditors over unsecured financing. First, when credit is secured by collateral, the collateral provides the creditor with a second chance for payment if the debtor defaults. The secured creditor can repossess and sell the collateral and apply the proceeds from the sale to pay off at least part of the balance owing on the credit after default. How much of the outstanding balance the collateral will cover varies greatly, depending on, among other things, whether the loan was fully secured, the nature of the collateral, and whether it was a commercial or consumer transaction. For example, consumer goods generally depreciate in value much more rapidly than does business collateral. The couch in your apartment that you paid $1,000 for last year for is not worth anything close to that after you and your friends have spilled guacamole dip on it while watching this season of Big Brother. Industrial equipment, on the other hand, if properly maintained, might retain considerable residual value even after prolonged use.

Second, collateral gives the secured creditor leverage it can use to control uncooperative debtors. The threat of immediate repossession might cause a defaulting debtor to re-prioritize its payment obligations. This is true even in the consumer context because we tend to think of our possessions in terms of what we originally paid for them, not what someone else might be willing to pay for them today. You paid $1,000 for your couch and that's what it's worth to you—it will cost you another $1,000 to replace it—even though it might fetch $100 tops at a garage sale. The lender's threat to repossess it might help you kick the $10-a-day frothy coconut latte habit. And the lender's threat to repossess a piece of equipment necessary to operate the debtor's business creates a powerful incentive for her to make sure the lender gets paid even when others don't.

Third, secured creditors do not have to be first in line at the courthouse door to protect their interests when the debtor suffers total financial melt-down—and maybe even ends up in bankruptcy. Most debtors have more than one creditor. When meltdown occurs, unsecured creditors compete with each other to grab as many of the debtors assets as necessary to satisfy their claims. Since meltdown usually means the debtor's liabilities exceed her assets, there won't be enough to satisfy all claims. The unsecured creditors who get to the courthouse, have their claim reduced to judgment, and are able to enforce their judgments against the debtor's property first, win. Everyone else loses. Except for secured creditors. A secured creditor has a claim to specifically identified assets of the debtor—the collateral—and that claim is superior to any unsecured creditor—even an unsecured creditor that has executed on its judgment. Unsecured creditors take a secured party's collateral subject to the security interest.

If the debtor ends up in bankruptcy, the race between the unsecured creditors is over. The Bankruptcy Code stays the enforcement of all claims against the debtor's assets and compels all unsecured creditors to share in the debtor's assets on a pro rata basis. Since liabilities exceed assets, no unsecured creditor gets paid in full. In fact, in most bankruptcies, unsecured creditors who get paid 10% of their claims will be doing better than average. And it can get worse. Unsecured creditors who happened to grab any of the debtor's assets within 90 days of the start of bankruptcy or who happened to be paid by the debtor during that period received what bankruptcy law calls a preference, and will have to pay back to the bankruptcy estate the value of whatever they got.

Secured creditors, on the other hand, fare much better in bankruptcy. Bankruptcy law recognizes their claim to their collateral, and although the bankruptcy stay prevents them from enforcing their claims against the collateral initially, the Bankruptcy Code does provide them with a process to get relief from that stay and enforce their claims against the collateral. In the alternative, bankruptcy law requires that secured creditors be paid the value of their collateral—they are not limited to a pro rata share from the total asset pool of the debtor like unsecured creditors are. And, secured creditors—subject to a few exceptions—cannot receive preferences; secured creditors get to keep whatever payments they received from the debtor or any collateral they repossessed within the 90 days preceding the start of the debtor's bankruptcy case.

Now, this summary of the advantages of the secured vs. the unsecured creditor is somewhat over-simplified. Sometimes a secured creditor is also an unsecured creditor—when the value of the collateral is less than the amount the debtor owes (the creditor is "undersecured")—the creditor wears the hat of both a secured an unsecured creditor. Often times there are secured creditors competing for the same collateral because the debtor has given a security interest in the collateral to each. But, the basic picture of why one might prefer to be a secured creditor rather than an unsecured creditor, is still helpful at this point as we begin our more detailed examination of Article 9 and secured financing.

CHAPTER 2

ARTICLE 9: SCOPE

We begin our journey through Article 9 by identifying the transactions to which it actually applies. Initially, Article 9 stakes out a very broad claim to the territory it covers but then proceeds to carve out of that territory those transactions not so important to commercial practice as to require the uniformity generally provided by the Code, or that are regulated elsewhere. The broad coverage was intended in part to prevent the proliferation of independent forms of secured financing that had undermined pre-Code statutory efforts to systematize specific forms of secured financing. The initial assessment of whether a transaction is covered by Article 9 is critical: If Article 9 applies, the parties must comply with the requirements of Article 9 or risk having their expectations upset by subsequent events.

The basic scope provision of Article 9, 9-109(a)(1), tells us that Article 9 cares about transactions that, regardless of their form, create security interests in personal property by contract. A security interest is defined in 1-201(35) as "an interest in personal property … that secures payment or performance of an obligation." So, Article 9 cares about transactions that create an interest in personal property for the purpose of securing the payment or performance of an obligation. But only when that interest in personal property is created "by contract". Is a lien asserted under the Internal Revenue Code against all of your property—real and personal—for delinquent taxes a security interest created by contract? It secures payment of your tax obligation. By limiting its scope to security interests created by contract, Article 9 is telling us that it cares about security interests created by agreement between the parties—consensual security interests. Security interests imposed by statute—like the IRS lien—are not consensual interests and therefore are not created by agreement. And because they are not created by agreement they are not covered by Article 9.

Section 9-109(a)(1) also tells us that Article 9 applies to consensual transactions that create interests in personal property to secure payment or performance of an obligation "regardless of form," making clear that Article 9 coverage is a matter of substance—function—rather than form. Comment 2 to 9-109 explains:

> When a security interest is created, this Article applies regardless of the form of the transaction or the name that parties have given to it. Likewise, the subjective intention of the parties with respect to the legal characterization of their transaction is irrelevant to whether this Article applies.

If, under the circumstances, an interest given in personal property functions to secure payment or performance of an obligation, it's a security interest and Article 9 cares about it no matter what the parties call it. A security interest can be created in the absence of terms like debtor, secured party, security interest, or collateral. You can call it a duck, a pig, or a cow, but if it functions as a security interest, that's what it is and if its consensual, Article 9 will care about it.

PROBLEM 2–1

Ray sells you a washer-dryer combo for $1200. You sign a contract that requires you to pay $100 each month until the purchase price plus finance charge is paid in full. You stop making payments after five months. Can Ray come and get the washer-dryer—repossess the washer-dryer?

Ray sells you a washer-dryer combo for $1200, but this time you sign a contract that requires you to pay $100 each month until the purchase price plus finance charge is paid in full and provides that Ray will retain title to the washer-dryer combo until you make the final payment. You stop making payments after five months. Can Ray repossess the washer-dryer combo? See 1-201(35).

You take your broken vacuum cleaner to Ray for repairs. When you stop by to pick it up a few days later, the repair charge is more than you expected so you tell Ray you'll pay him next week when your student loan comes in. Ray informs you that under a state statute, he has a lien on the vacuum until you pay for the repairs, so he will keep it at the shop until you pay. Can Ray keep your vacuum cleaner if he has not taken the steps required by Article 9 to create a security interest in it? See 9-109(a)(1) and (d)(2).

Ray leases you a washer-dryer combo for one year, at a rent of $100 per month. The lease requires you to return the washer-dryer combo to Ray at the end of the twelfth month. Does Article 9 care about the interest in the washer-dryer combo that Ray retains as lessor?

A. LEASE OR DISGUISED SALE ON CREDIT?

Not so long ago, most of us assumed that the only way to acquire the things we needed or wanted was to buy them—and in the case of items like cars, major appliances, furniture, and the like, that meant buying on credit. But today more and more of us are finding that leasing is a viable alternative to acquiring such things on credit. The leasing of personal property is hardly a new concept, businesses have been acquiring the machines and equipment necessary for their operations by lease for many years. Commercial equipment leasing is a $725 billion industry.

Why has leasing been so important to businesses and why is it becoming so important to consumers? The answer lies in the core differences between a lease and a sale on credit, and the implications of those differences. In a sale on credit, the buyer becomes the owner of the goods—it acquires both title and the right to use the goods. The seller does not expect to get the goods back—it retains only the inchoate right to take the goods back on the buyer's default, to "repossess" the goods. The repossessed goods are then sold, and the proceeds applied to pay down the buyer's obligation. In a lease, the lessee acquires the right to use the goods for the term of the lease—title (ownership) stays with the lessor and thus the lessor expects to get the goods back at the end of the term. The lessor is entitled to take the goods back on default, but the lessee gets no credit for their value against any remaining payments owed under the lease.

Because the lessee does not become the owner of the goods, the economics of a lease can be more favorable to a lessee than a credit transaction. Leases are usually 100% financed—so no down payment is required. Since the lessee is only acquiring the use of the goods for a period of time, rent payments are often lower than credit payments. Poor credit scores may preclude a sale on credit but not a lease. Or a debtor may have agreed with its other creditors not to encumber its personal property. If the goods are only needed for a limited purpose, there may be no reason to acquire the goods for a period longer than necessary to fulfill the purpose. Rent payments are deductible in their entirety as a business expense; a buyer can only deduct interest expense and depreciation. Lease expenses are not required to be carried as debt on a company's balance sheet, improving the debt to equity ratio which could help attract investors.

In the consumer context, the lower monthly payments under a lease and the ability to walk away from the goods at the end of the lease can make a lease more attractive than a sale on credit.

By now you're probably wondering what any of this has to do with Article 9. Leases can implicate Article 9 if they are structured so as to give the lessee more than just a right to use the goods. Remember, under Article 9 substance trumps form. If the actual effect of a transaction in the form of a lease is to create a security interest, then Article 9 claims it regardless of what the parties call it. The parties can't disguise a secured transaction as a lease and avoid the requirements of Article 9. But why would they try to do so? If I lease for five years a combine that has a working life of 10 years, at the end of the lease I have to turn it over to the lessor even though I may have paid 100%

(my lease payments) of the total purchase price for 50% of the useful life of the combine. That's the way a "true" lease works—my lease payments do not get me an ownership interest. But I want all of the benefits of a lease and I also want my lease payments to give me something more than just possession of the combine—I also want the equity a buyer on credit would have in the combine. So, I want the lease structured to give me the benefits of leasing and buying the combine.

The issue of whether a lease was a disguised secured transaction was frequently litigated under pre-Code law. As Gilmore explained:

> [A] considerable body of case law developed on the distinction btwen "true" leases ... and "false" ones which would be treated as [a] disguised security transaction. ... With respect to leases, the pre-Code distinction between true leases and security leases was usually said to depend on whether or not the "lessee" had the option of becoming the owner of the property after paying an amount of "rent" equivalent to the purchase price of the goods. If he had such an option, the lease was a security lease; if not, not.

Gilmore at 337–38.

As the *Marhoffer* case illustrates, the Code rejected this single factor test and instead instructed the courts to consider the totality of the circumstances. Unfortunately, the Code's failure to provide more specific guidelines for determining whether a lease was a lease or a disguised secured transaction resulted in a body of case law that was confused and inconsistent at best. The 1987 amendments to the definition of security interest in Article 1 addressed the problem, and these amendments have been carried forward into Revised Article 1. Although the *Marhoffer* case was decided before the 1987 amendments to Article 1, those amendments clearly were derived from the analysis of the lease versus secured transaction issue reflected in *Marhoefer* and cases like it.

IN THE MATTER OF: MARHOEFER PACKING COMPANY, INC.
United States Court of Appeals for the Seventh Circuit
674 F.2d 1139 (7th Cir. 1982)

PELL, *Circuit Judge*.

This appeal involves a dispute between the trustee of the bankrupt Marhoefer Packing Company, Inc., ("Marhoefer") and Robert Reiser & Company, Inc., ("Reiser") over certain equipment held by Marhoefer at the time of bankruptcy. The issue presented is whether the written agreement between Marhoefer and Reiser covering the equipment is a true lease under which Reiser is entitled to reclaim its property from the bankrupt estate, or whether it is actually a lease intended as security in which case Reiser's failure to file a financing statement to perfect its interest renders it subordinate to the trustee.

I.

In December of 1976, Marhoefer Packing Co., Inc., of Muncie, Indiana, entered into negotiations with Reiser, a Massachusetts based corporation engaged in the business of selling and leasing food processing equipment, for the acquisition of one or possibly two Vemag Model 3007-1 Continuous Sausage Stuffers. Reiser informed Marhoefer that the units could be acquired by outright purchase, conditional sale contract or lease. Marhoefer ultimately acquired two sausage stuffers from Reiser. It purchased one under a conditional sale contract. Pursuant to the contract, Reiser retained a security interest in the machine, which it subsequently perfected by filing a financing statement with the Indiana Secretary of State. Title to that stuffer is not here in dispute. The other stuffer was delivered to Marhoefer under a written "Lease Agreement."

The Lease Agreement provided for monthly payments of $665.00 over a term of 48 months. The last nine months' payments, totaling $5,985.00, were payable upon execution of the lease. If at the end of the lease term the machine was to be returned, it was to be shipped prepaid to Boston or similar destination "in the same condition as when received, reasonable wear and tear resulting from proper use alone excepted, and fully crated." The remaining terms and conditions of the agreement were as follows:

1. Any State or local taxes and/or excises are for the account of the Buyer.

2. The equipment shall at all times be located at

    Marhoefer Packing Co., Inc.
    1500 North Elm & 13th Street
    Muncie, Indiana

    and shall not be removed from said location without the written consent of Robert Reiser & Co. The equipment can only be used in conjunction with the manufacture of meat or similar products unless written consent is given by Robert Reiser & Co.

3. The equipment will carry a ninety-day guarantee for workmanship and materials and shall be maintained and operated safely and carefully in conformity with the instructions issued by our operators and the maintenance manual. Service and repairs of the equipment after the ninety-day period will be subject to a reasonable and fair charge.

4. If, after due warning, our maintenance instructions should be violated repeatedly, Robert Reiser & Co. will have the right to cancel the lease contract on seven days notice and remove the said equipment. In that case, lease fees would be refunded pro rata.

5. It is mutually agreed that in case of lessee, Marhoefer Packing Co., Inc., violating any of the above conditions, or shall default in the payment of

any lease charge hereunder, or shall become bankrupt, make or execute any assignment or become party to any instrument or proceedings for the benefit of its creditors, Robert Reiser & Co. shall have the right at any time without trespass, to enter upon the premises and remove the aforesaid equipment, and if removed, lessee agrees to pay Robert Reiser & Co. the total lease fees, including all installments due or to become due for the full unexpired term of this lease agreement and including the cost for removal of the equipment and counsel fees incurred in collecting sums due hereunder.

6. It is agreed that the equipment shall remain personal property of Robert Reiser & Co. and retain its character as such no matter in what manner affixed or attached to the premises.

In a letter accompanying the lease, Reiser added two option provisions to the agreement. The first provided that at the end of the four-year term, Marhoefer could purchase the stuffer for $9,968.00. In the alternative, it could elect to renew the lease for an additional four years at an annual rate of $2,990.00, payable in advance. At the conclusion of the second four-year term, Marhoefer would be allowed to purchase the stuffer for one dollar.

Marhoefer never exercised either option. Approximately one year after the Vemag stuffer was delivered to its plant, it ceased all payments under the lease and shortly thereafter filed a voluntary petition in bankruptcy. On July 12, 1978, the trustee of the bankrupt corporation applied to the bankruptcy court for leave to sell the stuffer free and clear of all liens on the ground that the "Lease Agreement" was in fact a lease intended as security within the meaning of the Uniform Commercial Code ("Code") and that Reiser's failure to perfect its interest as required by Article 9 of the Code rendered it subordinate to that of the trustee. Reiser responded with an answer and counterclaim in which it alleged that the agreement was in fact a true lease, Marhoefer was in default under the lease, and its equipment should therefore be returned.

Following a trial on this issue, the bankruptcy court concluded that the agreement between Marhoefer and Reiser was in fact a true lease and ordered the trustee to return the Vemag stuffer to Reiser. The trustee appealed to the district court, which reversed on the ground that the bankruptcy court had erred as a matter of law in finding the agreement to be a true lease. We now reverse the judgment of the district court.

II.

The dispute in this case centers on *section 1-201(37) of the Uniform Commercial Code*. In applying this section, the bankruptcy court concluded that "the presence of the option to renew the lease for an additional four years and to acquire the Vemag Stuffer at the conclusion of the second four-year term by the payment of One Dollar ($1.00) did not, in and of itself, make the lease one intended for security."

* * *

The district court disagreed. It held that the presence of an option to purchase the stuffer for one dollar gave rise to a conclusive presumption under clause (b) of *section 1-201(37)* that the lease was intended as security. Although it acknowledged that the option to purchase the stuffer for only one dollar would not have come into play unless Marhoefer chose to renew the lease for an additional four-year term, the district court concluded that this fact did not require a different result. "It would be anomalous," said the court, "to rule that the lease was a genuine lease for four years after its creation but was one intended for security eight years after its creation."

Reiser, relying on Peter F. Coogan's detailed analysis of *section 1-201(37)*, Coogan, Hogan & Vagts, Secured Transactions Under the Uniform Commercial Code, ch. 4A, (1981) (hereinafter "Secured Transactions Under U.C.C."), argues that the district court erred in construing clause (b)[1] of that section as creating a conclusive presumption that a lease is intended as security where the lease contains an option for the lessee to become the owner of the leased property for no additional consideration or for only nominal consideration. It contends that by interpreting clause (b) in this way, the district court totally ignored the first part of that sentence which states that "whether a lease is intended as security is to be determined by the facts of each case." Reiser claims that because the totality of facts surrounding the transaction indicate that the lease was not intended as security, notwithstanding the presence of the option to purchase the stuffer for one dollar, the district court erred in reversing the bankruptcy court's determination.

We agree that the district court erred in concluding that because the Lease Agreement contained an option for Marhoefer to purchase the Vemag stuffer at the end of a second four-year term, it was conclusively presumed to be a lease intended as security. However, in our view, the district court's error lies not in its reading of clause (b) of *section 1-201(37)* as giving rise to such a presumption, but rather in its conclusion that clause (b) applies under the facts of this case.

* * *

The primary issue to be decided in determining whether a lease is "intended as security" is whether it is in effect a conditional sale in which the "lessor" retains an interest in the "leased" goods as security for the purchase price. 1C

---

1   [Editor's Note: At the time this case was decided, clause b of 1-201(37) read:

     an agreement that upon compliance with the terms of the lease the lessee shall become or has the option to become the owner of the property for no additional consideration or for a nominal consideration does make the lease one intended for security.]

Secured Transactions Under U.C.C. §29A.05[1][C], p. 2939. By defining the term "security interest" to include a lease intended as security, the drafters of the Code intended such disguised security interests to be governed by the same rules that apply to other security interests. *See* U.C.C., Art. 9. In this respect, *section 1-201(37)* represents the drafter's refusal to recognize form over substance.

Clearly, where a lease is structured so that the lessee is contractually bound to pay rent over a set period of time at the conclusion of which he automatically or for only nominal consideration becomes the owner of the leased goods, the transaction is in substance a conditional sale and should be treated as such. It is to this type of lease that clause (b) properly applies. Here, however, Marhoefer was under no contractual obligation to pay rent until such time as the option to purchase the Vemag stuffer for one dollar was to arise. In fact, in order to acquire that option, Marhoefer would have had to exercise its earlier option to renew the lease for a second four-year term and pay Reiser an additional $11,960 in "rent." In effect, Marhoefer was given a right to terminate the agreement after the first four years and cease making payments without that option ever becoming operative.

Despite this fact, the district court concluded as a matter of law that the lease was intended as security. It held that, under clause (b) of *section 1-201(37)*, a lease containing an option for the lessee to purchase the leased goods for nominal consideration is conclusively presumed to be one intended as security. This presumption applies, the court concluded, regardless of any other options the lease may contain.

We think the district court's reading of clause (b) is in error. In our view, the conclusive presumption provided under clause (b) applies only where the option to purchase for nominal consideration necessarily arises upon compliance with the lease. It does not apply where the lessee has the right to terminate the lease before that option arises with no further obligation to continue paying rent. For where the lessee has the right to terminate the transaction, it is not a conditional sale.

Moreover, to hold that a lease containing such an option is intended as security, even though the lessee has no contractual obligation to pay the full amount contemplated by the agreement, would lead to clearly erroneous results under other provisions of the Code. Under section 9-506 [Now 9-623] of the Code, for example, a debtor in default on his obligation to a secured party has a right to redeem the collateral by tendering full payment of that obligation. The same right is also enjoyed by a lessee under a lease intended as security. A lessee who defaults on a lease intended as security is entitled to purchase the leased goods by paying the full amount of his obligation under the lease. But if the lessee has the right to terminate the lease at any time during the lease term, his obligation under the lease may be only a small part of the total purchase price of the goods leased. To afford the lessee a right of redemption under such circumstances would clearly be wrong. There is no evidence that the drafters of the Code intended such a result.

* * *

We therefore hold that while *section 1-201(37)(b)* does provide a conclusive test of when a lease is intended as security, that test does not apply in every case in which the disputed lease contains an option to purchase for nominal or no consideration. An option of this type makes a lease one intended as security only when it necessarily arises upon compliance with the terms of the lease.

* * *

Applying *section 1-201(37)*, so construed, to the facts of this case, it is clear that the district court erred in concluding that the possibility of Marhoefer's purchasing the stuffer for one dollar at the conclusion of a second four-year term was determinative. Because Marhoefer could have fully complied with the lease without that option ever arising, the district court was mistaken in thinking that the existence of that option alone made the lease a conditional sale. Certainly, if Marhoefer had elected to renew the lease for another term, in which case the nominal purchase option would necessarily have arisen, then the clause (b) test would apply.[2] But that is not the case we are faced with here. Marhoefer was not required to make any payments beyond the first four years. The fact that, at the conclusion of that term, it could have elected to renew the lease and obtain an option to purchase the stuffer for one dollar at the end of the second term does not transform the original transaction into a conditional sale.

This fact does not end our inquiry under clause (b), however, for the trustee also argues that, even if the district court erred in considering the one dollar purchase option as determinative, the lease should nevertheless be considered a conditional sale because the initial option price of $9,968 is also nominal when all of the operative facts are properly considered. We agree that if the clause (b) test is to apply at all in this case, this is the option that must be considered. For this is the option that was to arise automatically upon Marhoefer's compliance with the lease. We do not agree, however, that under the circumstances presented here the $9,968 option price can properly be considered nominal.

It is true that an option price may be more than a few dollars and still be considered nominal within the meaning of *section 1-201(37)*. Because clause

---

2   Reiser concedes that had Marhoefer elected to renew the lease after the first term, the transaction would have been transformed into a sale. George Vetie, Reiser's treasurer, testified that the renewal option was actually intended as a financing mechanism to allow Marhoefer to purchase the stuffer at the end of the lease if it desired to do so but was either unable or unwilling to pay the initial purchase price of $9,968.

(b) speaks of nominal "consideration" and not a nominal "sum" or "amount," it has been held to apply not only where the option price is very small in absolute terms, but also where the price is insubstantial in relation to the fair market value of the leased goods at the time the option arises.[3] *See e.g. Percival Const. Co. v. Miller & Miller Auctioneers, 532 F.2d 166 (10th Cir. 1977)* ($8,040 option price found to be nominal); *Citicorp Leasing, Inc. v. Allied Institutional, Etc., 454 F. Supp. 511 (W.D. Okla. 1977)* (option price of $1,253.71 nominal); *Chandler Leasing Corp. v. Samoset Associates, 24 U.C.C. Rep. 510 (Bankr. D. Me. 1978)* ($47,000 option price held nominal).

Here, however, the evidence revealed that the initial option price of $9,968 was not nominal even under this standard. George Vetie, Reiser's treasurer and the person chiefly responsible for the terms of the lease, testified at trial that the purchase price for the Vemag stuffer at the time the parties entered into the transaction was $33,225. He testified that the initial option price of $9,968 was arrived at by taking thirty percent of the purchase price, which was what he felt a four-year-old Vemag stuffer would be worth based on Reiser's past experience.

The trustee, relying on the testimony of its expert appraiser, argues that in fact the stuffer would have been worth between eighteen and twenty thousand dollars at the end of the first four-year term. Because the initial option price is substantially less than this amount, he claims that it is nominal within the meaning of clause (b) and the lease is therefore one intended as security.

Even assuming this appraisal to be accurate, an issue on which the bankruptcy court made no finding, we would not find the initial option price of $9,968 so small by comparison that the clause (b) presumption would apply. While it is difficult to state any bright line percentage test for determining when an option price could properly be considered nominal as compared to the fair market value of the leased goods, an option price of almost ten thousand dollars, which amounts to fifty percent of the fair market value, is not nominal by any standard.

Furthermore, in determining whether an option price is nominal, the proper figure to compare it with is not the actual fair market value of the leased goods at the time the option arises, but their fair market value at that time as anticipated by the parties when the lease is signed. Here, for example, Vetie testified that his estimate of the fair market value of a four-year-old Vemag stuffer was based on records from a period of time in which the economy was relatively stable. Since that time, a high rate of inflation has caused the

---

3   The trustee argues that the determination of whether the option price is nominal is to be made by comparing it to the fair market value of the equipment at the time the parties enter into the lease, instead of the date the option arises. Although some courts have applied such a test, *In re Wheatland Electric Products Co., 237 F. Supp. 820 (W.D. Pa. 1964)*; *In re Oak Mfg., Inc., 6 U.C.C. Rep. 1273 (Bankr. S.D. N.Y. 1969)*, the better approach is to compare the option price with the fair market value of the goods at the time the option was to be exercised. *In re Universal Medical Services, Inc., 8 U.C.C. Rep. 614 (Bankr. E.D. Pa. 1970)*.

machines to lose their value more slowly. As a result, the actual fair market value of a machine may turn out to be significantly more than the parties anticipated it would be several years earlier. When this occurs, the lessee's option to purchase the leased goods may be much more favorable than either party intended, but it does not change the true character of the transaction.

We conclude, therefore, that neither option to purchase contained in the lease between Marhoefer and Reiser gives rise to a conclusive presumption under *section 1-201(37)(b)* that the lease is one intended as security. This being so, we now turn to the other facts surrounding the transaction.

III.

Although *section 1-201(37)* states that "whether a lease is intended as security is to be determined by the facts of each case," it is completely silent as to what facts, other than the option to purchase, are to be considered in making that determination. Facts that the courts have found relevant include the total amount of rent the lessee is required to pay under the lease, *Chandler Leasing Corp. v. Samoset Associates, supra, 24 U.C.C. Rep. at 516*; whether the lessee acquires any equity in the leased property, *Matter of Tillery, 571 F.2d 1361, 1365 (5th Cir. 1978)*; the useful life of the leased goods, *In re Lakeshore Transit-Kenosha, Inc., 7 U.C.C. Rep. 607 (Bankr. E.D. Wis. 1969)*; the nature of the lessor's business, *In re Industro Transistor Corp., 14 U.C.C. Rep. 522, 523 (Bankr. E.D. N.Y. 1973)*; and the payment of taxes, insurance and other charges normally imposed on ownership, *Rainier National Bank v. Inland Machinery Co., 29 Wash. App. 725, 631 P.2d 389 (1981)*. Consideration of the facts of this case in light of these factors leads us to conclude that the lease in question was not intended as security.

First, Marhoefer was under no obligation to pay the full purchase price for the stuffer. Over the first four-year term, its payments under the lease were to have amounted to $31,920. Although this amount may not be substantially less than the original purchase price of $33,225 in absolute terms, it becomes so when one factors in the interest rate over four years that would have been charged had Marhoefer elected to purchase the machine under a conditional sale contract.[4] The fact that the total amount of rent Marhoefer was to pay under the lease was substantially less than that amount shows that a sale was not intended.

It is also significant that the useful life of the Vemag stuffer exceeded the term of the lease. An essential characteristic of a true lease is that there be something of value to return to the lessor after the term. Where the term of the lease is substantially equal to the life of the leased property such that there will be nothing of value to return at the end of the lease, the transaction is in

---

4   The bankruptcy court found that Reiser was originally willing to sell Marhoefer the stuffer under a conditional sale contract the terms of which would have been $7,225 down and monthly installments of $1,224 over a twenty-four month period. The total payments under such an agreement would have amounted to $36,601, substantially more than the amount Marhoefer was required to pay over four years under the lease.

essence a sale. *In re Lakeshore Transit-Kenosha, Inc., supra.* Here, the evidence revealed that the useful life of a Vemag stuffer was eight to ten years.

Finally, the bankruptcy court specifically found that "there was no express or implied provision in the lease agreement dated February 28, 1977, which gave Marhoefer any equity interest in the leased Vemag stuffer." This fact clearly reveals the agreement between Marhoefer and Reiser to be a true lease. *See* Hawkland, The Impact of the Uniform Commercial Code on Equipment Leasing, 1972 Ill. L. Forum 446, 453 ("The difference between a true lease and a security transaction lies in whether the lessee acquires an equity of ownership through his rent payments."). Had Marhoefer remained solvent and elected not to exercise its option to renew its lease with Reiser, it would have received nothing for its previous lease payments. And in order to exercise that option, Marhoefer would have had to pay what Reiser anticipated would then be the machine's fair market value. An option of this kind is not the mark of a lease intended as security. *See In re Alpha Creamery Company, 4 U.C.C. Rep. 794, 798 (Bankr. W.D. Mich. 1967).*

Although Marhoefer was required to pay state and local taxes and the cost of repairs, this fact does not require a contrary result. Costs such as taxes, insurance and repairs are necessarily borne by one party or the other. They reflect less the true character of the transaction than the strength of the parties' respective bargaining positions. *See also Rainier National Bank, supra, 631 P.2d at 395* ("The lessor is either going to include those costs within the rental charge or agree to a lower rent if the lessee takes responsibility for them.").

IV.

We conclude from the foregoing that the district court erred in its application of *section 1-201(37) of the Uniform Commercial Code* to the facts of this case. Neither the option to purchase the Vemag stuffer for one dollar at the conclusion of a second four-year term, nor the initial option to purchase it for $9,968 after the first four years, gives rise to a conclusive presumption under clause (b) of *section 1-201(37)* that the lease is intended as security. From all of the facts surrounding the transaction, we conclude that the agreement between Marhoefer and Reiser is a true lease. The judgment of the district court is therefore reversed.

IN RE MORRIS

United States Bankruptcy Court for the Eastern District of Missouri, Eastern Division 150 B.R. 446 (E.D. Mo. 1992)

SCHERMER, *District Judge.*

The issue before the Court in this objection to plan confirmation is whether a "rent-to-own" contract is a true lease or a conditional sales contract. Resolving this question brings into conflict the applicability of two Missouri statutes: (1) *section 400.1-201(37)* of Missouri's Commercial Code and (2) section 407.662(6) of Missouri's Rental Purchase Agreement Law. The creditor asserts that §407.662(6) of Missouri's Rental Purchase Agreement Law governs and that the contract is a true lease. If the contract represents an unexpired lease, the debtor must either assume or reject the lease as an executory contract pursuant to *§1322(b)(7)*. The Debtors, however, insist that Missouri's Commercial Code governs the transaction and that the contract is a conditional sales agreement under which the Creditor retains a security interest. If the contract represents a security agreement, the Debtors' plan must propose to pay the creditor the present value of its collateral and treat the balance of the claim as an unsecured obligation under *§506(a) of the Bankruptcy Code*.

* * *

FACTS

Wilford and Marinda Morris, husband and wife (hereinafter "the Debtors") filed a joint petition for relief under Chapter 13 of the U.S. Bankruptcy Code. Debtors scheduled National Rent-to-Own (hereinafter "National") as a secured creditor and filed a proof of claim on National's behalf. In the proof of claim, Debtors stated that National's collateral had a present value of zero, leaving National with an unsecured claim of $1,155.50. D.L. Cole & Associates, Inc., a Missouri corporation doing business as National Rent-to-Own, filed an objection to confirmation of Debtors' Chapter 13 plan asserting that Debtors' plan mischaracterizes Debtors as "owners" rather than as "renters" of certain property acquired by Debtors under National's rental purchase agreement.

National asserts that its rental purchase agreement is a true lease and insists that the Debtors are merely lessees of the property. Accordingly, National maintains that Debtors must accept the lease and continue making regular lease payments if they wish to retain the property. In support of its position, National directs the Court to Missouri's Rental Purchase Agreement Law, *Mo. Rev. Stat. §§407.660-407.665* (Supp. 1991) which both defines rental purchase agreements and specifies that they are not to be construed as, nor governed by, the security interest provisions of subdivision (37) of *Mo. Rev. Stat. §400.1-201*. Thus, National maintains Debtors have no ownership interest in the property and may not treat National's claim as bifurcated into secured and unsecured obligations.

Debtors, conversely, believe they have an ownership interest and cite the Court to *Mo. Rev. Stat. §400.1-201(37)(b)* (1986 & Supp. 1991). Debtors insist that their right to automatically acquire ownership of the property upon completion of all payments under the agreement makes the transaction a conditional sale with National merely retaining a security interest in the merchandise pursuant to *§400.1-201(37)(b)*.

THE AGREEMENT

The language of the rental purchase agreement is particularly instructive in determining whether the agreement reflects a purchase or lease transaction.

Under the contract Debtors were to make weekly payments of $22.15 for a period of 52 weeks. At the end of the 52 week period, if all lease payments were made, Debtors were to acquire ownership of the property. The lease ran for terms of one week and was renewable at the Debtors' option by making each weekly lease payment in advance. Debtors could terminate the lease at any time by ceasing payments and returning the property. The agreement also provided Debtors with the option of purchasing the property at any time by paying one and one half times the remaining cash value of the merchandise. Debtors carried all risk of loss or damage during the term of the lease although ordinary maintenance was the responsibility of National. Finally, the agreement explicitly provided that it was a lease agreement and not intended to convey any ownership interests until completion of all 52 lease payments. In its most relevant part, the agreement read as follows:

> THIS IS A LEASE AGREEMENT ONLY: This lease is for week to week possession of the property only. You will not acquire any equity in the property by making lease payments. … YOU ACQUIRE NO OWNERSHIP RIGHTS IN THE PROPERTY UNTIL ALL PAYMENTS ARE MADE UNDER THE OWNERSHIP TERMS OF THIS AGREEMENT.

DISCUSSION

Generally, the existence, nature and extent of a security interest in property is governed by state law. *In re Powers, 138 Bankr. 916, 917 (C.D. Ill. 1992)* citing, *Butner v. United States, 440 U.S. 48, 99 S. Ct. 914, 59 L. Ed. 2d 136: (1979).* Whether a lease is one intended as security is determined under Missouri law by *Mo.Rev.Stat. §400.1-201(37)* which states in part:

> Whether a lease is intended as security is to be determined by the facts of each case; however, (a) the inclusion of an option to purchase does not of itself make the lease one intended for security, and **(b) an agreement that upon compliance with the terms of the lease the lessee shall become or has the option to become the owner of the property for no additional consideration or for a nominal consideration** does **make the lease one intended for security.**

Mo.Rev.Stat. §400.1-201(37) (1986 & Supp.1991) (emphasis added).

Debtors insist that because they shall become the owners of the property upon completion of all lease payments, the transaction is, in fact, a conditional sale and the lease is one intended as security under subsection (b) of *§400.1-201(37).*

The Eighth Circuit, applying Missouri law, has stated that the existence of an **absolute obligation** by the lessee to purchase rental property is the touchstone in determining whether a security interest was intended. *Carlson v. Tandy Computer Leasing, 803 F.2d 391, 396 (8th Cir. 1986)* citing, *RCA Corp. v. State Tax Commission, 513 S.W.2d 313, 316 (Mo. 1974).* In *RCA Corp.*, the Missouri Supreme Court explained:

... if the transferee is obligated and bound to pay the purchase price it is a conditional sale, but if the agreement requires or permits the transferee to return the property in lieu of paying the purchase price the instrument will be a lease. In a conditional sale 'the purchaser undertakes an absolute obligation to pay for the property.' *Globe Securities Co. v. Gardner Motor Co., 337 Mo. 177, 85 S.W.2d 561, 567 (1935)*. ... 'Before there can be a conditional sales contract there must be a binding, absolute obligation on the part of the buyer to pay the full amount of the purchase price.' *17 Ariz. App. 520,: 498 P.2d 594, 597 (1972)*.

> *RCA Corp.*, 513, S.W.2d at 317.

In the instant case, there is no absolute obligation on the Debtors to purchase, pay for or assume title to the merchandise. Whether they become owners of the property is entirely at their option. Debtors may choose to continue making weekly lease payments until they acquire ownership rights in the property or they may cease making payments at any time and terminate the purchase agreement. Because the Debtors are not obligated by the terms of the rental purchase agreement to make payments until such time as the option to own arises, the agreement cannot be a conditional sale or a lease intended as security under *§400.1-201(37)*.

This holding and the rationale therefore is consistent with the position of courts in most jurisdictions. *See, In re Powers, 138 Bankr. 916, 921 (C.D. Ill. 1992)*, (while section 1-201(37) does provide a conclusive test when a lease is intended as security, that test does not apply where the lessee has the right to terminate the lease before the option arises with no further obligation to continue paying rent, *citing, In re Marhoefer Packing Co., Inc., 674 F.2d 1139 (7th Cir. 1982))*; *In re Taylor, 130 Bankr. 849 (Bankr. E.D. Ark. 1991)*; *In re Armstrong, 84 Bankr. 94 (Bankr. W.D.Tex. 1988)*; *In re Blevins, 119 Bankr. 814, 817 (Bankr. N.D. Okla. 1990)* ("... the lessee is not required to make the payments but can, at any time, unilaterally terminate the agreement and return the property. This is the essence of a lease."); *In re Frady, 141 Bankr. 600 (Bankr. W.D. N.C. 1991)*.

In addition to case law interpretation, Missouri statutes specifically provide for the existence and treatment of rental purchase agreements as leases. Missouri's Rental Purchase Agreement Law *§§407.660 - 407.665* delineates the requirements for creating such agreements and prohibits interpretation of such agreements as creating, among other things, a credit sale (*§407.661(6) (a)*) or a security interest (*§407.661(6)(f)*)[5]. National's rental purchase agreement complies with the requirements of *§407.661(6)* for classification as a Missouri rental purchase agreement. Subsection (6)(f) of *§407.661* therefore

---

5 Subsection (6)(f) states:

A rental-purchase agreement shall not be construed to be nor be governed by any of the following ... (f) A security interest as defined in subdivision (37) of *section 400.1-201(37) RSMo*;

precludes construction of National's agreement as a security interest under *subdivision (37) of §400.1-201.*

This Court notes that one District has not adopted the "termination" or "walk-away" test relied on by this Court and those courts cited above in determining whether a transaction is a true lease or a disguised installment sale with a security interest. The Northern District of Alabama, Western Division rejects the termination test in favor of a multi-factor test designed to measure the intent of the parties. *See, In re Burton, 128 Bankr. 807, 813 (Bankr. N.D. Ala. 1989) aff'd 128 Bankr. 820 (D.N.D. Ala. 1989), In re Brown, 128 Bankr. 815 (Bankr. N.D. Ala. 1989).* According to these decisions the termination test is inappropriate because a consumer's right to terminate is essentially meaningless where the consumer must choose between continued payments or forfeiture of its merchandise. These decisions explain that because most rental purchase agreement consumers are unsophisticated and "on the lower economic rung of the ladder," *(In re Burton, 128 Bankr. at 814)*, they have no place else to go in order to purchase household furnishings. Thus, by focusing on the economic realities of the consumer and merchant, these decisions conclude that rental purchase agreements must be disguised sales rather than true leases.

This court is not persuaded by the reasoning of such decisions. Were the documents obfuscatory or Missouri's Rental-Purchase Agreement Law less clear, then perhaps the economic realities of the situation might compel a conclusion that the agreement was a disguised sale transaction. However, this is not the case. The agreement is clear and repeatedly indicates that the consumer is only leasing the merchandise. The agreement plainly states that the consumer acquires no ownership rights in the merchandise until after making all lease payments and further states that the consumer may cancel the agreement at anytime by ceasing weekly payments. Under these circumstances, the court concludes that National's rental purchase agreement is in fact a true lease and not a conditional sale or lease intended as security.

Accordingly,

IT IS ORDERED that the Objection to confirmation of Plan by D.L. Cole & Associates, Inc. is SUSTAINED and confirmation of Debtors' Plan is DENIED.

PROBLEM 2–2

Ray leases as many appliances as he sells. Most of the appliances he leases last about ten years before they need to be replaced and can be sold for 25–30 percent of their original purchase price after they have been used for five years. The terms of the leases—especially duration, rent, and options—vary greatly from lease to lease. Until recently, Ray had always assumed that his leases were not subject to Article 9. But a number of his lessees have filed bankruptcy this year during the original terms of their leases, and Ray is now worried that the bankruptcy trustees are going to claim that some of the leases are not actually leases. Ray has asked you to review the following files to determine whether the leases are subject to Article 9: ①✓

File 1:   Ten-year lease of refrigerator at $15 per month, refrigerator to be returned to Ray at end of lease. Original purchase price of refrigerator was $1200. Lessee had option to terminate lease on thirty days notice at any time before the end of the ninth year.

LEASE

File 2:   One-year lease of washer at $100 per month. Original purchase price $1000. Lessee not required to return washer at end of lease.

$0 = Nom. Consideraton

File 3:   Ten-year lease of commercial freezer at $500 per year. Original purchase price of freezer was $4000. Lessee must return freezer to Ray and end of lease. ①✓

Def Term = Econ Life = SJ

File 4:   Five-year lease of industrial capacity dryer at $75 per month. Original purchase price $6000. Lessee must renew for additional five-year term at $50 per month. Lessee must return dryer to Ray at end of second term.

Have to Renew > Econ = SJ

File 5:   Five-year lease of industrial capacity washer-dryer combo at $150 per month. Original purchase price $10,000. Lessee has option to renew for second five-year term at $50 per month or to return combo to Ray. Lessee must return combo to Ray at end of second term.

LEASE

File 6:   Five-year lease of refrigerator at $40 per month. Original purchase price $2000. Lessee has option to purchase at end of lease for $100. Lessee must return refrigerator to Ray if option not exercised.

File 7:   Five-year lease of commercial walk-in freezer at $1000 per month. Original purchase price $55,000. Lessee has option to purchase at end of first term for $13,000. Lessee must return unit to manufacturer if option not exercised. Cost of dismantling and shipping to manufacturer $15,000.

Cost to Sent Back ($15k)

_>_

Option Price ($13k)

Per se = Nominal

B. Sales of Accounts

The basic Article 9 scope provision stakes out the range of secured transactions that Article 9 cares about. But there are other types of transactions that can create problems analogous to the ostensible ownership problem which can also be solved by public recording. When intangibles like account receivables are sold outright there's nothing about the transaction itself that would serve to alert subsequent parties who deal with the seller that it no longer owns the accounts generated by the business—there's no physical evidence to reflect the presence or the absence of the accounts as assets of the business. You can prevent Ray from using the wash machine you buy as collateral for a loan by taking it home with you. That's not an option with the sale of intangibles like accounts.

Financing by way of the sale of accounts—called "factoring"—was an important part of commercial financing when Article 9 was originally enacted. Instead of using its accounts receivable to secure a loan which it would then pay back, a business could "assign' its accounts to a "factor" in return for the cash it needed to operate. The "assignment" was in effect a sale of the accounts—the factor looked to the accounts for pay back—not the business that had assigned the accounts. The "sales price" was discounted to reflect the risk that the accounts would not be collected in full and the time needed for collection. Factoring was already regulated by statute when the drafting of Article 9 began, so including the sale of accounts within the scope of Article 9 was only logical.

The *Octagon Gas* case and the Problems that follow it develop Article 9's coverage of transactions involving sales of accounts.

OCTAGON GAS SYSTEMS, INC. v. ROY T. RIMMER
United States Court of Appeals for the Tenth Circuit
995 F.2d 948 (10th Cir. 1993)

BALDOCK, *Circuit Judge*.

[Poll Gas, Inc. operated a natural gas gathering system in Oklahoma. In separate transactions, Rimmer acquired a 5% "perpetual overriding royalty interest on all proceeds payable to" Poll under its gathering system. Poll filed for bankruptcy protection in 1988 and pursuant to its plan of reorganization, the gathering system was conveyed to one of Poll's creditors, "free and clear of liens, claims, interests, and encumbrances." The system was later conveyed to Octagon, the defendant in this proceeding, which refused to recognize Rimmer's interest and failed to make payments on that interest to Rimmer. This litigation was initiated to determine the effect of Poll's plan of reorganization on Rimmer's interest.]

* * *

On cross motions for summary judgement, the bankruptcy court held that Rimmer owned a five percent interest in the proceeds of gas sold through the Poll System which was not affected by the Plan or the transfer of the Poll System to Octagon. The court, rejecting Octagon's argument that Article 9 of the Uniform Commercial Code ("U.C.C.") applied, reasoned that Rimmer's partial interest in the proceeds from the sale of gas was a "good" and amounted to a proportionate ownership right. The court found that Rimmer's interest was not property of Poll's bankruptcy estate and therefore could not be transferred by the estate to Octagon. The bankruptcy court granted summary judgment in favor of Rimmer, and the district court summarily affirmed.

On appeal Octagon raises numerous issues, among them: ... (2) whether the bankruptcy court erred in determining that Article 9 of the U.C.C. was inapplicable to Rimmer's interest. Because we remand in order for the court to apply Article 9, we do not address Octagon's remaining issues.

* * *

II.

Throughout this litigation, Octagon has maintained that Rimmer's interest is an "account" governed by Article 9 of the U.C.C. as adopted by Oklahoma. Rimmer has conceded that his interest is an "account," but argues that regardless of Article 9, he "owns" the interest, not Poll, and therefore his interest has never been property of Poll's bankruptcy estate. The bankruptcy court held that Article 9 was inapplicable because Article 9 provides a classification of interests for the purpose of determining competing secured interests, "not a classification for the creation of an ownership right in personal property."

"Article [9 of the U.C.C.] sets out a comprehensive scheme for the regulation of security interests in personal property and fixtures." *Okla. Stat. Ann. tit. 12A, 9-101* (West 1963) (Official Comment). The aim of Article 9 is "to provide a simple and unified structure within which the immense variety of present-day secured financing transactions can go forward with less cost and with greater certainty." *Id.* As a means towards achieving this end, Article 9 lays out the steps a party must take to create a valid security interest. These steps include "attachment" of a security interest, and "perfection" of the interest. Article 9 also provides for priority among competing claims of purchasers and creditors of the debtor. Although Article 9 applies mainly to transactions intended to create security interests, it also applies to sales of accounts, ..., because sales of wholly intangible interests in accounts create the same risks of secret liens inherent in secured transactions.

As a starting point in our analysis, we must determine whether Rimmer's interest in the Poll System's gas sale proceeds is an "account" as defined by Article 9 of the U.C.C. as adopted by Oklahoma. Article 9 applies to transactions involving personal property. One form of personal property to which Article 9 applies is an "account" which is defined as "any right to payment for goods sold ... which is not evidenced by an instrument or chattel paper." Okla. Stat. Ann. tit. 12A, 9-106 [Now 9-102(2)] (West Supp. 1993). Section 9-105(1)(h) [Now 9-102(44)] states that "goods" includes "all things which are movable at the time the security interest attaches ... but does not include ... minerals or the like, including oil and gas, *before extraction*." *Id.* 9-105(1)(h) [Now 9-102(44)] (emphasis added).

Natural gas, once extracted, becomes personal property in Oklahoma, ..., and as such, is subject to Article 9. Also, by negative implication, section 9-105(1)(h) [Now 9-102(44)] indicates that minerals, including gas, *following extraction*, come within Article 9's definition of a "good." Here, the gas sold is extracted. Because extracted gas is a "good," Poll's right to payment for gas sold, as well as Rimmer's five percent interest in Poll's right to payment, is an account.

Having determined that the interest acquired by Rimmer is an account under Article 9, it follows that Article 9 applies to Rimmer's five percent interest in the Poll System's gas sale proceeds (hereinafter referred to as "Rimmer's account"), even though the transactions giving rise to Rimmer's account were not intended to secure a debt. The U.C.C. Official Comment 2 to *Okla. Stat. Ann. tit. 12A, 9-102* [Now 9-109] (West Supp. 1993), explains that in the case of commercial financing on the basis of accounts, "the distinction between a security transfer and a sale is blurred, and a sale of such property is therefore covered by [9-102(1)(b)] *whether intended for security or not.* The buyer is then treated as a secured party and his interest as a security interest." (emphasis added). *Section 9-102(1)(b)* [Now 9-109(a)(3)] states that Article 9 applies "to any outright sale of accounts." Further, the term "security interest" as defined by Article 9, expressly includes "any interest of a buyer of accounts," *Okla. Stat. Ann. tit. 12A, 1-201(37)* [Now 1-201(35)] (West Supp. 1993), and "secured party" includes "a person to whom accounts … have been sold." *Id.* 9-105(1)(m) [Now 9-102(73)]. Additionally, section 9-105(1)(d) [Now 9-102(25)] defines "debtor" as including "the seller of accounts," and, under section 9-105(1)(c) [Now 9-102(12)], "collateral" includes "accounts … which have been sold." These provisions clearly indicate that the buyer of an account is treated as a secured party, his interest in the account is treated as a security interest, the seller of the account is a debtor, and the account sold is treated as collateral.

PROBLEM 2–3

Which, if any, of the following transactions are subject to Article 9:

Transaction 1: Every six months, Ray assigns his delinquent accounts to a collection agency for collection. See 9-109(d)(5).

Transaction 2: When one of Ray's customers falls behind on her payments, Ray agrees to accept an assignment of the customer's right to payment for services she provided as a photographer to a client in full satisfaction of the customer's obligation to Ray. See 9-109(d)(7).

Transaction 3: Many of Ray's customers sign up for extended service agreements when they purchase their appliances. The three-year agreements provide that in return for an annual fee, Ray will service their appliance at no cost to the customer. Ray assigns all service agreements for the refrigerators he sells to his brother who specializes in refrigeration. See 9-109(d)(6).

PROBLEM 2–4

Ray has agreed to purchase a discount appliance store across town from his uncle. Ray is to pay cash for everything—the inventory, accounts, equipment, and the building. He plans to consolidate the two stores eventually at a new location. In the meantime, he will operate them as separate businesses. Because there is no loan or collateral involved in the transaction, Ray is assuming there are no Article 9 issues. Has Ray missed anything? See 9-109(d)(4).

[handwritten margin note: Sale of Accounts Receivable But Buying whole Biz So No Rattner issue]

C. PREEMPTION

Section 9-109(c) states the obvious: federal law supersedes state law. Article 9, as a creation of state law, gives way to federal law that applies to transactions that fall within its scope. But this really overstates the concession made in 9-109(c) to federal law. Article 9 gives way "only to the extent" that federal law "preempts" Article 9. Thus, the mere existence of a federal law that covers a transaction or a particular part of a transaction otherwise addressed by Article 9 does not displace Article 9 in its entirety, as the following case illustrates. Because the preemption contemplated by 9-109(c) is usually the result of federal law creating an alternative system for recording interests and the transfer of interests in particular types of property, Article 9 will continue to control, at a minimum, priorities between competing claimants and enforcement of interests in the property at issue. See, e.g. Ship Mortgage Act, 46 U.S.C. §§31301 - 30; Civil Aeronautics Act 49 U.S.C §§1403, 1404; Interstate Commerce Act, 49 U.S.C. §§.1 et seq.

IN RE MCLEAN INDUSTRIES, INC.

United States Bankruptcy Court for the Southern District of New York
132 B.R. 271 (S.D.N.Y. 1991)

BLACKSHEAR, *Bankruptcy Judge.*

This adversary proceeding ensues from an accident involving the cargo ship Delta Sud (the "Vessel"). Subsequent to the accident, the owner, United States Lines (S.A.), Inc. ("SA" or the "Debtor") filed a petition under chapter 11 of the Bankruptcy Code (the "Code"). Upon approving a settlement between the Debtor and its insurance underwriters over the insurance payment due resulting from the accident, Judge Buschman ordered that the insurance proceeds be paid into an escrow account pending the resolution of the competing claims to the proceeds.

On or about May 17, 1989, SA and Chemical Bank each instituted adversary proceedings against each other and against the United States of America, naming the Department of Transportation, Maritime Administration. By stipulation and order, these adversary proceedings were consolidated. The United States of America filed an answer to Chemical Bank's and SA's respective complaints; in each instance seeking reformation of the existing insurance policies and the rights to the insurance proceeds.

At the outset this Court notes that this matter involves some novel legal arguments raising issues of first impression for this Court, this district and this circuit.

FACTS

[Chemical Bank ("Chemical") loaned the Debtor's predecessor $50 million which was secured by a "fleet mortgage" which gave Chemical a security interest in the Debtor's ships including the Vessel. Chemical perfected its security interest in the collateral. The loan agreement and mortgage were amended from time-to-time. At the time the Debtor acquired the Vessel, it was subject to another security interest which secured a loan made by Whitney Bank. The Debtor's obligation to Whitney was in effect guaranteed by United States Department of Transportation ("USDOT"). When the Debtor defaulted on the Whitney Bank loan, USDOT paid off Whitney and was assigned Whitney Bank's claim against the Debtor and the Vessel.

Chemical's fleet mortgage required the Debtor to insure the Debtor's ships, including Vessel, for the benefit of Chemical, and the Debtor initially obtained the required insurance from Johnson & Higgins, but subsequently obtained the required insurance from another provider, Alexander & Alexander ("A&A"). Because some of the paper work the Debtor provided to A&A when it switched polices was outdated, the coverage certificates ultimately issued by A&A failed to name Chemical as a loss payee or an assured under the new policy. After the accident involving the Vessel – which was essentially totaled and sold for scrap – A&A settled the Debtor's claim under its policy for $6.5 million. Because the coverage certificates did not name Chemical as a loss payee, the Debtor asserted Chemical was not entitled to any of the insurance proceeds paid on the Vessel. Chemical argued, among other things, that the proceeds were proceeds of its security interest in the Vessel. We will examine the concept of proceeds in more detail in Chapter 8, but for purposes of the issues in this case, proceeds are whatever the debtor gets in exchange for the secured party's collateral.]

DISCUSSION

* * *

Although this Court's analysis could end here, this Court will consider the Uniform Commercial Code arguments. This Court believes that the Uniform Commercial Code further supports Chemical's and MARAD's rights to the insurance proceeds. The issue is whether the Uniform Commercial Code is applicable to a security interest perfected under the Ship Mortgage Act of 1920 (the "Ship Mortgage Act") where the Ship Mortgage Act is silent as to whether such security interest extends to insurance proceeds realized as a result of damage to a collateral vessel. The Debtor in the case sub judice, argues that Article 9 of the New York Commercial Code (the "N.Y.U.C.C.") does not apply to the order of entitlement to the insurance proceeds because the agreements between the parties are governed expressly by the Ship Mortgage Act. The Debtor argues that the Ship Mortgage Act, under which the MARAD and Chemical Mortgages were duly recorded and executed, has no provision expressly dealing with the rights of a mortgage holder to insurance proceeds and Chemical and MARAD cannot assert any rights to those proceeds under the N.Y.U.C.C. greater than what is offered under the Ship Mortgage Act. See generally *46 U.S.C. §911 et seq. (1988)* (repealed January 1, 1989, but which does not affect the mortgages in this case). The Debtor argues that the Ship Mortgage Act purports to deal with security interests in specific types of vessels, which term is defined to mean physical watercraft only, and thereby excludes a mortgagee's rights to insurance proceeds. The Debtor references specific language from the Chemical Mortgage which states that it covers only the physical watercrafts within the meaning of the Ship Mortgage Act.

Section 9-104(a) [Now 9-109(c)] provides that Article 9 does not apply to "a security interest subject to any statute of the United States to the extent that such statute governs the rights of the parties to … transactions in particular types of property." N.Y.*U.C.C. §9-104(a)*. Accordingly, the Debtor argues that since the mortgages are governed by the Ship Mortgage Act, the N.Y.U.C.C. does not apply. The Debtor also argues that if this Court needs to direct inquiry elsewhere, it should turn to federal maritime common law.

Official comment 1 to *§9-104* [Now 9-109(c)(1)] explains the purpose and reasoning for excluding certain types of security agreements from its coverage: "Where a federal statute regulates the incidents of security interests in particular types of property, those security interests are of course governed by the federal statute and excluded from this article. The Ship Mortgage Act of 1920 is an example of such a federal act." But the commentator also recognized that such a broad statement is not without qualification:

> Even such a statute as the Ship Mortgage Act is far from a comprehensive regulation of all aspects of ship mortgage financing. That Act contains provisions on formal requisites, on recordation and on foreclosure but not much more. If problems arise under a ship mortgage which are not covered by the Act, the federal court must decide whether to improvise an answer under federal law or to follow the law of some state with which the mortgage transaction has appropriate contacts. *The exclusionary language in paragraph (a) is that this Article does not apply to such security interest "to the extent" that the federal statute governs the rights of the parties. Thus, if the federal statute contained no relevant provision this Article could be looked to for an answer.*
>
> N.Y.*U.C.C. §9-104 [Now 9-109(c)(1)]*, official comment 1
> (emphasis added).

Since the Ship Mortgage Act does not address the issue of entitlement to insurance proceeds, this Court must look to the New York Uniform

Commercial Code for guidance. The Supreme Court noted in *United States v. Kimbell Foods, Inc., 440 U.S. 715, 717, 99 S. Ct. 1448, 1452, 59 L. Ed. 2d 711 (1979)*, that when a national rule is unnecessary to protect federal interests, "the prudent course is to adopt the readymade body of state law as the federal rule of decision until Congress strikes a different accommodation." *Id.*

Pursuant to N.Y. *U.C.C. §9-302(3)* and (4) [Now 9-311], the filing of a financing statement otherwise required by Article 9 is not necessary or effective to perfect a security interest in property subject to "(a) a statute or treaty of the United States which provides for a national registration." N.Y. *U.C.C. §9-302(3)* & (4) [Now 9-311]. Additionally, compliance with a statute or treaty is "equivalent to the filing of a financing statement under this Article, and a security interest in property subject to the statute or treaty can be perfected only by compliance therewith." See N.Y. *U.C.C. §9-302(4)*. Both MARAD and Chemical have complied with the registration and perfection requirements of the Ship Mortgage Act. Consequently, both hold perfected security interests in the Vessel which are recognized under the N.Y.U.C.C.

The N.Y.U.C.C. provides instructions for the disposition of insurance proceeds to secured parties. Courts have agreed that insurance payable by reason of loss to the collateral constitutes proceeds covered by the N.Y. *U.C.C. Section 9-306* [Now 9-315] provides that if a creditor holds a perfected security interest in property, that creditor also holds a perfected security interest in the proceeds of that collateral:

> (1) Proceeds includes whatever is received upon the sale, exchange, collection, or other disposition of collateral or proceeds. Insurance payable by reason of loss or damage to the collateral is proceeds. ...

> N.Y. *U.C.C. §9-306* [Now 9-315(a)] (McKinney 1984)

... Therefore, both MARAD's and Chemical's perfected security interests in the Vessel extends to the insurance proceeds.

This Court's resort should not be surprising since courts have traditionally applied the Uniform Commercial Code to fill gaps in federal statutes. See *Personal Jet Inc. v. Callihan, 624 F.2d 562 (5th Cir. 1980)* (Article 9 applied to fill void in Federal Aviation Act); *Morgan Guaranty Trust Co. v. M/V Grigorios C. IV, 615 F. Supp. 1444, 1451 (E.D. La. 1985)* (the court looked to the N.Y.U.C.C. to fill the gap in the Ship Mortgage Act).

The Debtor alternatively argues that even if the N.Y.U.C.C. is applicable, Chemical's and MARAD's security interests in the Vessel do not vest in the insurance proceeds without affirmative steps by the parties to assure secured status. This is not true. First, disregarding Article 9 momentarily, Chemical and MARAD did indeed take affirmative steps to guarantee their interests in the insurance proceeds. Both parties, relied on assurances made by the Debtor and A&A that the insurance policies would contain the correct revised loss payee and assured clauses. But through the error of A&A, the clauses never reached the London underwriters. Chemical and MARAD did not learn that their interests were not protected in the insurance policies, nor did they have reason to believe so, until after the damage to the Vessel. In light of these circumstances, Chemical and MARAD did all that they possibly could to secure their respective positions. Any argument by the Debtor that Chemical and MARAD did not take affirmative action to protect their interests is disingenuous.

Second, returning to Article 9, *section 9-306(3)* [Now 9-315(c)-(e)] clearly demonstrates that a creditor's security interest in collateral continues in proceeds until ten days after the proceeds are fully converted to cash. *Section 9-306(3)* [Now 9-315(c)-(e)] states the following:

> The security interest in proceeds is a continuously perfected security interest if the interest in the original collateral was perfected but it ceases to be a perfected security interest and becomes unperfected ten days after receipt of the proceeds by the debtor unless

* * *

> (3) a filed financing statement covers the original collateral and the proceeds are identifiable cash proceeds.

N.Y.*U.C.C.* *§9-306* [Now 9-315(c)-(e)] (McKinney 1984).

Chemical and MARAD, having filed such financing statements under the Ship Mortgage Act, are protected under the N.Y.U.C.C. See N.Y.*U.C.C.* *§9-312(6)* [Now 9-322(b)] official comment 8. Subsection (6) to official comment 8 of §9-312(6) [Now 9-322(b)] provides that the filing as to original collateral determines the date of filing as to proceeds thereof. This rule implies, of course, that the filing as to the original collateral is effective as to proceeds under *section 9-306(3)* [Now 9-315(c)-(e)]. Additionally, the proceeds are clearly identifiable since they remain in escrow. Accordingly, Chemical's and MARAD's perfected security interest as to the Vessel, runs to the insurance proceeds of the Vessel.

The Debtor also asserts that since at the commencement of the Debtor's chapter 11 case there were no proceeds in existence, the proceeds represent after acquired property which, pursuant to §552 of the Code, the Debtor can claim free and clear of any prepetition liens.

Generally, *section 552* provides that after-acquired property of the estate is not subject to any lien resulting from any security agreement entered into by a debtor prior to the commencement of the bankruptcy case. See *Collier on Bankruptcy para. 552.01* at 552-1-4 (15th ed. 1986). But this general rule is limited by the exceptions found in *section 552(b)* which allows a prepetition security agreement to extend to proceeds when the security agreement and non-bankruptcy law so provide. This rule is subject to further limitation by the equitable powers of the bankruptcy court which may "after notice and hearing and based on the equities of the case, order … otherwise." *11 U.S.C. §552(b).* "[However], if nonbankruptcy law covers proceeds, it is not necessary that the security agreement do so." *Collier on Bankruptcy, supra, para. 552.02.* Accordingly, since their financing statements covers proceeds, under the N.Y.U.C.C., Chemical's and MARAD's security interests in the insurance proceeds remain intact even though the proceeds came into existence after the commencement of the bankruptcy case. *Section 552* does not apply in this context.

In addition, *§9-306* [Now 9-315] clearly defines proceeds as "insurance payable by reason of loss of damage to the collateral ..." not merely insurance paid at the time of the commencement of the case. The intent of *§9-306* to cover "insurance proceeds" cannot be defeated merely because the insurance proceeds did not exist when the Debtor filed its chapter 11 petition. See *PPG Indus., Inc. v. Hartford Fire Ins. Co., 531 F.2d 58 (2d Cir. 1976)* (the insurance proceeds became proceeds on the date of the damage to the collateral).

When a transaction involves intellectual property—patents, trademarks, or copyrights—the relationship between federal law and Article 9 is more difficult to navigate. There are alternative federal recording systems for each, but there are variations within and between them with respect to the nature of the interests in intellectual property that are covered by each. For example, the trademark recording system applies to registered trademarks but not to unregistered trademarks. *See, Aerocon Engineering, Inc. V. Silicon Valley Bank, 303 F.3rd 1120 (9th Cir. 2002).* As a result, a transaction involving intellectual property may be subject to both the Article 9 filing system and an alternative federal recording system.

D. REAL ESTATE TRANSACTIONS

Article 9 does not apply to a security interest created in real property other than fixtures.[6] If your aunt loans you money to buy a home and by mortgage takes an interest in the property to secure your promise to repay the loan, Article 9 does not apply. But what if your aunt borrows money and gives her lender an interest in the promissory note that reflects your promise to pay her back: does the fact that the note is secured by an interest in real property take the transaction out of Article 9? As the following case illustrates, determining the point at which Old Article 9 gave way to real property law was not easy even in light of the comments which were intended to address the issue.

---

6 A fixture starts life as personal property but becomes connected to real property in such a way that it is then governed by real property law. We will examine the conflict between Article 9 and real property law triggered by the creation of a fixture in Chapter 7.

IN RE FREEBORN, ET AL. v. SEATTLE TRUST & SAVINGS BANK, ET AL.

Supreme Court of Washington
617 P.2d 424 (Wash. 1980)

WRIGHT, *Justice.*

This matter is before the court upon certification from the United States District Court for the Western District of Washington upon the authority of *RCW 2.60.010-.030* and *Rule of Appellate Procedure 16.16.* Two cases involving substantially identical questions have been consolidated. The primary question is whether an assignee of a vendor's right to receive payments in an executory contract for the sale of real property has priority over subsequent lien creditors (including a trustee in bankruptcy) if the assignment is recorded under *RCW 65.08.070* but not filed under the Uniform Commercial Code (U.C.C.), RCW 62A.9-101 *et seq.*

In re Freeborn stems from a loan by Seattle Trust and Savings Bank (Seattle Trust) to William and Clara Freeborn which was secured by an assignment of their vendors' interest in a real estate contract. The document of assignment, entitled "Deed and Seller's Assignment of Real Estate Contract," expressly (a) assigns the contract and (b) conveys the real estate. The face of the document includes a statement that the transfer is "for security purposes only". Although the assignment was recorded with the King County Auditor, Seattle Trust did not file a financing statement with the Secretary of State pursuant to U.C.C. article 9.

The Freeborns subsequently filed a petition in bankruptcy. Plaintiff Warren L. Erickson was appointed trustee. The bankruptcy court, Kenneth S. Treadwell, Judge, granted the trustee's motion for summary judgment. He held that in Washington a vendor under a real estate contract has a right to receive contract payments, which is personal property, and a right to hold legal title to the real property until fully paid. He further held that the transfer for security of the right to receive payments was a transfer of personal property which must be perfected under U.C.C. article 9. In the bankruptcy court's view, because the assignment was not perfected under the U.C.C. the trustee had the right to collect contract payments and Seattle Trust had only general creditor status. We affirm the bankruptcy court.

In re Hyak Skiing Corporation arose from a loan by Marie L. Hillman to Hyak Skiing Corporation (Corporation) secured by an assignment of a vendor's interests in real estate contracts. The document of assignment is entitled, "Seller's Assignment of Contracts and Deed". However, the deed portion of the document is not completed or executed. Hillman recorded the assignment but did not file a financing statement pursuant to U.C.C. article 9. The corporation subsequently applied for bankruptcy relief.

Aldo Patricelli and David O. Hamlin, respectively chairman of the creditors' committee and an unsecured creditor of debtor corporation, brought an action against Marie L. Hillman, a secured creditor, to invalidate or set aside her security and relegate her to general creditor status. Plaintiffs argued the security interest—the right to receive real estate contract payments—had not been properly perfected by filing a financing statement under the U.C.C.

The bankruptcy court judge, Sidney C. Volinn, deferred action on motions for summary judgment pending the decision of the district court in the appeal in Freeborn. When that case was certified, the defendant Bruce T. Thurston moved for certification in *Hyak*. The district court granted that motion.

I.

Initially we must decide if the right to receive real estate contract payments is personal property. We hold that it is personal property.

Washington case law supports the conclusion that the right to receive contract payments under a contract for the sale of real property is personal property. In *Cascade Sec. Bank v. Butler, 88 Wn.2d 777, 567 P.2d 631 (1977)*, we said at page 782: "Specifically we here hold that a real estate contract vendee's interest is 'real estate' within the meaning of the judgment lien statute." In *Cascade* we cited numerous Washington cases supporting the characterization of a vendee's interest as real property and a vendor's interest as personal property.

II.

The next issue is: Does U.C.C. article 9 apply to the assignment of a vendor's right to real estate contract payments?

Defendants Thurston and Seattle Trust argue that the respective assignments are excluded from the U.C.C. by two provisions—RCW 62A.9-102(1) [Now 1-109(a)] and RCW 62A.9-104(j) [Now 9-109(d)(11)]. RCW 62A.9-102(1) [Now 1-109(a)] reads in part:

> Except as otherwise provided ... in RCW 62A.9-104 on excluded transactions, *this Article applies so far as concerns any personal property* and fixtures within the jurisdiction of this state
>
> (a) to any transaction (regardless of its form) which is *intended to create a security interest in personal property* or fixtures including goods, documents, instruments, general intangibles, chattel paper, accounts or contract rights ...

RCW 62A.9-104(j) [Now 109(d)(11)] provides:

This Article does not apply

> (j) except to the extent that provision is made for fixtures in RCW 62A.9-313, *to the creation or transfer of an interest in or lien on real estate*, including a lease or rents thereunder; ...

(Italics ours.) The essence of the argument of defendants Seattle Trust and Thurston is that the contract right is an interest in realty and thus is excluded by RCW 62A.9-102(1)(a) [Now 9-109(a)] and 62A.9-104(j) [Now 9-109(d)(11)]. However, because we hold that a vendor's right to receive real estate contract payments is personal property it is evident U.C.C. article 9 applies.

A bankruptcy court considering the same contention made by Seattle Trust and Thurston held, as we do, that the transfer of rights in the contract is a transfer of personalty. *Hughes v. Russo, 20 U.C.C. Rep. Serv. 1349 (S.D. Fla. 1976).* The *Russo* court stated at page 1354:

> A right to contract proceeds is surely not an interest in land. No interest in land passes to a third party who obtains a right to collections on the contract as security for a loan obligation. Nor is the pledge of contracts an interest in land ...

> Thus, Article Nine is not applicable to execution of the subject contracts for the sale of land. ... However, when the vendor pledges his contract rights to defendants, Article Nine applies to the security interest created therein.

See also H. & Val J. Rothschild, Inc. v. Northwestern Nat'l Bank, 309 Minn. 35, 242 N.W.2d 844 (1976) (assignment for security of contractor's rights to receive payments under construction contracts creates security interest in contract rights covered by U.C.C. article 9).

Defendants Thurston and Seattle Trust next focus on RCW 62A.9-102(3) [Now 9-109(b)] and Official Comment 4 to U.C.C. §9-102. RCW 62A.9-102(3) [Now 9-109(b)] reads:

> The application of this Article to a security interest in a secured obligation is not affected by the fact that the obligation is itself secured by a transaction or interest to which this Article does not apply.

Official Comment 4 reads:

> An illustration of subsection (3) is as follows:

> The owner of Blackacre borrows $ 10,000 from his neighbor, and secures his note by a mortgage on Blackacre. This Article is not applicable to the creation of the real estate mortgage. Nor is it applicable to a sale of the note by the mortgagee, even though the mortgage continues to secure the note. However, *when the mortgagee pledges the note to secure his own obligation to X, this Article applies to the security interest thus created, which is a security interest in an instrument even though the instrument is secured by a real estate mortgage.*

> (Italics ours.)

Defendant Thurston acknowledges the applicability of the U.C.C. to the pledge of a note to secure the mortgagee's own obligation to a third party but nonetheless argues the U.C.C. is only "tangentially" involved because the security interest in the note can be perfected by possession. However, the situation in the comment set out above—where the mortgagee pledges the note to secure his own obligation to a third party—is analogous to the instant case. Here, the vendor and holder of legal title assigned the right to receive real estate contract payments in order to secure his obligation to a third party. *Hughes v. Russo, supra*, relies on an earlier but very similar version of Official Comment 4 to U.C.C. §9-102 [Now 9-109] in concluding that the giving of a mortgage along with the assignment of land sale contracts as collateral created a security interest (in the contracts) subject to article 9. The *Russo* court at page 1353 n.3 approvingly quoted J. White & R. Summers, *Uniform Commercial Code* §22-6, at 773 (1972), "It appears that Article Nine applies to security interests in 'realty paper'". In summary, RCW 62A.9-102(3) [Now-109(b)], U.C.C. §9-102, [Now 9-109] Official Comment 4 and *Russo* demonstrate that article 9 applies to the assignment of the legal title and contract together (Freeborn), requiring U.C.C. filing as to the contract right in order to perfect a security interest, as well as to the assignment of contract rights alone *(In re Hyak Skiing Corporation)*.

We hold that where the right to real estate contract payments *alone* is assigned and the legal title held by the vendor is not simultaneously conveyed by deed, as in *In re Hyak Skiing Corporation*, the assignee must file pursuant to U.C.C. article 9, RCW 62A.9-101 *et seq.*, in order to have priority over subsequent lien creditors, purchasers and encumbrancers, including a trustee in bankruptcy. While we strongly recommend that the assignment also be recorded pursuant to *RCW 65.08.070*, recording is not legally required because only an interest in personal property—unaccompanied by the vendor's legal title—has been transferred.

We further hold that where the vendor in a real estate contract executes a "Deed and Seller's Assignment of Real Estate Contract" by which he or she (a) assigns the contract and (b) conveys the real estate (legal title), as in *In re Freeborn*, the assignee-grantee must both file pursuant to U.C.C. article 9 (RCW 62A.9-101 *et seq.*) *and* record pursuant to *RCW 65.08.070* in order to have priority over subsequent lien creditors, purchasers and encumbrancers. The U.C.C. filing is necessary as to the right to receive contract payments. Recording is required because legal title is conveyed by the same instrument.

The clerk of this court shall certify this opinion to the federal district court in accordance with *RAP 16.16(g)* in answer to the questions of Washington law submitted.

Old Article 9 relied on what is now 9-109(b) to guide courts in determining when Article 9 was supposed to give way to real property law. But as the *Freeborn* case demonstrates, that provision often worked to obfuscate rather than to guide. In Revised Article 9, 9-109(b) now has a supporting cast to assist with its mission. First, the illustration from the comments to 9–109 quoted in *Freeborn* now makes clear that when your aunt uses your note to secure her obligation to the bank, Article 9 applies to the bank's security interest:

> The security interest in the promissory note is covered by this
> Article even though the note is secured by a real-property mortgage.

Comment 7, 9–109. Second, Revised 9–203(g) provides that the bank's
security interest in your note also gives the bank a security interest in the
mortgage you gave your aunt on your home. And third, Revised 9–308 provides that when the bank perfects its security interest in your note, it perfects
its security interest in the mortgage. Together, these provisions and comments
make clear what was not clear before the revision:

> … an attempt to obtain or perfect a security interest in a secured
> obligation by complying with non-Article 9 law, as by an assign-
> ment of record of a real-property mortgage, would be ineffective.

Comment 7, 9–109.

In other words, under Revised Article 9, because the mortgage (the interest in real property) always follows the obligation that it secures, it is not
treated as an independent interest in real property. When the note becomes
collateral in an Article 9 transaction, so too does the mortgage. And Article 9
applies to the whole package.

E. CONSIGNMENTS

Revised Article 9 accepts full custody of consignment transactions, replac-
ing the shared custody of Articles 2 and 9 that operated before the revision.
Consignments facilitate the sale of goods by allowing the owner (consignor)
to place goods with someone (consignee) who has the expertise, contacts, and/
or market presence, necessary to get the goods into the hands of the intended
end user. The attraction of a consignment as opposed to a sale on credit is
that the consignee is not obligated to pay for the goods unless they are sold
(and can ultimately return them if they are not) and the consignor retains
ownership of the goods and control of the ultimate terms on which they are
sold. Because title remains with the consignor, possession by the consignee is
without risk as the consignee has no interest in the goods that can be reached
by her creditors. And because the consignee is not obligated to pay for and
can return the goods unless sold, the consignee does not assume the risk of
getting stuck with them if they do not sell. Thus, for some, consignment—like
leasing—might be preferable to sale on credit.

But just as a secured transaction can be disguised as a lease, it can also be
disguised as a consignment. Even before revision, Article 9's substance trumps
form principal snared consignments intended for security and subjected them
to Article 9's general requirements. In a "true" consignment, the consignee
is simply the agent of the consignor, and as such follows the instructions of
the consignor with respect to the consigned goods. Title remains with the
consignor and on sale passes directly to the purchaser. The consignor sets
the price and other terms of the sale and pays the consignee a commission on
sale. Most importantly, the consignee has no obligation to pay for the goods

and remits the proceeds of any sales to the consignor less its commission. The consignee has the right to return to the consignor all goods not sold and owes nothing on the goods so returned. If the consignment requires the consignee to pay for any of the goods it cannot sell, it is not a true consignment, regardless of the other terms of the consignment.

All of this seems to suggest that whether Article 9 applies to a consignment turns simply on whether the consignment was a true consignment or one intended for security. A quick glance at the Code's treatment of consignments prior to Revised Article 9 would not have suggested otherwise. The Code appeared to deal with them as Article 2 (Sales of Goods) transactions. But as the following case demonstrates, upon a closer read of the Code, it would have become evident that most consignments, regardless of their nature, would be covered by Article 9. But that should come as no real surprise. Like security interests in personal property, consignments separate possession from ownership—the consignee has possession of the goods but the consignor claims to own them. It's the ostensible ownership problem—the form is different, but the evil is the same: people who deal with the consignee will not be aware of the secret claim of the consignor to the goods in possession of the consignee.

The *Excel Bank* case shows how Revised Article 9 dispenses with the Article 2 charade and brings most consignments within its coverage.

EXCEL BANK v. NATIONAL BANK OF KANSAS CITY
Court of Appeals of Missouri, Western District, Division Three
290 S.W.3d 801 (Mo. Ct. App. 2009)

ELLIS, *Justice*.

Excel Bank ("Excel") appeals from a summary judgment in favor of National Bank of Kansas City d/b/a Great American Acceptance Company ("GAAC") on Excel's replevin action concerning eighteen vehicles that GAAC seized from a used car dealer, Miles Truck and Auto ("Miles"). For the following reasons, we affirm.

The underlying facts are undisputed. On March 5, 2004, GAAC advanced money to Miles under a floor plan financing arrangement.[7] Miles granted GAAC a security interest in, among other things, all inventory that Miles "own[s] or ha[s] sufficient rights in which to transfer an interest, now or in the future ... and all proceeds and products" therefrom. Inventory was defined as "[a]ll inventory which [Miles] hold[s] for sale, lease, rental or demonstration and/or which [GAAC] ha[s] financed." GAAC filed a financing statement with the Missouri Secretary of State a few days later, identifying Miles as the debtor and describing the property in which it had a security interest.

---

7   "Floor plan financing is a method of financing where a lender provides money for the purpose of allowing a dealer of goods to buy inventory that is later resold to the consumer." *Citizens Nat'l Bank v. Maries County Bank, 244 S.W.3d 266, 269 (Mo. App. S.D. 2008).*

Miles defaulted on the financing agreement, and on January 12, 2008, GAAC seized certain vehicles from Miles's place of business. Shortly thereafter, Excel contacted GAAC, claiming an interest in eighteen of the seized vehicles and demanding their return. As evidence of its interest, Excel relied on a September 13, 2007 letter agreement with Miles stating:

> All remaining inventory for Eastland Auto Plaza, L.L.C. has been delivered to Miles Truck and Auto, 23110 E 40 HWY, Blue Springs, MO 64015. Miles has agreed to sell remaining inventory, receiving the amount of $400.00 per vehicle. This amount will cover sales commissions, advertisements, and any other cost incurred to sell the vehicles with the exception of repairs. Miles must call Excel Bank with all bids before any repairs are made. It will be the banks [*sic*] call whether or not to fix the vehicles. The bank will reimburse Miles for any repairs requested by the bank as long as he supplies invoices for all work done. Miles will call the bank concerning all bids to sell the vehicles and the bank will decide whether or not to take what is offered.

Excel further relied on the fact that it retained possession of the original certificates of title for the eighteen vehicles, which reflected Excel as the owner. Excel had not filed a financing statement with the Missouri Secretary of State concerning the disputed vehicles, it had not notified GAAC of any claimed interest prior to delivering the vehicles to Miles, and none of the vehicles were identified on Miles's lot as being subject to any claim or interest by Excel. GAAC refused to return the disputed vehicles.

On January 22, 2008, Excel filed a petition for replevin against GAAC in the Circuit Court of Jackson County. GAAC responded with an answer and a motion for summary judgment. Excel opposed the motion and filed its own motion for summary judgment. After a hearing, the court sustained GAAC's motion and denied Excel's motion, issuing its findings of fact, conclusions of law, and judgment on May 22, 2008. The court concluded that the relationship between Excel and Miles concerning the disputed vehicles was a consignment subject to the perfection requirements of the Uniform Commercial Code ("UCC"), that possession of the certificates of title in Excel's name was insufficient to perfect Excel's interest, and that Excel had an unperfected purchase money security interest. The court further concluded that GAAC had a validly perfected security interest in Miles's entire inventory, that GAAC's interest was superior to Excel's interest, and that GAAC was entitled to retain possession of the disputed vehicles. This appeal follows.

* * *

In its sole point of error, Excel asserts that the circuit court erred in granting summary judgment in favor of GAAC because the court erroneously concluded that the relationship between Excel and Miles concerning the disputed vehicles was a consignment subject to the requirements of the UCC instead of a simple bailment to which GAAC's security interest did not attach. Excel concedes that, if the circuit court correctly concluded that the relationship was a consignment, then GAAC had a superior security interest in the disputed vehicles and was entitled to seize them.

The UCC is intended "'(a) to simplify, clarify and modernize the law governing commercial transactions;' and '(c) to make uniform law among the various jurisdictions.'" *Dean Mach. Co. v. Union Bank, 106 S.W.3d 510, 517 (Mo. App. W.D. 2003)* (quoting §400.1-102(2)). Because there is very little Missouri case law concerning consignments under the UCC, we look to decisions from other jurisdictions for guidance. *Id.* In addition, "Official Comments to uniform laws adopted by the legislature, though not controlling, are a persuasive aid in determining legislative intent." *Mamoulian v. St. Louis Univ., 732 S.W.2d 512, 516 n.10 (Mo. banc 1987).*

"A 'bailment' in its ordinary legal sense signifies a contract resulting from the delivery of a thing by the bailor to the bailee with the condition that it be restored to the bailor in accordance with his directions as soon as the purpose for which it was bailed is satisfied." *K.C. Landsmen, L.L.C. v. Lowe-Guido, 35 S.W.3d 917, 922 (Mo. App. W.D. 2001).* "A consignment is a type of bailment where the goods are entrusted for sale." *Eagle Boats, Ltd. v. Cont'l Ins. Co. Marine Office of Am., Corp., 968 S.W.2d 734, 737 (Mo. App. E.D. 1998).*

The UCC was substantially revised effective July 1, 2001. Under both the prior and current versions, *§2-326* provides that, "[u]nless otherwise agreed, if delivered goods may be returned by the buyer even though they conform to the contract, the transaction is … a 'sale or return' if the goods are delivered primarily for resale." Goods held on "sale or return" are subject to the claims of the buyer's creditors while in the buyer's possession. §2-326(2). Prior to July 1, 2001, *§2-326(3)* provided:

> Where goods are delivered to a person for sale and such person maintains a place of business at which he deals in goods of the kind involved, under a name other than the name of the person making delivery, then with respect to claims of creditors of the person conducting the business the goods are deemed to be on sale or return. The provisions of this subsection are applicable even though an agreement purports to reserve title to the person making delivery until payment or resale or uses such words as "on consignment" or "on memorandum". However, this subsection is not applicable if the person making delivery
>
> (a) complies with an applicable law providing for a consignor's interest or the like to be evidenced by a sign, or
>
> (b) establishes that the person conducting the business is generally known by his creditors to be substantially engaged in selling the goods of others, or

(c) complies with the filing provisions of the Article on secured transactions (Article 9). ...

§2-326(3) (2000).

Section 9-114 then provided that "[a] person who delivers goods under a consignment which is not a security interest and would be required to file under [Article 9] by *paragraph (3)(c) of Section 2-326* has priority over a secured party who is or becomes a creditor of the consignee and who would have a perfected security interest in the goods if they were the property of the consignee" if the consignor complies with specified notice requirements.

"'[C]ertain true consignment transactions were dealt with in the former *Sections 2-326(3)* and *9-114*,'" but those provisions were deleted effective July 1, 2001, and were replaced by *§§9-109(a)(4)*, *9-103(d)* and *9-319*. As a result, *§2-326* no longer applies to consignments. "If a transaction is a 'sale or return,' as defined in revised *Section 2-326*, it is not a 'consignment.' In a 'sale or return' transaction, the buyer becomes the owner of the goods, and the seller may obtain an enforceable security interest in the goods only by satisfying the requirements of *Section 9-203*." UCC *§9-109 cmt. 6*; *see also In re Haley & Steele, Inc.*, (A "sale or return" requires a "present sale," where a "sale" is defined as "the passing of title from the seller to the buyer for a price," *§2-106(1)*, and that "is not what happens when goods pass from a consignor to a consignee.").

Under the current version of the UCC, Article 9 applies to every "consignment" as defined in *§9-102*. *See* §9-109(a)(4); Goss v. Morgansen's Ltd., *2005 U.S. Dist. LEXIS 43600, at *18-19 (E.D.N.Y. Sept. 27, 2005)* (Former *§2-326* governed "true" consignments and Article 9 governed consignments intended as security interests, but *§2-326* was amended in 2001 "so that transactions involving consignments would generally be covered by Article 9."). A consignment is defined as:

> a transaction, regardless of its form, in which a person delivers goods to a merchant for the purpose of sale and:
>
> (A) The merchant:
>
> > (i) Deals in goods of that kind under a name other than the name of the person making delivery;
> >
> > (ii) Is not an auctioneer; and
> >
> > (iii) Is not generally known by its creditors to be substantially engaged in selling the goods of others;
>
> (B) With respect to each delivery, the aggregate value of the goods is one thousand dollars or more at the time of delivery;
>
> (C) The goods are not consumer goods immediately before delivery; and
>
> (D) The transaction does not create a security interest that secures an obligation[.]

UCC §9-102(a)(20). This definition "includes many but not all 'true' consignments (i.e., bailments for the purpose of sale)." *UCC §9-109 cmt. 6.* Subparagraphs (B) and (C) exclude "transactions for which filing would be inappropriate or of insufficient benefit to justify the costs." *UCC §9-102 cmt. 14.* In addition, "consignments intended for security" are excluded from the definition of "consignment" because they "are not bailments but secured transactions" and are subject to all of the provisions of Article 9. *Id.*

"Once the transaction is determined to fall within the revised *UCC §§9-102(a)(20)* definition of consignment, then revised *UCC §9-319(a)* applies when a creditor of the consignee seeks to recover against the consigned goods." *Section 9-319(a)* provides that, "for purposes of determining the rights of creditors of … a consignee, while the goods are in the possession of the consignee, the consignee is deemed to have rights and title to the goods identical to those the consignor had." "Insofar as creditors of the consignee are concerned, [Article 9] to a considerable extent reformulates the former law, which appeared in former *Sections 2-326* and 9-114, without changing the results." *UCC §9-319 cmt. 2.*

Section 9-103(d) provides that "[t]he security interest of a consignor in goods that are the subject of a consignment is a purchase-money security interest in inventory." Accordingly, the perfection and priority rules concerning competing security interests apply to consigned goods. *UCC §9-109 cmt. 6.* With certain exceptions, a financing statement must be filed to perfect all security interests. §9-310(a). In general, a financing statement need not be filed to perfect a security interest in a motor vehicle because it may be perfected by complying with *§§301.600 to 301.660, RSMo*, which concern motor vehicle liens and registration. §9-310(b)(3); §9-311(a)(2). However, this exception to the filing requirement does not apply to security interests created by a dealer of motor vehicles who holds the vehicles for sale. §301.650.1(3); §9-311(d). In the case at bar, it is undisputed that GAAC had a validly perfected security interest in Miles's after-acquired inventory and that Excel did not take the required steps to perfect any interest it may have had under the UCC. "A perfected security interest … has priority over a conflicting unperfected security interest. …" §9-322(a)(2).

The Article 9 definition of a consignment is very similar to the definition under former *§2-326(3)*. Both sections require that (1) the goods be delivered to a person for sale where that person maintains a place of business at which he deals in goods of the kind involved under a name other than the name of the person making delivery and (2) the person conducting the business is not generally known by his creditors to be substantially engaged in selling the goods of others. In the case at bar, Excel argues that its relationship with Miles concerning the disputed vehicles was not a consignment because Miles was not holding the vehicles "for sale." It contends that the relationship was more like a "parking garage" than a consignment because Excel retained the certificates of title, which listed Excel as the owner, and Miles did not have authority to transfer title without Excel's approval but was only procuring offers for purchase.

Excel relies on several cases interpreting former §2-326(3) where the courts stated the general definition of a consignment and/or held that a consignment existed where there was no evidence of restrictions on the dealer's authority to transfer property to a buyer. However, none of these cases stands for the proposition that a dealer must have unrestricted authority to transfer title for a consignment to exist. Excel further relies on several bankruptcy cases involving competing claims to grain deposited in a grain elevator, but farm products are subject to special rules under both the UCC and the Bankruptcy Code, so those cases are inapplicable to the facts at hand. At common law, consignors often prevailed over creditors who had extended credit to a consignee based on the consignee's apparent ownership of consigned goods. Consignors prevailed because they still held title in the goods; a consignee's creditors were therefore viewed as unable to take any interest through the consignee." *In re State Street Auto Sales, Inc., 81 B.R. 215, 218 (Bankr. D. Mass. 1988).*

"The purpose of former *UCC §2-326(3)* and now revised *UCC §§9-102(a) (20) & 9-319(a)* is to protect general creditors of the consignee from claims of consignors that have undisclosed consignment arrangements with the consignee that create secret liens on the inventory." *In re Valley Media, Inc., 279 B.R. at 125.*

> The basis for this hostility to consignment arrangements … is fairly obvious. Regardless of the legal theory of the consignment, in practical operation it looks like a sales transaction in which the unpaid seller retains a secret lien in his goods. *From a creditor's point of view, the consigned goods appear to be part of the regular inventory of the consignee which, therefore, ought to be subject to their claims.* What is more, … there is no public filing or other notoriety respecting the consignment to warn the creditors that the consignor may have rights in the goods which are superior to theirs.

*Goss, 2005 U.S. Dist. LEXIS 43600, at *16* (quoting *In re Truck Accessories Distributing, Inc., 238 B.R. 444, 448 (Bankr. E. D. Ark. 1999)).* "The policy of the UCC would be undermined if an owner could show by proof of undisclosed mental operations that the transaction was something other than a consignment." *ITT Commercial Fin. Corp. v. Unlimited Auto., Inc., 166 B.R. 637, 644 (N.D. Ill. 1994); see also Bischoff v. Thomasson, 400 So.2d 359, 367 (Ala. 1981)).* The primary difference after the 2001 revisions is that consignors may no longer rely on notice through the posting of signs and/or written notification to other creditors, and they must now file a financing statement to protect their interests.

Many courts have described the concept of a "true" consignment, as opposed to a sale or a consignment intended as a security interest, both before and after the 2001 revisions to the UCC. "A consignment of goods for sale does not pass the title at any time, nor does it contemplate that it should be passed. … In effect, a consignment is a special kind of agency involving the delivery of goods to one … for the purpose of finding a buyer." *Bischoff, 400 So. 2d at 364* (internal quotations omitted). A consignment "exists where one party ... transfers possession of goods to another ... who in turn resells the goods to third-party consumers," where "[t]itle and the right to immediate possession of the goods remains with the consignor" until the consignee exercises its option to take title once certain conditions are met. *Nektalov, 440 F.Supp.2d at 298*; *see also Cherry-Air, Inc. v. OK Turbines, Inc.*, No. 00-42141-BJH-11, 2001 Bankr. LEXIS 2243, at *11 (Bankr. N.D. Tex. Apr. 17, 2001) ("'[A] true consignment is one in which the consignor retains extensive control over the goods but gives up possession with the intent that they be sold to a third party and in which the consignee may return the goods at any time and is not obligated to pay a fixed price for them.'" (quoting *3A Ronald A. Anderson, Anderson on the Uniform Commercial Code* §2-326:48 (3d ed. 1995)).

"[T]he UCC looks to the outwardly visible aspects of a transaction in determining whether an arrangement for the sale of goods is a consignment." *ITT Commercial Fin. Corp.*, 166 B.R. at 644; *see also Bischoff*, 400 So.2d at 367. The term "for sale" in the UCC definition of consignment "refers to a transaction's ultimate purpose and not ... to the question of whether the person to whom the goods were entrusted had the independent authority to sell them." *Berk v. State Bank of India*, No. 96 CIV. 4972 (MBM), 1998 U.S. Dist. LEXIS 13696, at *11 (S.D.N.Y. Aug. 28, 1998). This is consistent with the principle that former *§2-326(3)*, and now *§§9-102(a)(20)* and *9-319(a)*, were "designed to allow creditors to make lending decisions on the basis of externally visible information, without having to investigate undisclosed side agreements that may seek to structure a transaction as something other than a [consignment]." *1998 U.S. Dist. LEXIS 13696, [WL] at *11-12.*

Factors indicating that the parties intended a "true" consignment include that the consignor retains control over the sale price, the consignee is given possession with authority to sell only upon consent of the consignor, the consignor may recall the goods at any time, and the consignee is to receive a commission instead of a profit from the sale. *In re Oriental Rug Warehouse Club*, 205 B.R. 407, 410 (Bankr. D. Minn. 1997); *see also Nektalov, 440 F.Supp.2d at 299* ("[A] 'true consignment' is characterized by the fact that the consignor retains ownership and sets the sale price; the consignee receives a commission and not the profits of the sale" (internal quotation omitted)). All of these factors are present in the case at bar. Miles was to attempt to "sell remaining inventory," he would receive $400 commission for each vehicle for whom he found a buyer willing to purchase a vehicle at a price approved by Excel, and he was not obligated to pay for any of the vehicles for which he did not find a buyer. The fact that Excel retained title and extensive control over the disputed vehicles does not prevent the transaction from being a consignment subject to the perfection requirements of the UCC. Although Miles was not given full authority to sell the vehicles to whomever he chose for any price, the vehicles were clearly entrusted to him for the ultimate purpose of sale.

* * *

In revising the UCC in 2001, the drafters of the UCC, and by extension the Missouri legislature, chose to remove the additional provisions that allowed consignors to protect their interests through actual or constructive notice and, instead, required them to file a UCC financing statement to protect their interests. Both Excel and GAAC are sophisticated parties with access to expert advice on the requirements of the UCC. Excel could easily have filed a financing statement to protect its interest in the vehicles, but it took no steps whatsoever to inform third parties that it retained any interest in the vehicles, other than retaining the certificates of title in its possession. Although GAAC could have checked the motor vehicle registry in addition to the UCC filings, it was not required to do so. Point denied.

The trial court's judgment is affirmed.

F. OTHER EXCLUSIONS

PROBLEM 2–5

Several years ago, Ray started selling insurance on the side—the extra income was helpful when sales at the store were slow. He worked out of his office in the store during the evening, responding by phone to online requests with quotes that several different insurance companies would forward to him each day. He received a commission on every policy he sold during these quote calls. Although he sold policies for several different insurance companies, most of his commissions were made selling GEICO policies. Ray's bank has agreed to loan him the money he needs to add a hot tub to his backyard deck in return for a security interest in commissions he's already earned and those he will earn in the future. Will the bank's security interest be subject to Article 9? See 9-109(d)(3).

PROBLEM 2–6

Earlier this year Ray obtained a judgment for breach of warranty against a manufacturer of appliances he had purchased to sell in his store. Ray has agreed to assign his interest in the judgment to his father-in-law in return for the loan he needs to pay for a new roof for the store. Is Ray's transaction with his father-in-law covered by Article 9? See 9-109(d)(9). If Ray's father-in-law had agreed to take a security interest in Ray's life insurance policy instead of the judgment as collateral for the loan, would that transaction be covered by Article 9? See 9-109(d)(8).

PROBLEM 2–7

Ray's bank has agreed to take a security interest in his personal checking account to secure a loan Ray needs to purchase new computer equipment for the store. Will the bank need to comply with Article 9 to protect its interest in the checking account against the claims of Ray's other creditors? See 9-109(d)(13).

CHAPTER 3

CREATING AND PROTECTING A SECURITY INTEREST

Whether the parties have created an enforceable security interest that Article 9 cares about depends on whether they have complied with the formal requirements of Article 9 for doing so. Similarly, whether the secured party has protected that Article 9 security interest against third parties claiming an interest in the collateral depends on whether the secured party has taken the steps required by Article 9 to "perfect" its security interest. Under Article 9, creation and perfection of a security interest are, with some exceptions, independent procedures and each has its own requirements for effectiveness. The different requirements make sense in light of the different purposes served. Creating the security interest establishes the relationship between the debtor and the secured party and therefore requires some form of an agreement evidencing that relationship. Perfection of the security interest is what provides notice of that security interest to others and therefore requires the creation of a public record that is available to those dealing with the debtor. Accordingly, we address the requirements of each separately in the materials that follow.

A. CREATION

Under Article 9, a security interest is effective when it has "attached" to the collateral. A security interest "attaches" to collateral when it has become enforceable against the debtor. 9-203(a). A security interest is enforceable against the debtor when (1) the debtor has authenticated a security agreement, (2) the secured party has given value, and (3) the debtor has rights in the collateral. 9-203(b). Thus, until the security interest has attached—until there is an actual agreement between the debtor and the secured party, the secured party has extended credit (usual way it gives value), and the debtor actually has some interest in the personal property that is intended to serve as collateral, there is no interest in property that secures the payment or performance of an obligation.

Although "attachment" has a metaphysical aura to it, it simply means that all of the events necessary to create a security interest have occurred. These events need not occur in any specific order or within a specified period of time. The debtor can execute the security agreement even if she doesn't have the intended collateral or even if the intended collateral does not yet exist. The security interest will attach—become enforceable against the collateral—the moment the last of these three events occurs.

The material that follows addresses in detail the requirements for a security agreement and what rights in the collateral the debtor must have. The third requirement for attachment, that the secured party give value, need not detain us long. In most cases, the giving of value by the secured party will take the form of an extension of credit. Ray sells you the washer on credit or the bank loans you the money to buy the washer from Ray. But as defined by the Code, value also includes a pre-existing debt[1]—taking property as security for a pre-existing claim. You give your best friend a security interest in your car on account of the money she loaned you last year to buy your books for law school. 1-204(2). And value as used in the Code also means "a binding commitment to extend credit" even though credit has not actually been extended. 1-204(1). The definition of value under the Code is so broad that it presents few problems for purposes of determining whether attachment has occurred.

1. CLASSIFICATION: GENERALLY

The process of creating (and protecting) a security interest in personal property requires us, initially, to understand how Article 9 classifies the many different kinds of personal property that a creditor might want to take as collateral for a loan or other extension of credit. Mastering Article 9's scheme of collateral classification is important for two reasons. First, a secured party may use Code classes for purposes of satisfying the requirement that the security agreement "describe" the collateral and the requirement that the financing statement "indicate" the collateral. Mistakes in classifying the collateral in the security agreement will cost the secured party its intended collateral. Classification mistakes in the financing statement will cost the secured party the protection it was expecting under Article 9 against the claims of other creditors. Second, classification of collateral determines whether special rules are applicable to the transaction. For example, purchase money security interests in consumer goods are automatically perfected; after-acquired property clauses are generally not effective against consumer goods; Article 9 applies to both the sale of and the grant of a security interest in accounts receivable; certain buyers of inventory will take free of a pre-existing security interest in inventory; buyers

---

1   There are specific provisions of Article 9 that require "new value," in which case a pre-existing debt would not satisfy the requirement. See, e.g., 9-330.

of chattel paper and instruments can take free of a security interest in the chattel paper or instruments; documents of title and instruments are subject to rules providing for temporary perfection. Classification mistakes that result in a failure to identify the transaction as subject to a special rule may preclude perfection of a security interest or worse.

Article 9 divides personal property into eleven classes which can be grouped into three general categories: goods, pledgeable intangibles, and pure intangibles. Goods are the kinds of things that most of us would think of as personal property on a day-to-day basis: Toasters, lawnmowers, micro waves, cars, and furniture. But goods also includes the washers and dryers in stock at Ray's store, as well as the cows grazing on grandpa's farm and the printing press at the local print shop. Pledgeable intangibles are essentially pieces of paper that represent a claim to goods or a right to payment, and the claim or right represented by the paper can be transferred or pledged by physical delivery of the paper. Checks, promissory notes, the forms you fill out to ship something with UPS, all fall within this category. Pure intangibles are rights or claims that have no tangible form—there is no physical manifestation of them that can be used to transfer them or to pledge them. Patents, trademarks, copyrights, licenses, accounts, all fall within this category.

The problems which follow introduce the eleven classes of collateral and develop the distinctions between the classes within each of the general categories we've already identified. We will explore most of these classes in more detail in the context of perfecting a security interest or resolving priority disputes between creditors competing for the same collateral.

PROBLEM 3-1

Using the Article 9 classification scheme, how would you classify the following collateral:

1. The vehicle you drove to school today. The vehicles Avis rents to its customers. The limos you can rent from the limousine service in town.

2. The textbooks for sale at your school's book store. The used textbooks you're offering to sell to a classmate. The textbooks a publisher provides for review by your professor.

3. The cans of Red Bull in the cooler at the local convenience store. The can of Red Bull in your hands after you've purchased it.

4. The printing press at the local print shop. The ink the print shop uses in the printing press.

5. The recliner in your professor's office. The carols in the law library.

6. The tomatoes you are growing in the garden behind your house. The tomatoes you're selling at your roadside stand.

7. The dairy cows your grandfather raises on his dairy farm. The tractor your grandfather uses to bale hay on his dairy farm. The calves born this year on your grandfather's dairy farm.

8. The sheep pelts at the yarn factory. The yarn for sale at the yarn shop. The sweater your grandmother knitted for you with yarn she purchased at the yarn shop.

9. The lap top computer you bought for law school. The lap top computer your law firm provides so you can work at home.

10. The candy bars in the vending machines downstairs. The vending machines themselves.

11. Your dad's collection of rare Beatles albums. The baseball cards bought and sold by a card collector. The autographed baseballs in the display case at the sports memorabilia shop across town.

PROBLEM 3–2

How would you classify the following collateral under Article 9:

1. Your checking account at the bank. A check you've written on that account.

2. The ticket you're given when you check your backpack at the museum. The baggage claim the airline gives you when you check your luggage. The receipt given to the farmer by the grain silo when she drops her corn off for storage.

3. The dry cleaner's right to be paid for cleaning your suits. An airplane voucher for a future flight.

4. Payments under a settlement agreement resolving a breach of contract claim. Payments under a settlement agreement resolving a tort claim.

5. Your parents' brokerage account. The 100 shares of IBM stock in your parents' brokerage account.

6. Your right to a tax refund. Your right to have your damage deposit returned when your apartment lease expires. Your apartment lease.

ART. 9 DOESN'T CARE
REAL PROP.

7. A promissory note stapled to a security agreement. The leases its customers sign when Avis rents them cars.

8. A one-year certificate of deposit. A passbook savings account.

9. Royalty payments for the songs you wrote before starting law school. Your patent for the ear buds you designed. The music you've downloaded to your iPod.

10. Your obligation to pay your aunt back for the money she loaned you to buy your law books. The paper you signed promising to pay her back.

The *Davenport* and *McGehee* cases illustrate how collateral classification can affect the interests of the parties to an Article 9 transaction, and how incorrectly classifying the collateral might leave a creditor without the protection it assumed it had acquired when it prepared the documents required by Article 9. But they also emphasize, as we tried to emphasize in Problems 3 – 1 and 3 – 2, that Article 9 classifies collateral based on how the individual debtor uses that collateral not on the generic use we might expect to be made of a particular kind of collateral.

DAVENPORT v. BATES
Court of Appeals of Tennessee
2006 WL 3627875 (Tenn. Ct. App. 2006)

HIGHERS, *Justice.*

* * *

I. FACTS & PROCEDURAL HISTORY

On May 1, 2000, Michael Davenport ('Buyer' or 'Appellee') purchased a 1995 Chevrolet Corvette from Rick Bates d/b/a RB Auto Sales ('Seller' or 'Appellant'). The Corvette was purchased pursuant to a written contract which provided that Buyer would make monthly payments to Seller, and Seller would retain a security interest in the vehicle. [Davenport also purchased a truck on credit from Bates]

* * *

On January 1, 2004, Buyer called Seller to say that he would be unable to make his January payments on time. … At that point, according to Seller, he informed Buyer that 'it [was] over,' he would no longer tolerate the late payments and was sending someone to repossess the car.

The Corvette was repossessed on January 6, 2004. Buyer claims he knew nothing about Seller's plans to repossess until he got home and the car was gone.

* * *

Seller subsequently resold both vehicles, receiving $12,500 from a wholesaler for the Corvette and $8,000 for the truck. At trial, conflicting evidence was presented regarding whether Seller notified Buyer of these sales. Buyer claims he never received notice of either sale, nor did he receive an explanation of whether a deficiency or surplus remained after the sale. Seller testified that it was his policy to send a letter of notice to a customer ten days prior to a sale of the customer's repossessed vehicle. He also acknowledged his policy of providing notice of any surplus or deficiency existing upon sale. Seller claimed that he complied with these policies in dealing with Buyer. According to his testimony, he sent the appropriate letters to Buyer's home address, but the letters were returned to him. When asked about the current location of these notices, Seller stated that he had provided the originals to Buyer's former attorney, and Seller had no copies. However, upon re-examination, Seller acknowledged his inconsistent deposition testimony, in which he had stated that no notice was given to Buyer prior to the sale.

Buyer had made payments on the Corvette over the course of three and a half years totaling approximately $22,700.00, leaving a balance of $7,624.61 owing at the time of repossession according to the balance shown on his last payment receipt. Prior to the sale, Seller performed repairs on the car in the amount of $847.00. Seller then resold the Corvette for about $12,500.00 wholesale. It is undisputed that Seller retained money from the sale beyond what he was owed on the car, and Buyer never received that 'surplus.'

* * *

Buyer filed an amended complaint in the Circuit Court for Davidson County on January 11, 2005, alleging that Seller repossessed the vehicles in violation of the sales contracts, violated the Tennessee Consumer Protection Act, and engaged in intentional and outrageous conduct entitling Buyer to punitive damages. Buyer's request for relief included ... statutory damages pursuant to Tenn. Code Ann. §47-9-625, which provides remedies to a buyer if a secured party fails to comply with proper procedures upon a buyer's default.

Seller's answer stated various defenses. ... Additionally, Seller included a counterclaim for payment of the balance owing under the two contracts.

Buyer's answer to Seller's countercomplaint asserted that Seller. ... could not recover because he failed to comply with the proper procedures for repossession under Tennessee law. He also cited other defenses which are not relevant to this appeal.

* * *

On May 6, 2005, the trial court entered an order based on the jury's factual findings. Buyer was awarded $7,777 statutory damages for Seller's failure to provide proper notice of the sale of the Corvette and $4,385 statutory damages for Seller's failure to provide proper notice of the sale of the truck. These statutory damages were calculated pursuant to Tenn. Code Ann. §47-9-625(c)(2) for 'consumer goods' collateral. In addition, Buyer was awarded $9,875.39 for the 'surplus' existing after the sale of the Corvette. ...

On June 3, 2005, Seller filed a motion to alter or amend the judgment, or in the alternative, to grant a new trial.

* * *

Seller challenged the court's award and calculation of statutory damages. The court had calculated those damages according to the statute's provision for 'consumer goods' transactions. Buyer had testified that both the car and the truck were used in his landscaping business. ...

On July 25, 2005, the trial court entered an order on the parties' post-trial motions. ... The court withdrew the $4,385 statutory damages for consumer collateral in regard to the truck, which reduced the total judgment against Seller to $15,824.25.

* * *

C. DAMAGES

1. CONSUMER OR COMMERCIAL TRANSACTION

When a secured party fails to comply with the statutory notice requirements, the debtor may recover damages for its loss. Tenn. Code Ann. §47-9-625 (2001). However, if the collateral is 'consumer goods,' the debtor is entitled to recover a minimum statutory penalty without regard to his actual loss or his ability to prove that he has been damaged at all. ... The consumer debtor may recover an amount not less than 10% of the cash price plus the time-price differential. Tenn. Code Ann. §47-9-625(c)(2).

* * *

The trial court awarded statutory damages to Buyer for Seller's failure to notify him of the sales pursuant to Tenn. Code Ann. §47-9-625(c)(2) (2001) for 'consumer goods' collateral. (Vol.I, p. 84). Initially, the award included $7,777 regarding the sale of the Corvette and $4,385 regarding the truck. On Seller's motion to alter or amend, the trial court withdrew the award for the truck, apparently concluding that it was not a 'consumer goods' transaction. The court did not alter the $7,777 statutory damage award regarding the Corvette.

On appeal, Seller argues that the trial court erred in calculating damages for a 'consumer goods' transaction because Buyer himself testified that he used the Corvette in his landscaping business.

* * *

We will next consider the trial judge's conclusion that the Corvette transaction involved 'consumer goods.' If the Corvette is considered 'consumer goods,' Buyer is entitled to the sizeable statutory penalty. ...

In secured transactions, collateral is defined by its type of primary use in the hands of the debtor. ... 'Consumer goods' are defined as 'goods that are used or bought for use primarily for personal, family, or household purposes.' Tenn. Code Ann. §47-9-102(a)(23) "UCC §9-102" (2001). 'Of course, broadly speaking, every buyer is a 'consumer.' *Int'l Harvester Credit Corp. v. Hill*, 496 F. Supp. 329, 333-34 (M.D.Tenn.1979). However, the fact that an item is personally used does not mean it was for 'personal use.' *Id.* at 334.

At trial, various witnesses gave lengthy testimony about the value of the Corvette and its condition. However, the testimony as to Buyer's use of the Corvette was fairly limited. The following exchange took place between Buyer and his counsel:

Q. Just tell me what you did with the Corvette once you purchased the Corvette.

A. I bought it and used it in my landscaping business.

Q. Okay. What-explain that to us.

A. Well, of course, I didn't haul dirt in it, it was a Corvette. I went and looked at jobs in it, went and collected money in it, and went and done proposals in it, things like that.

Buyer also stated that one of his landscaping employees was paid to keep the car clean. In addition, when questioned about his failure to insure the vehicles as required by the contract, Buyer stated that he had attempted to have the Corvette and the dually put on one commercial insurance policy. He also provided documentation to Seller of his application for a commercial insurance policy. For some time, Seller was under the impression that the commercial policy covered the vehicles.

Buyer now contends that his testimony, along with that of his witnesses, demonstrates that the Corvette was a collector's item, and thus, inherently for personal use. He refers to his testimony that he kept the Corvette in excellent condition and had it cleaned on a regular basis. He also notes that he referred to the car as his 'baby' and said he loved the car. Also, he testified that he kept the car in a garage and did not drive it in the rain. According to Buyer, this is 'conclusive proof' that the vehicle was purchased for personal use. We disagree.

In searching the extensive transcript of the testimony in this case, we are unable to locate a single reference to an occasion of Buyer driving the car for personal or family use. To the contrary, all of Buyer's testimony relates to his use of the car in his business. When a debtor would benefit if the collateral constituted 'consumer goods,' the debtor has the burden of proving the nature of the collateral. 10 Ronald A. Anderson, *Anderson on the Uniform Commercial Code §9-507:77* (3rd ed.1999) (citing *Wilmington Trust Co. v. Conner*, 415 A.2d 773, 781 (Del.1980); *Bundrick v. First Nat'l Bank*, 570 S.W.2d 12, (Tex.Civ.App.1978)). In borderline cases of classifying collateral, the principal use of the property is determinative. *In re Frazier*, 16 B.R. 674, 680 (Bankr.M.D.Tenn.1981). Buyer simply did not produce any evidence that the vehicle was 'used or bought for use primarily for personal, family, or household purposes.' Tenn.Code Ann. §47-9-102(a)(23) (2001) [UCC §9-102].

Buyer, on appeal, cites two cases in support of his argument that the Corvette was a 'consumer good.' First, he notes that just because a vehicle is used for a particular purpose does not necessarily place the vehicle in that particular category, and he cites *Int'l Harvester Credit Corp. v. Hill*, 496 F.Supp. 329, 333-34 (M.D.Tenn.1979). We agree with Buyer's statement. We must consider the 'primary use' of the collateral in the hands of the debtor. *Walker*, 673 S.W.2d at 522. In *Int'l Harvester*, the collateral at issue was a tractor. 496 F.Supp. at 333. The court classified it as equipment, stating that just because an item is personally used does not mean it was for 'personal use' under the statute. *Id.* at 334. The court also said, '[i]t is the actual use to which the equipment is put and not the occupational status of the owner which is determinative.' *Id.* at 333. In this case, just because Buyer is a landscaper does not mean he could not use the Corvette for commercial purposes. Buyer himself acknowledged the peculiarity of his using the Corvette in his landscaping business. He explained, 'of course, I didn't haul dirt in it, it was a Corvette. I went and looked at jobs in it, went and collected money in it, and went and done proposals in it, things like that.' He hauled dirt and materials in the dually. His testimony demonstrates that he had a need for another vehicle in which he could easily travel to potential job sites and interact with customers, and he used the Corvette for those purposes.

Buyer also discusses *Mallicoat v. Volunteer Fin. & Loan Corp.*, 415 S.W.2d 347 (Tenn.Ct.App.1966), in which the court briefly discussed the classification of collateral. The court stated:

> There is no proof that [the buyer] was in a business requiring the use of an automobile. He testified he bought it to use in going to and from his place of employment. It is clearly not 'equipment', 'farm products' or 'inventory' as defined by T.C.A. §47-9-109. We,

therefore, hold that it falls within the category of 'consumer goods' as defined by the same Section of the Act.

Id. at 349-50.

Buyer now asserts that he used the Corvette in precisely the same way-to travel to and from his employment. He argues that he was not in a business to need a Corvette. However, as we have already discussed, Buyer's testimony revealed that he used the Corvette for various commercial reasons. In our opinion, Buyer's occupation would qualify as a business requiring the use of an automobile. He did not merely drive to and from an office everyday with no occasion to use the car for business reasons. Although he may not have needed a Corvette, specifically, he needed some type of vehicle and chose to purchase a Corvette. If Buyer had used another truck or a less expensive car and testified that he used it for these same commercial purposes, the vehicle would clearly not be classified as a consumer good. We will not accept Buyer's argument on appeal that the Corvette is 'inherently' a collector's item, and therefore for personal use, when the evidence he presented at trial does not support that conclusion.

In sum, we conclude that the evidence presented in this case does not support a finding that the Corvette was purchased in a 'consumer goods' transaction. Therefore, the statutory penalty available in consumer transactions was awarded in error. We vacate the trial court's award of $7,777 to Buyer regarding the Corvette. We find it unnecessary to address the issue Seller presented regarding the trial court's alleged error in calculating the award.

McGEHEE v. EXCHANGE BANK & TRUST CO.

Court of Civil Appeals of Texas, Waco
561 S.W.2d 926 (Tex. Civ. App. 1978)

JAMES, *Justice*.

This is a suit concerning conversion of a boat. Plaintiff-Appellee Exchange Bank and Trust Company sued Defendant-Appellants Lynn and H. G. McGehee (husband and wife) for damages for conversion of the boat in controversy against which Exchange Bank held a security interest. After jury trial the trial court entered judgment for Plaintiff Exchange Bank against Defendants McGehees for $15,222.39 plus interest and costs, from which the McGehees appeal. We affirm the trial court's judgment after reforming same as hereinafter shown.

On October 26, 1971, one Harry W. Baer, a resident of Tarrant County, Texas, executed a promissory note in the amount of $17,895.75 in favor of Plaintiff Exchange Bank, and also executed a security agreement and financing statement with respect to the boat in question which Baer at that time purchased. Then on November 1, 1971, Exchange Bank filed the financing statement in the office of the County Clerk of Tarrant County, Texas, the county of residence of Baer.

Thereafter Baer made periodic payments on the note and made two renewals of said note, the first time on January 26, 1972, for $22,785.00 and again on November 27, 1974, for $13,063.76. This last 1974 renewal note was never paid in full and on October 29, 1975, Exchange Bank took a default judgment against Baer in a Dallas County District Court for $12,509.44 plus $1212.95 interest and $1500.00 attorneys' fees and costs. Prior to this default judgment, however, in June of 1974, Baer sold the boat to the Defendant McGehees.

When the McGehees bought the boat from Baer in June of 1974, they had no knowledge of the Exchange Bank lien against it. Before buying the boat, Mr. McGehee specifically asked Baer whether he owed any money on the boat and Baer told him he did not.

Neither of the McGehees ever inquired with the Secretary of State or of the County Clerk of Tarrant County about a financing statement on the boat before they bought it, nor did anyone else ever check on same in their behalf.

The McGehees borrowed from Reisel Bank the funds necessary to buy the boat. Mr. McGehee testified that he asked Mr. Gary Welch, vice-president of Reisel Bank, to be sure there was no lien against the boat before Reisel Bank paid Baer the purchase price for the boat; however, Mr. Welch denied that McGehee ever asked him prior to McGehee's purchase of the boat, to check the lien records of the Secretary of State or the Tarrant County Clerk's office to determine whether there was a lien on the boat. Welch testified that he never made any such check. At any rate, the McGehees had no actual knowledge of Exchange Bank's lien on the boat when they bought it from Baer in 1974, and did not learn about it until 1975.

Trial was had to a jury in which the trial court submitted two special issues as follows:

(1) "Do you find from a preponderance of the evidence that the financing statement filed by Plaintiff, Exchange Bank and Trust Co., gave sufficient notice for a reasonable, prudent person to discover a lien existing on the said property herein?"

To this issue the jury answered: "It was sufficient."

(2) "Do you find from a preponderance of the evidence that in 1971, at the time the lien was filed, the boat in question was primarily used for personal and family use, or was in a contract for service?"

"Answer: 'It was used primarily for personal and family use' or 'It was used primarily for a contract of service.'"

The jury in response to Issue No. 2 answered: "It was used primarily for a contract of service."

The trial court's judgment recited: "The Court is of the opinion and finds that Special Issue No. 2 is not an ultimate issue of fact in this case and is not supported by the evidence and should be disregarded;" whereupon the judgment awarded Plaintiff Exchange Bank recovery against the Defendants McGehee in the amount of $15,222.39 plus interest at 6% Per annum from August 1, 1975 (the recited date of conversion) until the entry of judgment (December 16, 1976) in the amount of $1265.00 plus interest from date of judgment at 9% Per annum and costs.

* * *

Appellants contend that the jury's answer to Special Issue No. 2 to the effect that the boat was primarily used for a "contract of service" as opposed to "personal and family use" caused the boat to be classified as "inventory" under the Texas Business and Commerce Code and not as "consumer goods", in which event Exchange Bank was required to file the financing statement with the Secretary of State in Austin in order to perfect its lien or security interest. Appellants then go on to say that since Exchange Bank did not file their financing statement with the Secretary of State, that said Bank never perfected its security interest or lien as against Appellants who purchased the boat without actual knowledge of Exchange Bank's lien.

In other words, Appellants contend that Exchange Bank simply filed its financing statement in the wrong place, and thereby did not perfect its lien against the boat, and therefore Appellants bought the boat from Baer free and clear of any security interest in favor of Exchange Bank. Appellant contends, and correctly so, that a financing statement filed in the wrong place does not protect the secured party against a purchaser without knowledge of the security interest, citing *Meadows v. Bierschwale* (Tex.1974), 516 S.W.2d 125, 133.

Therefore the question we are obliged to answer is whether Exchange Bank by filing its financing statement in the Tarrant County Clerk's office filed same in the right place in order to perfect its security interest in the boat. In order to answer this question we first must determine whether the boat in question is classified as "consumer goods" or as "inventory."

Article 9.109 [Now 9.102(44)]of the Texas Business and Commerce Code in its pertinent parts provides:

"Goods are

(1) 'consumer goods' if they are used or bought for use primarily for personal, family or household purposes;

(2) 'equipment' (not applicable to our case);

(3) 'farm products' (not applicable to our case);

(4) 'inventory' if they are held by a person who holds them for sale or lease or to be furnished under contracts of service or if he has so furnished them, or if they are raw materials, work in process or

materials used or consumed in a business. Inventory of a person is not to be classified as his equipment."

Article 9.401 [Now 9.501], Texas Business and Commerce Code, deals with the place of filing financing statements, and in its pertinent parts provides:

"(a) The proper place to file in order to perfect a security interest is as follows:

(1) when the collateral is consumer goods, then in the office of the County Clerk in the county of the debtor's residence;

(2) when the collateral is timber to be cut (not applicable to this case);

(3) in all other cases, in the office of the Secretary of State."

From the above statutes we see that if the boat was "consumer goods," the Exchange Bank had filed in the right place and thereby perfected their security interest; whereas if the boat was "inventory," then Exchange Bank had not perfected its lien.

Appellant contends that since the jury by its answer to Special Issue No. 2 found that the boat was primarily used in a "contract of service" at the time the lien was filed in 1971, that the boat is "inventory," which in turn meant that the financing statement should have been filed with the Secretary of State, that Exchange Bank thereby had no lien and that Defendant-Appellants were entitled to judgment in their favor. We do not agree.

We are of the opinion and hold that the evidence conclusively established as a matter of law that the boat in question fell into the classification of "consumer goods" because it was bought and used primarily for personal and family use. This being so, the trial court properly disregarded the jury's answer to Special Issue No. 2 and properly entered judgment in favor of Plaintiff-Appellee Exchange Bank.

As we understand it, the intent of the debtor-purchaser at the time of the sale when Exchange Bank's security instrument attached to the collateral is controlling, and no creditor is required to monitor the use of collateral in order to ascertain its proper classification. *See Commercial Credit Equipment Corporation v. Carter* (1973), 83 Wash.2d 136, 516 P.2d 767, 769, in which the Uniform Commercial Code of Washington provided definitions of "consumer goods" and "inventory" in language identical to our own Business and Commerce Code. *Also see* Article 9.401 [Repealed] of our Code in subsection (c) thereof wherein it provides: "A change in the use of the collateral does not impair the effectiveness of the original filing."

In the case at bar, Baer in 1971 financed the purchase of the boat in question from Exchange Bank and at the same time secured insurance and represented that the boat was for private purposes only and at said time noted that he would be using it in the Coast Guard Auxiliary. Both Mr. William Jones, the collections officer for Exchange Bank, as well as Mr. Charles Gagnon, the

Allstate man who insured the boat, testified that the boat in question was a pleasure craft as opposed to being used for commercial purposes. Baer insured it as a pleasure craft. Insurance on boats used for commercial purposes is much higher than for pleasure craft, Gagnon testified.

When Baer insured the boat, he told the insurance man he would be using the boat in the Coast Guard Auxiliary which entitled him to a 10% Discount in the policy premiums.

The Coast Guard Auxiliary is a volunteer non-profit organization which any citizen can join provided he has a boat or a radio or an airplane which he can use to perform the sole function of water safety patrol. Any member of the Coast Guard Auxiliary can simply run its flag up on his boat and he is acting under the auspices of the Coast Guard Auxiliary, according to Baer's testimony. When the boat is on patrol for the Coast Guard Auxiliary, the boat owner is reimbursed for his gas and oil used, and no more, and during such times of patrol, the Coast Guard assumes responsibility for the boat in case of accidents, thereby relieving the insurance carrier. In cases of emergency, the U.S. Coast Guard can call Auxiliary members and their boats out to patrol the waters. Baer testified that his use of his boat for Coast Guard Auxiliary purposes was not inconsistent with his use of his boat as a pleasure craft, and this was not contradicted. In summary, the boat was purchased for and used as "combination personal and Coast Guard use" and was not used for commercial purposes or for hire. Baer used this boat about 80% of the time for the Coast Guard Auxiliary, and for a time commanded a flotilla for the Auxiliary on the Eagle Mountain Lake, in which all the flotilla members used a pleasure boat of some type.

Captain Boden, the marine expert who surveyed the boat before the McGehees purchased it from Baer, testified that the boat was designed for use as a pleasure craft, and not for commercial purposes.

Baer earned his livelihood as an insurance man, with a full time job as such. The use of the boat in question was for his and his family's hobbies of fishing, boating, and Coast Guard Auxiliary activity. All of these uses of the boat were to implement his and his family's hobbies, which meant that the boat was purchased for and used as a pleasure craft. In summary, the evidence conclusively shows and we hold as a matter of law that the boat was used for personal and family uses, thereby causing the boat to be "consumer goods" under the Code definition thereof. *See* the Uniform Commercial Code Comment, paragraph 3 under Article 9.109 [Now 9.102(23)], Texas Business and Commerce Code, which sheds light upon the meaning of the terms "inventory" and "(goods) furnished under a contract of service." In our opinion, none of Baer's activities with the Coast Guard Auxiliary constitute a "contract of service" contemplated by Article 9.109(4) of the Texas Business and Commerce Code. Moreover, there is no evidence in the record of any contract, written or oral, between Baer and the Coast Guard Auxiliary. Appellants' points one through five are accordingly overruled.

* * * *

---

2. THE SECURITY AGREEMENT

Before attachment can occur, Article 9 requires a record—a security agreement—that evidences the creation of a security interest.[2] 9-203(b)(3)(A). Although the security agreement need only be authenticated by the debtor and describe the collateral to satisfy the requirements of Article 9, because it controls the relationship between the secured party and the debtor, it will need to do much more. For example, although Article 9 provides in detail the procedures available to the secured party for enforcing its claim against the collateral on default by the debtor, it does not define what constitutes the necessary default. The parties themselves must define it in the security agreement. The Code leaves it to the parties to work out the precise parameters of their relationship.

The security agreement must be "authenticated" by the debtor. 9-203(b)(3)(A). Originally, the debtor merely had to "sign" the security agreement—but in anticipation of a paperless world, the term authentication was introduced into the Code to provide for alternative ways of accomplishing what the parties used to accomplish by "signing" a document. But signing is still a form of authentication, and so as long as we are still creating paper security agreements, the requirement that the security agreement be authenticated by the debtor is satisfied by the debtor's signature on the agreement. 9-102(a)(7). But "signed" as used in the Code includes more than just inscribing one's name onto paper. Signed means doing anything to the paper with the "present intention to adopt or accept the writing." 1-201(b)(37). Stamping your name or a symbol on the paper, scrawling an X on the paper with a crayon, or putting the agreement on letterhead, if done with the intent to associate yourself with that paper, will satisfy the authenticate requirement.

BROAD INTERPRETATION

The security agreement must also "describe" the collateral. Generally, a description of collateral is sufficient if "it reasonably identifies what is described." 9-108(a). This same general standard for sufficiency of description was applied inconsistently under Old Article 9. For example, courts disagreed as to whether a description by item (washing machine) was required or if a description by collateral type (appliance) was sufficient under the standard. Revised Article 9 attempts to provide for more consistency by creating a number of safe harbors for collateral description. Under 9-108(b) collateral is reasonably identified if described by specific listing, category, Code type, quantity, or computational or allocational formula. Revised Article 9 also

---

2 There are some exceptions to the writing requirement. For example, if the collateral is in the possession of the secured party, no written security agreement is required before attachment can occur. 9-203(b)(3)(B).

provides that super generic descriptions—all of the debtor's assets or all of the debtor's personal property—do not reasonably identify the collateral, resolving an issue that had split the courts under Old Article 9.

With the safe harbors and additional guidance provided under Revised Article 9, it might seem as though collateral description would not be a problem anymore. But the following cases prove otherwise.

ALLETE, INC. v. GEC ENG'G, INC.
Court of Appeals of Minnesota
726 N.W.2d 520 (Minn. Ct. App. 2007)

MINGE, *Justice*.

Appellant claimed a security interest in, and sought to garnish, property originally located in Missouri which had been acquired by respondent, a Texas resident, and moved to Texas. Appellant challenges the district court's summary judgment determination that it did not have a security interest in the property. Respondent challenges the jurisdiction of Minnesota courts. Because we conclude appellant did not have a security interest in the property, we affirm.

FACTS

In December of 2000, appellant Minnesota Power, Inc. negotiated an economic-development loan with respondent GEC Engineering, Inc. (GEC), a start-up company that was attempting to develop technology to convert diesel engines to run on cleaner-burning propane or natural gas. GEC and appellant are Minnesota corporations. To secure the loan, GEC executed a security agreement dated December 28, 2000. As collateral for the loan, the security agreement granted appellant a security interest in, "[a]ll equipment and inventory located at Borrower's facility at 510 W. 3rd Avenue North, Aurora, Minnesota." A financing statement listing equipment and inventory located at that Minnesota site was filed in this state.

Appellant's agreement to make a loan to GEC was based on its understanding that GEC, then operating in Missouri, was relocating to appellant's service area in Aurora, Minnesota. But by April 15, 2001, the target moving date, GEC had not relocated to Aurora and was experiencing financial difficulty. Appellant and GEC then filed a standard Minnesota UCC-1[3] financing statement in Missouri. The financing statement states:

> This financing statement covers the following types or items of property. ...
>
> A. All equipment and inventory located at Borrower's facility located at 116 Holloway Road, Ballwin, MO[.]

---

3   Article 9 of the UCC was revised and, as revised, enacted effective July 1, 2001. See 2000 Minn. Laws ch. 399, Art. 1, §130, at 672. The parties do not claim and it does not appear that this revision has any effect on the matters at issue in this appeal. For ease of reference, all citations and quotations are from the currently effective law.

The financing statement was recorded on May 3, 2001 and signed by respondent Jerry Brougher, the then-president of GEC. GEC never moved to Aurora, and early in 2002, the company ceased its operations and became insolvent. GEC failed to repay its loan with appellant, and appellant obtained a default judgment against GEC in Minnesota.

The subject of this dispute is a diesel engine that GEC purchased in Minnesota on April 15, 1999, to develop a prototype engine that would enable it to design and manufacture conversion kits for other engines. GEC bought the engine in South St. Paul and shipped the engine to CK Engineering (CK) in Ballwin, Missouri. GEC used CK's Missouri location for its operations. CK assisted in the testing and development of the engine. But GEC never paid CK for its services, and apparently abandoned the engine and other property at CK's site when it ceased operating. To recover some of the money owed to CK for its work on and storage of the engine, CK sought to sell the engine. In the summer of 2004, respondent Danielle Dellhomme[4] purchased the engine from CK Engineering for $18,000. Respondent was an investor in and former director of GEC. She is a Texas resident. CK shipped the engine to respondent in Texas, where it is currently stored. The engine was never located in Aurora, Minnesota. Although it appears that respondent was aware of appellant's loan to GEC and that she had visited Minnesota as a part of GEC's business, the record does not indicate that she was personally involved with or personally liable for GEC's debt to appellant.

During its post-judgment collection process in Minnesota state courts, appellant learned respondent was in possession of the engine and the testing equipment attached to it, property it claims was collateral for its loan to GEC. Appellant served respondent with Minnesota garnishment pleadings and moved the Minnesota district court for an order requiring her to surrender and deliver the engine to appellant. Respondent claimed that the Minnesota court lacked subject matter and personal jurisdiction, that appellant did not have a security interest in the engine, that even if it once had a security interest, it was displaced by the possessory mechanics lien of CK, and that the rights she acquired from CK were superior to the claims of appellant. After discovery, the district court granted summary judgment in favor of respondent and found that appellant never held a security interest in the engine. This appeal followed.

ISSUE

Does appellant have a valid security interest in the disputed engine?

ANALYSIS

The threshold question is which state's law governs the determination of whether appellant has a valid security interest in the disputed engine. As

---

4   Although this action started as a collection proceeding against GEC and its former president, they are not involved in the present garnishment action and appeal. "Respondent" in this opinion only refers to Dellhomme.

a commercial transaction, this dispute is subject to the UCC. We note that Minnesota, Missouri, and Texas have all adopted the UCC. See Minn.Stat. ch. 336 (2006); Mo. Ann. Stat. ch. 400 (West 2006); Tex. Bus. & Com.Code Ann. §§1.101-9.709 (Vernon 2006). There is also no claim that either the UCC or the caselaw in the various states differs with respect to the issue before us, and the parties do not dispute the proper choice of law. Under the circumstances, this is what is often called a "false conflict." See *Alside, Inc. v. Larson*, 300 Minn. 285, 293, 220 N.W.2d 274, 279 (1974); Restatement (Second) of Conflict of Laws §186 cmt. c (1971); 16 Am.Jur.2d Conflict of Laws §85 (1998). Accordingly, we apply Minnesota law.

The issue is whether appellant has a security interest in the disputed engine. ...

Minn.Stat. §336.9-203 (2006) governs the attachment and enforceability of security interests. Subdivision (a) of that section provides that "[a] security interest attaches to collateral when it becomes enforceable against the debtor. ..." Minn.Stat. §336.9-203(a). A security interest in collateral "is enforceable against the debtor and third parties" if three conditions are met:

(1) value has been given;

(2) the debtor has rights in the collateral or the power to transfer rights in the collateral ... and

(3) one of the following conditions is met:

(A) the debtor has authenticated a security agreement that provides a description of the collateral

Minn.Stat. §336.9-203(b).

Here, the parties do not dispute that value was given or that GEC had rights in the engine. The parties only dispute whether GEC "authenticated" a security agreement that provides a description of the collateral, sufficient to create a security interest in the engine.

* * *

We do not understand appellant to claim that the parties' original security agreement created a security interest in the engine. Nor could it. The plain language of the security agreement only grants appellant a security interest in equipment "located at Borrower's facility at 510 W. 3rd Avenue North, Aurora, Minnesota." It is undisputed that the engine was never located in Aurora. We consistently give a contract its "plain and ordinary meaning ... even if the result is harsh." *Denelsbeck v. Wells Fargo & Co.*, 666 N.W.2d 339, 346-47 (Minn.2003) (quotation omitted).

Appellant seizes on the UCC's flexible definitions of "security agreement" and "agreement" to argue that the financing statement the parties filed in Missouri creates a material fact issue as to whether the parties amended the original security agreement to give appellant a security interest in the engine.

Although the UCC does not explicitly address the question of whether a financing statement can boot strap a lender into a secured status, there are several provisions that are relevant to the answer.

The drafters of the UCC contemplated a distinction between a security agreement and a financing statement, and defined the two terms differently. See Minn.Stat. §336.9-102(a)(39), (73) (2006). It follows that the drafters understood the two documents to have different functions. Our caselaw confirms that the purpose of a financing statement is different from an agreement creating a security interest in collateral. "In contrast [to a security agreement], the financing statement serves the purpose of putting nonparties such as other subsequent creditors on notice that the debtor's property is encumbered." *Prod. Credit Ass'n of W. Cent. Minn. v. Bartos*, 430 N.W.2d 238, 241 (Minn.App.1988).

The language used in security agreements and financing statements reflects their functions. The security agreement must somehow state that a lien is created in identifiable collateral. Minn.Stat. §336.9-102(a)(73). By contrast, the financing statement is a bare-bones document that simply gives names and addresses and a description of property. In fact, until recently, the Minnesota standard form financing statement had no language that mentioned the term "security interest" or even referred to the described property as "collateral." *Compare* Minn. R. 8260.0600, subp. 3 (1995), *with* Minn. R. 8280.0040, subp. 2 (2005) (setting forth earlier and current standard forms for UCC-1, the latter of which uses the word "collateral" in the heading above the space provided for a description of the property).

The question we face is whether a financing statement with limited language can amend the plain and unambiguous description of collateral in a security agreement. We recognize that courts have found that a financing statement, in conjunction with other writings, constitutes a security agreement creating a security interest in property. See *In re Numeric Corp.*, 485 F.2d 1328, 1332 (1st Cir.1973) ("[A]n adequate [security] agreement can be found when a financing statement is considered together with other documents."). But we are aware of no court that has held that a standard financing statement, standing alone or with only parol evidence, is sufficient as a matter of law to create a security interest in collateral, or to amend an unambiguous security agreement. *See id.* at 1331 ("A considerable body of case law has developed to the effect that a standard form financing statement, taken alone, cannot also be considered a 'security agreement' that satisfies §9-203(1)(b).").

Here, the security agreement contains an explicit description of property that is limited to equipment located at a specific address in Aurora, Minnesota and certain other assets. There is nothing in the original security agreement that even implies that the security interest extends to equipment not located at that site. Appellant is correct that the Missouri financing statement implies a willingness to grant a security interest in the engine which is located in Missouri. Further, there is evidence that GEC's business plan for moving to Minnesota had collapsed, that appellant had advanced funds, and that the engine in question was of interest to appellant as collateral. Appellant's argument has a certain appeal. But there is nothing from the debtor that grants appellant a security interest in the collateral located in Missouri. The financing statement used in this proceeding has no reference to the described property as collateral. Other than the financing statement, appellant offers only obscure references to the engine in various items of correspondence as evidence of such an amendment. These references are largely comments by appellant's employees. The comments from GEC are oblique at best and require considerable interpolation.

If we were simply dealing with the imponderables of what constitutes adequate evidence of negligence, summary judgment dismissal of appellant's claim would be premature. However, the case before us does not turn on the weight of the evidence. Instead, we must determine the level of formality needed to establish a prima facie case that the parties amended a written contract with an explicit definition of collateral. Appellant's claims compete with rights of not just a debtor, whose interests in property that is not collateral can be overridden by executing on a judgment, but of other interested parties. Thus, we require an objective standard. Absent an indication that there is admissible evidence that the claimed amendment meets the core requirements needed to establish a security interest in the claimed additional collateral, there is not an adequate showing that appellant's claim can survive summary judgment. These core requirements include words granting a lien or security interest. *See* Minn.Stat. §336.9-203(b). Some written evidence or acceptable substitute is needed to establish that such a grant of a lien was made.

Here, because there is no admissible evidence in the record that GEC actually granted a security interest in the equipment in Missouri to appellant, we conclude that appellant has no security interest in the disputed engine as a matter of law and that the district court did not err in ordering summary judgment.

Because we conclude that appellant does not have a security interest, we do not reach the questions of whether Minnesota courts had jurisdiction over respondent or whether the interest she acquired from CK Engineering was superior to appellants.

DECISION

Because, on the undisputed facts of this case, appellant has no valid security interest in the disputed property as a matter of law, we affirm.

SHELBY COUNTY STATE BANK v. VAN DIEST SUPPLY CO.
United States Court of Appeals, Seventh Circuit
303 F.3d 832 (7th Cir. 2002)

WOOD, *Circuit Judge*.

Hennings Feed & Crop Care, Inc. (Hennings) filed a voluntary bankruptcy petition under Chapter 11 on August 23, 1999, after Van Diest Supply Co.

(Van Diest), one of its creditors, filed a complaint against it in the Central District of Illinois. Shelby County State Bank (the Bank), another creditor of Hennings, brought this action in the bankruptcy proceeding against Van Diest and the Trustee for Hennings to assert the validity of the Bank's security interest in certain assets of Hennings. ...

I.

Hennings, a corporation based in Iowa, was in the business of selling agricultural chemicals and products. As is customary, several of Hennings's suppliers extended credit to it from time to time to finance its business operations, and obtained liens or other security interests in Hennings's property and inventory to safeguard their advances.

The Bank is among Hennings's creditors. In December 1997, the Bank extended credit to Hennings for $500,000. In May 1998, the Bank increased this amount to a revolving line of credit of some $4,000,000. Hennings in return granted the Bank a security interest in certain of its assets, including inventory and general intangibles. Van Diest, also a creditor, entered into several security agreements with Hennings and its predecessor over the years to protect its financing of materials supplied to Hennings. These agreements were covered by the Uniform Commercial Code, which Iowa has adopted (including the revised Article 9), see Iowa Code §§554.9101-554.9507 (1999).

* * *

On August 29, 1983, Hennings and Van Diest entered into a new security agreement (the Security Agreement), the language of which is at the core of this dispute. The Security Agreement was based on a preprinted standard "Business Security Agreement" form. In the field for the description of collateral, the parties entered the following language, drafted by Van Diest, describing the security interest as being in:

> [a]ll inventory, including but not limited to agricultural chemicals, fertilizers, and fertilizer materials sold to Debtor by Van Diest Supply Co. whether now owned or hereafter acquired, including all replacements, substitutions and additions thereto, and the accounts, notes, and any other proceeds therefrom.

The Security Agreement contained a further preprinted clause providing:

> as additional collateral all additions to and replacements of all such collateral and all accessories, accessions, parts and equipment now or hereafter affixed thereto or used in connection with and the proceeds from all such collateral (including negotiable or non-negotiable warehouse receipts now or hereafter issued for storage of collateral).

The bankruptcy court found that the language of the Security Agreement was ambiguous and susceptible on its face to two interpretations: under one, the security interest extended to all of Hennings's inventory; under the other, it was limited to inventory sold to Hennings by Van Diest. Proceeding under Iowa law, that court applied several canons of contract interpretation to resolve the ambiguity. The upshot was that the court rejected the use of parol evidence and concluded that the Security Agreement extended only to inventory sold to Hennings by Van Diest.

The district court disagreed. It found that the bankruptcy court had created an ambiguity out of thin air and that the language of the Security Agreement supported only the view that the collateral included all inventory. It relied on the presence of the "after-acquired clause," which provides for future inventory to be deemed part of the collateral. Such a clause ensures that an entity having an interest in inventory retains the interest even when the original goods have been sold and replaced in the course of business, given the natural turnaround of inventory. *See, e.g., Larsen v. Warrington,* 348 N.W.2d 637, 639 (1984). To reach this conclusion, the district court found that the qualifier phrase mentioning specific items found in the first paragraph quoted above, while it concededly modified the term "inventory," was mere surplusage. Accordingly, it found that the description of "collateral" must have extended to "[a]ll inventory," and reversed the bankruptcy court's findings.

II.

* * *

The facts underlying the contract interpretation are not disputed in this case.

A. AMBIGUITY OF THE "AFTER-ACQUIRED" CLAUSE

In the process of divining the meaning of a contractual clause, a court must first establish whether the language in dispute supports more than one interpretation. The existence of such an ambiguity is a question of law, and under Iowa law, "[t]he test for ambiguity is objective: whether the language is fairly susceptible to two interpretations." *DeJong v. Sioux Ctr., Iowa,* 168 F.3d 1115, 1119 (8th Cir.1999).

The description of the security interest in this case is a textbook example of ambiguous language: a term (all inventory) is followed by a qualifier (including all …) and then another (sold to Debtor by Van Diest). It is a basic rule of English syntax (of all syntax, in fact) that a modifier should be placed directly next to the element it aims to modify: placing two modifiers in a row leads to the question whether the latter one modifies only the first modifier, or modifies the entire term. In the first edition of his book on statutory interpretation, Sutherland described the "doctrine of the last antecedent" as providing that "[r]elative and qualifying phrases, grammatically and legally, where no contrary intention appears, refer solely to the last antecedent." J.G. Sutherland, *Statutes and Statutory Construction* §267, at 349 (1st ed. 1891).

The Supreme Court recognized the existence of the "last antecedent" rule as early as 1799 in *Sims' Lessee v. Irvine*, 3 U.S. (3 Dall.) 425, 444, 1 L.Ed. 665 n.a (1799) ("The rule is, that 'such' applies to the last antecedent, unless the sense of the passage requires a different construction."). The Supreme Court of Iowa has also often endorsed resort to the doctrine in an attempt to resolve problems caused by ambiguously placed modifiers. *See, e.g., State v. Lohr*, 266 N.W.2d 1, 3 (Iowa 1978) (recognizing grammatical as well as legal origins of the rule.)

* * *

B. CANONS OF INTERPRETATION AND EXTRINSIC EVIDENCE

As a linguistic matter, therefore, the sentence is ambiguous. As both the Supreme Court and Iowa courts have recognized (and, indeed, as Sutherland himself pointed out) the rule is helpful in determining the existence of the ambiguity, but not in solving the puzzle when both readings are plausible. *See, e.g., Nobelman v. American Sav. Bank*, 508 U.S. 324, 330, 113 S.Ct. 2106, 124 L.Ed.2d 228 (1993); *In re: Kruse's Estate*, 250 N.W.2d 432, 433-34 (Iowa 1977). Unless one always followed a rigid formalistic approach, the rule would not cast light on which of the two interpretations should prevail. Instead, courts (including those in Iowa) turn to other canons of interpretation. Under Iowa law, those other canons should be used to resolve an ambiguity before parol evidence may be introduced. … The rules in Iowa are the familiar ones used in contract interpretation in United States courts: the contract must be construed as a whole; the court requires a fair and reasonable construction; avoid illegality; the interpretation must account for surrounding circumstances; and the parties' own practical construction is relevant. Iowa also applies the rule requiring the court to construe terms against the drafter of the instrument (still known to those fond of Latin phrases as the rule of contra proferentem); it favors specific terms over general terms; and it favors handwriting to typing and typing to printing.

Construing the contract before us as a whole leaves as many doubts as we had at the outset: nothing within it bears on the intended scope of the phrase "including but not limited to agricultural chemicals, fertilizers, and fertilizer materials sold to Debtor by Van Diest Supply Company." Van Diest could have acquired a security interest in everything that Hennings owned in inventory (as it had done, for instance, with the 1981 security agreement), or it could have limited its interest to the goods it supplied to Hennings. Without resort to other interpretive principles or to outside evidence, such as evidence of custom in the trade, it is impossible for a court to decide which reading the parties intended to adopt.

We do agree with the Bank's claim, however, that it would be bizarre as a commercial matter to claim a lien in everything, and then to describe in detail only a smaller part of that whole. This is not to say that there is no use for descriptive clauses of inclusion, so as to make clear the kind of entities that ought to be included ... But if all goods of any kind are to be included, why mention only a few? A court required to give "reasonable and effective meaning to all terms," *AmerUs Bank v. Pinnacle Bank*, 51 F.Supp.2d 994, 999 (S.D.Iowa 1999), must shy away from finding that a significant phrase (like the lengthy description of chemicals and fertilizers we have here) is nothing but surplusage.

Iowa law permits courts to consider the parties' conduct, such as the prior security agreements that Van Diest entered into with Hennings, as one way of resolving the ambiguity. Those earlier agreements at times provided for a blanket security with collateral in all inventory. This, too, is not terribly help-ful here. On the one hand, the prior use of a general claim for all inventory demonstrates the availability in the trade of such a term and the willingness of Hennings, on occasion at least, to enter into such broad lien grants. On the other hand, it tends to show that the parties knew how to achieve such a result if they wanted to. There must be a reason why the historically used "all inventory," was modified in this case.

More useful is the parties' own practical construction of this particular agreement—a source that Iowa courts agree may be consulted without open-ing the door entirely to parol evidence. *See Ackerman v. Lauver*, 242 N.W.2d 342, 347 (Iowa 1976). After the Security Agreement was executed, Van Diest sent to other lenders notices of its interest thereunder. In all the notices, it claimed a "purchase money security interest" only in the inventory it sold to Hennings. In a July 1993 letter to the Bank, for instance, Van Diest described its security interest as being in "[a]ll of Debtor's property (including without limitation all inventory of agricultural chemicals and additives thereto) pur-chased or otherwise acquired from the Secured Party. ..." In the parenthetical, Van Diest then construed its own interest as being limited to the goods it sold to Hennings-not to the whole of Hennings's inventory, as it now claims.

It is true that this canon of construction treads remarkably close to the ground covered by extrinsic evidence. Furthermore, the course of dealing between principal parties A and B is not likely to shed light on the way that third party C should have understood an agreement. Where a third party disputes a reading of a contract, it is not in a good position to use course of dealing or other extrinsic evidence to support its position. It was not a part of the negotiations and does not have the access that we otherwise presume of both parties to outside materials relating to the contract.

The Bank also argues that contractual terms must be interpreted in a "com-mercially reasonable" fashion, even though the Bank has not supported this specific proposition with references to Iowa law. Nevertheless, the somewhat broader requirement of a generally fair and reasonable construction is amply recognized in Iowa. *See Dental Prosthetic Servs., Inc. v. Hurst*, 463 N.W.2d 36, 38-39 (Iowa 1990). Of two plausible interpretations, we should assume the parties meant one that was fair and reasonable. The problem once again is that there is nothing inherently commercially unreasonable about either of the two possible readings. Under the circumstances, it would have been quite reasonable for Van Diest to get as much security from Hennings as it could, as the latter managed to ratchet up millions of dollars in debt before it went bust (it owes the Bank some $1,412,233.10; Van Diest had, at the time of the petition, some $2,890,288.75 in unpaid invoices; countless other creditors have lined up). On the other hand, it might have been unreasonable for Hennings to commit all of its potential collateral to Van Diest, if so doing might have made it more difficult for the company to obtain credit from others.

C. CONTRA PROFERENTEM

As between the two parties to a contract, there is another doctrine that often resolves ambiguities: it is the rule requiring that ambiguous language must be construed against its drafter. Not only should the drafter be penalized by bearing the costs ex post of having cut corners ex ante, the penalty of interpretation against the drafter also aims to avoid overbearing behavior between contracting parties where the drafter, often the one in the better bargaining position, tries to pull a fast one over the party who can merely accept or reject the contract as a whole. Although this doctrine of contra proferentem is perhaps on the wane in some jurisdictions, it is alive and well in Iowa, *e.g.*, ... *Continental Ins. Co. v. Bones*, 596 N.W.2d 552, 558 (Iowa 1999) ...

Unlike many jurisdictions that relegate the contra proferentem rule to the status of "tie-breaker," *see, e.g., Baker v. America's Mortgage Servicing, Inc.*, 58 F.3d 321, 327 (7th Cir.1995) (Illinois law), Iowa takes a strong view of the rule, holding that ambiguous language is to be "strictly construed against the drafter." *Iowa Fuel & Minerals, Inc. v. Iowa State Bd. of Regents*, 471 N.W.2d 859, 863 (Iowa 1991) ...

Here, the drafting party was Van Diest. It was Van Diest that was trying to obtain a security interest in certain property of Hennings, in order to protect its advances to the latter. At least if this were a case against Hennings, the use of the contra proferentem rule would provide a way out of the ambiguity in the key contractual language: construing it against Van Diest, the security interest extends only to the products Van Diest sold to Hennings, not to "all inventory." It is not such a case, however, and so we turn to the final consideration that persuades us that the Bank must prevail.

D. THIRD-PARTY INTERESTS

The most compelling reason to construe the language of this agreement against Van Diest is the fact that it was Van Diest that drafted the security agreement, and that the language of that agreement plays an important part for third-party creditors. Those creditors have no way of knowing what transpired between the parties; there is no parol evidence to which they may turn; and they have no way to resolve ambiguities internal to a contract. Here, we are not facing a garden-variety breach of contract action between the two contracting parties, both of whom were present during the negotiations. Instead, this case involves the effect of a contract between two parties (Hennings and Van Diest) on a third party (the Bank). The Bank, as we have already mentioned, is a stranger to the agreement, albeit one whose rights are affected by it. As the Bank could not have invested resources ex ante to avoid problems arising from ambiguous language, while Van Diest could have, it should be Van Diest who pays the price ex post.

A security agreement is a special kind of contract for which an important audience is third parties who need to know how much collateral has become encumbered. A potential creditor's decision whether to provide credit to Hennings (or anyone else), is contingent on the creditor's understanding of the extent of pre-existing security interests. An unclear statement of that extent should be avoided at all costs: if the creditor reads it reasonably, but too narrowly, when extending credit, it will be out of luck when the debtor defaults. If the potential creditor on the other hand takes a more conservative position and, fearful of the ambiguity, decides not to extend credit, the party seeking that credit is penalized in its access to capital by the shoddy work of its prior creditor—another result to be avoided.

By perfecting its security interest, Van Diest purported to give prospective creditors of Hennings notice of Van Diest's existing interest in Hennings's goods. A prospective creditor should have been able to look at Van Diest's filing and determine on that basis whether to extend credit to Hennings. Here, the Bank presumably did so, especially when it received Van Diest's letter in July 1993 telling it that the Van Diest security interest covered only goods bought from Van Diest. Whether this statement alone would have justified reliance on the Bank's part is debatable; but coupled with the language in the perfected Security Agreement that was susceptible to this interpretation, reliance was certainly reasonable.

The Supreme Court has also noted the special position that third parties occupy, given their limited ways of learning about the existence or the precise extent of a security interest. In *United States v. McDermott*, 507 U.S. 447, 113 S.Ct. 1526, 123 L.Ed.2d 128 (1993), the Court expressed concern over the possibility that an after-acquired security interest clause might prevent the Government from asserting its interests. Like the Bank, the Government could not have protected itself by contracting with the parties or by analyzing the terms of the clause. The underlying rationale for the decision is equally applicable here: for the notice requirement to be a valid instrument of protection for potential creditors, that notice must be clearly expressed, and it must be such as is needed to inform the behavior of the potential creditor. "When two private lenders both exact from the same debtor security agreements with after-acquired-property clauses, the second lender knows, by reason of the earlier recording, that that category of property will be subject to another claim, and if the remaining security is inadequate he may avoid the difficulty by declining to extend credit." *Id.* at 454, 113 S.Ct. 1526. When the earlier recording is ambiguous, the "second lender" does not know what collateral will be at its disposal.

* * *

Similarly, security agreements should be construed if at all possible without resort to external evidence, and they should be construed in a way that recognizes the important role they play for third-party creditors. Doing so here leads to the same result we have already reached: Van Diest's security interest extends only to the inventory it furnished. The limiting clause modifies the term "all inventory," and it is not surplusage.

III

For these reasons, we REVERSE the judgment of the district court and REMAND the case to the bankruptcy court for the entry of judgment in favor of the Bank.

PROBLEM 3–3

When the bank agreed to finance Ray's inventory purchase for the store, the bank filled out a security agreement and sent it to Ray for his review and signature. Ray instructed his office assistant to type his name on the line reserved for the debtor's signature, intending to actually sign it above the typed name before he returned it to the bank. The store got busy and he forgot to sign it before sending it back to the bank. The loan officer at the bank did not notice there was no actual signature before he placed the agreement in Ray's file and put it away. Has the bank's security interest attached to Ray's inventory? See 9-203, 9-102(7), and 1-201(37).

PROBLEM 3–4

Would your answer in the last Problem be different if instead of having his name typed on the security agreement, Ray had used a rubber stamp made of his signature to stamp his name on the security agreement?

PROBLEM 3–5

Ray sold a commercial grade freezer to the yogurt shop down the street from his store. He instructed his office assistant to fill out the security agreement. In the description of the collateral paragraph, the assistant copied the description from the financing agreement Ray had prepared for the transaction: "All Personal Property of the Debtor." Ray did not review the agreement before the owner of the yogurt shop signed it. Has Ray's security interest attached to the freezer?

PROBLEM 3–6

The freezer Ray sold the yogurt shop in the last problem was a General Electric Model 2140C. If instead of typing the super generic description on the security agreement, the assistant had typed "General Selectric Model 2140C," would Ray have an enforceable security interest in the freezer he sold the yogurt shop?

PROBLEM 3–7

When Ray filled out the security agreement for a refrigerator he sold on credit to a local customer for use in her home, in the collateral description paragraph he typed in "Consumer Goods." Can Ray enforce the security interest against the refrigerator? See 9-108(e).

3. THE COMPOSITE DOCUMENT THEORY

What happens when there is no document that satisfies the requirements of 9-203 produced in connection with a transaction, but the debtor and the secured party assume they have created a security interest and act accordingly? Is the absence of a single document that meets each of the requirements of 9-203 fatal to the recognition of the security interest they thought they had created? As the *O'Dowd* case explains, courts have been willing to enforce security interests in the absence of a definitive writing that meets the requirements for a security agreement, at least where the court is able to cobble together the missing security agreement from various writings produced by the parties in connection with their transaction. This process of cobbling together a security agreement is known as the Composite Document Theory. Does the court's application of the theory in the *O'Dowd* case imply that a security agreement requires more than just an authenticated record that describes the collateral? If it does, what is that additional requirement?

IN RE O'DOWD

United States Bankruptcy Court for the District of Montana
2005 Bankr. LEXIS 3095 (D. Mont. Feb. 2, 2005)

KIRSCHER, *Judge.*

In this Chapter 7 bankruptcy, after due notice, a hearing was held December 7, 2004, at Butte, on the Motion to Modify Stay filed by Gallatin Valley Furniture Co. ("GVF"). … This memorandum contains the Court's findings of fact and conclusions of law.

[Gallatin Valley Furniture ("GVF") sold Debtor over $50,000 of furniture, draperies, and other items on credit over a 10-month period. No security agreement was ever prepared but the Debtor did sign a promissory note at the end of the 10-month period that made reference to a security interest that would be filed. GVF filed a financing statement identifying the collateral in which it claimed a security interest.]

* * *

With regard to the items of property at issue, MCA §30-9A-201 provides: "Except as otherwise provided in chapters 1 through 9A, a security agreement is effective according to its terms between the parties". *Pursuant to* MCA §30-9A-203, "a security interest is enforceable against the debtor and third parties with respect to the collateral only if: (a) value has been given; (b) the debtor has rights in the collateral or the power to transfer rights in the collateral to a secured party; and (c) one of the following conditions is met: (i) the debtor has authenticated a security agreement that provides a description of the collateral[.]"

Based upon the testimony of Debtor and the arguments of her counsel, it is obvious that Debtor does not dispute that value has been given or that Debtor has rights in the collateral. At issue is whether Debtor has authenticated a security agreement that provides a description of the collateral. The Bankruptcy Appellate Panel of the First Circuit has recognized that under the Uniform Commercial Code:

> [T]here is no magic language required to constitute a security agreement. "A writing or writings, regardless of label, which adequately describes the collateral, carries the signature of the debtor, *and establishes that in fact a security interest was agreed upon,* [satisfies] the formal requirements of the statute and the policies behind it."

Empresas Berrios v. Ortiz (In re Ortiz), 295 B.R 158, 164 (1st Cir. BAP 2003) (emphasis in original).

Debtor acknowledges that her signature appears on both the promissory note and the UCC-1 Financing Statement. Additionally, MCA § 30-9A-108(1) states that "a description of personal ... property is sufficient, whether or not it is specific, if it reasonably identifies what is described. MCA § 30-9A-108(2) clarifies that "a description of collateral reasonably identifies the collateral if it identifies the collateral by: ... any other method, if the identity of the collateral is objectively determinable."

As previously noted, Debtor signed both the promissory note and the UCC-1 Financing Statement. The promissory note makes reference to the "Form UCC-1 for merchandise delivered to date". The UCC-1 Financing Statement signed by Debtor, and filed by GVF with the Gallatin County Clerk and Recorder, specifically identifies all items of collateral. Therefore, the Court finds that the identity of the collateral is "objectively determinable" as required by *MCA §30-9A-108.*

Thus, the remaining issues before this Court are whether the promissory note and financing statement constitutes a security agreement between the parties and whether such agreement creates or provides for a security interest in the merchandise. ... The promissory note that Debtor signed provides in pertinent part in the last paragraph: "Security interest will be filed at Court House on Form UCC-1 for merchandise delivered to date and security interest shall be retained on merchandise in storage. Merchandise shall remain in storage till paid in full. [GVF] shall have immediate access to secured merchandise for purpose of recovery of amount due should any payment be not made in a timely manner as state above."

Under the revised Uniform Commercial Code, a "'security agreement' means an agreement that creates or provides for a security interest." MCA §30-9A-102(uuu). An "'agreement' means the bargain of the parties in fact as found in their language or by implication from other circumstances, including course of dealing or usage of trade or course of performance. ..." MCA §30-1-201(3). A "'security interest' means an interest in personal property or fixtures that secures payment or performance of an obligation." MCA §30-1-202(37)(a). In bankruptcy, state law governs security interests in property. *Butner v. United States*, 440 U.S. 48, 55, 99 S.Ct. 914, 59 L. Ed. 2d 136 (1979). The revised Article 9 provisions of the Uniform Commercial Code apply as this case was filed on July 28, 2004, after the Article 9 revisions, which became effective date [sic] of July 16 2001. *See In re Wiersma*, 283 B.R. 294, 299 (Bankr. D. Idaho 2002).

"Case law [on the issue of what creates or provides for a security interest] under old Article 9 should continue to apply under the revision, bearing in mind that Revised Section 9-203 requires an authenticated record rather than a signed writing." 1 Coogan, SECURED TRANSACTIONS UNDER THE UNIFORM COMMERCIAL CODE 2004, §2A.04, p. 2A-29. The Montana Supreme Court in *Wagner v. Glasgow Livestock Sales Co.*, 222 Mont. 385, 390, 722 P.2d 1165, 1168 (1986) confirms the requirements for the enforcement of a security agreement under the old MCA §30-9-203, which are consistent with the requirements of the revised MCA §30-9A-203(2), except for the distinction between an authenticated record and a signed writing.

> Nowhere in either *Former Article 9* or *Revised Article 9* is there a requirement that a security agreement contain language "granting" the secured party a security interest. While there are some courts that have held that granting language is required in a security agreement, the prevailing rule is that while no "magic words" are required, the writings, taken together, must demonstrate an intent on the debtor's part to create a security interest in the collateral. [footnotes omitted].

Juliet M. Moringiello, *Revised Article 9, Liens from the Fringe, and Why Sometimes Signatures Don't Matter, 10 Widener J. Pub. L. 135, 154-55 (2001)*. ...

"In addition, the court [in *Owens*] observed that no special words are necessary to create a security interest, ... that form [should] not prevail over substance and that, whenever possible; effect should be given to the parties' intent. Given this instruction, the touchstone question in determining if a security interest was created [or provided for] is whether the transaction was intended by the parties to have the effect of giving security." *Wiersma*, 283 B.R. at 306. Also "a security agreement does not have to consist of a single writing.

The necessary elements may appear in several writings, provided they are tied together as relating to the same transaction and the debtor signs each." 1 Coogan, SECURED TRANSACTIONS UNDER THE UNIFORM COMMERCIAL CODE 2004, §2A.04[2][a], p. 2A-31-32. The several writings theory is better known as the "composite document" theory derived from the analysis undertaken by the court in *In re Numeric Corp.*, 485 F.2d 1328 (1st Cir. 1973) and followed by many courts, including *Matter of Bollinger Corp.*, 614 F.2d 924, 927 (3rd Cir. 1980). In *In re Ace Lumber Supply, Inc.*, 7 Mont. B.R. 500, 105 B.R. 964, 967 (Bankr. D. Mont. 1989), Judge Peterson concluded "under Montana law the composite document rule is available to provide evidentiary support to create a security [interest] in collateral."

> In general, we are sympathetic to the claim that an authenticated security agreement can be proven by the use of multiple documents, as in the leading case of [*Numeric*]. In that case the person claiming to be a secured creditor was unable to produce a written, signed security agreement. Although he maintained there was such an agreement, all he could produce was a financing statement that listed the collateral and the minutes of the board of directors of the debtor that approved the granting of a security interest. The court concluded that the financing statement satisfied the Statute of Frauds requirement in *9-203* and that the directors' resolution established that an agreement in fact existed to give security. Noting that the UCC should be "liberally construed", the court found that the secured creditor had proved an enforceable security agreement. Even when there is no fully formed security agreement, in most cases, the loan will be manifest. Notes, payments, and other performance will show it. There will also be considerable evidence of intention to grant security (written inventories of collateral, identification of collateral in one way or another, and filed financing statements). It is likely that a court will read documents together and hold that they satisfy the objective test of *9-203* when they have been executed as part of a whole, they include internal cross references, prior course of dealing indicates they should be read together, the documents include a financing statement, other documents indicate that the parties assumed an unsigned security agreement was in force, course of performance, and testimonial and other nondocumentary evidence shows the parties plainly intended to create a security interest. (Technically, this last factor may not be strictly relevant, for the question is whether the objective writing requirement of *9-203* is satisfied.)

4 James J. White & Robert S. Summers, UNIFORM COMMERCIAL CODE §31-3 (5th ed., 2004 update). Another commentator provided the following insight.

> Although a particular security agreement does not expressly grant or reserve a security interest, it satisfies the requirements of the

Code if it recognizes that the creditor has the security interest in the collateral. That is, any language recognizing the existence of a security interest is sufficient and it is not necessary that there be language expressly "granting" a security interest to the creditor. Similarly, it is sufficient to recite that certain personal property is encumbered as security for an obligation. When the seller reserves title until paid, the reservation constitutes a security interest and therefore it is unnecessary for the agreement to expressly state that the seller has or is given a security interest. A promissory note given by the buyer to the lender that recites that upon default the lender has the right to goods purchased by the buyer constitutes a security agreement.

8A Anderson, UNIFORM COMMERCIAL CODE, §9-203:89 (2004 update). Judge Peterson, in *Ace Lumber Supply, 105 B.R. at 968*, quoting from *In re Murray Bros., Inc., 53 B.R. 281, 284-85 (Bankr. E.D.N.C. 1985)*, stated:

The determination of whether a security interest exists is a two-step process. First, the court must determine as a question of law whether the language in the writing required by [9-203] objectively indicates that the parties intended to create a security interest. If the statute of frauds requirement is met, then the factfinder must determine whether the parties actually intended to create a security interest. Parol evidence may be admitted to interpret an ambiguous writing but may not be introduced to satisfy the statute of frauds requirement.

In the considering [sic] the facts in the case *sub judice* and the instructive commentary and case law referenced above, the Court concludes that under the composite document theory that the promissory note and the financing statement are sufficient, as a matter of law, to create a security interest in Debtor's personal property described on the financing statement. The promissory note signed by Debtor specifically references that a "[s]ecurity interest will be filed ... on Form UCC-1 for merchandise delivered to date and security interest shall be retained on merchandise in storage. ... [GVF] shall have immediate access to secured merchandise for purpose of recovery of amount due should any payment be not made in a timely manner. ..." The financing statement, signed contemporaneously with the promissory note, by the Debtor, contains a complete description of personal property.

The Court further concludes, given the contents of the promissory note and financing statement and the testimony of the witnesses, as a question of fact, that Debtor and [GVF] actually intended to create a security through the terms of the promissory note and financing statement. When the Debtor signed the promissory note and the financing statement does not alter the above analysis. The date when the promissory note and financing statement were signed and the corresponding date of attachment and perfection may, but not in this case, have been critical to a trustee's preference investigation.

See MCA §§30-9A-324(1) (perfection when debtor receives possession or within 20 days thereafter), 30-9A-309(1) (perfection on attachment regarding consumer goods), 30-9A-203(2) (attachment and enforcement when value and rights and powers pass and one of three conditions are met, e.g., authentication; and 11 U.S.C. §547(c)(3) (exception to avoidance when security interest created and perfected on or before 20 days after debtor takes possession).

While the above identified language in the promissory note is certainly not the best language to use in a security agreement, it clearly provides that GVF is entitled to possession of its collateral in the event Debtor defaults under the terms of the promissory note. The Court thus finds that such language does indeed create and provide for a security interest for [GVF] in the furniture purchased by Debtor from GVF.

Debtor admits that she has not made a payment to GVF since March of 2004. Given the foregoing and the fact that GVF's collateral is declining in value on a daily basis, the Court finds that cause exists under 11 U.S.C. §362 to grant GVF its requested relief.

Although 9-203 on its face requires only that the security agreement be an authenticated record that describes the collateral, courts often seem to imply there is something else necessary to create an effective security agreement. At least one court was so bold as to actually read an additional requirement into the predecessor of 9-203. In *American Card Co. V. H.M.H. Co.*, 196 A.2d 150 (R.I. 1965), the court refused to accept a filed financing statement as the required security agreement because the financing statement did not contain words granting a security interest to the secured party. This case has been subjected to much criticism by other courts and by commentators, for reading into the Code a requirement that the security agreement contain words of grant. But in many of the opinions rejecting the words of grant requirement of *American Card* under old Article 9, the courts refuse to accept a financing statement, on its own, as a substitute for the security agreement required by 9-203. Since a financing statement under old Article 9 named the debtor, described the collateral *and* had to be signed by the debtor, it seems that there was something more required. Of course, under Revised Article 9, the financing statement cannot satisfy the express requirements of 9-203, since it is not signed by the debtor. Even *O'Dowd*, which rejects any words of grant requirement, requires evidence of intent to create a security interest—are not words of grant simply the best evidence of such an intent?

4. RIGHTS IN THE COLLATERAL

Article 9 requires that the debtor have rights in the collateral before a security interest attaches, but the determination of whether the debtor has such rights is not controlled by Article 9. Whether the debtor has an interest in the collateral and the extent of that interest will be determined by common law property rules or applicable statutes, including Article 2 of the Code when the transaction involves a sale of goods. Article 9 "does not specify the quantum of 'rights' a debtor must have in collateral to support a security interest,"[5] but the debtor must, at a minimum, have "the power to transfer rights in the collateral to a secured party." 9-203(b)(2). Something less than exclusive ownership will do. The debtor as lessee of equipment can convey a security interest in its right to use the equipment under the lease. Under old Article 9, it was generally presumed that the debtor could only convey what it actually had—the security interest only attached to the quantum of rights the debtor actually had in the collateral. But the comments to 9-203 explain that the phrase "the power to transfer rights in the collateral" was added in the revision to acknowledge that there were circumstances under which a debtor could transfer greater rights than it had. 9-203, Comment 6. See, White and Summers, Uniform Commercial Code (West, 6th ed. 2010) at 1193.

The cases that follow illustrate some of the issues associated with the rights in the collateral requirement of 9-203: that things may not always be as they seem (Manger) or as you intended them to be (First National Bank of Phillip and State Bank of Young).

MANGER v. DAVIS
Supreme Court of Utah
619 P.2d. 687 (1980)

MAUGHAN, *Justice*.

Plaintiff, alleging her ownership of a valuable diamond ring, initiated this action to recover possession from Word Making Productions, Ltd., hereinafter "W.M.P." Plaintiff's consignee, Steven Davis, authorized Jack Anderson and Michael Allred to pledge the ring to W.M.P. The trial court ruled plaintiff's ownership was subject to the perfected security interest of W.M.P. in the ring, securing sums advanced by the pledgee. The judgment of the trial court is reversed, and the cause is remanded to the trial court for disposition in accordance with this opinion. ...

Plaintiff is an octogenerian and widow of an Academy Award recipient, movie star, Warner Baxter. In the 1930's he gave her a diamond ring containing an emerald cut diamond of approximately 9.72 carats with six baguettes totalling .967 of a carat. Plaintiff met Davis at a dinner party given by her niece, whose husband was a successful Hollywood producer and friend of Davis. Plaintiff was in need of funds and Davis, a recent graduate of a school of gemology, informed her he could find a buyer for the ring. She gave him possession and a writing, which stated:

---

5   Gilmore, at 353 (referring to the same "rights" requirement under old Article 9).

Dear Mr. Davis—It would please me so much—if you would sell my emerald cut diamond ring for me—at whatever percent you consider OK. It was nice meeting you and your charming wife.

4/18/76

Sincerely

Winifred Manger

There was an explicit understanding between plaintiff and Davis that any offer to purchase was to be submitted to plaintiff for approval. Davis made a brief attempt to sell the ring in San Francisco, but the offer to purchase was unsatisfactory. Davis took the ring to Salt Lake City, where he assured plaintiff, through telephonic communication, that it was secured in a vault in a bank. From time to time he informed plaintiff of prospective sales, but the transaction always failed.

Without plaintiff's knowledge or consent Davis embarked on a peculiar course of action. He testified that he did not apprise her of his actions because she was too old to understand. Davis had met two promoters named Jack Anderson and Michael Allred, who owned stock in a local company, CD&M. The promoters explained that if they effected certain mergers of CD&M with companies in Colorado and Texas, they would be able to borrow money to purchase the ring. Davis gave possession of the ring to Anderson, who without the knowledge or authority of Davis, took the ring to Zions Bank, represented it was his property and pledged it to secure a personal loan for $10,000. The promoters gave Davis some stock certificates they represented to be worth $200,000.00. He determined the stock was worthless and returned it on October 12, 1976.

Thereafter, Allred approached James B. Medlin, President of W.M.P., which is a close corporation, to seek further loans, offering a valuable ring as security. Allred was indebted to Medlin, who knew Allred had few assets, and Medlin was suspicious about the proffered security. Allred explained that Davis was the owner of the ring and had consented to the pledge. Subsequently, Anderson, Allred, and Davis met with Medlin to arrange the loan and pledge. At this time Medlin required Davis to execute an affidavit, which provided:

"Steve Davis, being first duly sworn on oath, deposes and says: As full payment for services rendered to the Estate of Winifred Manger, on or about August, 1975, I received the following described ring:

The ring has been appraised with a retail replacement value of approximately $140,000.00.

I am a certified diamond appraiser and have been duly certified by the Gemological Institute of America. My appraised value was $165,000.00.

I have entered into an agreement with Michael Allred and Jack Anderson to allow them to use my ring as collateral to raise money for their private ventures in exchange for securities which they have allowed me to use as collateral for my own private ventures.

> I understand that Jack Anderson and Michael Allred may be using the above-described ring as collateral to borrow money from Word Making Productions and/or James B. Medlin, and agree that said ring may be used as collateral for said loan in any manner in which Jack Anderson and Michael Allred see fit to use it.
>
> Dated this 18th day of October, 1976.
>
> Steve Davis."

Medlin, who is also an attorney, did not inquire what type of services were rendered by Davis, who was a young man, to receive this substantial compensation. Neither was Medlin curious about verification of the existence of such an estate, which he was informed was in Los Angeles, nor the unorthodox manner of compensation for services. He testified he relied on the statements of Allred and Anderson that the father of Davis was a prominent business man to verify the ownership of the ring. Medlin was similarly disinterested as to the motive of Davis to exchange a valuable asset with the promoters, one of whom was a debtor of Medlin and without assets, to further his own business interests. Medlin further arranged an agreement to notify the bank holding the ring as security for Anderson's loan of his subsequent security interest and appointing the bank as escrow agent to hold possession as a means of perfecting Medlin's security interest.

Plaintiff's ring was thus pledged to W.M.P. by the promoters to secure a loan of $20,000. Allred paid $5,000 of this loan to Medlin to discharge his prior indebtedness. Subsequently, Allred, alone, received an additional advance of $10,000, which was also secured by the pledge.

The promoters defaulted on all the loans and Anderson died. W.M.P. paid the bank $10,625 to discharge the prior indebtedness and took possession of the ring. The trial court ruled W.M.P. had a perfected security interest, securing payment of the following amounts: $10,625, plus interest; $20,450, plus interest; and $10,000, plus interest and court costs.

Since the other defendants do not claim any interest in the ring, only plaintiff and W.M.P. are involved in this appeal.

The trial court found the ring was delivered to Davis on a consignment to sell in April, 1976, and plaintiff did not file a financing statement or take any other action designed to perfect a security interest in the collateral. There was a finding that plaintiff had no knowledge of any of the transactions except for the delivery to Davis for purpose of sale. Davis was found not to be a merchant dealing in diamond rings or goods of that kind, and there was no valid or effective sale of the ring ever made to CD&M Co.

In its conclusions of law, the trial court ruled that W.M.P., as a lender and pledgee, was a purchaser of the ring as defined in 70A-1-201(32) [Now 1-201(30)]. The court further ruled that pursuant to the ... Uniform Commercial Code ... W.M.P. had a perfected security interest in the ring by possession, which was prior to plaintiff's ownership interest. The lien of

W.M.P. was obtained prior to any attempt by plaintiff to withdraw or rescind the authority of her agent, Davis.

* * *

In an analysis of this rather complex case, the appropriate point to begin is Section 70A-9-204(1) [Now 9-203], which provides that a security interest cannot attach until the debtor has rights in the collateral. Unless Davis had rights in the ring, so he could authorize the pledge by Allred and Anderson, the security interest of W.M.P. could not attach.

The Code does not clearly establish the meaning of "rights in the collateral." Although a debtor has possession of the collateral, that fact does not give him rights. If a security transaction relates to a sale, Article 2 may determine whether the debtor has rights. If there be no authority to subject property to a security interest, the creditor has no security interest therein.

* * *

The trial court found the transaction to be a consignment to sell between plaintiff and Davis. There is a degree of confusion in the findings and conclusions of law of the trial court in regard to this relationship.

* * *

The undisputed evidence in this case establishes that the transaction between plaintiff and Davis was a true consignment, establishing a principal-agent relationship. Davis was given possession with authority to sell only upon the express consent of plaintiff as to the sale price. Davis was to receive a commission and not a profit on the sale. Such a transaction does not fall within the purview of Section 70A-2-401, a provision cited by the trial court, for it was not a sale with title passing to the buyer. Further, Davis did not have the status of a buyer as that term is defined in 70A-2-103(1)(a):

" 'Buyer' means a person who buys or contracts to buy goods."

In 2 Anderson, Uniform Commercial Code (2nd ed.), Section 2-401:10, p. 11, it is explained:

"The authority of an agent to transfer title is distinct from the transfer of title which is the sale. Ordinarily the agent to sell, being clothed with no more than authority to make a transfer, does not hold title to the goods. ..."

To sustain its ruling, the trial court further cited the provisions in Section 70A-2-403. These provisions are of no aid to W.M.P. because Davis had no title as a consignee. The basic pre-Code concept that a possessor cannot pass title was not altered by the Code, in the absence of circumstances bringing the case within the scope of Section 2-403 ... W.M.P anticipated the problem of applying either sections 70A–2-403 or 2-401 to the circumstances of this transaction; therefore, it has urged in its brief that the trial court erred in its finding that Davis was not a merchant dealing in diamond rings or goods of that kind, and thus the consignment would fall within the provisions of 70A-2-326(3) [which would make it subject to the claims of his creditors]. Without detailing the record, a survey thereof clearly sustains the finding of the trial court that in his participation in this transaction, Davis was not a person who maintained a place of business at which he dealt in goods of the kind involved. It is even more apparent that this provision is inapplicable when its purpose is reviewed, viz., to prevent credit from being extended to a dealer on the basis of his ostensible ownership of the inventory, which was protected from the claims of creditors.

At this juncture, it is apparent that the transaction between plaintiff and Davis was a true consignment, and the law of agency resolves the conflicting claims between plaintiff and W.M.P. Restatement, Agency (2d), Section 201, provides:

> "(1) Apart from statute and except as stated in Subsection (3), the interests of an undisclosed principal who entrusts an agent with a chattel other than a commercial document representing a chattel or chose in action with directions to deal with it in a particular way, as by sale, barter, pledge or mortgage is not thereby affected by a transaction of a kind different from that authorized.
>
> (2) The interests of the principal are affected by an unauthorized transaction of the same kind as that authorized if it is conducted in the usual and ordinary course of business by an agent with one who reasonably believes the agent to be the owner and who pays value."

Comment (a), following Section 201, refers to the Comments on Section 175. Comment (e), following Section 175, states:

> What transactions are considered to be of a kind different from those authorized is a matter of degree. For the purpose of this Section, authority to barter does not give power to the agent to pledge or to mortgage the property. ..."

The authority conferred on Davis by plaintiff to sell the ring did not give him the right or power to pledge it in his own interest as an incident to his express authority. The pledge to W.M.P. was a transaction of a different kind than that authorized by plaintiff and therefore her interest in the ring was not affected thereby. Since Davis had no authority to pledge the ring, the pledgee, W.M.P., did not acquire a valid security interest therein, and plaintiff is entitled to recover unencumbered possession thereof.

Costs are awarded to plaintiff.

Possession may give the appearance that the debtor has something it can convey, but as *Manger* shows, appearances can be deceiving when it comes to rights in the collateral. Medlin's real mistake in *Manger* was not that he relied on Davis's possession of the ring, but that he did so in light of the questionable means by which Davis claimed to have acquired the ring and the suspicious circumstances under which it was offered to him as collateral.

FIRST NAT. BANK OF PHILIP v. TEMPLE
Supreme Court of South Dakota
2002 S.D. 36 (2002)

STEELE, *Justice*.

Doug Temple appeals from a judgment ordering that First National Bank of Philip held a perfected security interest in and to certain livestock as a result of loan instruments executed by Merle Temple. We affirm.

FACTS

Beginning in 1990, Merle Temple (Merle) obtained loans from First National Bank in Philip, South Dakota (FNB). To secure the loans, he pledged as collateral cattle bearing one or more brands owned by him. FNB perfected a security interest in all the cattle so branded, their products and proceeds, after first determining that no other security interest appeared of record to suggest any prior lien.

In 1992 Doug Temple (Doug), Merle's father, delivered thirty head of cattle bearing Doug's brand to Merle. These cattle were to be cared for by Merle. In exchange Merle would be entitled to all calves produced from these thirty head. Merle was also expected to work for Doug from time to time in general ranching activities.

In December 1993 Doug purchased twenty heifers which were branded with Merle's brand at Doug's direction. In October 1995 Doug purchased an additional twenty-nine heifers, again branding them with Merle's brand. All cattle were branded at their location of purchase and then delivered to Range Unit # 508, under Merle's control.

In his 1996 financial statement, Merle reported that he owned seventy-six cows and ten replacement heifers. This reflected an increase over the thirty-one cows and six replacement heifers reported in the 1995 financial statement. Merle claimed that the twenty head acquired in 1993 and the twenty-nine head acquired in 1995, all branded with his brand, were his cows. FNB understood that Merle was running thirty cows for his father and that Merle received all of the increase.

The relationship between Doug and Merle began to deteriorate. In March 1999 Doug removed part of the original thirty cows bearing his brand from Merle's care.

In early September 1999 Doug made his first and only contact with FNB, and apprised FNB of his claim of an ownership interest in Merle's cattle. He claimed that the livestock acquired in 1993 and 1995 were to remain his cows.

They were only branded with Merle's brand to distinguish the pasture to which they were assigned, despite the fact that Doug already had thirty head branded with his own brand in the same pasture. Shortly thereafter, Doug obtained an ex parte order from the Ogalala Sioux Tribal Court authorizing seizure of forty-nine to fifty head of cattle. These cattle were seized and sold at Belle Fourche Livestock Auction. The proceeds of the sale were paid into escrow and this action for declaratory judgment was brought in circuit court.

* * *

ISSUE THREE

Did the trial court err when it concluded that FNB held a valid and perfected security interest in the cattle in question?

To claim a valid, perfected security interest in collateral, the security interest must attach to the collateral. A security interest attaches when (1) there is an agreement that it attach; (2) value has been given by the secured party; and (3) the debtor has rights in the collateral. SDCL 57A-9-203; *First Nat. Bank v. Pleasant Hollow Farm*, 532 N.W.2d 60, 62 (S.D.1995). The issue in this case is whether the debtor had sufficient rights in the collateral enabling the security interest to attach.

"The phrase 'rights in collateral' as used in [SDCL 57A-9-203] has no clear definition." Continental Grain Co. v. Brandenburg, 1998 SD 118, ¶ 17, 587 N.W.2d 196, 200. The doctrine of derivative rights helps to define and explain this phrase. Essentially, a security interest does not attach to the described asset; it attaches to the debtor's rights in the asset. William H. Lawrence et al., *Understanding Secured Transactions* 88-90 (2000).

Furthermore,

> The common conceptualization of property rights as consisting of a bundle of sticks is helpful in understanding when a debtor has sufficient rights in an asset to grant an enforceable Article 9 security interest. Full ownership of an asset includes, inter alia, the rights to possess and use the asset. All or some of the owner's rights can be transferred by way of sale, lease, or license. A person with transferable rights can grant an enforceable security interest in those rights. In the full ownership situations, the security interest attaches to the full panoply of rights, ... debtor with only limited rights in an asset can convey no more than the extent of its own interest. The limitations on the debtor's rights also constitute limitations on the interest taken by the secured party and on the interest that can be conveyed to a foreclosure-sale buyer. ... A secured party's rights expand as additional parties with rights in the collateral consent to have their rights encumbered. ... Even a person who has not actually consented to a security interest may be estopped to deny its effectiveness. ... Estoppel can result from either a common-law

rule or a statute and is inevitably based on the estopped person's actions in clothing the debtor with indicia of ownership.

Id. (internal citations omitted).

(*See also Pleasant View Farms, Inc. v. Ness*, 455 N.W.2d 602 (S.D.1990). If the owner of collateral allows another to appear as the owner or to dispose of the collateral, such that a third party is led into dealing with the apparent owner as though he were the actual owner, then the owner will be estopped from asserting that the apparent owner did not have rights in the collateral).

This Court addressed the phrase "rights in the collateral" in *Continental Grain*, 1998 SD 118 at ¶ 17, 587 N.W.2d at 200:

> In an Article 9 transaction, the rule is mere possession of the collateral by the debtor is not enough to grant sufficient rights for the security interest to attach. Yet, as with many rules, there are exceptions. This Court has found formal title is not required for a debtor to have sufficient 'rights in the collateral' to allow a security interest to attach. A debtor may have sufficient rights to create a security interest when he does so with an authorization from the actual owner of the collateral. Also, a debtor may have sufficient rights in the collateral if he has something more than 'naked possession.' Essentially, the debtor normally can only convey something once it has something and that something may be less than the full bundle of rights that one may hold in such property. (internal citations omitted).

"In *Pleasant Hollow*, this Court stated that control over the collateral is the factor that determines the debtor's rights in the collateral, not ownership." *Continental Grain*, 1998 SD 118 at ¶ 18, 587 N.W.2d at 200.

> [E]ven if a party retains ownership interest in a piece of collateral, a debtor who retains that collateral is still able to mislead potential creditors by exercising his "rights" of possession and control over the collateral. It is the outward appearance of a debtor's rights of ownership and control in the collateral that determines whether attachment of a security interest is effective and not the right of a party who may have title to the collateral.

Id. (*quoting First Nat. Bank v. Pleasant Hollow Farm*, 532 N.W.2d at 63.)

In the case before us, Merle at all times had every outward appearance of ownership and control of the livestock. The livestock were, at all times, possessed by the debtor and had his healed brand on them. (*See also Continental Grain*, 1998 SD 118 at ¶ 32, 587 N.W.2d at 204, fn. 9 stating that SDCL 40-19-24 provides a registered brand is prima facie evidence of ownership of livestock). He cared for the cattle at his sole expense using his own land, facilities, equipment and feed. He made all decisions relative to culling, selling and care of the livestock. Furthermore, it is undisputed that he signed all documents necessary to secure the collateral for his loans. Doug gave Merle the outward appearance of ownership and control over the cattle. It was under his direction that the cattle were branded with Merle's brand. Doug argues that this was done to distinguish the pasture to which they were assigned. However, Doug's original thirty head, branded with his brand and which are not part of this controversy, were in the same pasture as the other cattle branded with Merle's brand. These facts compel this Court to conclude that the debtor, Merle, had the necessary rights in the collateral in order for FNB to properly perfect its security interest.

Doug argues that FNB knew or should have known that the cattle were his. Doug contends that FNB cannot take a valid security interest in those cattle through Merle if it can be shown that they knew, or should have known, that the cattle were not Merle's. He cites no direct authority to support this proposition. …

FNB did everything legally necessary to protect its interest. Doug failed to protect his interest under the law and clothed his son with all indices of ownership. FNB cannot be penalized for Doug's own failures.

Under the facts of this case, we conclude that FNB held a valid security interest in the livestock in question and is entitled to the escrowed proceeds of the sale.

Accordingly, we affirm the judgment of the trial court.

STATE BANK OF YOUNG AM. v. VIDMAR IRON WORKS, INC.
Supreme Court of Minnesota
292 N.W.2d 244 (1980)

YETKA, *Justice.*

The appellant State Bank of Young America brought this action against Vidmar Iron Works, Inc., to recover under security interests it held securing the unpaid debts of Adaptable Industries, Inc. Trial was held before the Carver County District Court, and the court entered findings and conclusions against the appellant. The appellant then moved for a new trial or, in the alternative, for amended findings and conclusions. The court denied that motion, and the appellant has appealed the order denying the motion. We reverse and remand.

This case presents the following issues for decision:

* * *

B. Did the bank's security interest in the inventory of Adaptable Industries cover raw materials owned by Vidmar Iron Works which Adaptable was converting into finished products to the extent of the value added by Adaptable?

* * *

CHAPTER 3. CREATING AND PROTECTING A SECURITY INTEREST

[Adaptable Industries ("Adaptable") was a metal goods fabricating shop that over the course of several years borrowed approximately $165,000 from the State Bank of Young America ("the Bank"). Because Adaptable made regular payments to the bank, the outstanding balance on its debt to the bank ranged from $500 to $30,000 at any one time. Three security agreements were executed during this same period of time granting the bank security interests in Adaptable's accounts receivable as well as its inventory and equipment. The bank filed financing statements in connection with each of the security agreements. Vidmar Iron Works ("Vidmar") contracted to have Adaptable do fabricating work on raw materials it supplied to Adaptable.]

* * *

On October 22, 1975, the bank sent Vidmar a certified letter notifying him of the bank's inventory security interest. At that time, Vidmar was making checks payable to the new company names. ...

The basis of the bank's right of action against Vidmar rather than Adaptable is found in the security agreements. The agreements provide that the bank may, at any time, make direct collection of the accounts or proceeds of goods secured. ... The agreements also authorize the bank to consider the debtor in default if it deems its security impaired or its risk materially increased. *Cf.* Minn.Stat. §336.1-208 (1978) [Now 1-309]. Vidmar does not deny that it is liable to the bank if the issues discussed below are resolved against it.

I.B.

Vidmar next argues that since it owned the steel which was processed by Adaptable, the bank's inventory security interest could not attach to it. The U.C.C. states that goods taken as collateral are classified as "inventory:"

> if they are held by a person who holds them for sale or lease or to be furnished under contracts of service or if he has so furnished them, or if they are raw materials, work in process or materials used or consumed in a business.

Minn.Stat. §336.9-109(4) (1978) [Now 9-102(a)(48)].

The U.C.C. does not require that collateral be owned by the debtor. In at least two instances, the U.C.C. specifically refers to situations in which the debtor is not the owner of the collateral. In defining the term "debtor," section 336.9-105(1)(d) [Now 9-102(18)] states "(w)here the debtor and the owner of the collateral are not the same person, the term 'debtor' means the owner of the collateral * * *." Section 336.9-112 [Omitted, Revised Art. 9] is entitled "Where Collateral is Not Owned by Debtor" and specifies certain rights of the owner which are not relevant here. The lack of a requirement of ownership of the collateral is consistent with the U.C.C.'s general non-reliance on the use of "title" to determine rights. *See* sections 336.2-401, 336.9-202.

Rather than requiring title, the U.C.C. only requires that the debtor have "rights in the collateral." Section 336.9-203(1). Professor Gilmore has written:

> The Article (Article 9) does not specify the quantum of "rights" which a debtor must have in collateral to support a security interest: evidently less than full "legal title" will do and the secured party will get whatever rights the debtor had * * *.

> 1G. Gilmore, Security Interests in Personal Property s 11.5 at 353 (1965).

Vidmar's argument that Adaptable had no rights in the steel is erroneous. Adaptable had contract rights in the goods to the extent of the amount due for its work and had a statutory lien in the goods to secure it. The lien would have been one granted for "personalty in possession" under Minn.Stat. ss 514.18-.22 (1978). Section 514.19(4) allows such a lien for anyone "(m)aking, altering or repairing any article, or expending any labor, skill or material thereon." Such a lien would even have had a priority over any perfected security interest in the steel held by Vidmar or its creditors. Section 336.9-310 (1978) [Now 9-333] states:

> When a person in the ordinary course of his business furnishes services or materials with respect to goods subject to a security interest, a lien upon goods in the possession of such person given by statute or rule of law for such materials or services takes priority over a perfected security interest unless the lien is statutory and the statute expressly provides otherwise.

This court has never considered whether the rights of one in Adaptable's position are sufficient to allow a security interest to attach. However, in *James Talcott, Inc. v. Franklin National Bank*, 292 Minn. 277, 194 N.W.2d 775 (1972), this court held that a security interest could attach to property purportedly leased by the debtor. Looking to the substance of the transaction, the court held that ownership for Article 9 purposes was not dependent upon formal title. The court stated:

> (T)he draftsmen of the code intended that its provisions should not be circumvented by manipulation of the locus of title. For this reason, consignment sales, conditional sales, and other arrangements or devices whereby title is retained in the seller for a period following possession by the debtor are all treated under Art. 9 as though title had been transferred to the debtor and the creditor-seller had retained only a security interest in the goods.

> 292 Minn. at 285, 194 N.W.2d at 781.

In a case dealing with facts identical to those of this case, the Oklahoma Supreme Court held that a security interest could attach. *Morton Booth Co. v. Tiara Furniture, Inc.*, 564 P.2d 210 (Okl.1977). The facts of that case were stated as follows:

> The mainstay of Tiara's business prior to its failure was a contract with Booth for the manufacture and sale of gun cabinets. Under the

terms of the contract Booth supplied most of the basic materials, i.e. glass, plywood, locks, hinges, pulls, felt, other hardware and packing cartons. Tiara was to supply the structural lumber and construct the cabinets to Booth's specifications. Upon completion of the cabinets, Tiara packed the cabinets in cartons fabricated from materials supplied by Booth and shipped them to Booth which would pay a reduced price for the finished product.

564 P.2d at 211.

Relying in part on the quoted passage from our decision in James Talcott, Inc., the court held that the debtor had sufficient "rights" in the material to allow the bank's inventory security interest to attach.

We hold that Adaptable had sufficient "rights in the collateral" under section 336.9-203(1) to allow the bank's inventory security interest to attach.

However, as Professor Gilmore stated, supra, the secured party only gets rights in the goods to the extent of the debtor's rights in them. Adaptable's rights in the goods were based on the payments due under the contracts from Vidmar. In this case, the bank properly seeks only to recoup those payments and is not claiming the value of the raw materials as supplied by Vidmar. The payments made are more than sufficient to cover the remaining unpaid debt of Adaptable.

* * *

Reversed and remanded.

B. PROTECTING THE SECURITY INTEREST

Once the security interest has attached, it is enforceable against the collateral. But Article 9 requires that the secured party take additional steps in order to protect that security interest against other creditors that assert competing claims to the collateral. When the secured party has taken the required steps, the security interest is "perfected." Perfection will give the secured party priority over many of the debtor's other creditors—perfection does not provide absolute priority, but in most cases, it provides a significant head start.

A secured party can perfect its security interest under Article 9 by filing a financing statement—a public notice of the security interest. It can also perfect its security interest by taking possession of the collateral. To perfect a security interest in certain types of collateral, the secured party will have to attain "control" of the collateral. And some security interest are automatically perfected when they attach—the secured party is not required to do anything to perfect the security interest after it has attached.

1. Filing

That a security interest in personal property could—or should—be perfected by some form of public filing was a well-established precept by the time the drafting of Article 9 began. Most of the pre-Code devices that had been legitimized by legislative action required some form of public filing. Article 9 made two significant improvements to pre-Code filing. First, it created a unified filing system for most types of secured financing. Article 9 replaced the "congeries of separate filing systems, mostly maintained on a local or county basis" that had developed around secured financing with "a unified system, maintained on a state-wide basis. ..."[6] The duplicity of these filing systems negated their purpose of

> providing creditors with an easily available method of checking on a borrower's financial status, while at the same time providing lenders who have made secured loans an easy and certain method of perfecting their security interests.[7]

Because there were so many ways of creating a security interest in the same property, a creditor had to incur the burden and expense of checking the filing system for each in order to assess a debtor's financial status.

Second, Article 9 implemented a notice filing system as opposed to the transaction filing systems that most pre-Code schemes had used. Transaction filing required the operative documents of the transaction between the debtor and the secured party—e.g., the chattel mortgage or the conditional sales contract—to be filed. The hyper-technical requirements of these operative documents meant that any change in the relationship had to be re-documented which then required refiling. For example, in inventory financing, whenever the secured party provided new inventory to replace what the debtor had sold a new agreement with the debtor was required which then had to be filed. This was not only expensive for the secured party, but made it unduly burdensome on subsequent creditors who would have to sort through the hundreds of agreements on file to ascertain the debtor's current financial status.

Article 9 creates a single notice-based filing system for most transactions involving a security interest in personal property. At center stage in the Article 9 filing system is the financing statement.

a. The Financing Statement

A notice filing system requires some form of standardized filing in order to facilitate discovery of the information on file. The standardized form used by Article 9 is the financing statement. Because the financing statement is intended only to alert subsequent parties dealing with the debtor that another claims an interest in the debtor's personal property, Article 9 only requires

---

6   Gilmore at 464–65.
7   Id. at 463.

that, to be effective when filed, a financing statement contain (1) the name of the debtor, (2) the name of the secured party, and (3) that it indicate the collateral it covers. 9-502(a). Financing statements covering realty-related collateral require additional information regarding the real property implicated. 9-502(b). Filings in the system are indexed by the name of the debtor, so assuring the accuracy of the debtor's name on filings is critical to the integrity (and utility) of the filing system. Accordingly, under Article 9, errors in the debtor's name that preclude discovery of the filing by parties searching the system render the filing a nullity. 9-506. In contrast, errors in the collateral description do not negate the overall effectiveness of the filing; instead, the security interest in some part of the intended collateral likely will be unperfected as a result of such errors. The secured party's name, while important as a resource for obtaining additional information about the transaction described, is not central to the integrity of the filing system. Errors in the name of the secured party will not negate the effectiveness of a filed financing statement.

Although the requirements necessary for a filed financing statement to be effective are minimal, as we will later see in this section, a financing statement is supposed to contain additional information before it is placed in the filing system.

I. ERRORS IN THE DEBTOR'S NAME

What is the debtor's name? Before we can determine whether there is an error in the debtor's name on a financing statement, we need to know what it is that Article 9 expects to see when it tells us to use the name of the debtor on the financing statement. Under Article 9, what the debtor's name is turns on what the debtor is. If the debtor is a 'registered organization," then the name of the debtor is the name that appears on the official registration documents—the public record—creating the debtor. 9-503(a)(1). A registered organization is any entity whose legal existence depends on recognition by the state. 9-102(a)(70). Corporations, limited partnerships, limited liability professional corporations, and the like are "registered organizations" under Article 9. If the debtor is an organization—as opposed to a registered organization—which actually has a name, then the name of the organization is the name of the debtor. 9-503(a)(4). If the organization does not have a name, then the Comments tell us to use the names of the individuals "who comprise" the organization. 9-503, Comment 2. If the debtor is an individual, the debtor's name for purposes of Article 9 will depend on which, if any, of the alternative 2010 amendments to section 9-503 that the controlling jurisdiction has adopted. The 2010 amendments provide that if the debtor has been issued a drivers license, the name on the license is the name of the debtor (mandatory) or is an acceptable form of the debtor's name (not mandatory).

When does an error in the name of the debtor on a financing statement matter? Since the purpose of notice filing is to alert subsequent parties to the existence of a security interest in identifiable property, an error in the debtor's name should matter when it prevents subsequent parties from discovering the financing statement intended to provide notice of the security interest. Under old Article 9, the courts did not agree on the kind of errors that would necessarily prevent discovery—in part because old Article was less than clear about how much of the discovery burden was placed on the searching party. As the case which follows explains, Revised Article 9 establishes a standard against which all financing statements are to be tested and which was intended to put all responsibility for non-discovery on the filing party. Under Revised Article 9, an error in the debtor's name will negate the effectiveness of a filed financing statement if the error makes the financing statement seriously misleading. A financing statement is seriously misleading when, using the standard search logic of the filing office where it has been filed, a search under the correct name of the debtor fails to produce the filed financing statement. In other words, if plugging the correct name of the debtor into the search engine used by the filing office does not retrieve a financing statement, the statement is seriously misleading and not effective to perfect the security interest it describes. If a search under the correct name of the debtor retrieves a financing statement with errors in the debtor's name, the statement is by definition not seriously misleading and is effective despite the errors in the debtor's name. The only burden on the searching party is to use the correct name of the debtor.

As you read the following case, consider whether the courts have managed to shift back to the searching party some part of the discovery burden despite the intent of Revised Article 9 to remove it completely.

HOST AMERICA CORP v. COASTLINE FIN., INC.
United States District Court, D. Utah, C.D
2006 WL 1579614 (D. Utah, C.D., May 30, 2006)

CAMPBELL, *Judge.*

Host America Corporation filed this action seeking a declaration that its security interest in goods owned by K.W.M. Electronics Corporation ('KWM') has priority over Coastline Financial, Inc.'s lessor's lien, which attached to the same goods. Host America moved for summary judgment, claiming that its interest is superior to Coastline's because either (1) Host America's security interest was perfected before Coastline's lessor's lien, or (2) Host America has perfected its security interest while Coastline has yet to perfect its lessor's lien.

Coastline opposed Host America's summary judgment motion and moved for partial summary judgment on the issue of perfection. Coastline argues that it perfected its lessor's lien no later than the fall of 2006 and that the security interest upon which Host America relies was not perfected at that time because the financing statement filed in connection with that security interest listed an incorrect debtor's name, rendering the financing statement 'seriously misleading' and precluding perfection. ...

As detailed below, the undisputed material facts establish that the initial financing statement filed in connection with Host America's security interest was seriously misleading. Although Host America has since attempted to correct the initial financing statement in an effort to ensure perfection of its security interest, the court concludes that Coastline perfected its lessor's lien before Host America undertook its corrective actions. Accordingly, the court concludes that Coastline's lessor's lien has priority over Host America's security interest.

Undisputed Facts

KWM, a manufacturer and assembler of electronic goods, leased space for its corporate facilities from Coastline. In late spring of 2001, KWM entered into a financing arrangement with Washington Mutual Bank. Pursuant to that agreement, KWM provided Washington Mutual with two security interests in certain collateral. Washington Mutual assigned those security interests to Coastline in the fall of 2002.

Desiring to wind up the financing obligations represented by the Coastline security interests, KWM sought alternative financing. As part of that process, KWM paid off the Coastline obligations and Coastline terminated the two financing statements evidencing its security interests. Around the same time, KWM granted Burton M. Sack a security interest in certain collateral. On May 12, 2003, Mr. Sack filed a financing statement to provide notice of his security interest and to perfect that interest. The financing statement listed the debtor as 'KWM Electronics Corporation' [as opposed to K.W.M.].

In the late summer of 2004, Coastline initiated an unlawful detainer action against KWM in the Third District Court for the State of Utah. Coastline initiated the action after KWM failed to pay rent. ... Accordingly, Coastline sought a writ of attachment, which it received on September 30, 2004, and ultimately obtained a default judgment against KWM on November 19, 2004. Coastline's lessor's lien attached to the goods identified as collateral in Mr. Sack's financing statement.

After obtaining the default judgment, Coastline seized the goods. But Host America, which had an ongoing business relationship with KWM, initiated legal action, claiming that it was the rightful owner of the seized goods. ... On December 9, 2005, Host America acquired the debt and the security interest held by Mr. Sack. On December 22, 2005, Host America filed a financing statement in connection with that debt and security interest, listing the debtor as 'K.W.M. Electronics Corporation.' On January 3, 2006, Host America filed the present action, claiming that its recently acquired security interest has priority over any lien held by Coastline. Two days later, Host America filed an additional financing statement in connection with the debt and security interest it acquired from Mr. Sack. That financing statement listed the debtor as 'K.W.M. Electronics Corporation.'

The key issue in the motions presently before the court is whether the security interest that Host America acquired from Mr. Sack has priority over Coastline's lessor's lien.

Analysis

Host America advances two arguments in support of its motion for summary judgment. First, Host America argues that Mr. Sack perfected his security interest when he filed the May 2003 financing statement. Because Mr. Sack's financing statement was filed well before Coastline attempted to foreclose on its lessor's lien, Host America contends that the security interest it acquired from Mr. Sack has priority. Second, and alternatively, Host America asserts that its security interest is superior to Coastline's lessor's lien because Host America perfected its security interest no later than January 5, 2006, the date on which it filed its most recent financing statement, and Coastline has yet to perfect its lessor's lien.

The court concludes that the financing statement filed by Mr. Sack in May of 2003 failed to sufficiently list the name of the debtor. Additionally, the court concludes that the financing statement was seriously misleading because a search of the state's records, conducted using filing office's standard search logic, would not have revealed the financing statement. As a result, the financing statement filed by Mr. Sack failed to perfect his security interest. Further, it is immaterial whether Host America eventually managed to cure the deficiency present in Mr. Sack's financing statement because Coastline perfected its lessor's lien well before Host America made such an attempt. The court will address each issue in turn.

I. Mr. Sack's May 2003 Financing Statement Was Seriously Misleading

Host America concedes that the financing statement Mr. Sack filed in May of 2003 did not provide KWM's correct name. The question before the court is whether the failure to list KWM's correct name on the financing statement rendered that statement 'seriously misleading.' If so, Mr. Sack's security interest remained unperfected until well after the time Coastline foreclosed its lessor's lien.

"The purpose behind the filing provisions is to provide notice to subsequent creditors in a manner which will give such creditors confidence that they are aware of any prior security interests in the collateral that may be superior to their own interest." *Pearson v. Salina Coffee House, Inc.*, 831 F.2d 1531, 1536 (10th Cir.1987). If a financing statement fails to provide adequate notice to subsequent creditors, the Utah Uniform Commercial Code will not allow the security interest evidenced by that filing to have priority over a subsequently perfected security interest. *See Diversified Holdings, L.C. v. Turner*, 2002 UT 129, ¶ 42, 63 P.3d 686. "Because notice of a secured interest in property is accomplished by searching the debtor's name, the requirement that a financing statement provide the debtor's name is particularly important." *Clark v. Deere & Co. (In re Kinderknecht)*, 308 B.R. 71, 74 (10th Cir.B.A.P.2004). Given the importance of the debtor's name, it should come as no surprise that a failure to adequately provide that name will render a financing statement 'seriously misleading.' *See* Utah Code Ann. §70A-9a-506.

Two sections of the Utah Uniform Commercial Code are relevant to determining whether Mr. Sack's May 2003 financing statement was seriously misleading: Utah Code section 70A-9a-503 and section 70A-9a-506. Both of these provisions were adopted by the Utah State Legislature during its 2000 session. The statutes are, in all relevant aspects, identical to revisions proposed by the National Conference of Commissioners on Uniform State Laws in 1998 ... The revisions "require[ ] more accuracy in filings, and place [ ] less burden on the searcher to seek out erroneous filings." *In re Summit Staffing Polk County, Inc.*, 305 B.R. 347, 354 (M.D.Fla.2003). "Prior to that time, courts struggled with whether names, such as trade names, in a financing statement sufficiently provided the name of the debtor. [The revisions were] meant to 'clarify when a debtor's name is correct and when an incorrect name is insufficient.'" *In re Kinderknecht*, 308 B.R. at 74-75 (*quoting* Official Uniform Commercial Code Comment 4.h).

When interpreting statutes, the court's "primary goal ... is to give effect to the legislative intent, as evidenced by the plain language, in light of the purpose the statute was meant to achieve." *Foutz v. City of S. Jordan*, 2004 UT 74 ¶ 11, 100 P.3d 1171 (internal quotation omitted). Accordingly, the court first turns to the plain language of the relevant statutes.

Section 70A-9a-503(1) provides that "[a] financing statement sufficiently provides the name of the debtor:

> (a) if the debtor is a registered organization, **only if the financing statement provides the name of the debtor indicated on the public record of the debtor's jurisdiction of organization. ...**" (emphasis added).

> **Section 70A-9a-506 states that, "[e]xcept as provided in Subsection (3), a financing statement** that fails sufficiently to provide the name of the debtor in accordance with Subsection 70A-9a-503(1) is seriously misleading. (emphasis added)."

Subsection (3) of the same statute provides an 'escape hatch' for creditors that fail to strictly comply with the Utah Code's requirement that the creditor of a registered organization list the name of that organization as it appears on the public record:

> If a search of the records of the filing office under the debtor's correct name, using the filing office's standard search logic, if any, would disclose a financing statement that fails sufficiently to provide the name of the debtor in accordance with Subsection, 70A-9a-503(1), the name provided does not make the financing statement seriously misleading.

Interestingly, the parties do not agree on KWM's correct name and therefore diverge on the question of what name would need to be listed on the financing statement to satisfy section 70A-9a-503(1). Host America contends that the public record lists KWM as "K. W. M. Electronics Corporation," with spaces between the periods; Coastline asserts that KWM's correct name is "K.W.M. Electronics Corporation," with no spaces between the periods. But the parties' dispute is immaterial because the financing statement filed by Mr. Sack failed to use any periods at all, and instead listed the debtor as "KWM Electronics Corporation." As mentioned, Host America concedes that by failing to indicate the presence of periods, Mr. Sack's financing statement did not comply with the requirements of section 70A-9a-503(1) of the Utah Code.

The plain language of section 70A-9a-506(2) dictates that Mr. Sack's failure to comply with the requirements of section 70A-9a-503(1) rendered his financing statement 'seriously misleading' unless saved by the escape hatch provision of subsection (3). In other words, if a search under KWM's correct name, using the filing office's standard search logic, would have revealed Mr. Sack's security interest, then the Utah Code would not consider Mr. Sack's financing statement 'seriously misleading.' *See id*. §70A-9a-506(3).

The parties provided the court with extensive information about the search logic used by the state's filing office, including multiple declarations from Kathy Berg, the director of the Division of Corporations and Commercial Code. The evidence is undisputed that a search under KWM's correct name using the filing office's standard search logic would not have revealed Mr. Sack's security interest at any point in time before Coastline seized the goods as part of its foreclosure activities. As a result, the conclusion seems foregone that the escape hatch provision of subsection (3) is not available to Host America.

What complicates that conclusion is that, until recently, the filing office's standard search logic was not capable of compensating for even minor errors in a debtor's name. As a result, Host America claims that the escape hatch provided by subsection (3) was completely illusory at the time Mr. Sack filed his financing statement. In essence, Host America argues that the limitations of the state filing office's search logic improperly eviscerated a creditor protection that the legislature intended to provide.

Although sympathetic with Host America's position, the court concludes that the historical limitations of the state's filing office-though severe indeed-do not excuse Mr. Sack's failure to comply with section 70A-9a-503(1). The plain language of section 70A-9a-506(3) establishes an escape hatch to creditors who list an improper debtor name only to the extent that the state's standard search logic can compensate for that error. By necessity, the breadth of the safe haven provided by section 70A-9a-506(3) will either expand or contract as the capabilities of the state's standard search logic change over time. The escape hatch provision is expressly tied to the state's search logic and allows no leeway for financing statements that remain undiscovered due to a creditor's failure to comply with section 70A-9a-503(1).

This is so even when, as here, a search under the debtor's correct name, using the filing office's standard search logic, fails to retrieve financing statements with relatively minor errors. The Utah Uniform Commercial Code, as it now stands, provides this court with no guidance on how to determine if a debtor's name is seriously misleading, other than referencing the filing office's standard search logic. *Cf.* Clark 308 B.R. at 75 ("The intent to clarify when a debtor's name is sufficient shows a desire to foreclose fact-intensive tests, such as those that existed under the former Article 9 of the UCC, inquiring into whether a person conducting a search would discover a filing under any given name. Requiring a financing statement to provide a debtor's legal name is a clear cut test that is in accord with that intent.") In short, the legislature elected to leave the fate of those creditors that fail to comply with the strict naming requirement of section 70A-9a-503(1) in the hands of those that develop and manage the filing office's search logic. *See* Note, *Good Technology and Bad Law: How Computerization Threatens Notice Filing Under Revised Article 9*, Meghan M. Sercombe, 84 Tex. L.Rev. 1065, 1068 (March 2006) ("[T]he drafters of the revised Article 9 opted for a bright-line rule, rejecting any language that would have measured validity against principles of fairness or equity.").

Following the plain language of the relevant statutes, the court concludes that Mr. Sack's May financing statement was seriously misleading and that his security interest was therefore unperfected at the time Coastline began foreclosing on its lessor's lien.

* * *

Conclusion

The financing statement filed by Mr. Sack in May of 2003 was seriously misleading because it failed to provide the correct name of the debtor and a search under the debtor's correct name, using the filing office's standard search logic, would not have revealed the financing statement. Coastline perfected its lessor's lien before Host America took steps to remedy the deficiency of Mr. Sack's financing statement. Accordingly, Coastline's lessor's lien has priority over Host America's security interest. ...

PROBLEM 3–8

In each of the following cases, determine whether the financing statement is effective to perfect the secured party's security interest: See 9-503 and 9-506.

Case 1: Ray sold a commercial grade freezer to the local yogurt shop, retaining a security interest in the freezer. The security agreement was signed by the owner of the shop, Rodger House, but the financing statement identified the debtor as "Roger House." See *Pankratz v. Citizens Nat.*, 33 Kan. App. 2d 279 (2004).

Case 2: Ray sold a double range oven to a local restaurant operating as "The Italian Eatery," which was owned by "Progreso Foods, Ltd." Ray retained a security interest in the oven and filed a financing statement to perfect his secuirty interest. The financing statement identified the debtor as "Progreso Food, Ltd." See *CHN Capital v. Progreso Materials*, 78 U.C.C. Rep. Serv. 2d 1007 (S.D. Tex. 2012).

Case 3: Ray sold a dishwasher to the local coffee shop, taking a security interest in the dishwasher to secure the buyer's promise to pay. The owner of the coffee shop was known around town as "Terry Kinderknecht" and that's the name Ray used on the financing statement he filed. As it turns out, the debtor's legal name is "Terrence Kinderknecht." See *In re Kinderknecht*, 308 Bankr. 71 (B.A.P. 10th Cir. 2004); *In re Green*, 79 U.C.C. Rep. Serv. 2d 42 (Bankr. D. N.M. 2012).

Problem 3–9

The local pet store bought a deep freezer from Ray—fresh frozen pet food for dogs and cats is all the rage with the wealthy pet owners in town. Ray had both the husband and wife, who ran the store, sign the security agreement on behalf of the store, and filed the financing statement under the name of the store, "Pet Partners." As it turns out, "Pet Partners" was just the trade name of the store—it was jointly owned by the married couple. Is Ray's security interest in the freezer perfected? See 9-503.

Problem 3–10

When Ray sold the local bakery an oven, refrigerator, and ductless air conditioner, the bakery's owner signed a security agreement giving Ray a security interest in the bakery's inventory and equipment. The financing statement Ray filed identified the collateral as "inventory, equipment, and accounts receivable." Can Ray enforce the security interest against the bakery's accounts receivable?

Problem 3–11

Ray agreed to put up his store's equipment as collateral for a loan the bank made to his daughter. Should the bank have Ray sign the security agreement even though it's not making the loan to him? Who should the bank identify as the debtor on the financing statement it files? See 9-102(a)(28) and (59).

PROBLEM 3–12

Ray sold a trash compactor to the local delicatessen, retaining a security interest in the compactor to secure the buyer's promise to pay for it. Ray had the owner of the delicatessen, Steve Nixon, sign the security agreement and filed his financing statement with Steve Nixon identified as the debtor. A few months later, the debtor legally changed his name to Nick Zen. When the bank searched the filing records before making a loan to Zen secured by the delicatessen's equipment, the search results did not produce Ray's financing statement. Zen stopped paying the bank and it repossessed all of the Delicatessen's equipment. The bank refuses to turn the compactor over to Ray. Should Ray have priority over the bank because he filed his financing statement first? See 9-507.

II. ERRORS IN COLLATERAL DESCRIPTION

When assessing the effect of collateral description errors in the financing statement it is important to keep in mind that the collateral description in the financing statement does not define the scope of the security interest—the extent of the debtor's property subject to a security interest is established by the collateral description in the security agreement. Instead, the collateral description in the financing statement defines the scope of the priority to which the security interest is entitled. The priority acquired by filing the financing statement extends only as far as the collateral description in the financing statement. For example, if the security agreement grants a security interest in the debtor's inventory and equipment, but the financing statement only identifies the debtor's inventory, the financing statement only perfects the security interest in the inventory; the security interest in the equipment would be unperfected.

Article 9 requires that the financing statement "indicate" the collateral it covers and provides that collateral is "sufficiently indicat[ed]" if the description satisfies the requirements of 9-108 (the "reasonably identifies" test) or if it states that it covers all of the debtor's assets or all of the debtor's personal property. The authorization of "super generic" terms like "all assets" or "all personal property" is new—and reverses the result reached by a majority of the courts under old Article 9 which was silent on the use of these terms in the financing statement.

The following problems illustrate some of the issues that arise in disputes about the collateral description in a financing statement.

PROBLEM 3–13

When Ray sold several commercial grade freezers to the local butcher shop, he took a security interest in the freezers he sold as well as the shop's other equipment. The security agreement the shop executed in connection with this transaction described the collateral as "all the debtor's equipment." The financing statement Ray filed for this transaction identified the collateral as "all appliances." Does Ray have a perfected security interest in "all the debtor's equipment"? See 9-504 and 9-108.

PROBLEM 3-14

If the financing statement Ray prepared in the last Problem had identified the collateral as "all equipment on Exhibit A attached hereto" but had been filed without the attached Exhibit A, would Ray have a perfected security interest in the collateral described in the security agreement? See 9-504 and 9-108.

B. THE MECHANICS OF FILING

Although a financing statement that has made its way into the system is effective if it provides only the name of the debtor, the name of the secured party, and indicates the collateral that it covers, Article 9 commands that a financing statement should not be accepted for filing by the clerk's office unless it contains additional information and is properly communicated to the clerk's office with the appropriate filing fee. 9-516(b). So, in theory, a filed financing statement will provide more than the minimum information required for effectiveness under 9-502.

The additional information required for filing provides further details about the parties that can be useful to parties searching the files in several ways. First, the address of the debtor as well as the organizational details about business debtors will help a subsequent creditor searching the files distinguish between debtors with the same or similar names. A search of the files under the name John Anderson may turn up dozens of financing statements. The addresses on each of the financing statements allow the searcher to identify which, if any, are filed against the John Anderson she cares about. The same is true with business debtors—you will be able to distinguish financing statements filed against the AAA Auto you care about based on the addresses as well as the organizational information provided for business debtors.

Second, requiring the address of the secured party facilitates further inquiry by subsequent creditors into the specifics of the relationship identified on a financing statement—the underlying transaction. Of course, secured parties are not obligated to provide information to anyone but the debtor, so access to the secured party for informational purposes is probably of limited utility. The secured party's address is perhaps most useful when Article 9 requires someone dealing with a debtor to provide notice to parties with financing statements on file. For example, in order to claim purchase money priority, a party taking a purchase money security interest in inventory is required to so notify any creditor with a financing statement on file claiming a security interest in the debtor's inventory.

Article 9 also commands that the clerk reject a financing statement that is not properly communicated to the clerk's office along with the applicable filing fee. Proper communication requires using the method or medium authorized by the specific clerk's office. Article 9 does not establish a uniform method or medium for sending a financing statement to the clerk's office and as a result what it takes to get a financing statement filed varies from jurisdiction to jurisdiction. This is especially true for electronic filing.

What happens if a financing statement does not contain the information required by 9-516(b) or is improperly communicated to the clerk's office or is sent without the applicable filing fee? Article 9 commands that the clerk reject any financing statement that is deficient in any or all of these ways. 9-520. These provisions were intended to negate any perception that filing or refusing to file a financing statement was a matter left to the discretion of the clerk. Substantive review of the form and content of financing statements by clerks under old Article 9 had caused problems, and Revised Article 9 makes clear that the filing clerks do not have any such authority. What if the clerk accepts and files a financing statement he was required to reject under 9-520? As long as the financing statement includes the names of the debtor and the secured party and identifies the collateral subject to the security interest, it is effective even though it should not have been placed in the file by the clerk. 9-520(c).

What if the clerk refuses to accept and file a financing statement for a reason other than those set out in 9-516(b)? Article 9 overrides the clerk's decision and the financing statement is deemed filed—it is effective as a filed record. 9-516(d). Of course it will not be discoverable by subsequent searchers because it's not actually in the file. Article 9 anticipates this problem and provides that although the improperly rejected financing statement is generally effective, it is not effective against a subsequent purchaser of the collateral described in the rejected financing statement who gives value in reasonable reliance on the absence of the financing statement from the file. 9-516(d). The "purchaser" protected here is both a buyer of the collateral and a creditor that takes a security interest in the collateral. See 1-201(29) and (30).

PROBLEM 3–15

In each of the following cases, determine (1) whether the clerk's actions were proper under 9-516 and 9-520, and (2) if the clerk acted improperly, the effect of the improper action on the filing party.

Case 1:   Ray communicated to the clerk's office a financing statement intended to perfect a security interest in the LCD television he sold to the local sports bar. He did not include his address on the financing statement. The clerk filed the financing statement.

Case 2:   Ray loaned the burger shop across the street from his store $10,000 and took a security interest in the shop's equipment.

The financing statement Ray communicated to the clerk's office did not identify any collateral. The clerk filed the financing statement.

Case 3: Instead of filling out the financing statement form on the web page of the clerk's office and submitting it as the web page instructed, Ray attached a PDF of the financing statement he prepared for the transaction to an email he sent to the clerk's office. The clerk rejected the financing statement.

Case 4: The address of the debtor was incorrect on the financing statement Ray communicated to the clerk's office to perfect his security interest in appliances Ray had sold to the debtor. The clerk filed the financing statement. See 9-338.

Case 5: The financing statement the bank communicated to the clerk's office to perfect its security interest in Ray's appliance inventory identified Ray's business as a Delaware corporation. The clerk knew that Ray had not incorporated and had no connection with Delaware, so she rejected the financing statement.

2. POSSESSION

Perfection by possession—the common law pledge we examined in Chapter 1—was really the first form of secured transaction recognized as legitimate by the courts. Because the secured party in the pledge transaction took possession of the collateral, there was no ostensible ownership problem. The debtor was not left in possession with apparent control over the property and consequently was not able to create a misleading picture of her creditworthiness. If the secured party was in possession, the debtor was not able to pass off the collateral as her own. Possession by the secured party provided the public notice of its claim that was later provided by the recording systems created by statute in the pre-Code days and which, as we have seen, was incorporated into Article 9. The pledge lives on in Article 9 where the secured party's possession of the collateral is made an act of perfection that protects the security interest against others claiming interests in the collateral. See 9-313.

Perfection by possession by its very nature must be limited to collateral that has a tangible existence—but as we have previously noted, under Article 9 tangible property includes more than just goods. In addition to a washer, a printing press, and a cow, a security interest in a promissory note, chattel paper, stock certificates, money, and UPS documents can also be perfected by possession.

Perfection by possession is fairly straightforward. When perfection of a security interest is based on possession, perfection occurs when the secured party takes possession of the collateral—provided that the security interest has attached. 9-313(d). The secured party either has the collateral or does not have it. However, because the secured party can perfect by using the possession of a third party—an agent, perfection by possession can be more complex. First, the third party on whose possession the secured party is relying cannot be the debtor, related to the debtor, or under the debtor's control. 9-313 Comment 3. What constitutes sufficient "relatedness to" or "control" over such third party by the debtor so as to preclude using the third party's possession to perfect the security interest will be determined ultimately by non-Code law. The Comments propose an effects test: has the debtor "retained effective possession, even though the person may have agreed to take possession on behalf of the secured party." 9-313 Comment 3.

Second, perfection based on the possession of a third party is not effective until the third party has acknowledged in an authenticated record that it holds possession or will hold possession of the collateral for the secured party's benefit. 9-313(c). The party in possession of the collateral does not have to provide the authenticated acknowledgment, and if it does not, the secured party will not be able to perfect its security interest by possession. 9-313(f). An acknowledging party does not owe any duty to the debtor or to the secured party for whom it holds possession, unless she agrees otherwise or non-Code law would impose a duty. 9-313(g).

As we've already noted, perfection by possession in transactions involving goods is usually not very practical—at least from the debtor's perspective. Most people acquire goods for the purpose of using them; buying washers on credit would not help Ray very much if they were not available for display and sale at his shop because Maytag retained possession of them to perfect its security interest. There are situations, however, where loss of use by the debtor is not a problem. For example, if the debtor has leased the collateral to another, perfection by possession—with the secured party relying on the lessee's possession—will not be impractical for the debtor since she was not expecting to have use of the collateral (at least not during the term of the lease).

PROBLEM 3–16

Ray agrees to lend $20,000 to his artist friend, taking a security interest in 10 of the artist's paintings that are currently on consignment at a local gallery. Ray and the artist agree that he will not perfect by filing—the artist does not want to frighten away any prospective purchasers of the paintings by making a public record of his loan from Ray. Instead, Ray agrees to perfect by possession, using the gallery's possession of the paintings as his own. The gallery owner agrees to hold the paintings for Ray in a voicemail she leaves on his cell phone. Is the gallery's possession of the paintings effective to perfect Ray's security interest? See 9-313.

3. AUTOMATIC PERFECTION

Generally, Article 9 expects secured parties to file a financing statement to perfect their security interests. 9-310. But, as we've seen, filing is not the exclusive way to perfect a security interest under Article 9 in all cases. A security interest in tangible property can also be perfected by possession. And as we will see in the next section, security interests in certain types of collateral cannot be perfected by filing. Article 9 also recognizes that in certain types of secured financing the marginal utility of the notice provided by a filing system is outweighed by the burdens of complying with a filing requirement. As a result, Article 9 exempts these transactions from its filing requirements. 9-309.

One such type of secured financing is that involving consumer goods. As Gilmore explained:

> The only justification for any filing system is that it is the best available method for giving certain information to people who need the information and who may be expected to use the files and get the information. People who extend credit to the typical [ ] consumer have not the faintest interest in whether any of his personal property (with the possible exception of his automobile) is encumbered; a store opening a charge account or a bank making a small loan is interested only in whether the customer or borrower has a regular job and a reputation for paying his bills. ... It is surely not unreasonable to conclude that a filing system in this area (leaving out automobiles) is useless; none of the creditors or purchasers for whose benefit the files are maintained will ever look at them, ...

> Gilmore at 534-35.

Accordingly, Article 9 does not require a filing to perfect all security interests in consumer goods. Purchase money security interests in consumer goods are automatically perfected under Article 9—no filing is necessary as they are deemed perfected when they attach. 9-309(1).

Purchase money security interests are defined in a Rube Goldberg-like manner in 9-103. Stripped to its basics, 9-103 describes two forms of purchase money security interests. When the seller retains a security interest in goods it sells on credit to secure the buyer's promise to pay for those goods, the seller's security interest is a purchase money security interest. When a lender loans money to enable its borrower to acquire specific goods and takes a security interest in those goods to secure the borrower's promise to repay the loan, the lender's security interest is a purchase money security interest. When the purchase money collateral is consumer goods, the security interest is automatically perfected when it attaches.

Although conceptually simple, in its application the purchase money definition can quickly take on an existential dimension when, as a result of a series of transactions between the secured party and the debtor, purchase money collateral secures more than its own purchase price. For example, you buy a washer from Ray's shop on credit, signing a security agreement that grants Ray a security interest in the washer to secure your promise to pay for it and also provides that the washer will secure any future obligation to Ray you incur. A few months later, you buy a refrigerator from Ray on credit signing another security agreement granting Ray a security interest in the refrigerator and providing that the refrigerator secures any other obligation you have to Ray. Ray would appear to have a purchase money security interest in both the washer and the refrigerator. But both also secure more than their own purchase price—the washer also secures your promise to pay for the refrigerator and the refrigerator also secures your promise to pay for the washer. Ray has 'overloaded" his purchase money security interests and the courts have not agreed on what effect, if any, this should have on the original purchase money security interest. The dissent in the *Ford* case which follows sets out the competing views on overloaded purchase money security interests developed by the courts under old Article 9. Revised Article 9 adopted one of these views for application to non-consumer transactions, but left it to the courts to determine the fate of the overloaded purchase money security interest in consumer transactions like those between you and Ray.

[handwritten: REVIEW!]

The 2005 amendments to the Bankruptcy Code have generated another split among the courts with respect to the scope of purchase money security interests when part of the loan made to acquire the purchase money collateral is used to pay off a pre-existing obligation. How much of the security interest created in such a transaction is entitled to purchase money status? That is the primary issue before the court in the *Ford* case.

IN RE FORD
United States Court of Appeals, Tenth Circuit
574 F.3d 1279 (10th Cir. 2009)

MURPHY, *Circuit Judge*.

I. INTRODUCTION

Appellants John Wesley Ford, Sr. and Cynthia Ford appeal an order of the Bankruptcy Court for the District of Kansas rejecting their proposed Chapter 13 bankruptcy plan. The Fords have an outstanding debt to Appellee Ford Motor Credit Company ("Ford Motor Credit") secured by their automobile. The debt includes the amount paid to discharge the "negative equity" on their trade-in vehicle. Negative equity is the amount owed on a loan in excess of the collateral's value. In their proposed bankruptcy plan, the Fords sought to bifurcate their automobile debt to Ford Motor Credit under 11 U.S.C. §506(a) into secured and unsecured claims. The unsecured claim would be the portion of the debt used to discharge the negative equity in the trade-in. Ford Motor Credit objected to the proposed plan, claiming the debt bifurcation was impermissible under the "hanging paragraph" of 11 U.S.C. §1325(a). The bankruptcy court sustained the objection, and the Fords sought an immediate appeal to this court. We conclude we have jurisdiction to hear this appeal under 28 U.S.C. §158(d)(2) and AFFIRM the ruling of the bankruptcy court.

II. BACKGROUND

The underlying facts of this case are not in dispute. The Fords purchased a 2007 Ford F-150 truck from Rusty Eck Ford on February 24, 2007. The Fords made a down payment of $1500 and received $40,168.30 in financing secured by the truck. At the same time, the Fords traded in their 2006 Ford truck. The 2006 truck was valued at $16,300, but the Fords owed $23,500 on it. $11,693.30 in financing covered "[a]mounts paid on [the Fords'] behalf." This included taxes, fees, a service contract, gap insurance, and $7200 to pay off the creditor on the 2006 truck for the amount owed on the vehicle in excess of its present value.

The Fords filed for Chapter 13 bankruptcy fewer than four months later. Under their proposed plan, they sought to reduce the secured debt on the 2007 truck by $7200, the amount of negative equity on their trade-in. That amount would be treated as an unsecured claim under the plan. Ford Motor Credit objected to the proposed treatment of its security interest.

Exercising jurisdiction pursuant to 28 U.S.C. §157(b)(2)(K), (L), the bankruptcy court concluded the negative equity financing was part of the creditor's purchase money security interest under the "hanging paragraph" in 11 U.S.C. §1325(a) and thus the debt could not be bifurcated and "crammed down" pursuant to 11 U.S.C. §506(a). The bankruptcy court sustained Ford Motor Credit's objection to the proposed plan and ordered the Fords to file an amended plan treating the entire Ford Motor Credit debt as secured debt.

* * *

III. DISCUSSION

The bankruptcy court's interpretation of the Bankruptcy Code is a question of law to be reviewed de novo. *Hamilton v. Lanning (In re Lanning)*, 545 F.3d 1269, 1274 (10th Cir.2008). When consumers enter Chapter 13 bankruptcy, they are normally permitted, if they wish, to bifurcate each secured debt into two claims: (1) an amount equal to the present value of the collateral, and (2) any excess. 11 U.S.C. §506(a)(1). The excess portion is converted into unsecured debt. Id. The plan can then be "crammed down," or confirmed over the secured creditor's objection, so long as the creditor receives a lien securing the claim and the plan provides for payments to the creditor over the life of the plan equal to the present value of the collateral. 11 U.S.C. §1325(a) (5)(B); Assocs. *Commercial Corp. v. Rash*, 520 U.S. 953, 957, 117 S.Ct. 1879, 138 L.Ed.2d 148 (1997). Whether debt is secured or unsecured is significant because secured creditors generally must be repaid in full before unsecured creditors receive anything. 11 U.S.C. §1325(a)(5), (b)(1).

In 2005, Congress enacted the Bankruptcy Abuse Prevention and Consumer Protection Act ("BAPCPA"). One provision of BAPCPA amended the Bankruptcy Code to remove certain secured consumer debts from bifurcation and cramdown. Pub.L. No. 109-8, §306(b), 119 Stat. 23, 80 (2005). At the end of 11 U.S.C. §1325(a), Congress added an unnumbered paragraph, now commonly known as the "hanging paragraph," which reads, in relevant part, as follows:

> For purposes of paragraph (5), section 506 shall not apply to a claim described in that paragraph if the creditor has a purchase money security interest securing the debt that is the subject of the claim, the debt was incurred within the 910-day [sic] preceding the date of the filing of the petition, and the collateral for that debt consists of a motor vehicle (as defined in section 30102 of title 49) acquired for the personal use of the debtor. ...

11 U.S.C. §1325(a).

The hanging paragraph protects creditors possessing a "purchase money security interest securing the debt that is the subject of the claim" from §506(a) bifurcation and cramdown. 11 U.S.C. §1325(a). The parties agree the collateral in this case is a motor vehicle acquired for the personal use of the debtors and the motor vehicle was acquired within 910 days of the bankruptcy filing. The only issue in dispute is the extent to which Ford Motor Credit has a "purchase money security interest."

The issue of whether, under the hanging paragraph, a creditor has a purchase money security interest in the negative equity on a trade-in vehicle has been litigated extensively throughout the country, and the rulings have not been consistent.[8] *See Graupner v. Nuvell Credit Corp. (In re Graupner)*, 537 F.3d 1295, 1300 (11th Cir.2008) (collecting cases). The Tenth Circuit Bankruptcy Appellate Panel recently held that creditors have a purchase money security interest in negative equity. *AmeriCredit Fin. Servs., Inc. v. Padgett (In re Padgett)*, 408 B.R. 374, 381-82 (10th Cir. BAP 2009). District courts and bankruptcy courts within this circuit have reached varied results on the question. *Compare, e.g., Citifinancial Auto v. Hernandez-Simpson*, 369 B.R. 36, 48 (D.Kan.2007) (holding bifurcation and cramdown are available because purchase money security interest does not include negative equity), *In re McCauley*, 398 B.R. 41, 45-46 (Bankr.D.Colo.2008) (same), *and In re Padgett*, 389 B.R. 203, 211-12 (Bankr.D.Kan.2008) (same), *rev'd sub nom., AmeriCredit Fin. Servs., Inc. v. Padgett (In re Padgett)* 408 B.R. 374, 381-82 (10th Cir. BAP 2009), *with In re Ford*, 387 B.R. 827, 833 (Bankr.D.Kan.2008) (holding bifurcation and cramdown are unavailable because negative equity is part of purchase money security interest), *and In re Austin*, 381 B.R. 892, 897 (Bankr.D.Utah 2008) (same). Two circuit courts to date have ruled on the question, both holding the purchase money security interest held by a creditor includes the negative

---

8 Although many courts have concluded, as this court does, that the issue is resolved by interpreting state law, the American Financial Services Association notes in its amicus brief that Article 9 of the U.C.C. has been adopted, at least in part, in every state. Therefore, although courts have been interpreting the laws of different states, they have been interpreting mostly identical statutory provisions.

equity on the trade-in vehicle. *In re Price*, 562 F.3d 618, 628 (4th Cir.2009); *In re Graupner*, 537 F.3d at 1301. The Second Circuit declined to rule on the issue, instead certifying the question to the New York Court of Appeals. *Reiber v. GMAC, LLC (In re Peaslee)*, 547 F.3d 177, 186 (2d Cir.2008). After certification the New York Court of Appeals concluded purchase money security interests include the negative equity. *In re Peaslee*, 13 N.Y.3d 75, 913 N.E.2d 387, 885 N.Y.S.2d 1, 2009 WL 1766000 (N.Y.2009). The issue previously came before this court, but the case was rendered moot before the court ruled on the merits. *Wells Fargo Bank, NA v. Griffin (In re Hunt)*, 550 F.3d 1002, 1004 (10th Cir.2008).

The Bankruptcy Code does not define the term purchase money security interest. Property interests referred to in the Bankruptcy Code are generally defined by state law. *Butner v. United States*, 440 U.S. 48, 54, 99 S.Ct. 914, 59 L.Ed.2d 136 (1979). This court, therefore, has looked to state law for a definition of the term as it is used elsewhere in the Bankruptcy Code. *Billings v. AVCO Colo. Indus. Bank (In re Billings)*, 838 F.2d 405, 406 (10th Cir.1988) ("[T]he courts have uniformly looked to the law of the state in which the security interest is created."). When Congress enacts a statute using a phrase that has a settled judicial interpretation, it is presumed to be aware of the prior interpretation. *Comm'r v. Keystone Consol. Indus., Inc.*, 508 U.S. 152, 159, 113 S.Ct. 2006, 124 L.Ed.2d 71 (1993). When Congress drafted BAPCPA in 2005, it chose to use the term "purchase money security interest" without defining it. Under settled case law, that term, when used in the Bankruptcy Code, is interpreted with reference to state law. As a consequence, we presume Congress intended that term as used in BAPCPA to be interpreted according to state law.

Kansas has adopted the relevant portion of Revised Article 9 of the Uniform Commercial Code ("U.C.C."), and it also lists the Official U.C.C. Comment in its statutory compilation. Kan. Stat. Ann. §84-9-103. Under Kansas law, "A security interest in goods is a purchase-money security interest: (1) To the extent that the goods are purchase-money collateral with respect to that security interest. . . ." *Id.* §84-9-103(b). Purchase-money collateral is defined as "goods or software that secures a purchase-money obligation incurred with respect to that collateral." *Id.* §84-9-103(a)(1). A purchase-money obligation is "an obligation of an obligor incurred as all or part of the price of the collateral or for value given to enable the debtor to acquire rights in or the use of the collateral if the value is in fact so used." *Id.* §84-9-103(a)(2). Whether something is a purchase-money security interest thus depends upon whether the underlying obligation was incurred to pay "all or part of the price of the collateral" or covers "value given to enable the debtor to acquire rights in or the use of the collateral." *Id.* §84-9-103(a).

The Official Comment to Kan. Stat. Ann. §84-9-103 provides additional guidance on what constitutes a purchase-money security interest. It states:

> [T]he "price" of collateral or the "value given to enable" includes obligations for expenses incurred in connection with acquiring

rights in the collateral, sales taxes, duties, finance charges, interest, freight charges, costs of storage in transit, demurrage, administrative charges, expenses of collection and enforcement, attorney's fees, and other similar obligations.

The concept of "purchase-money security interest" requires a close nexus between the acquisition of collateral and the secured obligation.

Id. §84-9-103 cmt. 3.

The issue is whether paying off negative equity in a trade-in car is part of the "price" of the new car or part of the "value given to enable" acquisition of the new car. The Fords point out that it is possible to acquire rights in a new car without paying off the negative equity in the old one. The debtor's rights in the two vehicles are distinct. The Fords further argue the trade-in encompasses two separate transactions: the transfer of rights in the trade-in vehicle and the transfer of rights in the new vehicle. They claim negative equity is different than the expenses listed in the Official Comment. In opposition to this position, Ford Motor Credit emphasizes that vehicle trade-ins are commonplace. It further argues that many vehicle trade-ins involve negative equity on the old vehicle and cites a study by J.D. Power and Associates estimating that approximately thirty-eight percent of new car buyers have negative equity at trade-in. It argues the trade-in of the old vehicle is directly related to the purchase of the new vehicle, and the former would not have occurred absent the latter. The Kansas Bankers Association, as amicus curiae, argues the Fords' position artificially breaks a single, package transaction into two parts.

The Fords' position has some logic, and it is not surprising that a number of courts have adopted it. On balance, however, it is not as persuasive as the position advanced by Ford Motor Credit. It may be theoretically possible to split the exchange of vehicles into two separate transactions, but that is not how the parties treated the deal. They signed a single agreement encompassing the trade-in of the old vehicle and the sale of the new vehicle. This type of transaction, moreover, is very common in the automobile industry. The very name "trade-in" implies the two vehicle exchanges are linked. The entire exchange would undoubtedly be a single transaction if the Fords did not have negative equity on the trade-in vehicle and the two parties were simply swapping items of value. As indicated by the data cited by Ford Motor Credit, the existence of negative equity on the trade-in vehicle has not prevented consumers from continuing to trade-in old vehicles for new ones, and it should not turn the swap into two separate transactions. As the Bankruptcy Court recognized, discharging negative equity is necessary to complete the trade-in because otherwise the dealer would take the old vehicle subject to a lien exceeding the vehicle's value. *In re Ford*, 387 B.R. at 831.

We conclude the trade-in exchange is essentially a single transaction. The expense incurred in retiring the lien on the trade-in vehicle, therefore, is an "expense[ ] incurred in connection with acquiring rights" in the new car. Kan. Stat. Ann. §84-9-103 cmt. 3. There is also the requisite "close nexus" between the acquisition of the new vehicle and the secured obligation. *Id.* The entire debt incurred by the debtors is therefore a "purchase-money obligation," the new vehicle is "purchase-money collateral" for the entire obligation, and the security interest in the entire debt is a purchase-money security interest under Kansas law. *Id.* §84-9-103(a)-(b). Because Ford Motor Credit has a purchase-money security interest in the full amount of the debt, it is entitled to the protection of the hanging paragraph. 11 U.S.C. §1325(a). The Bankruptcy Court was correct, therefore, in sustaining Ford Motor Credit's objection to the proposed plan.

The Fords contend, as does the dissent, that the phrase "expenses incurred in connection with acquiring rights" must be interpreted in light of its proximity to the other examples listed in the Official Comment. This is undoubtedly true, but we discern no significant difference between the expense of discharging negative equity on a trade-in and some of the other examples listed in the Official Comment. The Official Comment lists "sales taxes, duties, finance charges, interest, freight charges, costs of storage in transit, demurrage, administrative charges, *expenses of collection and enforcement, attorney's fees*, and other similar obligations" as expenses that can be part of a purchase-money security interest. Kan. Stat. Ann. §84-9-103 cmt. 3 (emphasis added). Collection and enforcement expenses and attorney's fees are costs incurred so that the creditor may realize the value of the security interest. The discharge of negative equity clears the title of the trade-in vehicle, per-mitting the creditor to realize the value of the vehicle it receives as part of the trade. Both categories of expenses allow the creditor to realize its benefit of the bargain. The dissent argues collection and enforcement expenses are distinguishable from negative equity because such expenses are transaction costs. *Dissenting Op.* at 1289. The term "transaction costs," however, is entirely absent from the statute and the Official Comment. Had the drafters of the U.C.C. intended to limit a purchase-money security interest to cash price plus transaction costs, they could easily have done so. Instead, we are left with the language the drafters actually used, which we conclude is broad enough to encompass negative equity on trade-in vehicles.

The Fords also argue this result will enable predatory lending on the part of automobile dealers by encouraging them to refinance antecedent debt secured by a new vehicle. For reasons well articulated by the Fourth Circuit, this concern is overstated. *See In re Price*, 562 F.3d at 627. The reasons for treating the trade of an old vehicle for a newer one as a single transaction include the similarity in function between the new and old vehicles. The vehi-cle trade-in is a common, established transaction in the automobile industry, and it makes sense for many consumers to discard their old vehicles when they acquire new ones. The discharge of unrelated antecedent debt, however, may not bear the required "close nexus" to the acquisition of a new vehicle. *Id.*; Kan. Stat. Ann. §84-9-103 cmt. 3. An automobile dealer who attempted to refinance unrelated antecedent debt and secure the new debt with the new car would present a question wholly different from the question presented here. *See In re Vega*, 344 B.R. 616, 617-18, 622 (Bankr.D.Kan.2006) (refusing to apply hanging paragraph to portion of car dealer's loan used to extinguish debt on previous car loan when consumer did not trade in the old vehicle).

IV. CONCLUSION

Under Kansas law, Ford Motor Credit holds a purchase-money security interest in the entire amount owed to it by the Fords. The debt therefore falls within the ambit of the hanging paragraph of 11 U.S.C. §1325, and the Fords may not bifurcate the debt for the purpose of a cramdown under 11 U.S.C. §506(a). The interlocutory order of the Bankruptcy Court is therefore AFFIRMED and the case is remanded to the Bankruptcy Court for further proceedings consistent with this opinion.

TYMKOVICH, *Circuit Judge*, dissenting.

I respectfully dissent because I read the Kansas Uniform Commercial Code, which controls the resolution of this case, as providing a narrower definition of "purchase money security interest" (PMSI) than the majority adopts.

In my view, Kansas law prohibits lenders from using a PMSI to secure a loan for negative equity, even if the loan is bundled with a standard car loan that is itself secured with a PMSI. Therefore, Ford Motor Credit Company does not have a PMSI covering the portion of the Fords' loan attributable to the $7,200 of negative equity in their truck. And because the hanging paragraph, 11 U.S.C. §1325(a)(*), applies only to PMSIs, the $7,200 is not protected from cram down. Even so, Kansas's dual-status rule preserves PMSI status for the remaining portion of the Fords' loan and that portion is therefore immune from cram down.

A. PMSIs GENERALLY

A PMSI is a "special type of security interest" that is created when a secured party (here, Ford Credit) "provides the credit that enables the debtor [the Fords] to obtain the collateral [the Fords' new truck]." Keith G. Meyer, *A Primer on Purchase Money Security Interests Under Revised Article 9 of the Uniform Commercial Code*, 50 Kan. L.Rev. 143, 152 (2001). In the consumer goods context, a common example of a transaction that creates a PMSI is a purchase using a store-issued credit card:

> Typical credit sales should be relatively familiar to all of us, though we may not always recognize them. Each time we use our Sears Card to buy a drill, a stereo, furniture, etc., we participate in a credit sale. Sears is granting us credit to purchase those items from the store, and we are granting the store a PMSI in that item until it is paid off.

In this example, the consumer is the debtor, and Sears is the purchase-money lender.

Aside from the benefit conferred by the hanging paragraph (i.e., protection from cram down for some car loans), purchase-money lenders receive additional advantages under the U.C.C. and other law. Most importantly, a purchase-money lender has "super-priority"—the lender's claim to the purchase-money collateral trumps the claims of other secured creditors. *See Matthews v. Transamerica Fin. Servs. (In re Matthews)*, 724 F.2d 798, 801 (9th Cir. 1984) ("Purchase money security is an exceptional category in the statutory scheme that affords priority to its holder over other creditors. ...").

Additionally, unlike other security interests, PMSIs in household goods cannot be "avoided" (i.e., extinguished) in bankruptcy. *See* 11 U.S.C. §522(f)(1)(B); *see also In re Billings*, 838 F.2d at 406 ("[I]f the security interest ... retains its status as a purchase money security interest ... then debtors may not avoid the security interest under §522(f)."). In the household goods context, PMSIs have yet another benefit: Federal Trade Commission regulations prohibit lenders from taking "a nonpossessory security interest in household goods *other than* a purchase money security interest." 16 C.F.R. §444.2(a)(4) (emphasis added).

Because of the advantages of PMSIs, lenders sometimes attempt to use them to secure obligations unrelated to purchase-money collateral. Indeed, "overloaded" PMSIs are a recurring concern in the law of secured transactions, and jurisdictions have adopted various mechanisms to prevent them. *See* Ann E. Conaway Stilson, *The "Overloaded" PMSI in Bankruptcy: A Problem in Search of a Resolution*, 60 Temp. L.Q. 1, 16 (1987).[9]

Some jurisdictions eliminate PMSI status if a lender attempts to secure a loan that exceeds the amount required for the debtor to obtain the collateral. *See* Marion W. Benfield, Jr., *Consumer Provisions in Revised Article 9*, 74 Chi.-Kent L. Rev. 1255, 1292 (1999). Under this so-called "transformation" rule, "a security interest that was originally a purchase money interest loses that status entirely if the debt is restructured and an additional nonpurchase money advance is made." *Id.*; *see also In re Matthews*, 724 F.2d at 801 (applying the transformation rule under California law).

Other jurisdictions, including Kansas, adopt the "dual-status" rule, which preserves an overloaded PMSI "to the extent that it secured the price of the

9   Several federal circuit cases from the 1980s addressed the treatment of overloaded PMSIs in bankruptcy, with respect to the anti-avoidance provision in §522(f). *See In re Billings*, 838 F.2d at 408 (suggesting that an obligation can "be considered only *partly* a purchase money debt," and therefore a security interest can still be considered a PMSI with respect to the portion that is not overloaded (emphasis added)); *Pristas v. Landaus of Plymouth, Inc. (In re Pristas)*, 742 F.2d 797, 801 (3d Cir. 1984) (adopting "pro tanto preservation of purchase-money security interests," but invalidating overloaded portions of PMSIs); *In re Matthews*, 724 F.2d at 801 (holding that when a creditor refinances a purchase money obligation, the PMSI is extinguished).

original goods even though the security agreement also secured the price of other items." Meyer, 50 U. Kan. L. Rev. at 155-56 & n.64; Kan. Stat. Ann. §84-9-103(f) (2007) ("[A] purchase-money security interest does not lose its status as such, even if: ... the purchase-money collateral also secures an obligation that is not a purchase-money obligation."); *see also Snap-On Tools, Inc. v. Freeman (In re Freeman)*, 956 F.2d 252, 254-55 (11th Cir. 1992) ("A security interest in collateral is 'purchase money' to the extent that the item secures a debt for the money required to make the purchase. If an item of collateral secures some other type of debt, e.g., antecedent debt, it is not purchase money.").

These principles underscore that the benefits of PMSIs come with certain limitations. When Congress chose to use the state law term PMSI to confine the scope of the hanging paragraph, it adopted these state law limitations as well and made them applicable in bankruptcy.

B. THE KANSAS DEFINITION OF PMSI

The items on Comment 3's list-such as sales tax, finance charges, freight charges, costs of storage in transit, attorney's fees, and collection costs-are all expenses that will be charged uniformly to any potential purchaser of a vehicle who chooses to finance the purchase. Each item is akin to a transaction cost, a cost that adds no particular value for either the buyer or the seller but is instead simply "the cost of using the price mechanism." R.H. Coase, *The Nature of the Firm*, 4 Economica 386, 390 (1937); *see also Black's Law Dictionary* 372 (8th ed. 2004) (defining "transaction cost" as "[a] cost connected with a process transaction, such as a broker's commission, the time and effort expended to arrange a deal, or the cost involved in litigating a dispute"); Harold Demsetz, *The Cost of Transacting*, 82 Q.J. Econ. 33, 35 (1968) ("Transaction cost may be defined as the cost of exchanging ownership titles.").

Negative equity is different. It is not a transaction cost, but a transfer of money for value. Much like a home equity loan used to pay a preexisting credit card debt, the portion of the auto loan attributed to negative equity is not used for the purchase of some new piece of collateral or the costs inherent in the purchase. It is used for another purpose altogether. *See Americredit Fin. Servs., Inc. v. Penrod (In re Penrod)*, 392 B.R. 835, 852 (9th Cir. BAP2008) ("[N]egative equity is nothing more than a refinancing of the preexisting debt owed on the trade-in. There is no necessary connection between this refinancing and the car's acquisition."). Unlike the other expenses listed in Comment 3, the amount (and even the existence) of negative equity depends upon circumstances completely unrelated to the price of the new vehicle and its financing or the costs associated with transfer of title. Indeed, negative equity differs vastly for each purchaser, depending in large part on the purchaser's past choices.

Thus, although the Fords and their dealer were free to use the new pickup as security for a loan to pay an antecedent debt, that does not mean paying the old debt was part of the "price" of the pickup. Nor does it mean the portion of a loan used to pay off the old debt was a purchase money security interest. As a Texas bankruptcy court stated:

> One may borrow money to buy something (*e.g.*, a new vehicle), and also borrow additional money for some other purpose (*e.g.*, to pay off the balance of a loan for the trade-in vehicle). The part used to buy something is purchase money obligation. The part used for some other purpose is not.
>
> *In re Sanders*, 377 B.R. 836, 853 (Bankr.W.D.Tex.2007), *rev'd*, 403 B.R. 435 (W.D.Tex.2009).

* * *

II. OTHER APPROACHES

I recognize my conclusion is at odds with the majority's reasoning, and with the reasoning of a number of other courts that have addressed the treatment of negative equity under the hanging paragraph.

Though the majority does not make all of these arguments, I take this opportunity to explain why I find them unpersuasive.

One common line of reasoning holds that negative equity is part of a "package deal" and cannot be separated from the remainder of the PMSI. The *In re Graupner* court, for example, viewed the financing of negative equity as "part of the same transaction" as the purchase of the new vehicle such that it was "properly regarded as a 'package deal.'" 537 F.3d at 1302. To the Eleventh Circuit, negative equity was an "integral part" of the purchase and was "inextricably intertwined" with the transaction. *Id.*; *see also In re Price*, 562 F.3d at 625 ("All of the Prices' debt … was incurred at the same time, in the same contract, and for the same purpose: acquiring the new car."). The majority adopts this approach, concluding that "the trade-in exchange is essentially a single transaction." *Maj. Op.* at 1285.

The intuitive difficulty with this position is that vehicle purchasers—even those that buy on credit—are not required to purchase the new vehicle by trading in an old one. Whether doing so is necessary or even desirable depends on their individual circumstances. Perhaps in this case it is true that the Fords could not have purchased their new pickup without trading in their old one. And perhaps financing the negative equity was "integral" to the Fords completing their purchase, because it was inconvenient or impossible for them to complete the purchase any other way.

The definition of PMSI, however, does not encompass any and every expense that might enable a particular purchaser to complete the purchase in the most convenient manner. If the Fords were unable to drive themselves to the dealership, we would not consider the cost of a taxi as part of the price of the new truck, even if the dealer was willing to pay for it and fold it into the sales contract. If the Fords did not qualify for a car loan because their resources were strained by too much credit card debt at high interest rates, they could not fold those debts into the PMSI for a new car even if the attendant lower interest rate solved their credit problem and enabled them to obtain the car loan.

Allowing a creditor to transform antecedent debt into a PMSI by refinancing the debt into a new contract amount that includes the purchase price of new collateral would convert the concept of "purchase money" from a defined term to one that can be expanded at the will of the parties. *See In re Conyers*, 379 B.R. 576, 582 (Bankr.M.D.N.C.2007) ("Allowing the Debtor to rollover negative equity into the new loan was simply an accommodation. It was an arrangement made as a favor to another."); *In re Westfall*, 365 B.R. 755, 762 (Bankr.N.D.Ohio 2007) (providing the extreme example of a "debtor [who] would not have made it to the dealer's lot were it not for the emergency appendectomy, [making] payment of the doctor's outstanding fee … an enabling expense"), *rev'd* in part, 376 B.R. 210.

Congress confined the hanging paragraph to PMSIs, and I cannot conclude the hanging paragraph protects any and every loan secured by an automobile.

* * * *

Another question that divided the courts under old Article 9 was the effect of refinancing on the purchase money status of a security interest. Can the purchase money lender substitute a new loan secured by the purchase money collateral for the original purchase money loan without affecting the purchase money status of its security interest? The *Gillie* case illustrates the issue and the competing views of the courts under old Article 9. Revised Article 9 solves the problem for non-consumer transactions but again leaves it for the courts to determine in consumer transactions.

IN RE GILLIE
United States Bankruptcy Court, N.D. Texas, Lubbock Division
96 B.R. 689 (Bankr. N.D. Tex. 1989)

AKARD, *Bankruptcy Judge*.

ISSUE

Does refinancing a purchase money loan by issuing a new loan destroy the purchase money nature of the original security interest for purposes of Bankruptcy Code §522(f)?

FACTS

First State Bank, Morton (Bank), advanced cash to Mrs. Gillie to purchase household furniture. On June 19, 1985, Mrs. Gillie signed a note in the amount of $6,370.92 payable to the Bank in 36 monthly installments of $176.97 each. The note represented $4,600.00 paid to Mrs. Gillie, credit life and credit health and accident premiums in the amount of $300.54 and $1,407.38 interest at 17.92% per annum. The note listed "Table & Chairs" as security for the loan. Mrs. Gillie signed a security agreement on the $6,370.92 note listing the collateral as: "2 Arm Chairs, 4 Side Chairs, 1 Table, 1 Entertainment Center" and classified the furniture as Consumer Goods. The Bank issued Cashier's Check No. 88992 dated June 19, 1985, payable to Doris Gillie, in the amount of $4,600.00. Mrs. Gillie used the funds to purchase the table, chairs, and entertainment center from Spears Furniture. The Bank filed a financing statement signed by Mrs. Gillie in the office of the County Clerk of Lamb County, Texas, on June 25, 1985. The financing statement listed the collateral as shown on the security agreement.

On April 21, 1986, Mr. Gillie signed a note in the amount of $6,166.02, including interest at 17.77% per annum payable to the Bank in 42 monthly installments of $146.81 each. The amount financed included credit life and credit health and accident premiums in the amount of $316.90. The noted listed "Table, Chairs, and Entertainment Center" as security for the loan. The note also recited the June 19, 1985 security agreement as security for the loan. Mr. Gillie signed no Security Agreement or Financing Statement. Although the Bank stamped the note signed by Mrs. Gillie "PAID BY RENEWAL", the note signed by Mr. Gillie did not recite that it renewed or extended the note signed by Mrs. Gillie.

On February 19, 1987, Mr. Gillie executed a note in the amount of $5,498.40, including interest at 12.51% per annum, payable to the Bank in 60 monthly installments of $91.64 each. The amount financed included credit life and credit health and accident premiums in the amount of $338.27. The note recited that it was secured by the June 19, 1985 security agreement and Table, Chairs and Entertainment Center. It also recited "Renew: 3245 1", but there is no number 3245 1 on either of the previous notes. Again, Mr. Gillie signed no Security Agreement or Financing Statement. The note of April 21, 1986 was stamped "Paid by Renewal."

The parties stipulated that all three notes related to the same transaction and that the Bank advanced no new funds and added no new collateral when the second and third notes were given. The Debtors seek to avoid the Bank's claimed purchase money security interest in the household goods.

DISCUSSION

Section 522(f)(2)(A) permits a debtor to avoid a non-possessory non-purchase money security interest in household furnishings, household goods, or appliances which are primarily used for the personal family or household use of the debtor or a dependent of the Debtor to the extent that the lien impairs an exemption to which the Debtor otherwise would be entitled. The Debtors selected the Federal Exemptions under §522(d).

The Bankruptcy Code does not define "purchase money security interest", therefore, we must look to state law. See *Roberts Furniture Co. v. Pierce (In re Manuel)*, 507 F.2d 990, 992 (5th Cir.1975). Tex.Bus. & Com.Code Ann. §9.107 [Now 9.103] (Vernon Supp.1989) defines a purchase money security interest as follows:

> A security interest is a "purchase money security interest" to the extent that it is
>
> (1) taken or retained by the seller of the collateral to secure all or part of its price; or
>
> (2) taken by a person who by making advances or incurring an obligation gives value to enable the debtor to acquire rights in or the use of collateral if such value is in fact so used.

There is no question but that the Bank qualified as the holder of a purchase money security interest with respect to the note, security agreement and financing statement signed by Mrs. Gillie. However, the second and third notes are another matter.

* * *

While the Fifth Circuit Court of Appeals has not spoken to this precise question, it has been squarely addressed and answered by the Ninth Circuit Court of Appeals in *Matthews v. Transamerica Financial Services (In re Matthews)*, 724 F.2d 798 (9th Cir.1984) (per curiam). The Matthews purchased a piano and a stereo with money borrowed from Transamerica Financial Services (Transamerica). The collateral listed as securing the loan included the piano, the stereo, and other household goods and other personal property of the Matthews. Subsequently, Transamerica refinanced the loan for a longer term at a lower monthly payment and issued a new loan. The Matthews used the new loan to pay off the old and, additionally, received $63.14 in cash and paid insurance charges of $279.23. The Matthews filed a petition for bankruptcy in November 1980. When Transamerica filed for relief from the Automatic Stay to repossess the collateral, the Debtors cross-complained to avoid Transamerica's lien. The Bankruptcy Court decided in favor of the Debtors on the ground that the remaining security interest was not purchase money. The Ninth Circuit Bankruptcy Appellate Panel reversed, holding that a security interest existed in the goods to the extent of the remaining indebtedness attributable to the purchase price.

The Ninth Circuit reviewed the Bankruptcy Appellate Panel's interpretation of §522(f) de novo as a question of law and reversed. *Id.* at 799. The Court decided that the transaction delineated above did not meet the definition of a purchase money security interest as contained in U.C.C. §9–107(b) [Now 9-103(a)(2)]. Although Transamerica gave purchase money value when it initially loaned money to the Debtors for the purchase of the piano and the stereo, the second loan was valued to enable the Debtors to pay off the first loan to receive cash and to pay insurance charges. *Id.* at 800. The Court cited with approval *In re Jones*, 5 B.R. 655 (Bankr.M.D.N.C.1980). In *Jones*, the Bankruptcy Judge stated: "The purpose of the renewal note was to payoff (sic) the original note, an antecedent debt. The purchase money character of the security interest was extinguished when the proceeds from the first renewal note were used to satisfy the original note." *Id.* at 657.

The Circuits are split on the issue. Agreeing with *Matthews*, supra, are courts from the 1st, 4th, 6th, 8th, 9th and 11th Circuits. *See, e.g., Dominion Bank of Cumberlands, N.A. v. Nuckolls*, 780 F.2d 408 (4th Cir.1985) (holding that under Virginia law, a bank's security interest, which secured a loan made to refinance pre-existing debt, was a non-possessory, non-purchase-money security interest); *Hipps v. Landmark Financial Services of Georgia, Inc. (In re Hipps)*, 89 B.R. 264, 18 B.C.D. 57 (Bankr.N.D.1988) (holding that in Georgia, pursuant to §9–107 [Now 9-103] of the U.C.C., refinancing of a promissory note transforms the obligation, thereby destroying purchase money nature of the security interest. Therefore, the creditor lost its purchase money security interest [PMSI] in a television set when the loans were consolidated, and lien was avoidable. *Id.* 89 B.R. 264, 18 B.C.D. 58); *Smiley v. Feldman Furniture Co. (In re Smiley)*, 84 B.R. 6 (D.R.I.1988) (holding that a creditor's pmsi in goods sold to debtors did not survive consolidation of the original installment contract with a later contract for the purchase of additional goods); (citing *In re Matthews*, supra, and *In re Manuel*, supra); *In re Wandler*, 77 B.R. 735 (Bankr.D.N.D.1987) (holding that under North Dakota law consolidation of a note secured by a PMSI in farm machinery with other goods resulted in a novation, destroying the creditor's PMSI); *In re Challinor*, 79 B.R. 19 (Bankr.D.Mont.1987) (holding that a note, which was a consolidation of the debtors' previous notes, did not give rise to a PMSI); *Franklin v. ITT Financial Services (In re Franklin)*, 75 B.R. 268 (Bankr.M.D.Ga.1986) (holding that under Georgia law a creditor's refinancing of a promissory note destroyed the purchase money nature of the creditor's security interest in a wall unit which served as collateral); *In re Faughn*, 69 B.R. 18 (Bankr.E.D.Mo.1986) (holding that the creditor's refinancing of an old loan at the time a new loan was executed extinguished the purchase money character of the original loan because proceeds of the new loan were not used to acquire rights in collateral and, thus, the creditor's liens in all but the most recently purchased household goods were avoidable); (disagreeing with Pristas, infra); *In re Janz*, 67 B.R. 553 (Bankr.D.N.D.1986) (holding that where a debtor borrowed money from a third party to pay off the holder of a PMSI in the collateral, the effect was to extinguish the PMSI. The court noted that a finding that the lender enabled the debtor to acquire rights in the collateral as §9–107 requires may be possible where a non-selling lender has given value prior to the time the debtor acquires rights in the collateral); *In re Mason*, 46 B.R. 119 (Bankr.E.D.Mich.S.D.1985) (holding that under Michigan law, when debtors paid off the initial loan with the proceeds of refinancing, the creditor's PMSI in stereo expired); *Booker v. Commercial Credit Corp. (In re Booker)*, 9 B.R. 710

(Bankr.M.D.Ga.1981) (holding that where a security agreement contained collateral other than collateral for which creditor advanced funds to debtor, since it secured antecedent debts as well as new debt and the agreement provided that the security interest secured payment and performance of the debtors' present and future debts to the creditor, the creditor did not have a PMSI and the debtors could avoid the creditor's lien on collateral claimed as exempt).

Disagreeing with *Matthews* are courts from the 3rd, 8th, 9th and 10th Circuits. *See, e.g., Pristas v. Landaus of Plymouth, Inc.*, 742 F.2d 797 (3rd Cir.1984) (holding that Pennsylvania law permits retention of the purchase-money security interest in goods that also secure later payments to extent the original items secure the unpaid part of their own price); *Billings v. Avco Colorado Industrial Park (In re Billings)*, 838 F.2d 405 (10th Cir.1988) (holding that under Colorado law, refinancing of a purchase money loan, whereby an old note and security agreement were canceled and replaced by a new note and security agreement, did not automatically extinguish the creditor's PMSI in the debtors' furniture. The parties did not intend the new note to extinguish the original debt and security interest in that identical collateral remained, almost no new money was advanced, and the document specifically stated an intent to continue the PMSI); *In re Hansen*, 85 B.R. 821 (N.D.Iowa 1988) (holding that post–1978 refinancing of a debt did not constitute a novation, thus debtor could not avoid liens on equipment it owned prior to the 1978 enactment of the Bankruptcy Code where no new money was advanced, no additional security was encumbered, and varying the term of years and interest rates was done to benefit the debtor); *In re Hemingson*, 84 B.R. 604 (Bankr.D.Minn.1988) (holding that under Minnesota law, refinancing and consolidation of purchase money loans did not destroy their "purchase money" character for bankruptcy "lien avoidance" purposes); *Geist v. Converse County Bank (In re Geist)*, 79 B.R. 939 (D.Wyo.1987) (holding that a creditor's refinancing by renewal does not destroy a PMSI to the extent that the balance remaining on the original loan is transferred to the renewal note); *Bond's Jewelers, Inc. v. Linklater (In re Linklater)*, 48 B.R. 916 (Bankr.D.Nev.1985) (holding that a purchase money security in jewelry was not lost when the perfected purchase money security interest was consolidated with a subsequent retail installment contract); *In re Schwartz*, 52 B.R. 314 (Bankr.E.D.Pa.1985) (holding that a purchase-money security interest did not lose its character as such for purposes of lien avoidance when debtor and creditor effected a novation of the loan agreement).

In *Manuel*, supra, the Fifth Circuit Court of Appeals considered a purchase money agreement between a buyer of household furniture and a seller. Since the agreement failed to indicate the order in which the purchases were paid off and the amounts still due on each item and secured by the paid-up items, the Court found that the agreement attempted to make collateral secure debt other than the price of that collateral. As a result, the statutory exception from the U.C.C. filing requirement did not apply and, since the seller did not perfect either by filing or retaining possession, it did not have a PMSI. The Manuel case is distinguishable from the instant case, however, because in Manuel the Court dealt with a revolving loan or "add-on" type situation, rather than a refinancing of the original purchase.

In re Snipes, 86 B.R. 1006 (Bankr.W.D.Mo.C.D.1988) presents a lucid analysis of the two lines of thought on the issue: (1) the "transformation rule," that if an item of collateral secures not only its own purchase price, but also that of other items, the security interest that existed before the "add on" procedures is transformed into nonpurchase money status, and (2) the "dual status" approach, that the presence of a nonpurchase money security interest does not destroy the purchase-money aspect. *Id.* at 1007. In Snipes, the Bankruptcy Court adopted the transformation approach because the consolidated agreement made the original collateral security for both the original loan and a second loan and did not provide for any separate allocation of payments. The court reasoned that since the second agreement did not provide that the collateral was just security for the remaining balance due on the first note, it changed the purchase money character of the security interest.

CONCLUSION

This Court finds the Matthews and Snipes cases persuasive and in harmony with the Texas cases. The first note was signed by Mrs. Gillie. The second note was signed by Mr. Gillie. He had no liability on the first note; she had no liability on the second. Clearly there was a novation and the second note paid off the first. The Bank's purchase money security interest was lost when the second note was signed. Therefore, the Court holds that the Debtors may avoid the Bank's lien pursuant to §522(f) of the Bankruptcy Code.

ORDER ACCORDINGLY.

---

4. CONTROL

Control as a method for perfecting a security interest is new to revised Article 9. Perfection by control is limited to deposit accounts, investment property, and letters of credit. Control is the only way to perfect a security interest in a deposit account, and the only direct method for perfecting a security interest in a letter of credit. Security interests in investment property can be perfected by filing or by control.

A. DEPOSIT ACCOUNTS

There are three ways to perfect a security interest in a deposit account by control. First, if the secured party is the depository institution where the account that is to serve as collateral is located, the secured party is deemed to have control. 9-104(a)(1). If the secured party is not the depository institution, then the secured party must either become the bank's customer on the account—turn the account into a joint account with the debtor or have the debtor transfer the account to the secured party—or execute a control agreement with the bank and the debtor. The control agreement must be between and authenticated by the secured party, the debtor, and the bank and provide that the bank will follow the secured party's directions with respect to the account, without further consent by the debtor, even if the secured party's directions contradict instructions given by the debtor. 9-104(a)(2) and (3).

The priority rules for deposit accounts have a rock-paper-scissors feel to them. First, control always trumps filing, even if filing preceded control. 9-327. A secured party with a security interest in a deposit account will always prevail over a party claiming an interest in the account that is perfected by a filed financing statement, even if the financing statement was filed before the competing party got control of the account. Second, when both parties claiming the account have perfected by control, the party that got control of the account first has priority. Except when one of the competing parties is the depository institution, in which case it will have priority even if the other party got control first. Unless, however, one of the competing parties got control by becoming the customer on the account, in which case it has priority even if the other party got control first or is the depository institution.

The following problems illustrate perfection of a security interest in a deposit account by control and the priority rules for resolving competing claims to a deposit account.

PROBLEM 3–17

The local finance company has agreed to loan Ray the money he needs to renovate and expand his store. To secure the loan, the finance company has agreed to take a security interest in the store's business account at the local bank that holds a security interest in Ray's inventory. What can finance company do to avoid being subordinated to the bank if Ray should give the bank a security interest in the same account? See 9-327.

PROBLEM 3–18

In the last Problem, if Ray deposits the money he receives from customers who buy appliances from the store in the account that will be collateral for the finance company's loan, the bank will have a security interest in the funds in Ray's account. The money Ray's customers pay him for the appliances that are subject to the bank's security interest is "proceeds" of the inventory and, as we will see in Chapter 8, the bank's security interest automatically attaches to the proceeds of its collateral—whatever Ray gets in exchange for the bank's collateral. If Ray defaults on his obligations, both the finance company and the bank will claim the funds in Ray's account. Which will have priority? See 9-327.

B. INVESTMENT PROPERTY

Security interests in investment property can be perfected by control—but they can also be perfected by filing. And perfection by control of tangible investment property is accomplished by possession of the bonds or securities. Perfecting a security interest in intangible investment property—securities accounts, security entitlements, commodity accounts and commodity contracts—by control is similar to perfecting a security interest by control in a deposit account. 9-106. A security interest in a security account or entitlement is perfected by control if (1) the secured party becomes the account or entitlement holder, or (2) the broker executes a control agreement, (3) another person has control of the account or entitlement on behalf of the secured party, or (4) the secured party is the securities broker where the entitlements account is located. A secured party with control over all of the entitlements in a securities account is deemed to have control of the account itself. A security interest in a commodity contract is perfected by control if (1) the secured party is the commodity broker for the account, or (2) the secured party executes a control agreement with the broker and the debtor which provides that the broker will follow the secured party's directions with respect to the account, without further consent from the debtor. A secured party with control over all of the contracts in a commodity account is deemed to have control of the account itself.

Generally, under the priority rules for investment property, perfection by control always trumps perfection by filing. A secured party that has perfected by control will prevail over a secured party that has perfected by filing, even if the filing occurred before control was attained. Second, when both parties claiming the investment property have perfected by control, the party that got control of the investment property first has priority. Except when one of the competing parties is the securities broker or the commodities broker, in which case it will have priority even if the other party got control first. 9-328.

C. LETTERS OF CREDIT

A letter of credit is a vehicle that parties use to facilitate an exchange in situations where neither party wants to perform before the other has performed. The seller does not want to ship the goods until the buyer pays for them and the buyer does not want to pay for the goods before the seller ships them. A letter of credit bridges the confidence gap between the parties by using a third party—usually a bank—as an intermediary. In a simple exchange of goods transaction, the buyer arranges for the issuance of a letter of credit by a bank, pursuant to which the bank agrees to pay the seller as the beneficiary of the letter of credit on behalf of the buyer upon presentation of evidence that the goods have been shipped by the seller. The seller is comfortable shipping the goods without payment because it has the promise of a reliable entity—the bank—that payment will be made if the seller presents documents proving it has shipped the goods to the buyer. The buyer is comfortable because the seller has, in effect, performed first—the bank will not pay the seller unless the seller can prove it turned over the goods to a carrier for delivery to the buyer. The seller no longer has possession over the goods.

The seller can also use the letter of credit as collateral in another transaction. For example, if the seller needed a loan to purchase the materials necessary to manufacture the goods to be exchanged under its agreement with the buyer, the seller could use the letter of credit as collateral for the loan by assigning its rights to the proceeds of the letter to the secured party.

A security interest taken directly in a letter of credit can only be perfected by control. And control here requires that the bank that issued the letter of credit give its consent to the seller's assignment of its right to the proceeds under the letter of credit. The following problems illustrate how Article 9 deals with letters of credit as collateral.

PROBLEM 3–19

Ray is the only U.S. seller of appliances made by Fisher-Paykel, a New Zealand company that has been manufacturing premium appliances for over fifty years. Last week, Ray received a large order for Fisher-Paykel products from a Seattle store that he has not done business with before. Since this is a new customer, Ray was unwilling to order the appliances from New Zealand and ship them to the buyer on credit. The buyer, likewise having never done business with Ray, was unwilling to pay for the goods before shipment. To resolve the standoff, the buyer agreed to have a letter of credit issued naming Ray as the beneficiary to cover the purchase price of the appliances it wanted. Ray wanted to use the letter of credit as collateral for a loan from the local finance company that he would need to pay Fisher-Paykel to ship the goods to the U.S. What does finance company need to do in order to perfect its security interest in the letter of credit? See 9-107.

PROBLEM 3–20

If the bank that issued the letter of credit in the last Problem refuses to re-designate the finance company as the beneficiary under the letter of credit, can the finance company still perfect a security interest in the letter of credit? See 9-102(a)(77), 9-203(f), and 9-308(d).

CHAPTER 4

CHOICE OF LAW

If the purpose of filing a financing statement is to enable discovery of the security interest by anyone dealing with the debtor, those who deal with the debtor must know where to look for the financing statement. When the debtor, the secured party, and the collateral are located in the same state, we might expect to find the notice filed within that state. But if the debtor and the secured party are not located in the same state or the debtor and the collateral are located in different states, where would we expect the financing statement to be filed? Under old Article 9, financing statements were sometimes filed where the goods were located and other times where the debtor was located. But often goods move from place to place and so do debtors. Revised Article 9 makes it easier to determine where a financing statement covering a transaction should be filed, making it more likely that someone dealing with the debtor will be able to find the filed financing statement.

A. BASIC RULES

The general rule under Revised Article 9 is that financing statements are filed in the jurisdiction—the state—where the debtor is located. 9-301(1). There are exceptions, but the exceptions are not surprising because they generally involve situations where there is some connection between the collateral and the real property where it is located. 9-301(4) Financing statements covering minerals to be mined or fixtures—personal property that has become connected to real property, are filed as real property interests in the real property files where the property is located. Otherwise, the location of the debtor determines where financing statements are filed.

Where a debtor is located turns on the nature of the debtor. Individual debtors are located at their "principal residence." 9-307(b)(1). "Principal" is not defined and, as a result, the Comments warn that when in doubt "prudence may dictate perfecting under the law of each jurisdiction that might be the debtor's 'principal residence.' " Comment 2, 9-307. A "registered organization" is located in the state in which it is registered. 9-307(e). Corporations, limited liability partnerships, and other forms of business operations that depend on formal recognition by a state in order to legally exist are "registered organizations" for purposes of Article 9. 9-102(a)(70). An organization—a business or entity that does not require "registration" to legally exist—is located at its place of business unless it has more than one place of business which are not all in the same state, in which case it is located where its chief executive office is located. 9-307(b)(2) and (3). While Article 9 does not define "chief executive office," it's the place where the people who manage the organization—make the important decisions—are located. According to the Comments, in most cases "it will be simple to determine" the debtor's chief executive office and the Comments assume that it will be "rare" to have more than two choices—in which case the secured party should file in both. Comment 2, 9-307.

The Aura Systems case looks at the choice of law determination under Revised Article 9 and the consequences of getting it wrong.

IN RE AURA SYSTEMS, INC.
United States Bankruptcy Court for the Central District of California
347 B.R. 720 (C.D. Cal. 2006)

BUFFORD, *Bankruptcy Judge.*

I. INTRODUCTION

This summary judgment motion raises the issue of whether, after the 2001 amendments to Division 9 of the California Commercial Code (the California version of the Uniform Commercial Code ("UCC")), a creditor can create a judicial lien against personal property belonging to a non-California corporation by filing a notice of judgment lien with the California Secretary of State. The court holds that a judicial lien on California personal property governed by Division 9 of the Commercial Code ("California Collateral") cannot be perfected against a non-California corporation by the filing of a notice of judgment lien with the California Secretary of State. Instead, perfection of a lien against such collateral can only be accomplished by an appropriate filing pursuant to the laws of the state where the corporation is incorporated.

II. RELEVANT FACTS

Debtor Aura Systems, Inc. ("Aura"), a Delaware corporation, filed a voluntary petition under chapter 11 of the bankruptcy code in 2005. In 1995, some ten years earlier, claimants filed a district court action for alleged violations of federal securities laws in connection with their purchase of Aura common stock. In 1999, the parties reached a global settlement, which provided for Aura to pay claimants a total of $4 million in installments.

In late 2002, Aura defaulted on the monthly payment due under the settlement. As a result, the district court entered a final judgment in favor of claimants for the sum of $923,250, the unpaid remainder of the settlement sum. The claimants filed a "Notice of Judgment Lien," using a "Form Jl-1," with the California Secretary of State on April 10, 2003. Claimants' proof of claim that [sic] states that the claim is secured by accounts receivable, equipment and inventory pursuant to a lien arising from this judgment.

In its motion for summary judgment on its claim objection, Aura contends that a judicial lien cannot be created against a non-California corporate debtor through the filing of a notice of judgment lien with the California Secretary of State. Thus, Aura argues, the claimants' claims are unsecured. The question for this court is whether a judicial lien can be created, after the UCC Article 9 amendments adopted in 2001, by filing a notice of judgment lien with the California Secretary of State against a non-California corporate debtor with property in California.

III. ANALYSIS

A. JUDGMENT LIEN UNDER CALIFORNIA LAW

In support of the secured status of their claim, claimants rely on California Code of Civil Procedure ("CCP") *§697.510*, which provides in relevant part: "A judgment lien on personal property described in *Section 697.530* is created by filing a notice of judgment lien in the office of the Secretary of State." *Section 697.530(a)* provides in relevant part:

> A judgment lien on personal property is a lien on all interests in the following personal property that are subject to enforcement of the money judgment against the judgment debtor ... at the time the lien is created *if a security interest in the property could be perfected under the Commercial Code by filing a financing statement at that time with the Secretary of State:*

> (1) Accounts receivable.

> (2) Chattel paper.

> (3) Equipment.

> (4) Farm products

> (5) Inventory

> (6) Negotiable documents of title.

See id. §697.530 (emphasis added).

Defendants contend that their judgment is secured by property of this description. The question before the court is whether a security interest in the California collateral can be perfected under the California Commercial Code by filing a financing statement with the California Secretary of State.

B. Security Interests in Personal Property

Security interests in personal property are governed generally by Article 9 of the UCC, as adopted in each state of the United States. Prior to July 2001, the California Commercial Code provided that, in perfecting a security interest in personal property, the location of the property and type of property determined which state's law controlled the perfection of a security interest thereon. *See CAL. COM. CODE §9103* (repealed 2001). However, in 2001, every state in the United States, including California, adopted substantial amendments to the UCC involving the perfection of security interests in personal property. These amendments took effect on July 1, 2001 in every state (except for four states, none relevant hereto, where the amendments took effect later that year).

California Commercial Code §9307 (the California version of *UCC §9-307*), effective July 1, 2001, determines the location of a debtor for the purposes of personal property security interests. *Section 9307(e)* specifies: "A registered organization that is organized under the law of a state [such as a corporation] is located in that state." Identical provisions were adopted in 2001 in every other state. Thus, for the perfection of a security interest in personal property, Aura is located in Delaware, because it is a Delaware corporation.

The consequence of Aura's location in Delaware is specified in *California Commercial Code §9301(1)*, also adopted in 2001, which provides in relevant part: "while a debtor is located in a jurisdiction, the local law of that jurisdiction governs perfection ... of a security interest in collateral." Again, the law of every other state is similar. Thus, California law dictates that the perfection of a security interest in Aura's California collateral is governed by the internal law of Delaware.

UCC §9-310, adopted in Delaware as *6 Del. C. 9-310*, provides the applicable Delaware law for perfecting a security interest in collateral. This provision states (with certain exceptions not relevant in this case): "a financing statement must be filed to perfect all security interests. ..." *Section 9-501 (a) of the UCC*, codified in Delaware as *6 Del. C. 9-501(a)*, provides the proper location for such a filing: "if the local law of this State governs perfection of a security interest ... the office in which to file a financing statement to perfect the security interest ... is ... the office of the [Delaware] Secretary of State. ..."

From these statutory provisions, it follows that, under both California and Delaware law, there is a single place to perfect a security interest in collateral owned by a Delaware corporation, wherever the collateral may be located. That location is the office of the Delaware Secretary of State. It also follows that there is no place in California to file a financing statement that would accomplish such perfection of a security interest in such collateral, including California collateral, belonging to a Delaware corporation.

There are strong policy considerations behind this result. One of the principal purposes of the 2001 changes in Article 9 of the UCC was to require that all UCC security interest filings for a given corporation be made in the corporation's state of incorporation.

Previous law provided that the state where the property was located was usually the proper location for perfecting a security interest. See Former *U.C.C. §9-103(1)(b)*. This law was unsatisfactory, for two reasons. First, a lender seeking a security interest in a corporation's collateral would have to examine the filings in all states where the corporation had collateral to make sure that there was no outstanding encumbrance in such collateral. In addition, such a lender was required to file its financing statement in every state where such collateral was located. This was a burdensome and duplicative process if the borrower was a large corporation.

Second, personal property is frequently moved from state to state. In consequence, a secured creditor could lose its security interest if it did not adequately keep track of the location of its collateral and take appropriate subsequent steps, within an appropriate time frame, to maintain its secured status by filing in the new state or states where the collateral came to rest. *See UCC §9-103* (1972) (amended effective July 1, 2001). In addition, a secured creditor would have to investigate the provenance of collateral to find out if it was subject to a prior perfected security interest in another state.

The goal was to make a UCC security interest filing permanent and easy to find. For a Delaware corporation, it is now necessary to examine only the UCC filings in Delaware to determine whether there is a perfected security interest for any collateral belonging to the corporation anywhere in the United States. This is far more efficient and less prone to error than the previous system.[1]

C. APPLICATION OF UCC LAW TO CALIFORNIA JUDGMENT LIENS

We come now to consider the application of the foregoing law to obtaining a judgment lien on California collateral. Under *CCP §697.530*, a judgment lien on such property can be created only by filing the requisite notice in the office of the Secretary of State. However, the statute provides that this procedure is effective to create a judgment lien only if the Commercial Code permits the perfection of a security interest in such collateral by a filing in the same office.

The parties devote much space to discussing which state's Secretary of State's office is specified by the statute. The court need not resolve this dispute. If the statute is interpreted to apply only to the California Secretary of State, the statute does not apply in this case, because the California Commercial Code does not permit the perfection of a security interest in

---

1   Similarly, a creditor needs to examine only the filings in the office of the California Secretary of State to determine if a California corporation's collateral, wherever it may be located in the United States, is subject to a prior lien.

collateral belonging to a Delaware corporation by filing a notice of judgment in California. On the other hand, if we take the California statute to create a judgment lien upon the filing of a notice of judgment lien in the Secretary of State's office in the appropriate state, claimants must lose because they filed their notice of judgment in the wrong state. They should have filed their notice in Delaware instead of in California.

We leave for another day the issue of whether a filing of a notice of judgment lien in Delaware, based on a California judgment with no domestication of the judgment in Delaware, is sufficient to create a judgment lien. In this case, there is no judgment lien because the claimants failed to file their notice of judgment lien in the proper state.

Prior to 2001, the controlling law governing perfection of security interests in California was mostly based on the location of the *property* rather than the location of the debtor. *See CAL. COM. CODE §9103* (West 1982) (repealed 2001). While the procedure regarding the perfection of security interest substantially changed after the amendments made to the California Commercial Code, the legislative comments regarding *§697.530* did not. Because the legislative comments to *§697.530* did not substantially change, the absence of comments regarding the problem of a nonresident debtor does not support the claimants' conclusion that Aura's location has no bearing on where to file a notice of judgment lien.

Aura's position is further supported by the fact that, in California, creating a judicial lien by filing a notice of judgment lien is not the only way to create a judicial lien on a debtor's property. If a debtor corporation is incorporated in another state, then, under *CCP §697.520*, creating a judicial lien by filing a notice of judgment lien with the Secretary of State is an "alternative or in addition to a lien created by levy under a writ of execution" or other enforcement procedures. *Id.* Thus, creditors generally have other enforcement remedies to obtain a judgment lien in California against a non-California resident.

Moreover, along with the other available remedies under California law, creditors seeking to impose a judgment lien on a non-California corporation may utilize the procedures in the state where the corporation is incorporated.

IV. CONCLUSION

In California, the filing of a notice of judgment lien with the California Secretary of State is no longer a valid means to create a judicial lien against the California collateral of a non-California corporation. After the 2001 revisions to the California Commercial Code, the location of the debtor, not the property, controls where a security interest can be perfected. Thus, a corporate judgment debtor must be incorporated in California to permit the creation of a judicial lien through the filing of a notice of judgment lien with the California Secretary of State. Because Aura is incorporated under the laws of Delaware, the claimants did not obtain a judgment lien on its California collateral through the filing of a notice of judgment lien with the California Secretary of State. Therefore, claimants' judgment against Aura only supports an unsecured claim in this case.

Summary judgment is granted to Aura.

PROBLEM 4–1

Determine where Ray should file his financing statement to perfect his security interest in the following transactions generated over the internet through the store's web page. In each transaction Ray retained a security interest in the appliance(s) he sold. See 9-301 and 9-307.

[handwritten: PMSI → NO NEED TO FILE]

Transaction 1:   Ray sold a commercial grade refrigerator on credit and shipped it to the buyer's home in Nevada. *[handwritten: INDIVIDUAL]*

Transaction 2:   Ray sold an electric cook top on credit to one of his local customers who had him ship it to the customer's summer home in Maine. *[handwritten: (NOT PRIMARY)]*

Transaction 3:   Ray sold a commercial grade range to the burger joint across the street from his store which is part of a national chain of burger joints owned by a company incorporated in Georgia. *[handwritten: REGISTERED ORG.]*

Transaction 4:   Ray's neighbor purchased a large capacity freezer for each of the 23 ice cream shops he operates around the state. *[handwritten: (SAME JURISDICTION)]*

Transaction 5:   Would your answer in transaction 4 change if the 23 ice cream shops were scattered across 3 states? *[handwritten: → YES, NEED CEO]*

Transaction 6:   The purchasing officer at Yogurt Stop headquarters in Seattle orders a commercial grade dishwasher for delivery and installation at the company owned store around the block from Ray's.

PROBLEM 4–2

A local customer bought a microwave convection oven from Ray on credit and had him ship it to his daughter who was attending college out of state. The oven was damaged in transit and the daughter took it in to the appliance repair shop close to campus for repairs. When she was unable to pay for the repairs, the shop refused to let her take the oven home, claiming that under a state statute, it had a lien on the oven for the cost of the repairs and was entitled to retain possession until she paid the repair bill. Ray retained a security interest in the oven and now wants to repossess it because the customer has stopped making payments on the oven since his daughter does not have it. If statutory liens for repairs cannot be asserted against consumer goods in Ray's state, which is where the debtor-customer is located, can Ray recover on

[handwritten: REVIEW]

a conversion claim against the repair shop if it refuses to turn the oven over so Ray can exercise his right to repossess it under Article 9? See 9-301(3)(C).

As we noted earlier, debtors move—what effect does a change in the debtor's location have on a filed financing statement? Assuming the secured party filed the financing statement in the correct jurisdiction at the time of the original transaction, should the secured party be penalized because the debtor has moved to a new jurisdiction? Or should subsequent parties who deal with the debtor, presuming it is now located, for Article 9 purposes, in the new jurisdiction assume the risk that financing statements may have been filed against the debtor in other jurisdictions? The problems which follow explore these questions.

PROBLEM 4–3

Ray sold a commercial range with grill top to a restaurant located in the next city up the interstate, retaining a security interest in the range and grill top to secure the buyer's promise to pay. A few months later, when business began to slow at the restaurant, the owner's father loaned him the money he needed to keep the doors open, taking a security interest in the restaurant's equipment and filing a financing statement in the correct place. When the lease expired on the building where the restaurant was located, the lessor refused to renew the lease and the owner was forced to find a new location for the restaurant. He decided to move it to a neighboring state. Ray found out about the move five months after the restaurant had relocated to the neighboring state. The owner's father, of course, knew of the move when it happened and had filed a financing statement in the new state shortly after the restaurant had relocated.

Does Ray's security interest still have priority over the security interest of the owner's father? See 9-316. If not, can Ray restore his perfected status and the priority it gave him by immediately filing a financing statement in the new state? Does it matter that the owner's father knew that Ray had a security interest in the range but did not notify Ray that his son had moved the restaurant?

PROBLEM 4–4

Would your answer to Problem 4–3 be different if the father had made the loan and taken a security interest in the restaurant equipment (and filed his financing statement in the new state) two months after the restaurant had moved to the new location? What if instead of taking a security interest in the equipment, the father had perfected a judgment lien against the restaurant's equipment? What if after relocating, the owner had sold the range subject to Ray's security interest to another restaurant that was unaware of Ray's security interest? See 9-316.

B. CERTIFICATES OF TITLE

Long before Article 9, security interests in certain types of personal property were subject to special legislation aimed primarily at addressing the uniquely mobile nature of the property covered. For example, automobiles—as opposed to washers and couches—move easily between jurisdictions and retain significant value even when not new, which makes auto theft both easy and profitable. As automobiles became a staple of American commerce, states acted quickly to counter the growing market in stolen autos that followed. The counter-measure of choice was the certificate of title. Certificates of title were issued in the name of the owner of an auto and were intended to be the exclusive "means for controlling property interests in goods like autos." Comment 4b to old 9-103. Unless a thief also acquired the certificate of title for an auto, the thief, in theory, would not be able to transfer an interest in the stolen vehicle superior to that of the person in whose name the certificate of title was issued.

By the time work began on Article 9, autos had become a common form of collateral and a section on certificates of title was included in an early draft of Article 9. That section was dropped from Article 9 to avert a turf war with an organization claiming jurisdiction over motor vehicle legislation. That did not mean, however, that Article 9 could ignore titled goods. As long as goods subject to certificates of title were being used as collateral, conflict between Article 9 and certificate of title acts was possible.

For our purposes, the primary consequence of certificate of title acts is that they preempt Article 9 by providing the exclusive method for creating and perfecting a security interest in the types of goods they cover. Perfection of a security interest in titled goods is by notation of the security interest on the actual certificate of title issued. A security interest in titled goods cannot be perfected by filing an Article 9 financing statement unless the goods are inventory in the hands of the debtor. 9-311(a). Because the certificate of title is an indispensable part of any transaction intended to create or convey an interest in the goods it covers, the notation of the security interest on the certificate of title provides notice to subsequent parties looking to acquire an interest in titled goods.

Even though the creation and perfection of a security interest in titled goods is not governed by Article 9, the following cases demonstrate that disputes involving claims to titled goods can still raise choice of law issues that Article 9 must resolve.

IN RE OWEN

United States Bankruptcy Court for the District of Idaho
Bankr. L. Rep. (CCH) ¶ 81,592 (Bankr. D. Idaho July 15, 2009)

MYERS, *Bankruptcy Judge.*

INTRODUCTION

This preference avoidance action involves a security interest in a motor vehicle [2007 Mercury Marguis]. That security interest was perfected in California. However, the debtors relocated themselves and the vehicle to Idaho. The vehicle was then titled in Idaho and, exactly 90 days later, the debtors filed for bankruptcy relief. Because of the manner in which the perfection of the security interest in Idaho took place, the chapter 7 trustee asserts a preferential transfer occurred.

This action presents an issue of statutory interpretation, and does so upon facts that the creditor's counsel lamented as "reverse serendipity." Though those facts required the creditor to defend its interest, the Court finds no preference has been established.

* * *

FACTS

Pursuant to the agreement and stipulation of the parties, and in light of the documents admitted into evidence, the facts are these.

On December 10, 2007, Debtors entered into an agreement with Defendant so they could purchase the Mercury. Under that agreement, Defendant agreed to finance a portion of the purchase price, and Debtors agreed to give Defendant a security interest in the Mercury to secure that obligation. Debtors took possession of the Mercury that same day.

Also on December 10, Defendant applied for a California certificate of title for the Mercury showing Debtors as the owners and Defendant as the lienholder. An electronic California title was issued noting the same. The parties agree that, under applicable California law, Defendant perfected its security interest in the Mercury on December 10, 2007.

In May 2008, Debtors moved to Idaho, bringing the Mercury with them.

On June 26, 2008, the Department of Motor Vehicles ("DMV") in Ada County, Idaho, sent Defendant a letter, stating that Debtors had filed an application to register and title the Mercury in Idaho and that this application listed Defendant as a lienholder. The letter requested that Defendant submit a "paper" out-of-state certificate of title. It further stated: "*If your lien is still active, it will be recorded on the Idaho title, which will in turn be mailed to you after issuance.*"

A paper California certificate of title was thereafter issued. It showed Debtors as owners of the Mercury, and it noted Defendant's lien. This paper California title had an "odometer date" of December 10, 2007 and an "issue date" of July 16, 2008. It contained no other date speaking to when Defendant's lien was perfected. However, the parties answered that question at trial by agreeing that the perfection date of the lien under California law was December 10, 2007.

The parties stipulated that sometime between July 16 and July 30, an application was made for an Idaho title for the Mercury. The Idaho title issued as a result of this application is dated August 6, 2008. It shows Debtors as owners and Defendant as lienholder. The Idaho title shows the "record" date for Defendant's lien as July 16, 2008—a date consistent with the "issue date" on the paper California title.

On October 14, 2008, Debtors filed their voluntary chapter 7 petition for relief. The parties stipulated that the petition date is exactly 90 days after July 16.

On these facts, Trustee alleges that Defendant perfected its lien pursuant to Idaho law on July 16, 2008. Thus, he asserts, this is a transfer avoidable as a preference, and that he can recover the vehicle or its value.

Defendant counters that its security interest was perfected on December 10, 2007 under California law and remained perfected as of the bankruptcy filing, thus resulting in no avoidable transfer.

DISCUSSION AND DISPOSITION

* * *

2. IDAHO LAW CONTROLS PERFECTION IN THIS CASE

The perfection of a security interest is governed by state law. *See Elliott v. Frontier Props. (In re Lewis W. Shurtleff, Inc.)*, 778 F.2d 1416, 1420 (9th Cir. 1985); *cf. Butner v. United States*, 440 U.S. 48, 55, 99 S. Ct. 914, 59 L. Ed. 2d 136 (1979) (stating that "[p]roperty interests are created and defined by state law.").

Idaho Code §28-9-303 addresses the perfection and priority of security interests in goods covered by a certificate of title, and it states:

> (a) This section applies to goods covered by a certificate of title, even if there is no other relationship between the jurisdiction under whose certificate of title the goods are covered and the goods or the debtor.
>
> (b) Goods become covered by a certificate of title when a valid application for the certificate of title and the applicable fee are delivered to the appropriate authority. Goods cease to be covered by a certificate of title at the earlier of the time the certificate of title ceases to be effective under the law of the issuing jurisdiction or the

time the goods become covered subsequently by a certificate of title issued by another jurisdiction.

(c) The local law of the jurisdiction under whose certificate of title the goods are covered governs perfection, the effect of perfection or nonperfection, and the priority of a security interest in goods covered by a certificate of title from the time the goods become covered by the certificate of title until the goods cease to be covered by the certificate of title.

Idaho Code §28-9-303. These principles regarding change in controlling law are illustrated by an example:

Debtor's automobile is covered by a certificate of title issued by Illinois. Lender perfects a security interest in the automobile by complying with Illinois' certificate-of-title statute. Thereafter, Debtor applies for a certificate of title in Indiana. ... *Under Section 9-303, Illinois law ceases to govern perfection; rather, once Debtor delivers the application and applicable fee to the appropriate Indiana authority, Indiana law governs.*

See Idaho Code §28-9-316, Official Comment 5, at example 8 (emphasis supplied).

Though there is no Idaho case law construing this provision, in interpreting other states' versions of §9-303 of Revised Article 9, courts have determined that a certificate of title on a vehicle issued by a foreign state ceases to control the issue of perfection of a security interest once application is made in the forum state for a new certificate of title. At that time, the law of the second jurisdiction governs perfection of a lien in the vehicle. For example, in *In re Cook, 2007 Bankr. LEXIS 780, 2007 WL 680170, at *2 (Bankr. W.D.Mo. Mar. 1, 2007),* the court held:

When the Debtor bought the [car], it was "covered" by the Illinois Certificate of Title. However, under *§9-303(b),* when the Missouri Department of Revenue issued its Certificate of Title on May 16, 2005, the [car] ceased to be covered by the Illinois Certificate of Title and became covered by the Missouri Certificate of Title. At that point, Missouri law became the local law of the jurisdiction under whose certificate of title the [car] was covered and, under *§9-303(c),* Missouri law governs perfection of liens on it.

Id. See also Metzger v. Americredit Fin. Servs., Inc., 273 Ga. App. 453, 615 S.E.2d 120, 124-25 (Ga. Ct. App. 2005) (stating that pursuant to Georgia's version of Revised *UCC §9-303,* "even when a security interest in goods has been perfected in another state, Georgia law determines perfection and priority issues once the goods become 'covered' by a Georgia certificate of title, which occurs when a valid application and fee are submitted to the Georgia DMV.")

Here, at the time Debtors moved to Idaho, the Mercury was subject to a perfected security interest in favor of Defendant under California law. That lien interest and its effective date of December 10, 2007, were reflected on the electronic California title, and the parties agree Defendant was perfected under California law.

However, between July 16 and July 30, Debtors applied for an Idaho certificate of title. This is significant. Under *Idaho Code §28-9-303(b)*, goods "cease to be covered" by a certificate of title "*at the earlier of*" (1) the time the certificate of title ceases to be effective under the law of the issuing jurisdiction [*i.e.*, California], *or* (2) "*the time the goods become covered subsequently by a certificate of title issued by another jurisdiction.*" The statute further establishes that the "[g]oods become covered" in that second jurisdiction [*i.e.*, Idaho] "when a valid application for the certificate of title and the applicable fee are delivered to the appropriate authority." *Id.*

Under these provisions, the Mercury ceased to be covered by the California certificate of title, and became covered by the Idaho certificate of title laws, on or about July 30, 2008, when the application and fees were tendered to the Idaho authorities. The Court must therefore look to Idaho law to address the question of Defendant's perfection of its security interest. *See* Revised *UCC § 9-303(c)*; *Idaho Code §28-9-303(c)* ("The local law of the jurisdiction under whose certificate of title the goods are covered governs perfection [and] the effect of perfection or nonperfection ... from the time the goods become covered by the certificate of title until the goods cease to be covered[.]")

3. THE LIEN'S PERFECTION IN CALIFORNIA REMAINED EFFECTIVE

The parties do not disagree with a fundamental proposition of Idaho law governing perfection of liens in motor vehicles found in *Idaho Code §49-510(3)*, which states:

> The filing of a lien or encumbrance and the notation of it shall be a condition of perfection and shall constitute constructive notice of the lien or encumbrance and its contents to creditors and subsequent purchasers and encumbrancers. *All liens or encumbrances so filed with the department shall be perfected and take priority according to the order in which the same are noted upon the certificate of title or entered into the electronic records of the department.*

(Emphasis supplied).

In applying this statute, this Court has stated that "a security interest is deemed perfected according to the date noted by the State [of Idaho] on the title certificate." *Walker*, 161 B.R. at 491. This is true even if the lien date on the Idaho title was recorded by administrative error.

Trustee emphasizes that Defendant's lien date as shown on the Idaho certificate of title is July 16, 2008. Ex. 208. He argues that whether the Idaho authorities erroneously listed this date based upon the July 16, 2008 "issue date" on the paper California certificate of title is not relevant to deciding the perfection issue.

Therefore, Trustee concludes, Defendant perfected its security interest in the Mercury under Idaho law on July 16, 2008. He contends that this provides the initial date required under *§547(e)(1)(B)* (providing that transfer of property other than real property is perfected when creditor on simple contract cannot acquire a judicial lien superior to the interest of the transferee). Then, because this date is more than 30 days after the transfer took effect between the transferor and the transferee (*i.e.*, the grant of the security interest by Debtors to Defendant in December, 2007), he contends that the transfer was made for preferences purposes on the date of perfection, July 16, 2008.

While the Court does not disagree with these authorities or the general analysis, Trustee's argument overlooks another provision of Idaho statutory law. Defendant contends—correctly—that its lien, perfected in December, 2007, under California law, remained perfected as of the October 14, 2008 bankruptcy filing pursuant to *Idaho Code §28-9-316*.

A. *IDAHO CODE §28-9-316* PROVIDES FOR CONTINUED PERFECTION

Idaho Code §28-9-316 is entitled "*Continued perfection of security interest following change in governing law*." It provides a general rule that perfection continues until the earliest of (1) the time it would cease under the initial state's law, (2) four months after the debtor's change of location to another state, or (3) one year after transfer of the collateral to another person that becomes a debtor and is located in another state. However, security interests in goods subject to certificates of title have special provisions. The relevant subsections of *Idaho Code §28-9-316* are *(d)* and *(e)*, which provide:

> (d) Except as otherwise provided in subsection (e) of this section, a security interest in goods covered by a certificate of title which is perfected by any method under the law of another jurisdiction when the goods become covered by a certificate of title from this state remains perfected until the security interest would have become unperfected under the law of the other jurisdiction had the goods not become so covered.
>
> (e) A security interest described in subsection (d) of this section becomes unperfected as against a purchaser of the goods for value and is deemed never to have been perfected as against a purchaser of the goods for value if the applicable requirements for perfection under section 28-9-311(b) or 28-9-313 are not satisfied before the earlier of:
>
> (1) The time the security interest would have become unperfected under the law of the other jurisdiction had the goods not become covered by a certificate of title from this state; or
>
> (2) The expiration of four (4) months after the goods had become so covered.

Idaho Code §28-9-316(d) provides a general rule that is key to the present dispute. Reordering and restating that rule, "when the goods become covered by a certificate of title from this state [Idaho]," a previously perfected security interest in those goods "under the laws of another jurisdiction ... remains perfected until [the time] the security interest would have become unperfected under the law of the other jurisdiction had the goods not become so covered [in Idaho]."

The Official Comments explain:

> 2. Continued Perfection. This section [9-316] deals with continued perfection of security interests that have been perfected under the law of another jurisdiction. The fact that the law of a particular jurisdiction ceases to govern perfection under Sections 9-301 through 9-307 does not necessarily mean that a security interest perfected under that law becomes unperfected. To the contrary: This section generally provides that a security interest perfected under the law of one jurisdiction remains perfected for a fixed period of time (four months or one year, depending on the circumstances), even though the jurisdiction whose law governs perfection changes. However, cessation of perfection under the law of the original jurisdiction cuts short the fixed period. The four-month and one-year periods are long enough for a secured party to discover in most cases that the law of a different jurisdiction governs perfection and to reperfect (typically by filing) under the law of that jurisdiction. If a secured party properly reperfects a security interest before it becomes unperfected under subsection (a), then the security interest remains perfected continuously thereafter.

> *Idaho Code §28-9-316*, Official Comment 2.

The comment to *Idaho Code §28-9-303*—the section that deals with change in the controlling law where the goods are subject to certificates of title—is consistent:

> 4. Continued perfection. The fact that the law of one State ceases to apply under subsection (b) does not mean that a security interest perfected under that law becomes unperfected automatically. In most cases, the security interest will remain perfected. *See Section 9-316(d)*, (e).

> *Idaho Code §28-9-303*, Official Comment 4.

Recall Official Comment 5, example 8, to *Idaho Code §28-9-316*, quoted *supra*, discussing that a vehicle perfected under Illinois law would become subject to Indiana law upon application in Indiana for a certificate of title given the operation of Revised *UCC §9-303(b)*. The balance of the comment addresses the issue of continued perfection:

> Example 8. Debtor's automobile is covered by a certificate of title issued by Illinois. Lender perfects a security interest in the automobile by complying with Illinois' certificate-of-title statute. Thereafter, Debtor applies for a certificate of title in Indiana. Six months thereafter, Creditor acquires a judicial lien on the

automobile. Under Section 9-303(b), Illinois law ceases to govern perfection; rather, once Debtor delivers the application and applicable fee to the appropriate Indiana authority, Indiana law governs. *Nevertheless, under Indiana's Section 9-316(d), Lender's security interest remains perfected until it would become unperfected under Illinois law had no certificate of title been issued by Indiana. … If Lender's security interest remains perfected, it is senior to Creditor's judicial lien.*

> *Idaho Code §28-9-316*, Official Comment 5, at example 8
> (emphasis supplied).

Under *Idaho Code §28-9-316(d)*, the inquiry here is whether and when Defendant's security interest would have become unperfected under California law.

B. THE LIEN WOULD NOT HAVE BECOME UNPERFECTED UNDER CALIFORNIA LAW

Under California law, a security interest in a motor vehicle is perfected only by compliance with the California Vehicle Code. *See Cal. Veh. Code §§6300-6303*. However, once perfected, *California Vehicle Code §6303* provides that "the effect of such perfection, and the creation, attachment, priority and validity of such security interest shall be governed by the Uniform Commercial Code."

California, like Idaho, has adopted *Revised UCC §§9-303* and *9-316* providing for the continued perfection of goods previously titled in one state after they become covered by a certificate of title in another state. Thus, in the absence of a provision in California's Uniform Commercial Code dictating the termination of a perfected interest in a motor vehicle upon the issuance of a certificate of title in another state, the provisions of *§§9303* and *9316* of its Uniform Commercial Code control.

Those provisions of the California Uniform Commercial Code do not cause Defendant's security interest in the Mercury to become unperfected upon the vehicle becoming covered by the certificate of title in Idaho. Nor has Trustee cited any other statutory authority or case law establishing that Defendant's interest became unperfected under California law on July 16, 2008, or elsewhere between July 16, 2008 and the petition date of October 14, 2008.

Therefore, pursuant to California's Uniform Commercial Code *§§9303* and *9316*, and absent identified law to the contrary, the Court concludes that Defendant's security interest was still perfected when Debtors filed their chapter 7 bankruptcy petition on October 14, 2008. Because Defendant's interest in the Mercury was so perfected, Trustee did not meet his burden of proving that a transfer was made on July 16, 2008.

CONCLUSION

Based on the foregoing, there was no transfer that occurred on July 16, 2008 under *§547(e)*. In the absence of such transfer, Trustee's preference action fails.

Judgment will be entered for Defendant. Its counsel will provide an appropriate form of judgment for entry by the Court.

PROBLEM 4–5

The license plates issued by the State of Alaska for vehicles have always been Ray's favorite American plates—the silhouette of climbers trudging over the Chilkoot Pass on the middle of the plates he found inspirational. So, when he bought a new service van he decided to get Alaska plates for it. Alaska only issues plates to vehicles with an Alaska certificate of title, which means that Ray will have to get the van titled in Alaska and that the bank financing his purchase of the van will have to get its security interest noted on the Alaska title. The loan officer handling the deal for the bank is worried that a notation on a certificate of title issued by a state other than the state where the debtor lives would not be effective to perfect its interest. Should the loan officer be worried? See 9-303(a).

Just need sec. int. noted on COT

IN RE LANCE
United States Bankruptcy Court for the Western District of Missouri
59 U.C.C. Rep. Serv. 2d (Callaghan) 632 (Bankr. W.D. Mo. 2006)

FEDERMAN, *Bankruptcy Judge.*

ORDER DENYING TRUSTEE'S MOTION TO COMPEL TURNOVER OF 2004 ARCTIC CAT SNOWMOBILE

The Chapter 7 Trustee filed a Motion to compel the Debtor to turn over a 2004 Arctic Cat Snowmobile (the "Snowmobile") identified on the Debtor's schedules. Both the Debtor and NW Preferred Federal Credit Union (the "Credit Union") responded to the Motion to Compel, each stating that the Credit Union has a perfected security interest in the Snowmobile and that there is no equity in it. For the reasons that follow, the Trustee's Motion to Compel is DENIED.

Although the loan documents were not submitted at the hearing on the Trustee's Motion, and the Trustee initially took the position that the Credit Union failed to provide proof of perfection in violation of Local Rules, it appeared at the hearing on the Motion that the Trustee has received copies of the loan documents and now concedes that they granted the Credit Union a purchase-money security interest in the Snowmobile. Rather, the only issue argued at hearing was whether the security interest was properly perfected. The Trustee asserts the security interest was not perfected because no UCC-1 financing statement was filed; the Credit Union asserts the Snowmobile is a "consumer good" under the Uniform Commercial Code and, therefore, perfection occurred when the security interest attached and that no filing was necessary.

According to the statements of counsel at hearing, the Debtor, who at all relevant times lived in Missouri, purchased the Snowmobile in Wisconsin on February 15, 2005. The Snowmobile is located in Minnesota, where the Debtor stores it at his brother's house. The Debtor uses it for recreational purposes when he visits his brother there. He has never brought it to Missouri.

The Debtor filed a voluntary Chapter 7 bankruptcy petition on October 6, 2005. He lists the Snowmobile with a value of $4,000, and a secured claim of $4,152 held by the Credit Union. His Statement of Intention indicates he intends to keep the Snowmobile and reaffirm the debt to the Credit Union.

The first issue is which state's laws apply in this situation, given that the Debtor lives in Missouri, but the Snowmobile was purchased in Wisconsin and is currently located in Minnesota. Bankruptcy courts apply the choice of law rules of the state in which they sit. In Missouri, the choice of law rule governing perfection of security interests is found in §400.9-301 of the Missouri Statutes. That section provides, in relevant part:

> Except as otherwise provided in *sections 400.9-303 through 400.9-306*, the following rules determine the law governing perfection, the effect of perfection or nonperfection, and the priority of a security interest in collateral:
>
> (1) Except as otherwise provided in this section, while a debtor is located in a jurisdiction, the local law of that jurisdiction governs perfection, the effect of perfection or nonperfection, and the priority of a security interest in collateral.

This general rule does not apply to certain types of collateral, such as those covered by a certificate of title, which are governed by §400.9-303.

In Missouri, "motor vehicles" are covered by certificates of title. *Section 301.010* of the Missouri Statutes defines "motor vehicle" as "any self-propelled vehicle not operated exclusively upon tracks, except farm tractors." "Vehicle" is defined as "any mechanical device on wheels, designed primarily for use, or used, on highways, except motorized bicycles, vehicles propelled or drawn by horses or human power, or vehicles used exclusively on fixed rails or tracks, or cotton trailers or motorized wheelchairs operated by handicapped persons." With regard to snowmobiles, as the Attorney General for Missouri has opined:

> A snowmobile, as we describe the machine, is a self-propelled vehicle not operated exclusively on tracks and would come within the definition of a motor vehicle … if it is a "vehicle." The term "vehicle," as used in this chapter, is defined as any mechanical device on wheels, designed primarily for use on highways, and is to be included in the definition of "motor vehicle" which has to be registered under this chapter. Unless it is a mechanical device on wheels, it does not come within the definition of a motor vehicle

which is required to be registered and licensed under Chapter 301
... It is our opinion that a snowmobile is not a mechanical device
on wheels since it gets its traction for mobility to move forward
from the revolution of the belts and not from wheels. Further, it
is our understanding snowmobiles are not designed primarily for
use on highways. Therefore, snowmobiles are not required to be
registered and licensed under Chapter 301 before being operated
on the highways of this state."

I agree. Because a snowmobile does not have wheels, nor is it used on
highways, it is not a "motor vehicle" under the clear language of the statute.

In addition, the Missouri Statutes contain a specific provision requiring
all-terrain vehicles be covered by a certificate of title. "All-terrain vehicles"
are defined as "any motorized vehicle manufactured and used exclusively for
off-highway use ... traveling on three, four or more low pressure tires." Again,
because a snowmobile does not have tires, it is not an "all-terrain vehicle" and
is not covered by a certificate of title.

Accordingly, because snowmobiles are not covered by certificates of title,
§400.9-301(1) provides that the local law of the jurisdiction where the Debtor
is located governs perfection of security interests in them. An individual is
"located," for purposes of the UCC, at his or her principal residence. Missouri
law, therefore, applies.

Under Missouri law, certain types of collateral require the filing of a financing statement in order to perfect a security interest in them. The Credit Union
asserts that the Snowmobile is a "consumer good," and therefore is excepted
from the filing requirements. Goods are classified as "consumer goods" if they
are "goods that are used or bought for use primarily for personal, family, or
household purposes." The determinative factor is the principal use to which
the property is put.

There is no dispute that the Debtor uses the Snowmobile for recreational
purposes when he visits his brother in Minnesota. Hence, I find that the
Debtor uses the Snowmobile primarily for personal purposes and it is, therefore, a "consumer good" under the UCC.

The UCC provides for the automatic perfection of purchase-money
security interests taken in consumer goods, other than goods covered
under Missouri's motor vehicle registration and licensing laws. Because the
Snowmobile is a "consumer good" and is not a motor vehicle subject to
registration and licensing laws, the Credit Union's purchase-money security
interest was perfected when it attached. The Credit Union was not required
to file a financing statement in order to perfect its security interest.

Accordingly, because NW Preferred Federal Credit Union has a perfected
security interest in the 2004 Arctic Cat Snowmobile and there is no equity in
it, the Trustee's Motion to Compel Turnover is DENIED.

Problem 4–6

Ray owned a service van which he had outfitted with the tools and equipment necessary to make repairs to his customer's appliances. The bank that loaned him the money to buy the van took a security interest in the van, which was noted on the certificate of title issued on the van. Ray sold the van to one of his out of state customers who drove it to his home state where he got the state department of motor vehicles to issue a new certificate of title on the van. He was able to do this without surrendering Ray's certificate of title on the van, and as a result, the bank's security interest in the van was not noted on the new certificate. Two months later he sold the van to a neighbor with no mention of the bank's security interest.

Ray had stopped making payments on the van after he sold it, and the bank declared a default and went looking for the van to repossess it. Late one evening, the bank's repo man found the van parked in the neighbor's driveway and towed it away. If the neighbor sues the bank for conversion, will he recover? See 9-316 and 9-337. Would your answer be different if instead of selling the van to his neighbor, Ray's customer had traded it in on a new van he purchased from a specialty van dealer?

Problem 4–7

Last winter Ray bought a snowmobile for his family from his cousin who lives in another state. Snowmobiles are subject to the certificate of title act in Ray's state but not in the state where his cousin lives. Ray has not gotten around to getting a certificate of title issued for his snowmobile. But he just discovered that the dealer that financed his cousin's purchase of the snowmobile had a security interest in the snowmobile that it had perfected by filing. Can the dealer enforce that security interest now that the snowmobile is in a different state? If Ray applies for a certificate of title for the snowmobile, does he have to tell the state department that issues titles about the dealer's security interest? See 9-316.

Problem 4–8

Would your analysis in Problem 4–7 be different if the snowmobile had moved from a state where snowmobiles were subject to certificates of title to a state where they were not? If the dealer failed to file a financing statement in the new state would it eventually lose the perfection it had in the original state based on the notation of its interest on the certificate of title issued for the snowmobile? See 9-316.

CHAPTER 5

PRIORITIES

What happens when more than one creditor claims an interest in the debtor's personal property? As long as the debtor is paying all of the creditors, there's usually little for Article 9 to do. But when the debtor stops paying one or more of these creditors and the unpaid creditors move to enforce their security interests against the collateral, how do we divide the collateral as between the parties claiming an interest in it if the total amount of the claims asserted against the collateral exceed the value of the collateral? Surprisingly, the various laws directed at secured transactions that were enacted before Article 9 generally "ignore[d] priority problems, leaving them to be solved, as they arose, by the courts on whatever principles occurred to the judges." Gilmore at 655. But, as its drafters recognized, if Article 9 was to function as a comprehensive system for the creation and enforcement of security interests in personal property, it would have to abandon the "tradition of sweeping all priority problems under the rug" and expressly confront the priority issues inherent in such a system. Gilmore at 656.

Article 9 incorporates a set of rules that will determine the winner in a dispute between creditors claiming an interest in the same collateral. It also provides for certain exceptions to these priority rules, which we will explore in the next Chapter. As we work through the priority rules, it is important to remember that not all claims to the collateral will be based on a security interest created under Article 9. Holders of judicial liens, buyers, and other transferees of the collateral can have interests in the collateral that compete with those of the holder of an Article 9 security interest in that collateral. Therefore, the Article 9 priority rules are not limited to resolving disputes between competing Article 9 security interests; the rules also resolve disputes between an Article 9 security interest and creditors (or others) asserting claims arising outside of Article 9.

A. Basic Rules

The basic priority rules we use to resolve disputes between competing claims to the collateral are set out in 9-317 and 9-322. Which rule applies turns on whether a security interest is perfected or unperfected. The priority of an unperfected security interest is determined under 9-317—unless the competing claim is also an unperfected Article 9 security interest, in which case 9-322 will determine priority. As we will see, an unperfected security interest usually loses to a competing claim. The priority of a perfected security interest is determined under 9-322—unless the security interest is a purchase money security interest. So, if we have a dispute involving an unperfected security interest, 9-317 would usually be our starting point. If we have a dispute involving a perfected security interest, we would start with 9-322. The following problems develop the basic Article 9 priority rules.

Problem 5–1

In each of the following cases, determine which of the competing claimants will have priority to the appliance:

Case 1:   Ray sold several washing machines to the local laundromat. Ray retained a security interest in the washers to secure the laundromat's promise to pay for the washers, but never filed the financing statement that he had prepared for the transaction. All of the laundromat's equipment was subject to a security interest retained by the local finance company to secure a loan it made to the debtor. The finance company's security agreement provided that its security interest attached to any future equipment acquired by the debtor. The finance company filed a financing statement covering its collateral. If the laundromat stops paying Ray and the finance company, which creditor will get the washers Ray sold? See 9-317.

Case 2:   If, after Ray had delivered the washers, the finance company in the last Case had not retained a security interest in the laundromat's equipment, but had instead obtained a judgment against the laundromat pursuant to which it had executed on the laundromat's personal property—including its equipment—would Ray have a better chance of getting his washers back? See 9-317.

Case 3:   Ray sold a large capacity freezer to the yogurt shop down the block from his store, retaining a security interest in the freezer. Several months passed before he filed the financing statement he had prepared for the transaction. Before Ray filed the financing statement, the yogurt shop sold the freezer to the corner convenience store. Can Ray repossess the freezer from the convenience store when the yogurt shop stops making payments? Would your answer be different if the owner of the convenience store knew that Ray had a security interest in the freezer when he bought it? See 9-317.

Case 4:   Would your answer in Case 3 change if instead of selling the freezer to the convenience store the yogurt shop leased the freezer before Ray got around to filing the financing statement? See 9-317.

PROBLEM 5–2

In each of the following cases, determine which of the competing claimants will have priority to the appliance:

Case 1:   Ray loaned his brother the $10,000 his brother needed to open an all-night café across from the junior college in town. Ray took a security interest in all of the cafe's equipment, including any equipment it acquired in the future. He filed his financing statement on February 14. The local bank also loaned his brother $10,000 for the café and, like Ray, took a security interest in the cafe's equipment. It filed its financing statement on March 1. If Ray's brother defaults on both of his loans, which secured party—Ray or the bank—will have priority to the cafe's equipment? If, at the time Ray filed his financing statement, he knew the bank had taken a security interest in the equipment but had not yet perfected it, would the bank be entitled to priority? See 9-322.

PERFECTED
V.
PERFECTED

Case 2:   Same facts as Case 1, but this time the bank filed its financing statement on February 1, and did not advance the $10,000 until Ray's brother had authenticated a security agreement on March 1. When Ray filed his financing statement on February 14, he had already advanced the $10,000 and obtained his brother's signature on a security agreement. If Ray's brother defaults on both loans, which secured party will have priority to the cafe's equipment?

Case 3:   Ray loaned his neighbor $20,000 and as collateral for the loan, took possession of a small painting by Picasso that his neighbor had inherited from his uncle. The neighbor subsequently borrowed $20,000 from the bank, giving the bank a security interest in the same Picasso painting. The bank filed its financing statement covering the painting shortly after it advanced the $20,000. Which secured party will have priority to the Picasso if the neighbor stops paying Ray and the bank? Does it matter that Ray never got an authenticated security agreement from the neighbor? See 9-322 and 9-203.

Case 4:   Would your answer in Case 3 be different if, before any default by the neighbor, Ray had let the neighbor take the painting to an art dealer in town to get it appraised? What if the neighbor had the painting for less than an hour when he returned it to Ray? See 9-322.

B. PURCHASE MONEY PRIORITY

Article 9 creates an exception to the first in time rule for purchase money security interests by affording them a "super" priority. 9-324. A secured party that takes a purchase money security interest and complies with the requirements for purchase money priority will prevail over other secured parties that have perfected their security interests before the purchase money security interest is perfected. Purchase money priority is best understood as a reaction to the development and recognition of the after acquired property clause. As we've seen, an after acquired property clause extends the secured party's security interest beyond property the debtor has at the inception of the security interest to include property the debtor acquires in the future. A broad after acquired property clause can make it difficult for the debtor to obtain credit for future purchases when the secured party itself is unwilling to provide the financing because the clause gives the secured party priority over future lenders who might be willing to extend credit in return for a security interest in what the debtor intends to purchase.

For example, where the debtor needs funds to replace failed or worn out equipment, but the bank with the security interest in the debtor's equipment and after acquired equipment is unwilling to advance the funds, a seller otherwise willing to sell equipment on credit to the debtor in return for a security interest in the equipment sold, would be less inclined to do so because its security interest would be subordinate to the security interest that the bank automatically acquired in the equipment sold as a result of its after acquired property clause. The after acquired property clause takes an entire category of the debtor's assets out of play as a source of collateral for funds needed to operate the business.

Purchase money priority allows the purchase money seller or lender to escape from the shadow of subordination created by an after acquired property clause which in turn opens the door to alternative financing for the debtor subject to an after acquired property clause. The cases and problems that follow explore purchase money priority in more detail.

IN RE DECKERS CONSTRUCTION, INC.
United States Bankruptcy Court for the District Puerto Rico.
461 B.R. 143 (Bankr. D.P.R. 2011)

FLORES, *Bankruptcy Judge.*

OPINION AND ORDER

The controversy before the Court revolves around competing security interests in accounts receivable of the Debtor, Deckers Construction, Inc. (hereafter referred to as "Debtor" or "Deckers"). Plaintiff, Eurobank, now Oriental Bank (hereafter referenced to as "Eurobank"), asserts that it has a super priority interest over Defendant, Westernbank Puerto Rico, now Banco Popular de Puerto Rico (hereafter referenced to as "Westernbank"), in the accounts receivable of Deckers even though Westernbank's security interest was recorded prior to Eurobank's. Eurobank contends that its junior security interest trumps Westernbank's because Eurobank's security interest falls within the scope of a purchase money security interest (hereafter referenced to as "PMSI"). Defendant disagrees and argues that the general rule of "first in time, first in right" governs rather than the exception of the purchase money security interest.

For the reasons set forth below, the Court holds that Eurobank's security interest does not fall within the scope of a PMSI under the Puerto Rico Uniform Commercial Code, and, consequently, the general rule of "first in time, first in right" governs in this case.

I. UNCONTESTED MATERIAL FACTS AND PROCEDURAL HISTORY

* * *

The relevant undisputed facts are as follows:

The Debtor, Deckers Construction, entered into two contracts with DVC pursuant to which it was to "construct mixed residence complex apartments for the elderly and for families that qualified for a social housing program." On February 6, 2003, Westernbank granted the Debtor a $1.5 million line of credit to fund Debtor's operational expenses under, among other things, the two contracts with DVC. Westernbank's credit line was secured by the accounts receivable from the two DVC contracts. Westernbank properly perfected its security interests by filing financing statements with the Puerto Rico Department of State on March 18, 2003. On November 26, the Debtor obtained a loan from Eurobank that was also secured by the accounts from the DVC contracts. Eurobank properly filed its financing statements to perfect its security interests on December 6, 2003.

On October 31, 2005, the Debtor filed for relief under Chapter 11 of the United States Bankruptcy Code. The case was later converted to a Chapter 7 proceeding. At the time of the Debtor's petition, DVC owed the Debtor $900,000 for work done under the two contracts. DVC has paid that amount to the Chapter 7 trustee, who holds it pending resolution of this matter. Westernbank and Eurobank have both asserted claims to the $900,000 owed under the DVC contracts.

II. LEGAL ANALYSIS

It is undisputed and admitted by both parties that their respective perfected security interests do, in fact, cover the accounts receivable over The Projects. Both parties agree that Westernbank's security interest was recorded before Eurobank's security interest at the Puerto Rico Department of State. However, Eurobank claims that the general rule of "first in time, first in right" does not apply to its security interest because the same is a PMSI, which is excepted from the general rule and takes priority over previously perfected security interests.

To resolve the super priority issue among these competing secured creditors, we begin our analysis by looking at the priority dispositions of the Puerto Rico Uniform Commercial Code.

A) Priorities under the Puerto Rico Uniform Commercial Code

The Puerto Rico Uniform Commercial Code, also known as the Commercial Transactions Act (known in the Spanish language as the "Ley de Transacciones Comerciales"), *19 L.P.R.A. §§401 et seq.*, was enacted through Law No. 208 of August 17, 1995 (hereafter referenced to as the "PR–UCC"). By creating the PR–UCC, the Puerto Rico legislature adopted nine (9) of the thirteen (13) articles of the Model Uniform Commercial Code (the "UCC"), the premier commercial statute which has been incorporated, either in whole or in part, by the fifty (50) states, the District of Columbia and the Virgin Islands.

Article 9 of the UCC, one of the articles adopted by the PR–UCC, contains provisions regarding security interests, negotiable instruments, and consignments. *19 L.P.R.A. §§2001–2207.* Those transactions covered by the Commercial Transactions Act shall be applicable to, including "any transaction (regardless of its form) which is intended to create a security interest in personal property or fixtures including goods, documents, instruments, general intangibles, chattel paper or accounts." *19 L.P.R.A. §2002(a).* In order for the security interest to be perfected over personal property, including chattel paper and accounts, the financing statement must be filed at the Puerto Rico Department of State. *19 L.P.R.A. §2151(b).*

Section 9–312 of the PR–UCC lists the order of priorities with regards to conflicting security interests over the same collateral. The same reads, at its pertinent parts:

> (1) ...
>
> (2) ...
>
> (3) A perfected purchase money security interest in inventory has priority over a conflicting security interest in the same inventory and also has priority in identifiable cash proceeds received on or before the delivery of the inventory to a buyer [under certain circumstances].
>
> (4) A purchase money security interest in collateral other than inventory has priority over a conflicting security interest in the same collateral or its proceeds if the purchase money security interest is perfected at the time the debtor receives possession of the collateral or within thirty (30) days thereafter.
>
> (5) In all cases not governed by other rules stated in this section (including cases of purchase money security interests which do not

qualify for the special priorities set forth in subsections (3) and (4) of this section), priority between conflicting security interests in the same collateral shall be determined according to the following rules:

(a) Conflicting security interests rank according to priority in time of filing or perfection. Priority dates from the time a filing is first made covering the collateral or the time the security interest is first perfected, whichever is earlier, provided that there is no period thereafter when there is neither filing nor perfection.

(b) So long as conflicting security interests are unperfected, the first to attach has priority.

(6) ...

(7) ...

19 L.P.R.A. §2112.

When there are more than one perfected security interests covering the same collateral, the general rule of priority is that the security interest whose financing statement was registered first at the Puerto Rico Department of State shall be superior over the security interest whose financing statement was registered later. *19 L.P.R.A. §2112(5).* This general maxim is known as the "first in time, first in right" rule. This rule, however, is not absolute. One of the exceptions to the same is the purchase money security interest. *19 L.P.R.A. §2112(3)-(4).*

1) PURCHASE MONEY SECURITY INTEREST ("PMSI")

The traditional concept of a PMSI is described as follows:

> The purchase money secured creditor is often the seller of a product who has retained a security interest [over said product] to secure its purchase price. ...

> James J. White & Robert S. Summers, Uniform Commercial Code, Hornbook Series, at 846 (5th ed. 2004).

In other words, "[a] purchase money security interest ... can be either an interest that a seller of property retains to secure the property's purchase price or an interest taken by a creditor who gives value to enable a debtor to acquire rights in the collateral." Dana L. McAlister, Purchase Money Security Interests and Their Continuing Priority as to Proceeds, *34 Boston College L.Rev. 655, 656 (1993).*

PMSIs are granted "super priority" over a prior security interest covering the same collateral in order to prevent a "stranglehold" by a floating lienor on debtor's future access to money from other creditors. By providing this preferential treatment to PMSIs, the UCC tries to avoid the situation where:

> an un-yielding creditor may be able to frustrate future outside borrowing by his debtor, since any future lender will be confronted with

the fait accompli of a prior perfected security interest that gives the al-ready [sic] secured party priority even for subsequent advances. Article 9 mitigates this undesirable consequence of the floating lien by affording a special priority to the 'purchase money' lender. The Code's favorable treatment of the purchase money lender rests on a general policy ... of giving new money priority protection over old.

Thomas H. Jackson & Anthony T. Kronman, A Plea for the Financing Buyer, Yale L.J., Vol. 85, No. 1–2, at 1 (1975).

See also, 1A–7B Secured Transactions under the UCC §7B.05("the purchase money priority 'frees' the debtor to turn to other financers when it decides to acquire new assets").

For these reasons, a PMSI will trump a previously perfected security interest and disregard the general rule of "first in time, first in right."

III. Discussion

In order to consider whether Eurobank's security interest qualifies for super priority status as a PMSI, Eurobank must show that it either complies with Section 9–107(a) or Section 9–107(b) of the PR–UCC, *19 L.P.R.A. §2007.*

Section 9–107 of the PR–UCC states:

> A security interest is a 'purchase money security interest' to the extent that it is
>
> (a) Taken or retained by the seller of the collateral to secure all or part of its price, or
>
> (b) taken by a person who by making advances or incurring an obligation gives value to enable the debtor to acquire rights in or the use of collateral if such value is in fact so used.

Id.

A PMSI under Section 9–107(a) is "inspired by the traditional conditional sales contract: the seller retaining 'title' to secure the purchase price of the goods ... ." 1A–7B Secured Transactions under the UCC §7B.04. Section 9–107(a) is inapplicable to the instant case in light of the fact that Eurobank's transaction consists of a financing transaction to provide funds for the construction of the Comerio and Villalba projects, and is not a sales agreement of any kind. Therefore, Eurobank's security interest does not qualify as a PMSI under Section 9–107(a).

Whether Eurobank's security interest qualifies as a PMSI under Section 9–107(b), the Court must consider if Eurobank, through the financing granted to Deckers, and the security interests created therein: (1) extended new value to Deckers; (2) to be used to enable Deckers to acquire rights in the accounts receivable; and (3) whether Deckers used said value for the intended purpose of acquiring rights over the accounts receivable of The Projects. See

MBank Alamo Nat'l Ass'n. v. Raytheon Co., 886 F.2d 1449, 1453 (5th Cir.1989) (the creditor moving for PMSI consideration over accounts receivable must show "(1) that it gave value; (2) that the value given enabled [the debtor] to acquire rights in the accounts receivable; and (3) that the accounts receivable qualify as collateral within the meaning of the statute.").

These factors must be scrutinized in the following fashion:

(1) *New value vs. antecedent debt.* The purchase money creditor took its interest to secure new value either in the form of an advance, an obligation or the delivery of the collateral itself. As comment 2 to old Section 9–107 stated: "any security interest taken as security for or in satisfaction of a preexisting claim or antecedent debt" is excluded from the purchase money category.

(2) *Acquisition vs. retention or production or generation.* **The purchase money creditor enabled the acquisition of the collateral rather than enabling the retention of the assets or their production or generation in the debtor enterprise …**

(3) *Intent vs. happenstance.* **A creditor who disbursed funds for general operational purposes that did not involve acquisitions was not moved into the purchase money category. …**

Secured Transactions under the UCC §7B.04 (emphasis added).

A) NEW VALUE

Both Eurobank's financing and security agreements over the Villalba and Comerio Projects indicate that Eurobank did, in fact, advance funds to Deckers. Said financing was for the construction of The Projects, guaranteed by a security interest in the accounts receivable that each of the construction projects would generate.

According to Section 1–201(44) of the PR–UCC, a person gives value when he acquires rights:

(a) In return for a binding commitment to extend credit or for the extension of immediately available credit whether or not drawn upon and whether or not a charge-back is provided for in the event of difficulties in collection; or

(b) as security for or in total or partial satisfaction of a pre-existing claim; or

(c) by accepting delivery pursuant to a preexisting contract for purchase, or

(d) generally, in return for any consideration sufficient to support a simple contract.

19 L.P.R.A. §451(44). See, e.g., MBank Alamo, 886 F.2d at 1452

("The value requirement is satisfied by any consideration sufficient to support a simple contract.").

Based on the above, it is clear from the contractual documentation that Eurobank, through the financing extended on November 26, 2003, meets the "value" portion of the PMSI analysis.

B) THE VALUE ENABLED THE ACQUISITION OF THE COLLATERAL

Both Eurobank and Westernbank cite the same case law to support their respective positions as to whether Eurobank's security interest over the accounts receivable of The Projects qualify as a PMSI under Section 9–107(b):[1] *Northwestern Nat'l Bank v. Lectro Syst., Inc., 262 N.W.2d 678 (Minn.1977), In re Woodworks Contemporary Furniture, Inc., 44 B.R. 971 (Bankr.W.D.Wis.1984), MBank, 886 F.2d 1449,* and *First Interstate Bank of Utah v. Internal Rev. Serv., 930 F.2d 1521 (10th Cir.1991).*

Of the four cases relied upon by the parties, the decision of *MBank Alamo, 886 F.2d 1449,* provides us with the most comprehensive discussion as to the general concept and requirements of PMSIs. In MBank Alamo, the Court of Appeals for the Fifth Circuit, with regards to the second and third prongs of the test, the court expressed that:

> To create a PMSI, **the value must be given in a manner that enables the debtor to acquire [an] interest in the collateral**. This is accomplished when a debtor uses an extension of credit or loan money to purchase a specific item. *See Ingram v. Ozark Prod. Credit Assoc., 468 F.2d 564, 565 (5th Cir.1972); In re Dillon, 18 Bankr. [B.R.] 252, 254 (Bkrtcy.E.D.Cal.1982)* (PMSI lien attaches to item actually purchased); Jackson & Kronman, Secured Financing and Priorities Among Creditors, 88 Yale L.J. 1143, 1165 (1979) (PMSI priority limited "to loans that can be traced to identifiable, discrete items of property.").
>
> *Id. at 1453*(emphasis added).

---

1   From a philosophical standpoint, there has been some debate as to whether accounts receivable can even enjoy PMSI status. Uniform Commercial Code, Hornbook Series, at 847("Except when they are proceeds, security interests in accounts receivable and other intangibles will not enjoy purchase money status."). However, it has been considered that, "although traditionally the only type of purchase money security interest the law has concerned itself with is that in goods, there is no reason why the purchase money concept should not apply to intangible property such as contract rights." *In re Woodworks, 44 B.R. at 972 (citing Gilmore, The Purchase Money Priority, 76 Harvard Law Review 1333, 1374).*

Defendant has not raised the issue of whether accounts receivable qualify for PMSI status. Therefore, the Court will make no determination whatsoever as to the applicability of one viewpoint over the other on this matter.

The decisive factors under the second and third prongs of the three part test rely on the interplay between "value given" and "acquisition of collateral." The collateral must be obtained on or after the debtor receives the new value, and that said collateral was obtained as a result of such value. *Id.*

The court in Northwestern reasoned that the definition of a PMSI "contemplates that the loaned funds be intended, and actually used, for the purchase of an identifiable asset which stands as the secured party's collateral." *262 N.W.2d at 680.* The Northwestern court denied the creditor super priority status because "[t]his is not a case in which funds were advanced and used for purchase of a receivable; the contract was already in existence between Agate and Lectro when Cox loaned funds to Agate and entered into a security agreement with it." *Id.* This case supports the notion that accounts receivable that stem from an already existing contract prior to obtaining new value by the creditor, may not qualify for PMSI status.

In the case of *Woodworks, 44 B.R. 971, 973,* which makes reference to the decision in Northwestern, the Bankruptcy Court for the Western District of Wisconsin expressed that transactions in which funds were loaned so that borrowers could perform under preexisting contracts do not fall within the scope of a PMSI.

Finally, in the case of *First Interstate, 930 F.2d at 1526–1527,* the Court of Appeals for the Tenth Circuit states that, in a situation where a lender advances funds to a debtor for operational expenses to allow the debtor to fulfill preexisting contractual obligations, and for which the debtor, in turn, extends a security interest over the accounts receivable of said obligations to the lender, said transaction does not constitute a PMSI.

> An important distinction exists between funds extended for asset acquisition and those extended for the ordinary operation of business. A brightline demarcation must always exist between these two purposes. To accept the lender's contention in this case would be to blur, if not eliminate, that line … Accordingly, we conclude that the right to perform the pre-existing executory contract in this case is not "collateral" or the "rights in collateral" within the requirements of the U.C.C.

> Id.

The instant case contains a similar situation to the one considered in *Woodworks* and *First Interstate.* Particularly as to the fact that:

> (1) we are dealing with a situation in which Deckers had already incurred in [sic] preexisting contractual obligations at the time it incurred in the financing with Eurobank (i.e., the constructions contracts entered between Deckers and DVC and Comerio Housing, as well as between Deckers and DVC and Villalba Housing);

> (2) the financing was obtained for purposes of allowing Deckers to perform under the preexisting construction contracts; and

(3) while the financing did allow Debtor to perform under the construction contracts, the advance was not intended, nor actually used, for the purchase of an identifiable asset which stands as Eurobank's collateral (i.e., the accounts receivable). *See Northwestern, 262 N.W.2d at 679; Woodworks, 44 B.R. at 973; First Interstate, 930 F.2d at 1526–1527.*

The "acquisition" of Decker's right to generate and receive accounts receivable under The Projects took place back on January 10, 2002, when Deckers entered into the construction contracts with DVC, Comerio Housing, and Villalba Housing. Through the financing provided, Eurobank supplied funds to Deckers for the construction of the Comerio and Villalba Projects, and not for the specific purpose to allow Deckers to purchase or acquire rights on any accounts receivable. The accounts receivable were given as a security for the repayment of the monies loaned for the construction of The Projects.

It is clear from the facts at hand that Eurobank's value enabled Deckers to fulfill its obligations under the preexisting construction contracts. Said value did not enable Deckers to acquire any rights or interest over the accounts receivable of The Projects. Furthermore, we are not faced with a situation in which the funds were advanced exclusively for purposes of allowing Deckers to acquire and/or purchase new accounts receivables. *Woodworks, 44 B.R. at 973; MBank Alamo, 886 F.2d at 1453.* In other words, Eurobank "did nothing more than fund the debtor's performance of its contracts in its ordinary business operations; it did not enable the debtor to acquire a discrete new asset." *First Interstate, 930 F.2d at 1524.*

In view of the foregoing, by having extended financing solely to permit Deckers to perform under a pre-existing executory contract, Eurobank's security interest in this case does not qualify as "collateral" or the "rights in collateral" within the scope of a PMSI pursuant to Section 9–107(b) of the PR–UCC.

* * *

For the reasons stated above, the Court finds that Eurobank's security interests do not fall within the scope of a PMSI under Section 9–107 of the PR–UCC, *19 L.P.R.A. §2007.* Consequently, the applicable priority scheme in the instant case is the general rule of "first in time, first in right" contained at Section 9–312(5) of the PR–UCC, *19 L.P.R.A. §2112(5).*

In light of the undisputed and admitted fact that Westernbank filed its financing statement before Eurobank at the Puerto Rico Department of State, the Court hereby finds that Westernbank's security interest has priority over Eurobank in the accounts receivable of the Villalba and Comerio projects.

PROBLEM 5-3

Ray sold a commercial grade refrigeration system to the only upscale restaurant in town. He retained a security interest in the system to secure the restaurant's promise to pay. The restaurant's equipment was already subject to a security interest held by the bank, and the bank had included an after acquired property clause in its security agreement, which covered equipment acquired by the restaurant. Ray filed a financing statement covering the transaction three days after the system was delivered to the restaurant. As between Ray and the bank, which secured party has priority to the refrigeration system? See 9-324.

PROBLEM 5-4

Would your answer be different in Problem 5-3 if Ray had filed his financing statement 23 days after the refrigeration system was delivered to the restaurant? See 9-324.

Still PMSI, No Super Priority

PROBLEM 5-5

Ray sold a commercial grade washer-dryer combo to the local laundromat, on credit, retaining a security interest in the combo. Four days after the combo was delivered, the bank loaned the laundromat $20,000 and took a security interest in all of the laundromat's equipment, including after acquired equipment. The bank filed a financing statement the same day it made the loan. Ray filed his financing statement covering the washer-dryer combo ten days after the bank filed its financing statement. When the laundromat stopped paying, the bank it repossessed all of the laundromat's equipment and has refused to turn the washer-dryer combo over to Ray, claiming that it has priority because Ray's security interest was unperfected at the time the bank filed its financing statement. Is the bank correct—does it have priority over Ray? Could the bank claim priority under the first to file rule—since it filed its financing statement before Ray filed his? See 9-317 and 9-324.

→ Bank wins under 1st in Time

PROBLEM 5-6

Ray leased a bakery oven to the local grocery store which had decided to make "homemade" baked goods available to its customers. The lease was for 12 months and included an option to purchase the oven that could be exercised any time prior to the expiration of the lease. At the time the lease was made, the bank had a security interest in all of the grocery store's equipment. The bank's security agreement included an after acquired property clause covering equipment. Six months into the lease, the grocery store exercised its option to purchase the oven and signed a security agreement giving Ray a security interest in the oven. Ray immediately filed a financing statement covering the oven. A representative of the bank has told Ray that if the grocery store

Even if Bank had PMSI, each Transaction has to independently qualify for PM status
✱ So Bank could have PMSI in initial equip but Not through AAPC ✱

defaulted on its obligations, the bank's security interest in the oven would have priority over Ray's security interest. Is the banker correct? Why might the bank believe it is entitled to priority? When does the 20 day filing period begin to run for a purchase money security interest? See 9-324.

IN RE LEADING EDGE PORK, LLC.
United States Bankruptcy Court, C.D. Illinois
No. 09-82789, 2010 Bankr. LEXIS 2299
(Bankr. C.D. Ill. July 26, 2010)

PERKINS, *Chief Bankruptcy Judge*.

This matter is before the Court on cross motions for partial summary judgment filed by each of the Defendants, Heritage Bank of Central Illinois (HERITAGE BANK or the BANK) and Lone Hollow, LLC (LONE HOLLOW). The Debtor, Leading Edge Pork, LLC (DEBTOR) is the Plaintiff but is not participating in the summary judgment process.

The two-count complaint seeks declaratory relief to resolve a priority dispute between the Defendants as to conflicting security interests in certain weaner pigs, and to determine whether LONE HOLLOW misapplied certain payments. The cross motions are "partial" because only the priority dispute is at issue.

FACTUAL AND PROCEDURAL BACKGROUND

The DEBTOR filed for relief under Chapter 11 of the Bankruptcy Code on September 1, 2009. This adversary complaint was filed on October 5, 2009. According to the complaint, the DEBTOR is a swine "integrator" in that it purchases piglets from third party sources and pays other third party growers to raise them to market weight. The DEBTOR retains ownership of the swine while in possession of the growers.

HERITAGE BANK has a lending relationship with the DEBTOR that dates back almost a decade. According to its proof of claim, the DEBTOR owed HERITAGE BANK in excess of $5.0M as of the petition date. HERITAGE BANK has a valid, perfected non-purchase money security interest in the DEBTOR'S livestock.

LONE HOLLOW sold the DEBTOR weaner pigs in 2009 on credit and took back a purchase money security interest (PMSI) in the pigs it sold, creating a priority conflict with HERITAGE BANK. Section 9–324 of the Uniform Commercial Code permits a purchase money livestock lender to prime a prior perfected non-PMSI livestock lender if four conditions are met:

(1) the purchase-money security interest is perfected when the debtor receives possession of the livestock;

(2) the purchase-money secured party sends an authenticated notification to the holder of the conflicting security interest;

(3) the holder of the conflicting security interest receives the notification within six months before the debtor receives possession of the livestock; and

(4) the notification states that the person sending the notification has or expects to acquire a purchase-money security interest in livestock of the debtor and describes the livestock.

810 ILCS 5/9–324(d).

It is undisputed that LONE HOLLOW perfected its security interest in the weaner pigs it sold DEBTOR by filing a properly completed UCC–1 Financing Statement with the Illinois Secretary of State on June 9, 2009. Thereafter, LONE HOLLOW made five sales of pigs to DEBTOR, on or about June 10, 2009, June 12, 2009, June 15, 2009, June 29, 2009 and July 13, 2009. HERITAGE BANK concedes that the four conditions required by Section 9–324(d) are met with respect to the later three sales; only the first two, the June 10 and June 12 sales, are challenged.

PERFECTED 6/9/09

Since the UCC–1 was filed on June 9, HERITAGE BANK concedes that the first of the four statutory conditions is satisfied. The latter three conditions are disputed. Two communications are at issue. An e-mail was sent on June 9, 2009, at 6:34 p.m. by Gary Donley on behalf of LONE HOLLOW. It was sent to HERITAGE BANK via a website maintained on behalf of HERITAGE BANK that is freely accessible by the general public and that offers website-based e-mail to the public as a convenient means of communicating with HERITAGE BANK. Donley named Scott Hedden as the intended recipient. Hedden is an officer of HERITAGE BANK who was identified to LONE HOLLOW by the DEBTOR (through Wayne Peugh) as the person to receive notices concerning PMSI's. HERITAGE BANK concedes that Hedden is an appropriate contact person. The e-mail, in its entirety, states:

> Scott—Wayne Peugh gave me your contact information with regard to Purchase Money Security Interest for pigs delivered from Lone Hollow.

E-mails sent from the website are manually routed, by HERITAGE BANK employees, to the individual recipients' e-mail inboxes. The Donley e-mail was forwarded to Hedden at 8:13 a.m. on June 10, 2009.

The second communication sent by Donley to Hedden was mailed from Carthage, Illinois, on Friday, June 12, 2009. The single page document is on LONE HOLLOW letterhead, addressed to Scott Hedden at HERITAGE BANK'S address in Trivoli, Illinois, and is manually signed by Donley. It bears the heading: NOTICE OF PURCHASE MONEY SECURITY INTEREST. The entire substance of the notice is as follows:

> Ladies and Gentlemen:

> We understand that you hold a security interest in the inventory of Leading Edge Pork LLC ("Buyer").

Pursuant to Section 9–324(b) of the Uniform Commercial Code, we hereby notify you that Lone Hollow LLC ("Seller") has acquired or expects to acquire a purchase money security interest in swine sold by Seller to Buyer at any time, wherever located, together with all proceeds thereof.

Please call me at [phone number omitted] if you have any questions regarding this security interest.

The record contains no direct evidence as to the date and time the mailed notice was delivered to HERITAGE BANK by the U.S. Postal Service. The record does contain an e-mail from Hedden to Peugh sent Tuesday, June 16, 2009, at 4:15 p.m. that refers to the mailed notice as an attachment.

ANALYSIS

Donley's second communication to Hedden cites Section 9–324(b) instead of 9–324(d). The reference to subsection (b) is incorrect, but immaterial. Subsection (b), providing for a 5–year effective period for a priming notice, applies to a PMSI in inventory. Subsection (d), providing only a 6–month effective period, covers a PMSI in livestock that are farm products. What if the livestock are also the farmer's inventory? The question is resolved by application of the canon of statutory construction that the specific controls the general. ... "Inventory" is more general than "livestock," which is often a particular subset of inventory. Thus, a seller of livestock is stuck with the shorter effective period in Section 9–324(d), like it or not, and may not weasel his way into the 5–year period in Section 9–324(b) by calling himself an inventory lender.[2] Nevertheless, there was no prejudice to HERITAGE BANK, so Donley's mistaken reference to Section 9–324(b) is immaterial.

A party seeking to enforce a statutory lien must strictly comply with the statutory requirements. *Meier v. Olivero, 279 Ill.App.3d 630, 216 Ill.Dec. 600, 665 N.E.2d 858 (Ill.App. 3 Dist.1996).* Actual notice by the party against whom the lien is sought to be enforced does not excuse a failure of strict compliance. *Id.* Strict compliance by those parties seeking to obtain the protections offered by Article 9 of the Uniform Commercial Code has long been required. See *In re Dittmer, 102 B.R. 143 (Bankr.C.D.Ill.1988); McCarthy v. BMW Bank of North America, 509 F.3d 528, 530 (D.C.Cir.2007).* Moreover, the priming lien obtainable by a PMSI lender upon compliance with the conditions of section 9–324 is in derogation of the long-standing principle of "first in time, first in right" that otherwise protects the holder of a prior perfected security interest, which is an additional reason why strict compliance with the statutory conditions should be required. See *In re Superior Equipment, Inc., 195 B.R. 77, 79 (Bankr.C.D.Ill.1996).* Significantly, the district court for this district recently ruled that strict compliance with the noticing requirements

_____

2   Presumably, the shorter period applicable to purchase money livestock lenders relates to the customary practice of long-term lenders making advances to farmers on an annual or semi-annual basis. So a PMSI livestock lender must send a new notice every 6 months to retain priming rights.

of section 9–324(b) is required of a purchase money lender.[3] *In re Sports Pub., Inc.*, 2010 WL 750008 (C.D.Ill.2010) (McCuskey, C.J.) (strict compliance required because a PMSI is an exception to general rule of first in time to perfect has priority). The district court rejected the suggestion that substantial compliance was sufficient, finding that giving the prior lender a copy of the security agreement which referred to "purchase money security interest" did not amount to the authenticated notice required by the statute.

There is no dispute about what Donley's June 9, 2009, e-mail says. Whether it satisfies the content requirements of section 9–324(d)(4) is a question of law that is properly decided at the summary judgment stage. In this Court's view, it does not. Most significantly, the e-mail fails to identify Leading Edge Pork, LLC, the BANK'S borrower, as the entity to whom purchase money credit sales of pigs were to be made. The reference to Wayne Peugh, an individual representative of the DEBTOR, is not an adequate substitute. Neither does the e-mail state that LONE HOLLOW has or expects to acquire a PMSI. The indefinite reference to Hedden as the contact person "with regard" to PMSI is not sufficient. Under the strict compliance standard, the e-mail does not meet the content requirements of section 9–324(d)(4).[4]

The second notice, mailed by Donley to Hedden on June 12, 2009, clearly satisfies the content requirements of section 9–324(d)(4). Signed by Donley, it is also properly authenticated as required by section 9–324(d)(2). *See* 810 ILCS 5/9–102(a)(7). So, the only possible issue is compliance with 9–324(d)(3). That subsection requires a comparison of the timing of two events: (1) the receipt of the notification by HERITAGE BANK, and (2) the receipt by the DEBTOR of the weaner pigs sold by LONE HOLLOW. In order to prevail, LONE HOLLOW must establish that the BANK received the notification before the DEBTOR received the pigs. The analysis permits no ties; if necessary, the timing must be established down to the minute that the event occurred.

The evidence in the record does not permit the timing of either event to be determined. The earliest that the mailed notice could have been received at the BANK is Saturday, June 13, 2009. Theoretically, it could have been brought to Hedden's attention that day for purposes of 810 ILCS 5/1–202(e)(1) or (f).

Although unlikely, it is also theoretically possible (as an inference that must be drawn in favor of LONE HOLLOW) that possession of the pigs sold by LONE HOLLOW on June 12, 2009, and even those sold on June 10,

---

3   Other than the period for which the notice is effective, the requirements of subsections (b) and (d) of section 9–324 are identical.

4   The cryptic e-mail reads as if it was intended as a prelude to the sending, subsequently, of more specific information about the LONE HOLLOW PMSI. Of course, the intent or state of mind of Donley, as sender, and Hedden, as recipient, is immaterial. Compliance with section 9–324(d) is accomplished by the delivery of a written "notification," and is not dependent upon "actual knowledge" of the recipient. See 810 ILCS 5/1–202.

2009, were not received by the DEBTOR until June 13, 2009, or later. The record contains no evidence of when the DEBTOR received possession of these two shipments.[5]

So there are three unresolved facts that preclude summary judgment: (1) when did the DEBTOR receive the pigs sold on June 10 and 12, 2009, (2) when did Hedden become aware of the mailed notification, and (3) when did HERITAGE BANK receive the mailed notification. If in fact, however, the pigs were received by the DEBTOR on or before June 12, 2009, then LONE HOLLOW'S priming claim must fail for lack of compliance with section 9–324(d)(3).

In light of these genuine issues of material fact, both motions must be denied. Nevertheless, the Court determines that section 9–324(d) is the provision applicable to the transactions in question. The Court further determines that the June 9, 2009, e-mail sent by Donley to Hedden does not constitute an authenticated notification that complies with the content requirements of section 9–324(d)(4). The Court further determines that the notice mailed by Donley to Hedden on June 12, 2009, satisfies the content requirements of section 9–324(d)(4) and the authentication requirement of section 9–324(d)(2).

PROBLEM 5–7

Ray wants to add Fisher-Paykel appliances to the product pool he sells at his store. Fisher-Paykel is willing to provide product on credit in return for a security interest in all appliances it delivers to the store. The only issue holding up an agreement with Fisher-Paykel is its concern that the bank's security interest in Ray's inventory, which includes after acquired inventory, will have priority over any security interest Fisher-Paykel takes in the product it delivers. What should Fisher-Paykel do to avoid having its security interest subordinated to the bank's security interest? See 9-324.

PROBLEM 5–8

Could Fisher-Paykel satisfy the notice requirement in the last Problem by simply calling up the bank and providing the details of its agreement with Ray? What if it sends the notice before delivering the appliances to Ray, but the bank does not actually receive the notice until after Ray has the appliances

---

5   Donley's affidavit, attached as an exhibit to Document No. 34, is direct evidence of when pigs sold on June 10 were loaded. The issue, however, is the time of delivery. Donley, apparently, has no personal knowledge of that fact. To the extent that an inference could be drawn (as Donley draws it) that delivery occurred at noon or in the afternoon on June 10, the Court is not permitted to draw that inference (no matter how likely it is) at this stage, where all inferences must favor the non-moving party.

in his store? The court in *Leading Edge Pork* determined that the notice must be received before the goods are delivered. Is that the only possible construction of 9-324(b)?

C. FUTURE ADVANCES

Commercial financing often involves a long-term relationship between a debtor and a lender during which the lender makes multiple loans to the debtor. If our appliance dealer, Ray, sells most of his inventory on credit, there may be times when he needs an infusion of cash to fund the day-to-day operations of the shop while he waits for his customers to make their monthly payments. If the bank with a security interest in his equipment and accounts receivable loans him additional cash during these low cash periods, are these new loans secured by the equipment and accounts receivable that served as collateral for the bank's first loan? And if they are collateral for the new loans, how do we determine the priority of the bank's security interest for each of the new loans? Does priority date from the time of each loan? Does it matter whether Ray has given another lender a security interest in the same equipment and accounts receivable between the bank's original loan and the new loans?

Whether the bank's original collateral also secures the new loans—what Article 9 calls future advances—depends initially on what the security agreement between the bank and Ray provides. Under Article 9, a security agreement can include a future advance clause, the effect of which is to make the collateral described serve as collateral for any future loans made by the secured party to the debtor. 9-204. But even if the security agreement does not include a future advance clause, the parties can accomplish the same thing by simply creating a new security agreement which provides that the new loan is secured by the original collateral. Thus, all a future advance clause does is save paper—eliminating the need to create a new security agreement for each new loan.

As to the priority of the bank's security interests for the new loans, the general rule is that priority does not date from the time of the advance—the bank has the same priority as to the future advances that it had with respect to its initial loan. If the bank perfected its original security interest by filing a financing statement on July 1, 2013, its priority for each of the new loans would date from July 1, 2013, even though the new loans were made long after July 1, 2013. There are several exceptions to the general rule, which we will explore in the problems that follow.

ALLIS-CHALMERS CREDIT CORP. v. CHENEY INV., INC.
Supreme Court of Kansas
227 Kan. 4 (1980)

PRAGER, *Justice.*

This is a dispute between two secured creditors over the priority of their security interests in an Allis-Chalmers combine. The facts in the case are undisputed and are covered generally by a stipulation of facts filed by the parties in district court. The factual circumstances giving rise to the controversy are set out in chronological order as follows:

On November 16, 1970, Lloyd Catlin executed a retail installment contract to Ochs, Inc., a dealer for Allis-Chalmers Corporation, to cover the purchase price of an Allis-Chalmers combine identified as G-7754. This contract was in a total amount of $10,149.44 including the financing charge. There was no provision in the contract for future advances. In the course of the opinion, this will be referred to as contract # 1. This contract was assigned to plaintiff-appellant, Allis-Chalmers Credit Corporation, who financed the transaction. On November 27, 1970, a financing statement covering combine G-7754 was filed by Allis-Chalmers with the register of deeds of Barber County, Kansas.

On December 19, 1970, Cheney Investment Company, Inc., the defendant-appellee, made a cash advance to Lloyd Catlin, taking a security interest (chattel mortgage) in combine G-7754. On December 24, 1970, Cheney Investment filed a financing statement covering combine G-7754 with the Barber County register of deeds. In the course of the opinion, we will refer to the security interest of Cheney Investment as the chattel mortgage. On September 17, 1971, Catlin purchased a new Allis-Chalmers combine G-17992 from Highway Garage and Implement Company, another dealer of Allis-Chalmers. The retail installment contract which created the security interest included both the new combine, G-17992, and the used combine, G-7754. This contract will be referred to in the opinion as contract # 2. Contract # 2 provided that contract # 1 was cancelled and the notation "Payoff ACCC-Wichita $4,542.00" was written on its first page. The balance owing under contract # 1 was included in the purchase price stated in contract # 2. There was no other reference to the prior security agreement or financing statement. On September 29, 1971, Allis-Chalmers Credit Corporation, as assignee of contract # 2 from Highway Garage and Implement Company, filed a financing statement covering both the new combine G-17992 and the used combine G-7754. On February 16, 1972, Allis-Chalmers notified Cheney Investment of its claim to a senior security interest on combine G-7754, as Cheney had taken possession of that combine when Catlin defaulted on his loan payments to Cheney Investment.

On May 30, 1972, Allis-Chalmers and Cheney Investment executed a letter agreement to allow combine G-7754 to be returned to Catlin, the debtor, with each party to notify the other if Catlin defaulted on either financing agreement. On September 11, 1973, after several revisions and amendments to contract # 2, Catlin sold combine G-17992 and paid Allis-Chalmers $11,641.12, leaving an unpaid balance of $8,300. A new payment schedule was prepared for the balance owing plus a new finance charge. Thereafter, Catlin defaulted on his payments, both to Allis-Chalmers and to Cheney Investment. On March 1, 1974, Cheney Investment sold combine G-7754 at a chattel mortgage sale, having taken possession shortly after Catlin defaulted on the Allis-Chalmers obligation. Allis-Chalmers participated in the sale but was not the purchaser. The sale proceeds totaled $8,560. Subtracting the amount then owing to Cheney Investment and costs, there remained $2,111.80 to satisfy the security interest of Allis-Chalmers.

Following the above events, the plaintiff, Allis-Chalmers, brought this action against Cheney Investment for conversion of combine G-7754, claiming a senior and prior security interest. At that time, Catlin's indebtedness to Allis-Chalmers was in the amount of $8,650 plus interest. In its answer, Cheney Investment claimed a first and prior lien against the combine in the amount of $6,093.79 plus interest. All of the above facts were stipulated by the parties. In addition to the stipulation, the case was submitted on the deposition of Richard F. Ellis, vice-president of Allis-Chalmers. In his deposition, Ellis testified that contract # 1 between Ochs, Inc., and Lloyd Catlin was paid off and canceled at the time contract # 2 was executed and the balance owing on contract # 1 was carried forward and became a part of the consideration for contract # 2. He agreed that contract # 2 was a new and separate contract.

The district court held in favor of defendant Cheney Investment, reasoning that contract # 2 cancelled the prior contract # 1 and was thus an entirely new and separate agreement which created an entirely new and distinct security interest. In its memorandum decision, the trial court emphasized that contract # 1 was one involving only the sale of combine G-7754 and, since it contained no provision covering future advances or sales, it was a distinct and separate transaction from contract # 2. The trial court then concluded that the advances made under contract # 2, dated September 17, 1971, did not relate back and were not covered by the financing statement filed by Allis-Chalmers on November 27, 1970. Thus, it concluded that the intervening security interest of Cheney Investment, created by its chattel mortgage on December 19, 1970, and perfected by the filing of its financing statement on December 24, 1970, was a security interest, senior and prior to the security interest of Allis-Chalmers created by contract # 2 in September of 1971. The trial court entered judgment in favor of defendant Cheney Investment, and Allis-Chalmers has appealed to this court.

The question of priority presented in this case is one of first impression in this state under the Kansas Uniform Commercial Code, K.S.A. 84-1-101 et seq. The subject of secured transactions is covered in Article 9 of the code (84-9-101 through 84-9-508). The question of priorities between conflicting security interests is controlled by K.S.A. 84-9-312(5)(A) [Now 9-322].

In this case, both of the parties have perfected their respective security interests. Simply stated, the issue to be determined is which of their security interests is entitled to priority over the other. Section 84-9-312(5)(A) [Now 9-322] governs the priority as between conflicting security interests. Prior to 1975, K.S.A. 84-9-312 provided in part as follows [Court quotes Kansas version of 9-312(g) [Now 9-323]]:

* * *

It is important to note that the security agreement itself is not filed of record. As pointed out in the official UCC comment to 84-9-402 [Now 9-501], this section adopts a system of "notice filing." The notice itself indicates merely that the secured party may have a security interest in the collateral described. The burden is placed upon other persons to make further inquiry from the parties concerned in order to obtain a disclosure of the complete state of affairs. The code philosophy is that a simple, filed notice that the secured party and debtor *may* be financing with respect to collateral described in the financing statement should be a "red flag" warning to third parties not to proceed with any financing on the same collateral of the debtor until investigation is made to see that the road ahead has been cleared. *See In Re Rivet, 299 F.Supp. 374, 379 (E.D.Mich.1969), citing Professor Roy L. Steinheimer, Jr., of the University of Michigan Law School, in a commentary on 9-402* [Now 9-501] *in 23 M.C.L.A. 467.* In his article, Professor Steinheimer suggests that if there is a prior filing, the second lender should do one of the following things:

> (1) Insist that the record be cleared by the filing of a termination statement under 9-404 [now 9-513], or

> (2) Enter into a subordination agreement with the first lender which appropriately apportions priorities in the collateral under 9-316 [Now 9-339].

The controversy arose in this case, as it has in other cases, because K.S.A. 84-9-312(5)(A) [Now 9-322], as originally adopted, did not have clear and specific language governing the right of a lender to include later advances made in subsequent transactions under the financing statement filed at the time of the original transaction. It should be noted that K.S.A. 84-9-204(5) provided that "(o)bligations covered by a security agreement may include future advances or other value whether or not the advances or value are given pursuant to commitment."

The issue as to the priority of the security interest of a lender, who made advances after the filing of the original financing statement, over the security interest of an intervening creditor came before a Rhode Island superior court in *Coin-O-Matic Service Co. v. Rhode Island Hospital Trust Co., 3 U.C.C.Rptr.Serv. 1112 (R.I.Super.Ct.1966).* The district court in the present case relied upon Coin-O-Matic in holding that the security interest of Cheney Investment was prior to the security interest of Allis-Chalmers. In *Coin-O-Matic,* the debtor gave a security interest in an automobile to the seller, who assigned the debt to Rhode Island Hospital Trust Company which filed a financing statement. One year later, the debtor gave Coin-O-Matic a security interest. It filed a financing statement. The following month, Rhode Island Hospital Trust Company loaned the debtor an additional sum of money, one-third of which was used to pay off the first note to Rhode Island Hospital Trust Company. The first note was cancelled, a new security agreement executed, and a new financing statement filed. When the debtor went into bankruptcy, both Coin-O-Matic Service Company and Rhode Island

Hospital Trust Company claimed a prior security interest in the automobile. Rhode Island Hospital Trust Company argued that the first financing statement was sufficient to protect the second contract, as it effectively put the whole world on notice that the collateral was subject to present and future security interests in favor of the filing party. This argument was rejected by the Rhode Island superior court. The *Coin-O-Matic* court first recognized that giving the first-to-file priority in all subsequent transactions placed the lender in an unusually strong position. The court reasoned that, under such a holding, the debtor would be precluded from obtaining a second loan, even to pay off the first, because subsequent lenders would be reluctant to lend money based on the collateral already mortgaged, as their security interest would always be subject to preemption by a subsequent security agreement in favor of the first creditor. The court stated that to construe the UCC to give the first lender an interest in collateral for future advances, absent future advance provisions in the security agreement, would render information obtained under 9-204 irrelevant. The court noted that the first creditor could easily protect future advances by including a future advance provision as authorized by 9-204(5).

The ultimate conclusion in *Coin-O-Matic* was that a reasonable interpretation of 9-312(5)(A) [Now 9-322] should be that a "single financing statement in connection with a security agreement, when no provision is made for future advances, is not an umbrella for future advances based upon new security agreements, notwithstanding the fact that involved is the same collateral." (3 U.C.C. Rptr.Serv. at 1120.) This portion of the decision in *Coin-O-Matic* caused controversy and widespread criticism of the rule announced therein.

The holding in *Coin-O-Matic*, requiring a future advance clause in the original security instrument in order for future advances to have 9-312 [Now 9-322] priority, has been rejected by the vast majority of the jurisdictions in subsequent cases. In rejecting *Coin-O-Matic*, those courts generally stress the "notice" or "red flag" function of the code and hold that a financing statement on file is notice to the entire world of present or future security interests in the collateral. Cases taking this approach which are contrary to the rule of *Coin-O-Matic* are the following:

> *In Re Rivet*, 299 F.Supp. 374; *First Nat. Bank & T. Co. of Vinita, Okl. v. Atlas Credit Corp.*, 417 F.2d 1081 (10th Cir. 1969); *James Talcott, Inc. v. Franklin National Bank*, 292 Minn. 277, 194 N.W.2d 775 (1972); *In re Wilson*, 13 U.C.C.Rptr.Serv. 1195 (E.D.Tenn.1973); *In Re Gilchrist Company*, 403 F.Supp. 197 (E.D.Pa.1975); *Index Store Fixture Co. v. Farmers' Trust Co.*, 536 S.W.2d 902 (Mo.App.1976); *Thorp Finance v. Ken Hodgins*, 73 Mich.App. 428, 251 N.W.2d 614 (1977); *Matter of Gruder*, 89 Misc.2d 477, 392 N.Y.S.2d 203 (1977); *Genn v. CIT Corp.*, 40 Md.App. 516, 392 A.2d 1135 (1978); *Chrysler Credit Corp. v. Community Banking Co.*, 35 Conn.Sup. 73, 395 A.2d 727 (1978).

The rationale found in *James Talcott, Inc. v. Franklin National Bank*, 292 Minn. at 290-292, 194 N.W.2d at 784, well illustrates the approach taken by those courts which have rejected the rule adopted in *Coin-O-Matic*:

> "Even where the parties originally contemplate a single debt, secured by a single item of property or a single group of items, the secured party and the debtor may enter into further transactions whereby the debtor obtains additional credit and the secured party is granted more security. The validity of such arrangements as against creditors, trustees in bankruptcy, and other secured parties has been widely recognized by many courts. *See, DuBay v. Williams*, 417 F.2d 1277 (9 Cir. 1969); *Grain Merchants of Indiana, Inc. v. Union Bank & Sav. Co.*, 408 F.2d 209 (7 Cir.), *certiorari denied sub nom. France v. Union Bank & Sav. Co.*, 396 U.S. 827, 90 S.Ct. 75, 24 L.Ed.2d 78 (1969); *Rosenberg v. Rudnick*, 262 F.Supp. 635 (D.Mass.1967).

Using future-advance clauses and using after-acquired property clauses in the original security agreement are not the only means by which perfected security interests can be obtained in subsequently contracted obligations or in goods the debtor may later come to own. There is nothing exclusive about s 336.9-204(3, 5). Parties may use future-advance and after-acquired clauses, and they are a great convenience. But, if they are not used, there is nothing in the code which prevents the parties from accomplishing the same result by entering into one or more additional security agreements.

> ... The better view holds that, where originally a security agreement is executed, an indebtedness created, and a financing statement describing the collateral filed, followed at a later date by another advance made pursuant to a subsequent security agreement covering the same collateral, the lender has a perfected security interest in the collateral not only for the original debt but also for the later advance.

Matter of Gruder, 89 Misc.2d at 481, 392 N.Y.S.2d at 206, reached the same result, quoting White & Summers, U.C.C. HB, s 25-4 at p. 908, as follows:

> We reject the *Coin-O-Matic* holding for three reasons. First, it provides little protection against overreaching, for a creditor can avoid the holding simply by including a future advance clause in his security agreement. Second, we suspect that the *Coin-O-Matic* court misunderstands commercial practice. We suspect that it is a rare banker who will lend against the same collateral which secures a prior loan; in our experience the commercial practice is for the second lender to pay off the first and so take a first priority as to all of the collateral. Finally, *Coin-O-Matic* conflicts with the most obvious and we think intended meaning of 9-312(5)(a); if the draftsmen had wished to qualify the rule as the *Coin-O-Matic* court did, they could have done so.

The only case supporting *Coin-O-Matic* called to our attention is *Texas Kenworth v. First Nat. Bank of Bethany, 564 P.2d 222 (Okl.1977)*. We have concluded that the district court in this case was not justified in relying upon the decision in *Coin-O-Matic*. The rule of *Coin-O-Matic* was immediately rejected by the UCC permanent editorial board. It conceded that under the 1962 code, as originally adopted, the position of an intervening creditor in reference to a subsequent advance by an earlier secured party was debatable. In order to clarify the matter, the editorial board suggested an amendment to 84-9-312 by the addition of a new subsection (7) which was subsequently adopted in various states. Subsection (7) was adopted by the Kansas legislature by amendment of K.S.A. 84-9-312 in 1975, effective January 1, 1976. The new subsection (7) may be found at K.S.A.1979 Supp. 84-9-312(7) [Now 9-323] and is as follows:

> (7) If future advances are made while a security interest is perfected by filing or the taking of possession, the security interest has the same priority for the purposes of subsection (5) with respect to the future advances as it does with respect to the first advance. If a commitment is made before or while the security interest is so perfected, the security interest has the same priority with respect to advances made pursuant thereto. In other cases a perfected security interest has priority from the date the advance is made.

The issue has clearly been laid to rest in Kansas by the adoption of the new subsection (7) of K.S.A.1979 Supp. 84-9-312 [Now 9-323] by the Kansas legislature in 1975. We note the official UCC comment to that section which is printed in the 1979 Supp. at p. 64, and which states as follows:

> 7. The application of the priority rules to future advances is complicated. In general, since any secured party must operate in reference to the Code's system of notice, he takes subject to future advances under a priority security interest while it is perfected through filing or possession, whether the advances are committed or non-committed, and to any advances subsequently made 'pursuant to commitment' (Section 9-105) during that period.

Comment (7) is followed by example 5, which sets forth a hypothetical factual situation involving a question of priority which essentially presents the same issue to be decided in this case. It states:

> Example 5. On February 1 A makes an advance against machinery in the debtor's possession and files his financing statement. On March 1 B makes an advance against the same machinery and files his financing statement. On April 1 A makes a further advance, under the original security agreement, against the same machinery (which is covered by the original financing statement and thus perfected when made). A has priority over B both as to the February 1 and as to the April 1 advance and it makes no difference whether or not A knows of B's intervening advance when he makes his second advance.

A wins, as to the April 1 advance, because he first filed even though B's interest attached, and indeed was perfected, before the April 1 advance. The same rule would apply if either A or B had perfected through possession. Section 9-204(3) and the Comment thereto should be consulted for the validation of future advances.

The same result would be reached even though A's April 1 advance was not under the original security agreement, but was under a new security agreement under A's same financing statement or during the continuation of A's possession.

Also note should be taken of the official UCC comment to K.S.A.1979 Supp. 84-9-402 [Now 9-501], which states on p. 75 of the 1979 Supp. as follows:

> However, even in the case of filings that do not necessarily involve a series of transactions the financing statement is effective to encompass transactions under a security agreement not in existence and not contemplated at the time the notice was filed, if the description of collateral in the financing statement is broad enough to encompass them. Similarly, the financing statement is valid to cover after-acquired property and future advances under security agreements whether or not mentioned in the financing statement.

It is clear that subsection (7) [Now 9-323] was adopted by the Kansas legislature to make it clear that K.S.A. 84-9-312(5)(A) [Now 9-322] should be applied to future advances made by the first creditor, whether such advances are "committed" or "noncommitted" thus making it immaterial whether or not there was a future advance provision in the original security agreement. We regard this amendment as a clarification of the original intent of the legislature when it adopted the Uniform Commercial Code in 1965.

On the basis of the reasoning set forth above, we hold that the security interest of Allis-Chalmers in combine G-7754 is prior and superior to the security interest of the defendant, Cheney Investment, Inc. Under the undisputed facts, the proceeds from the sale of the Allis-Chalmers combine G-7754 totaled $8,650. At the time the suit was filed, Catlin's indebtedness to Allis-Chalmers was in the total amount of $8,650 plus interest. Since the security interest of Allis-Chalmers equals or exceeds the amount of the net proceeds received from the sale of the combine, after expenses of sale, Allis-Chalmers is entitled to apply the net proceeds to its debt.

The judgment of the district court is reversed and the case is remanded to the district court with directions to enter judgment in favor of the plaintiff Allis-Chalmers, awarding it the net proceeds from the sale of combine G-7754, after deducting the expenses of sale, together with interest as allowed by law and for the costs of the action.

PROBLEM 5–9

Last week, Ray made the last payment on his loan from the local bank—his obligation is paid in full. The bank had retained a security interest in his inventory and after acquired inventory and it had filed a financing statement to perfect its security interest. Ray now wants to work with a different lender—a national bank with greater resources. National Bank has agreed to loan Ray the money he needs to renovate and expand his store, in return for a security interest in all of his inventory and equipment, including after acquired inventory and equipment. Ray provides the cancelled note from his loan with the local bank—which was stamped "Paid in Full" by the local bank—to the loan officer at National Bank as proof that the local bank no longer had a claim to his inventory. National Bank filed a financing statement to perfect its security interest. Six months after National Bank makes its loan to Ray, Ray needs additional funds to complete the renovation and expansion project. National Bank declines to advance any additional funds, so Ray borrows the rest of the money he needs to finish the project from the local bank. Which bank now has priority to Ray's inventory? Does the local bank's priority turn on whether it had a future advance clause in its security agreement? Does the local bank need to file a new financing statement to obtain priority? See 9-323.

PROBLEM 5–10

As in the last Problem, Ray has paid off the loan he received from local bank in full. The bank has returned the promissory note from the loan to Ray stamped "Paid in Full." One of Ray's disgruntled customers obtains a judgment against Ray and executes the judgment against Ray's inventory. Ray does not inform the bank about the judgment creditor's claim on his inventory when he asks the bank for a new loan he needs to renovate the store. The bank has Ray sign a new security agreement giving it a security interest in the store's inventory and advances him the funds he requests. The bank does not file a new financing statement. As between the bank and the judgment creditor, who has priority to Ray's inventory? Would it matter if the bank knew about the judgment creditor at the time it made the new loan? See 9-323.

PROBLEM 5–11

If in the last Problem, one of Ray's employees had sold a 56" LCD TV to a friend late one night from the loading dock of the store before Ray got the new loan from the bank, could the bank enforce its security interest in the TV—as it was inventory—against the friend? Would it matter if the bank knew about the sale when it made the new loan? What if the new loan was made two months after the sale? See 9-320 and 9-323.

The absence of any express limitation on the use of a future advance clause has troubled many courts. Early on Gilmore had warned:

> Legitimate future advance arrangements are validated under the Code, as indeed they generally were under pre-Code law. This useful device can, however, be abused; it is abused when a lender, relying on a broadly drafted clause, seeks to bring within the shelter of his security arrangement claims against the debtor which are unrelated to the course of financing that was contemplated by the parties.

Gilmore at 932.

Pre-Code courts construing such clauses, which came to be known rather unflatteringly as "dragnet clauses," imposed a "relatedness" requirement on such clauses: a future advance—a new loan—would be secured only to the extent that there was some relationship between the original credit extension and the future advance. In its most simplistic form, the relatedness requirement was articulated in terms of class: the future advance must be of the same class as the original extension of credit. Thus, if the original transaction was in the nature of a consumer transaction, the future advance clause only covered future transactions that involved the personal, household, or family affairs of the debtor. An extension of credit to the debtor's business would not be covered by the future advance clause. But other courts rejected this simplistic categorical approach to demarcating the reach of a future advance clause, relying instead on conventional rules of contract interpretation to discern the agreement of the parties as expressed by the language used in the security agreement itself.

So, when it came time to revise Article 9, there were competing views of how a court should determine the scope of a future advance clause. The following case explains how Revised Article 9 addressed the issue.

FRONTIER FIN. CREDIT UNION v. DUMLAO (IN RE DUMLAO)
United States Bankruptcy Appellate Panel of the Ninth Circuit
2011 WL 4501402 (B.A.P. 9th Cir. Aug. 5, 2011)

JURY, HOLLOWELL, and KWAN, *Bankruptcy Judges*.

This appeal involves the enforceability of a cross collateral clause contained in a security agreement that was signed prepetition by chapter 7 debtor Deborah Dumlao.

In a Memorandum Decision and Order, the bankruptcy court granted summary judgment for debtor, finding that appellant, Frontier Financial Credit Union ("FFCU"), violated the §524 discharge injunction because its asserted lien against debtor's car for her Visa credit card debt was unenforceable. ...

FFCU appeals the bankruptcy court's judgment, arguing that the court erred by ... (2) denying FFCU's motion to dismiss or, in the alterative, for summary judgment because the cross collateral clause was valid and enforceable under Nevada's Uniform Commercial Code ("U.C.C."). ...

For the reasons stated, we REVERSE the bankruptcy court's decision granting summary judgment for debtor and REMAND the case to the bankruptcy court for further proceedings consistent with this disposition.

I. FACTS

Debtor had a credit relationship with FFCU since 2002.

On February 7, 2002, debtor obtained a Visa card from FFCU. Paragraph 8 of the Visa Classic Silver Credit Card Agreement provided that the Visa card debt was secured by debtor's shares in an individual or joint account. It also stated that "[c]ollateral securing other loans you have with the Credit Union may also secure this loan ... ." Debtor had no other loans with FFCU at that time.

On February 3, 2005, debtor and her husband applied for, and obtained, a signature (unsecured) loan for $6,000 through FFCU's Loanliner program. Under the Loanliner program, the member signs a credit agreement. Once the credit agreement has been executed, the member may apply for extensions of credit under the Loanliner Plan (the "Plan"). The Plan provides for the advancement of monies through various subaccounts. When an advance is made, it is memorialized in a document called an advance request voucher. A subaccount advance can be unsecured (signature loan) or secured.

Paragraph 6 of the credit agreement, which was initialed by debtor and her husband, provided:

> Additional security for the Plan may be required at the time of an advance. If a subaccount identifies a type of property (such as "New Cars") you must give that type of property as security when you get an advance under the subaccount. A subaccount name such as "Other Secured" means you must provide security acceptable to us when you obtain an advance under that subaccount. Property you give as security will secure all amounts owed under the Plan and all other loans you have with us now or in the Future, except any loan secured by your principal dwelling. Property securing other loans you have with us may also secure the Plan.

On October 16, 2006, debtor and her husband borrowed $16,285 from FFCU under the Loanliner program to refinance a 2002 Acura RSX Sport vehicle (the "Acura"). In conjunction with the loan, they executed a Loanliner Open–End Voucher and Security Agreement. Under the heading of "Security Offered," the advance loan voucher stated: "[t]he advance is secured by your shares, all property securing other Plan advances and loans received in the past or in the future, and the following property: Acura RSX S Sport, 2002. ..." The voucher further provided below the "Signatures" heading: "[b]y signing below ... you agree ... [t]o make and be bound by the terms of this Security Agreement including the cross collateral clause."

Paragraph 2 of the attached Security Agreement provided:

> What the Security Interest Covers—The security interest secures the advance and any extensions renewals or refinancings of the advance. It also secures any other advances you have now or receive in the future under the Plan and any other amounts or loans, including any credit card loan, you owe us for any reason now or in the future except any loan secured by your principal residence.

On March 25, 2009, debtor filed her chapter 7 bankruptcy petition. In Schedule D, debtor listed FFCU as a creditor owed $10,816 secured by the Acura. In Schedule F, debtor listed FFCU as an unsecured creditor for the $2562 balance owing on her Visa card. FFCU had notice of debtor's bankruptcy, but did not participate in the proceedings. On July 8, 2009, debtor received her discharge and a final decree was entered December 10, 2009.

On February 1, 2010, debtor paid off the loan on her Acura in full and made a demand on FFCU to transfer title. FFCU refused, asserting that the cross collateral clause in the Security Agreement provided that the Acura secured all debt owed to FFCU, including amounts owed on her Visa card. In a March 10, 2010 letter to debtor's attorney, FFCU stated that unless debtor arranged to make payments on her Visa card, FFCU would repossess her car. The letter further stated that FFCU was not seeking to collect a debt against debtor personally.

On June 11, 2010, the court granted debtor's motion to reopen her bankruptcy case.

On June 17, 2010, debtor filed an adversary complaint against FFCU, alleging that her credit card debt was unsecured and discharged in her bankruptcy. Debtor's complaint was not the model of clarity. ...

Recognizing that the central issue was whether FFCU's lien on debtor's Acura also secured her credit card debt, i.e., the validity of the cross collateral clause, FFCU moved to dismiss debtor's complaint or, in the alternative, for summary judgment on July 20, 2010. FFCU argued that the cross collateral clause in the Security Agreement was valid under Nevada Revised Statute ("NRS") 104.9204 so long as the obligations secured by the collateral were within the intent of the parties' agreement. FFCU asserted that the clause was clear and unambiguous and, therefore, valid and enforceable against debtor as a matter of law.

Debtor opposed FFCU's motion, arguing that the cross collateral clause was invalid as to consumer goods (her car) and that Nevada's U.C.C. imposed an obligation of good faith, which FFCU breached. In her opposition, debtor asked the court to deny FFCU's motions or enter judgment for her on the pleadings. ...

Debtor also asserted in a separate statement of undisputed facts, among other things, that (1) when she applied for her Visa card, FFCU did not inform her that if she were to finance an automobile through FFCU that it would become security for charges made on her Visa card; (2) her signature loan agreement mentioned only her and her husband's deposit/share accounts as security, but did not mention credit card debt; and (3) no one from FFCU asked her or her husband to initial any portion of the car loan Security Agreement nor did anyone tell them that the Acura might be used as security for payment of credit card obligations.

On November 3, 2010, the bankruptcy court heard FFCU's motion and took the matter under submission. On November 30, 2010, the court entered its Memorandum Decision and Order granting summary judgment for debtor, finding that the cross collateral clause was unenforceable as a matter of law. The bankruptcy court's few factual findings make it unclear whether the court properly applied the law. The court simply stated that it refused to enforce adhesion agreements and their dragnet clauses, but it offered no reasoning for its conclusion. Moreover, the court construed the credit agreement and later Security Agreement as ambiguous because they did not clearly reference the 2002 Visa Classic Silver Credit Card Agreement. As a result of these conclusions, the court found that debtor's credit card debt was discharged and that FFCU had violated the §524 discharge injunction.

FFCU timely appealed and debtor cross appealed on the issue of damages.

III. ISSUE

Whether the bankruptcy court erred in granting summary judgment for debtor and denying FFCU's motion to dismiss or, in the alternative, for summary judgment.

* * *

V. DISCUSSION

Nevada adopted the revised U.C.C., effective July 1, 2001. Nevada's version of U.C.C. §9–204 on after-acquired property and future advances provides that "[a] security agreement may provide that collateral secures ... future advances or other value, whether or not the advances or value are given pursuant to commitment." NRS 104.9204. Official Comment 5 explains this provision:

> [C]ollateral may secure future as well as past or present advances if the security agreement so provides. This is in line with the policy of this Article toward security interests in after-acquired property under subsection (a). Indeed, the parties are free to agree that a security interest secures any obligation whatsoever. Determining the obligations secured by collateral is solely a matter of construing the parties' agreement under applicable law. This Article rejects the holdings of cases decided under former Article 9 that applied other tests, such as whether a future advance or other subsequently incurred obligation was of the same or a similar type or class as earlier advances and obligations secured by the collateral.

Through adoption of the revised U.C.C. §9–204, Nevada gives effect to cross collateral clauses. However, there is no controlling precedent or persuasive authority from Nevada's state courts (or federal courts) on the construction or validity of such clauses under the revised statute. Therefore, we are left to predict how the state's highest appellate court would rule if presented with the issue before us. ...

We have previously recognized the usefulness of the Official Comments in interpreting the U.C.C. *See NetBank, FSB v. Kipperman (In re Commer. Money Ctr., Inc.)*, 350 B.R. 465, 475 (9th Cir.BAP2006). The directive of Official Comment 5 is sufficiently clear—the enforceability of a cross collateral clause is based on contract, which requires us to construe the parties' agreement under applicable law. *See also* NRS 104.9201 (a security agreement is effective according to its terms between the parties).

Moreover, the comment provides that revised U.C.C. §9–204 rejects the holdings of cases decided prior to its adoption that have applied other tests, such as the relationship of the loans test or the reliance on the security test. *See In re Auza*, 181 B.R. 63, 69–70 (9th Cir.BAP 1995) (finding Arizona law to employ both these tests). Therefore, we are not convinced that debtor's citations to *Auza, In re Kim*, 256 B.R. 793 (Bankr.S.D.Cal.2000), *In re Wollin*, 249 B.R. 555 (Bankr.D.Or.2000), or *In re Gibson*, 234 B.R. 776 (Bankr.N.D.Cal.1999) have any bearing on the outcome of this appeal, as all those cases were decided prior to the adoption of the revised U.C.C. §9–204.

Accordingly, we look to Nevada law governing contracts to ascertain the parties' intent. Under Nevada law, whether or not a document is ambiguous is a question of law for the court. *Margrave v. Doormat Props., Inc.*, 110 Nev. 824, 878 P.2d 291, 293 (Nev.1994). "A contract is ambiguous if it is reasonably susceptible to more than one interpretation." *Id.* If there is an ambiguity requiring extrinsic evidence to discern the parties' intent, summary judgment is improper. *Id.* However, an unambiguous contract is construed from the language of the document. *Chwialkowski v. Sachs*, 108 Nev. 404, 834 P.2d 405 (Nev.1992).

The relevant contractual language in the Security Agreement reads: "[w]hat the Security Interest Covers—The security interest secures ... any other advances you have now or receive in the future under the Plan and any other amounts or loans, including any credit card loan, you owe us for any reason now or in the future. ..." We do not perceive that the clause is reasonably susceptible to more than one interpretation. It unambiguously states that FFCU holds a security interest in the Acura not only for the advance given, but for any other loans, including any credit card loan. Because the terms of an unambiguous private contract must be enforced irrespective of the parties' subjective intent, *see* 11 R. Lord, Williston on Contracts §30:4 (4th ed.1999), "[t]hat is the end of the inquiry." *Nagata*, 2006 WL 2131318, at *2.

However, our conclusion does not end the litigation between the parties. On this record, we are not convinced that FFCU was entitled to summary judgment as FFCU contends on appeal. Although not artfully argued, debtor had raised the issue of whether applying the cross collateral clause would violate the duty of good faith under the U.C.C., which includes a requirement of "reasonable commercial standards of fair dealing." NRS 104.1201(t). Good faith is a question of fact. … The bankruptcy court never addressed this argument when entering summary judgment for debtor. Therefore, we remand this issue to the bankruptcy court.

Moreover, in her statement of undisputed facts, debtor referred to the "fine print" in her Visa card application and she also refers to font sizes and paragraph labels in her brief. These arguments implicate an analysis of adhesion contracts and their enforceability under Nevada law. Nevada courts define an adhesion contract as "'a standardized contract form offered to consumers … on a 'take it or leave it' basis, without affording the consumer a realistic opportunity to bargain.'" *Burch v. Second Jud. Dist. Ct. of State ex rel. County of Washoe*, 118 Nev. 438, 49 P.3d 647, 649 (Nev.2002). Under Nevada law, an adhesion contract may be enforced where there is "'plain and clear notification of the terms and an understanding consent[,]' and 'if it falls within the reasonable expectations of the weaker … party.'" Nevada courts do not enforce a contract, or any clause of a contract, that is unconscionable. *Id.*

NRS 104.1201(j) provides:

'Conspicuous,' with reference to a term, means so written, displayed or presented that a reasonable person against which it is to operate ought to have noticed it. Whether a term is 'conspicuous' or not is a decision for the court. Conspicuous terms include the following:

(1) A heading in capitals equal to or greater in size than the surrounding text, or in contrasting type, font or color to the surrounding text of the same or lesser size; and

(2) Language in the body of a record or display in larger type than the surrounding text, or in contrasting type, font or color to the surrounding text of the same size, or set off from surrounding text of the same size by symbols or other marks that call attention to the language.

Further, "[i]f the court as a matter of law finds the contract or any clause of the contract to have been unconscionable at the time it was made the court may refuse to enforce the contract, or it may enforce the remainder of the contract without the unconscionable clause. …" *See* NRS 104.2303. Accordingly, we remand this claim to the bankruptcy court to determine these issues in the first instance.

* * *

VI. CONCLUSION

In sum, we REVERSE the bankruptcy court's grant of summary judgment for debtor on the limited issue discussed above. However, we decline to enter summary judgment for FFCU. The bankruptcy court did not address whether the application of the cross collateral clause would violate the duty of good faith or whether the agreements at issue were unenforceable adhesion contracts under Nevada's U.C.C. Accordingly, we REMAND those remaining claims to the bankruptcy court for further proceedings.

PROBLEM 5–12

REVIEW!

The security agreement that Ray signed giving the local bank a security interest in the store's inventory provided that the inventory would secure any and all other obligations, past, present, or future, of Ray to the bank. Ray later applied for and was issued a VISA credit card by the bank for his personal use. Ray got behind on his payments on the credit card and the bank declared a default under its security agreement and repossessed Ray's appliance inventory. Can the bank assert his personal debt against his business collateral? See 9-323.

CHAPTER 6

EXCEPTIONS

In this chapter we will examine some of the special priority rules that apply to specific transactions that would otherwise be covered by the general priority rules in 9-317 and 9-322. In some cases, these transactions were treated specially under pre-Code law and Article 9 simply adopts this pre-Code treatment. In other cases, Article 9's special rules were adopted to address priority problems that were not adequately addressed under pre-Code law and which were not adequately resolved under Article 9's general priority rules. In most of these cases, there's a fairly obvious and practical justification for not treating the transaction under the general Article 9 priority rules.

A. BUYERS IN THE ORDINARY COURSE

Generally, when the debtor sells (or transfers) a secured party's collateral, the security interest follows the collateral. 9-315(a)(1).[1] In other words, the secured party can enforce its security interest against the collateral even though it's now in the hands of someone who is not a party to the security agreement that created the security interest—regardless of whether the buyer knew about the security interest at the time of the transfer. Does this mean that the vendors who retained security interests in the appliances they sold on credit to Ray can start repossessing the washers and dryers Ray sold to his customers if Ray stops paying the vendors? Probably not, for one of two reasons. First, the vendors most likely authorized Ray in their security agreements to sell the collateral free of their security interests. The vendors anticipate—need—Ray to sell their collateral in order to generate the funds necessary to pay them for the appliances they have sold him on credit. Customers will be unwilling

---

1   If the security interest is not perfected, however, the secured party is subordinated to the buyer under 9-317—as we saw in Chapter 5.

to buy those appliances if their right to keep and use them is outside of their control—dependent on whether Ray can pay his own bills. To facilitate sales by Ray, the vendors will have to authorize Ray to sell their collateral free of the security interests in that collateral. They may, however, place restrictions on how Ray sells the appliances—the sales must be on certain terms or conditions, for example.

Second, even if the vendors have not authorized a sale of the appliances free of their security interests, Ray's customers who qualify as buyers in the ordinary course of business will take free of the vendors' security interests. 9-320(a). A buyer in the ordinary course of business "buys goods in good faith, without knowledge that the sale violates the rights of another person in the goods, and in the ordinary course from a person … in the business of selling goods of that kind." 1-201(9). In the pre-Code period, courts and, eventually, legislatures, had acted to protect certain buyers of collateral even when the security interest was filed of record and the buyer knew of the security interest. Gilmore at 678–79. As the following materials illustrate, Article 9 continues this tradition of protecting certain buyers in 9-320.

1. BUYERS OUT OF INVENTORY

Not all buyers of goods subject to a security interest are protected under 9-320(a). By definition, a buyer in the ordinary course is a buyer who buys out of inventory—buys from "a person that is in the business of selling goods of that kind." So, 9-320(a) only protects buyers who buy out of a seller's inventory. 9-102(a)(48) (goods held for sale classified as inventory). Buyers of farm products are expressly excluded from protection under 9-320(a)—for reasons that we will explore later. And although buyers of consumer goods are given protection under 9-320(b), buyers of consumer goods are not protected if, unlike buyers out of inventory, they know of the security interest or if the security interest has been perfected by filing.

The *Hockensmith* case and problems that follow it develop the basic requirements of the buyer in the ordinary course exception.

HOCKENSMITH v. FIFTH THIRD BANK
United States District Court for the Southern District of Ohio,
Western Division
2012 WL 5969654 (S.D. Ohio Nov. 29, 2012)

* * *

I. BACKGROUND

The dispute in this case centers on three vintage and very valuable Chevrolet Corvette automobiles, a 1967 project 435 Corvette, VIN# 194677S106186, a black 1967 Corvette Coupe, VIN# 194377S100405, and a white 1967

Corvette convertible, VIN# 194377S117307. The rival claimants for these cars are Plaintiff Randall Hockensmith, a citizen of Florida, and Defendant Fifth Third Bank ("Fifth Third"), a bank organized under the laws of the State of Ohio. The other important entity in this case is Performance Plus Motor Sports, Inc. ("Performance Plus"), which was a corporation formerly in the business of buying, restoring, and selling automobiles, particularly Corvettes.

Fifth Third provided floor plan financing to Performance Plus under an agreement dated August 3, 2007. As collateral for the loan, Performance Plus gave Fifth Third a security interest in a number of assets, including its inventory. The Floor Plan Agreement defines "inventory" as:

> all now owned, or hereafter acquired, goods, supplies, wares, merchandises [sic], and other tangible personal property, including raw materials, work in progress, supplies and components, and finished goods, including but not limited to all new and used automobiles, trucks, vans and other motor vehicles, and all parts, accessories, additions or accessions thereto, whether held for sale or lease, or furnished or to be furnished under any contract for service, or used or consumed in business, and also including rents, issues, proceeds, products of and accessions to inventory, packing and shipping materials, and all documents of title evidencing any of the foregoing, whether negotiable or non-negotiable, representing any of the foregoing.

Fifth Third filed a U.C.C.–1 financing statement perfecting its security interest in Performance Plus's inventory on August 3, 2007.

Plaintiff is a self-described collector of classic and exotic automobiles. Although Plaintiff calls his car collecting activities a hobby, his affidavit and deposition reflect that he had an informal but nevertheless tangible business relationship with Performance Plus with respect to Corvettes. Noel Grace, the president of Performance Plus, would identify Corvettes he thought Plaintiff would be interested in buying. Plaintiff would send funds to Performance Plus, who would then buy the Corvette on his behalf. Performance Plus would restore the Corvette to Plaintiff's specifications and then Performance Plus would sell the Corvette to another buyer on Plaintiff's behalf. Plaintiff and Performance Plus would split any profits resulting from the sale. Performance Plus usually retained Plaintiff's profits so they could be rolled into the purchase of another Corvette. On other occasions, Plaintiff and Performance Plus would simply trade one Corvette for another Corvette, or for another Corvette and cash. The rather ad hoc nature of the dealings between Plaintiff and Performance Plus is reflected in the convoluted provenance of the three Corvettes at issue in this case. (reflecting an extended series of purchases, restorations, sales or trades which culminated in the acquisitions of the three Corvettes).

There are several noteworthy aspects of the relationship between Plaintiff and Performance Plus. First, the Corvettes were usually titled to Performance

Plus, instead of Plaintiff, because that made it easier for Performance Plus to enter the Corvettes into competitions. Second, once the restoration of a car was completed, it was available for sale or trade at Performance Plus. Third, Plaintiff authorized Performance Plus to buy, sell, or barter the cars on his behalf, albeit Performance Plus normally obtained Plaintiff's consent before concluding a transaction.

Performance Plus defaulted on its floor plan agreement with Fifth Third on or about August 2, 2009. At around this time, Grace informed Plaintiff that Fifth Third "was systematically putting him [Grace] out of business over his floor plan[.]" The Corvettes involved in this case were titled to Performance Plus at this time and were located on its premises. Plaintiff instructed Grace to transfer the titles to the three Corvettes to him immediately and move them from Performance Plus's property because "when they [Fifth Third] come in they're going to want everything and I don't want them having what's mine." Grace transferred the title to the three Corvettes to Plaintiff on August 10, 2009.

Grace, however, did not move the Corvettes from Performance Plus's property.[2] Fifth Third obtained a judgment against Performance Plus on October 26, 2009. On December 21, 2009, Fifth Third executed its judgment against Performance Plus. The sheriff entered Performance Plus's property and seized all the personal property there, including the three Corvettes. Plaintiff demanded that Fifth Third return the Corvettes to him, but Fifth Third has refused.

Plaintiff filed suit against Fifth Third in March 2011, asserting state law claims for replevin, conversion, and civil theft of the Corvettes. Fifth Third answered and filed counterclaims asserting that it has perfected security interests in the Corvettes and that Performance Plus's transfers of the Corvettes to Plaintiff violated its rights as a secured creditor. Fifth Third, therefore, seeks a judgment that it is entitled to liquidate the Corvettes and apply the proceeds to the obligations owed to it by Performance Plus. The Court has subject matter jurisdiction over this matter because the parties are diverse and the amount in controversy exceeds $75,000.

Following the close of discovery, Plaintiff filed a motion for summary judgment on each of his claims and on Fifth Third's counterclaims. Plaintiff also seeks an order directing his immediate possession of the three Corvettes. Plaintiff's motion for summary judgment has been fully briefed and is ready for disposition.

* * *

2   Fifth Third asserted during oral argument, and again in its objections to the Report and Recommendation, that Performance Plus moved the Corvettes off of its place of business and into an off-site storage location. Fifth Third, however, did not provide a record citation to support this assertion. Nevertheless, even if true, it is undisputed that the Corvettes remained either in Performance Plus's and/or Noel Grace's custody and control after the default.

III. ANALYSIS

Although a number of legal theories are at play in this case, the basic and dispositive issue in the case is whose interest in the Corvettes is superior, Fifth Third's or Plaintiff's. Plaintiff contends that he was a buyer in the ordinary course of business of the Corvettes, thus terminating any security interest Fifth Third had in the Corvettes ... Fifth Third argues that its interest in the Corvettes is superior to Plaintiff's due to its perfected security interest in Performance Plus's inventory. Plaintiff responds that Fifth Third never perfected its interest in the Corvettes because notations of its security interests were never made on the certificates of title.

* * *

B. A REASONABLE JUROR COULD CONCLUDE THAT FIFTH THIRD HAS A PERFECTED SECURITY INTEREST IN THE CORVETTES

Plaintiff argues that Fifth Third does not have a security interest in the Corvettes because there is no notation of its lien on the certificates of title. Plaintiff is generally correct that the Certificate of Motor Vehicle Title Act requires a security interest in a motor vehicle to be perfected by either noting the lien on the title itself or by electronically entering the lien with the clerk of court. *Ohio Rev.Code §4505.13(B); In re McAlmont, 385 B.R. 191, 195 (Bkrtcy.S.D.Ohio 2008)* (stating that a security interest in a motor vehicle may only be perfected by complying with the Certificate of Motor Vehicle Title Act). The court in McAlmont specifically noted that a security interest in a motor vehicle cannot be perfected merely by filing a financing statement. *385 B.R. at 195* ("Under Ohio law, the filing of a financing statement does *not* result in the perfection of a security interest in goods—such as the Debtor's motorcycle—that are subject to Ohio's certificate of title statute.") (emphasis in original).

As Fifth Third correctly argues, however, the certificate of title act provides an exception when a motor vehicle is being held as inventory. Section 4505.13(A)(2) provides that the perfection provisions of Chapter 1309 apply when a dealer holds a motor vehicle as inventory. Furthermore, this section provides that neither a notation of the security interest on the certificate of title nor a electronic notation by the clerk of court is required to perfect a security interest in a motor vehicle held as inventory.

Stated more specifically, if a motor vehicle is being held as inventory by a dealer, the perfection provisions of Chapter 1309 [Article 9] prevail over the perfection provisions of the certificate of title act. See Heartland, supra, at 755. Therefore, if a motor vehicle is being held as inventory by a dealer, a creditor may perfect its security interest in the motor vehicle by filing a U.C.C. financing statement on the debtor's inventory. *See* Ohio Rev.Code

§1309.311(D), and Comment 4 ("Compliance with a certificate-of-title statute is both unnecessary and ineffective to perfect a security interest in inventory to which this subsection applies. Thus, a secured party who finances an automobile dealer that is in the business of selling and leasing its inventory of automobiles can perfect a security interest in all the automobiles by filing a financing statement but not by compliance with a certificate-of-title statute.").

A reasonable juror could find that Performance Plus was holding the Corvettes as inventory for sale and that, therefore, Fifth Third has a perfected security interest in the cars.

First, a reasonable juror could find that Performance Plus was a dealer in automobiles, and, more specifically, vintage or collectible Corvettes. The Certificate of Motor Vehicle Title Act defines "dealer" as including both a "new motor vehicle dealer" and a "used motor vehicle dealer." Ohio Rev. Code §4505.13(H) (2) & Ohio Rev.Code §4517.01(J). In turn, a "used motor vehicle dealer" is "any person engaged in the business of selling, displaying, offering for sale, or dealing in used motor vehicles, at retail or wholesale." Ohio Rev.Code §4517.01(L). In this case, the complaint alleges that Performance Plus "was in the business of buying, restoring, and selling automobiles, especially Chevrolet Corvettes." Similarly, Plaintiff's deposition and affidavit indicate that Performance Plus bought and sold used Corvettes. Therefore, a reasonable juror could conclude that Performance Plus was a "used motor vehicle dealer."

Second, a reasonable juror could conclude that Performance Plus was holding the Corvettes as inventory. "Inventory" means, inter alia, "goods, other than farm products that ... are being held for sale or lease[.]" Ohio Rev.Code §4505.13(H)(4) & Ohio Rev.Code §1309.102(48)(b). Although Plaintiff's brief characterizes the Corvettes as being part of his collection for his personal use and enjoyment, his deposition testimony indicates otherwise. In his deposition, Plaintiff indicates that the Corvettes were "investment" cars, i.e., cars that were involved in his informal arrangement with Performance Plus to buy, restore, and re-sell Corvettes. Additionally, Plaintiff's affidavit states that the Corvettes he purchased were generally available for sale or trade at Performance Plus. Accordingly, a reasonable juror could conclude that the Corvettes were being held as inventory by Performance Plus.

Noel Grace's affidavit denies that Performance Plus was holding the Corvettes as inventory. As Fifth Third accurately argues, however, based on the entire record, a reasonable juror could conclude that the Corvettes were acquired in the course of Plaintiff's agreement with Performance Plus to buy, restore, and re-sell Corvettes. Thus, a reasonable juror could conclude that the Corvettes were in inventory and available for sale by Performance Plus until Plaintiff learned that Performance Plus had defaulted on its floor plan agreement. As discussed further, infra at 15–17, a reasonable juror could conclude that the conveyance of the Corvettes to Plaintiff was fraudulent.

Since a juror could conclude that the Corvettes were being held as inventory by Performance Plus, the perfection provisions of §1309.311(D) apply. As already stated, a security interest in motor vehicles being held as inventory is perfected by filing a U.C.C. financing statement on the debtor's inventory. Fifth Third perfected its security interest in Performance Plus's inventory by timely filing a U.C.C. financing statement. Therefore, a reasonable juror could conclude that Fifth Third has a perfected security interest in the Corvettes.

C. A REASONABLE JUROR COULD CONCLUDE THAT PLAINTIFF WAS NOT A BUYER OF THE CORVETTES IN THE ORDINARY COURSE OF BUSINESS

Plaintiff argues that even if Fifth Third has a perfected security interest in the Corvettes, he was a buyer in the ordinary course of business of the Corvettes and, therefore, extinguished Fifth Third's security interest in them. A buyer of goods in the ordinary course of business takes free of a perfected security interest in the goods created by his seller. Ohio Rev.Code §1309.320(A). A "buyer in ordinary course of business" means:

> a person that buys goods in good faith, without knowledge that the sale violates the rights of another person in the goods, and in the ordinary course from a person, other than a pawnbroker, in the business of selling goods of that kind. A person buys goods in the ordinary course if the sale to the person comports with the usual or customary practices in the kind of business in which the seller is engaged or with the seller's own usual or customary practices. A person that sells oil, gas, or other minerals at the wellhead or minehead is a person in the business of selling goods of that kind. A buyer in ordinary course of business may buy for cash, by exchange of other property, or on secured or unsecured credit, and may acquire goods or documents of title under a preexisting contract for sale. *Only a buyer that takes possession of the goods* or has a right to recover the goods from the seller under Chapter 1302 of the Revised Code may be a buyer in ordinary course of business. "Buyer in ordinary course of business" does not include a person that acquires goods in a transfer in bulk or as security for or in total or partial satisfaction of a money debt.

> Ohio Rev.Code §1301.201(B)(9) (emphasis added).[3]

---

3   Plaintiff has argued that he is a buyer in the ordinary course of business pursuant to Ohio Rev.Code §1309.209(B). Fifth Third has argued that Plaintiff cannot be a buyer in the ordinary course of business under this section because he bought the Corvettes as investments and not for household or personal use. Section 1309.209 is Ohio's codified version of U.C.C. §9–320. As explained by White and Summers, §9–320(B) is for sales "by amateurs to amateurs." 4 JAMES J. WHITE, ET. AL., UNIFORM COMMERCIAL CODE §33–8 (6th ed.2012). Section 9–320(B) only applies when the seller used the goods primarily for personal, family, or household purposes and the buyer intends to use the goods primarily for personal, family, or

There are three problems with Plaintiff's contention that he was a buyer of the Corvettes in the ordinary course of business. First, although Plaintiff adduced evidence showing wire transfers of cash to Performance Plus, at least two of the certificates of title indicate $0 as the purchase price of the car. In order to be a buyer in the ordinary course of business, however, the purchaser must give some value for the goods. *See* Ohio Rev.Code §1301.201(9) ("A buyer in ordinary course of business may buy for cash, by exchange of other property, or on secured or unsecured credit, and may acquire goods or documents of title under a preexisting contract for sale."); Ohio Rev.Code §1302.01(A)(11) ("A 'sale' consists in the passing of title from the seller to the buyer *for a price*.") (emphasis added); see also Ohio Rev.Code §4505.07(B)(12) (requiring the purchase price of the motor vehicle to be reflected on the face of the certificate of title). Viewing the record in the light most favorable to Fifth Third, these certificates of title indicate that Plaintiff did not give value for at least two of the Corvettes. Additionally, as Fifth Third points out in its memorandum in opposition, Plaintiff has not adduced any bills of sale evidencing a purchase of the Corvettes from Performance Plus. A reasonable juror could conclude from these facts that Plaintiff did not give value to Performance Plus for the Corvettes.

Second, as Fifth Third correctly points out, Plaintiff never took possession of the Corvettes-indeed, he has never actually even seen them. Therefore, Plaintiff's failure to take possession of the Corvettes arguably disqualifies him from being a "buyer in the ordinary course of business." But see Ace Equip. Sales, Inc. v. H.O. Penn Mach. Co., Inc., 88 Conn.App. 687, 871 A.2d 402, 406 (Conn.Ct.App.2005) (buyer was buyer in the ordinary course of business, despite failure to take physical possession of rock crusher, because custom of the industry was not to take physical possession of heavy equipment because of prohibitive cost of transportation); *In re Havens Steel Co.*, 317 B.R. 75, 87–88 (Bkrtcy.W.D.Mo.2004) (constructive possession sufficient to confer "buyer in the ordinary course of business" status).

Plaintiff contends that he was a buyer in the ordinary course of business, even though he did not take actual possession of the Corvettes, because he had the right to take possession of the Corvettes from Performance Plus. Plaintiff cites for this proposition §1301.201(9) where it states that a purchaser may be

---

household purposes. Id. This section does not apply if the seller is in the business of selling goods of the kind. Id. In this case, regardless of whether Plaintiff bought the Corvettes for personal use or as an investment, §1309.320(B) would not apply to determine Plaintiff's buyer in the ordinary course of business status because the alleged seller of the Corvettes to Plaintiff, Performance Plus, was a seller of goods of the kind. In other words, Performance Plus was in the business of selling Corvettes; it did not own the Corvettes primarily for personal, family or household purposes. Plaintiff, nevertheless, could still be a buyer in the ordinary course of business under §1301.201(B)(9) and/or §1309.320(A). In any event, §1309.320 does not actually define who is a buyer in the ordinary course of business; rather, it only provides the rule that a buyer in the ordinary course of business takes free of a security interest created by his seller.

a buyer in the ordinary course of business when he has "the right to recover the goods from the seller." A full reading of this clause, however, shows that it is not conferring buyer in the ordinary course of business status on a purchaser who has a generalized right to take possession of the goods, which is what Plaintiff argues. Rather, §1301.201(9) states that a purchaser may be a buyer in the ordinary course of business where he has "a *right to recover the goods from the seller under Chapter 1302.*" Ohio Rev.Code 1301.201(9) (emphasis added). In turn, the Official Comments to §1301.201(9) indicate that "the right to recover the goods from the seller" is a term of art. The commentary states: "Concerning when a buyer obtains possessory rights, see Sections 2–502 and 2–716." Ohio Rev.Code §1301.201, Official Comment 9. In other words, according to these provisions, in order to be a buyer in the ordinary course of business without taking possession of the goods, the buyer must have the right to recover the goods from the seller under either U.C.C. 2–502 or U.C.C. 2–716. See 1 James J. White, et. al., Uniform Commercial Code §1:8 (6th ed. 2012) ("A court may still find that the buyer 'has the right to recover the goods from the seller under Article 2.' Buyers may recover goods from seller under §§2–502(1)(b) and 2–716(1), (3)).").

In turn, U.C.C. §2–502 provides the buyer a right to recover the goods where the seller repudiates the sales contract and maintains possession of goods after the buyer makes a down payment for goods. U.C.C. §2–716 provides the buyer a right to specific performance or replevin of the goods upon breach of contract by seller. These sections are not applicable in this case, however, because Performance Plus did not retain possession of the Corvettes in breach of a contract to sell them to Plaintiff. Plaintiff is not a buyer in the ordinary course of business merely because he could have taken possession of the Corvettes from Performance Plus whenever he desired.

Third, a buyer in the ordinary course of business only takes free of a security interest created by his seller. Ohio Rev.Code §1309.320(A). In this case, while the evidence shows that Performance Plus created the security interests in the Corvettes, Plaintiff did not buy the Corvettes from Performance Plus. Rather, the evidence shows that Performance Plus located sellers of Corvettes for Plaintiff and bought or traded for Corvettes from third-parties on his behalf. Stated another way, Performance Plus acted as Plaintiff's purchasing agent for the Corvettes. Plaintiff's affidavit in fact states that he bought Corvettes through Performance Plus and not from Performance Plus. Thus, the record shows that the actual sellers of the Corvettes to Plaintiff were third parties, not Performance Plus. Since Performance Plus, and not the actual sellers of the Corvettes, created the security interests in the Corvettes, Plaintiff was not a buyer of the Corvettes in the ordinary course of business from Performance Plus. See United States v. Continental Grain Co., 691 F.Supp. 1193, 1198 (W.D.Wis.1988) ("[T]he buyer loses this protection [buyer in the ordinary course of business] where the buyer purchases farm products from a person engaged in farming operations, *or where the buyer's seller did not create the security interest in the goods sold.*") (emphasis added). While Plaintiff might be a buyer of the Corvettes in the ordinary course of business vis-à-vis the third parties, a reasonable juror could find that he was not a buyer of the Corvettes from Performance Plus in the ordinary course of business.

PROBLEM 6–1

Ray's bank has a security interest in the store's appliance inventory which it perfected by filing a financing statement. Which of the following buyers of appliances from Ray's store would take the appliance they purchased free of the bank's security interest under 9-320(a)?

> Transaction 1: Ray's neighbor stops by the store and purchases a new microwave oven using his VISA card. He takes the oven home with him. Would it matter under 9-320(a) that the neighbor, based on his many backyard conversations with Ray, knew that the bank had a security interest in the store's inventory? —————➤ NO

> Transaction 2: Would your answer in Transaction 1 change if Ray had decided to close the store and the neighbor had purchased the oven at the store's "Going Out of Business Sale"? ————➤ MAYBE

> Transaction 3: The store was running a special sale on "demos"— appliances that had been used as display models for customers to examine before making their purchases. The display models were sold at steep discounts in order to move them quickly. Ray's high school history teacher buys a refrigerator demo at a discounted price.

> Transaction 4: One of Ray's employees promises a friend that he can get her a "sweet deal" on a 48" LCD television. The only catch is that the friend will have to pick up the TV at the store's loading dock after midnight when the store is closed. The friend shows up as arranged and drives off with a new TV.

PROBLEM 6–2

Ray sells a complete set of commercial grade appliances to a new restaurant opening in town. Ray retains a security interest in the appliances. After several months of operating the restaurant, the owner decides he does not need the trash compactor he bought from Ray, so he sells it to one of the restaurant's customers who operates the ice cream shop around the corner. Can Ray enforce the security interest against the ice cream shop?

PROBLEM 6–3

Business has been bad and Ray needs cash to keep the store open. He contacts the other appliance store in town and offers to sell it 10 of the refrigerators he's got in stock at a price well below his own cost to purchase the refrigerators. The owner of the other store agrees to purchase the refrigerators, but when Ray delivers them he presents a sales invoice indicating that in addition to cash, the buyer has traded a number of other appliances for the refrigerators. When the value of the traded items is added to the cash purchase price Ray had offered, the total consideration received for the refrigerators is equal to their cost to Ray. The buyer signs the invoice even though he knows it does not represent the actual terms of his deal with Ray. Several days later, when a representative of Ray's bank calls to confirm the details of the transaction, the buyer affirms that the invoice accurately stated the terms of his transaction with Ray. Will 9-320(a) prevent the bank from enforcing its security interest in the 10 refrigerators against the other appliance store? See, *International Harvester v. Glendenning*, 505 S.W.2d 320 (Tex. 1974).

PROBLEM 6–4

Earlier this year Ray sold a Sub-Zero refrigerator-freezer to one of the store's regular customers. Ray retained a security interest in the refrigerator. After using the refrigerator for several months, the customer decided it was too small and sold it to Discount Appliances, the used appliance store in town. The customer told Discount about Ray's security interest in the refrigerator. Discount never contacted Ray and did not make any payments on the refrigerator to Ray. It later resold the refrigerator to a local architect but did not tell her about Ray's security interest. Ray was unaware that the refrigerator had been sold and resold until his customer stopped making payments. The architect has refused to turn over the refrigerator and Ray has threatened to sue her for conversion. If Ray does sue, will 9-320(a) protect the architect?

Agricultural lenders have often been the beneficiaries of special protections unavailable to the rest of the lending community, and so it comes as no surprise that buyers of farm products from a farmer are not given the same protection as are buyers out of inventory under 9-320(a)—even though

> [t]here may seem to be a formal resemblance between the situation of the business which holds goods for sale as inventory and that of a farmer or stockman who raises and sells crops or livestock.

> Gilmore at 707.

Justification for the special treatment of agricultural lenders was incomplete if not absent altogether. After years of criticism levied at the farm products exception in Article 9 from many different groups, Congress weighed in and preempted the farms products exclusion of 9-320 by enacting the Food Security Act of 1985.

The *Fin Ag.* case examines the protection given to buyers of farm products under the Food Security Act.

FIN AG, INC. v. HUFNAGLE, INC.
Supreme Court of Minnesota
720 N.W.2d 579 (Minn. 2006)

HANSON, *Justice*.

This case concerns the impact of grain "fronting" on the respective rights of buyers of farm products and those who hold a security interest in those products.

* * *

A. THE STATUTORY FRAMEWORK

To develop a proper framework for the analysis of this case, we must consider the interaction between the state and federal statutes that address the conflict between the rights of buyers of farm products and the rights of those who hold a security interest in those farm products. Because the Minnesota statutes governing security interests in farm products have been revised from time to time, it is helpful to first consider what that interaction was when Congress first enacted *7 U.S.C.§1631* in response to perceived shortcomings in the Uniform Commercial Code (UCC).

Prior to 1985, the UCC generally reflected a policy that favored the rights of the holders of security interests, presumably to promote the availability of credit on reasonable terms. Thus, *UCC section 9-201* recognized that "a security agreement is effective according to its terms between the parties, against purchasers of the collateral and against creditors." U.C.C.§9-201 (1972) (amended 2000), 3A U.L.A. 651-52 (2000). And the general rule embodied in *UCC section 9-306* was that a security interest in goods continues despite the sale of those goods by the debtor. U.C.C.§9-306 (1972) (amended 2000), 3B U.L.A. 33-34 (2002). That general rule was subject to an exception under *UCC section 9-307*, where a "buyer in the ordinary course of business" could take the goods free of some security interests, but only those that were "created by his seller." U.C.C.§9-307 (1972) (amended 2000), 3B U.L.A. 154 (2002). But that exception did not apply to buyers of "farm products." *Id.* Thus, the UCC protected buyers in the ordinary course of business only from security interests created by the buyer's seller; and buyers of farm products were excluded from even this narrow protection.

The practical effect of the exclusion of farm products from *UCC section 9-307* was that buyers of farm products became guarantors of their seller's debt. As a result, more than a third of the states amended *UCC section 9-307* in various ways, generally attempting to reduce the bias in favor of lenders by providing mechanisms that would assist buyers in protecting their interests.

Charles W. Wolfe, *Section 1324 of the Food Security Act of 1985: Congress Preempts the "Farm Products Exception" of Section 9-307(1) of the Uniform Commercial Code*, 55 UMKC L. Rev. 454, 461-64 (1987). The various state amendments were not consistent with one another and diluted the uniformity goals of the UCC. Wolfe, *supra*, at 455, 461-64.

Congress became concerned with the impact of the UCC on buyers of farm products and with the inconsistent amendments to *UCC section 9-307* by many states. Wolfe, *supra*, at 463. Often, buyers of farm products did not know of a security interest or have any practical way to discover it and thus were required to pay twice for the product—once to the seller and a second time to the security holder if the seller defaulted on the debt. *See 7 U.S.C.§1631(a)*. To address this situation, Congress in 1985 enacted *7 U.S.C.§1631* (titled "Protection for purchasers of farm products"). Where it applies, *section 1631* preempts all conflicting state laws. *See 7 U.S.C.§1631(d)* (prefacing the statutory rule by stating "notwithstanding any other provision of Federal, State, or local law").

The title and congressional findings of *section 1631* suggest that it was intended to protect buyers of farm products from having to make "double payment for the products, once at the time of purchase, and again when the seller fails to repay the lender." *7 U.S.C.§1631(a)(2)*. But the protection actually provided by *section 1631* was not as sweeping as the statement of intent might suggest. As explained below, *section 1631* did not provide that the buyer would take free of all security interests, but instead only established a notice system that provided a mechanism for buyers to protect themselves from some, but not all, security interests.

Section 1631 established, contrary to the UCC, that a buyer of farm products in the ordinary course of business takes free of security interests created by the seller. *Section 1631(d)* provides:

> Except as provided in subsection (e) of this section and notwithstanding any other provision of Federal, State, or local law, a buyer who in the ordinary course of business buys a farm product from a seller engaged in farming operations *shall take free of a security interest created by the seller*, even though the security interest is perfected; and the buyer knows of the existence of such interest.

7 U.S.C.§1631(d) (emphasis added). Notably, *section 1631(d)* adopted the same narrow scope of protection as provided in *section 9-307 of the UCC*—it only provides protection against a security interest "created by the seller." Therefore, this language provides no protection for a buyer of farm products from any valid security interest that was created by someone other than the immediate seller.

The federal statute does provide exceptions to *section 1631(d)*. Under these exceptions a buyer of farm products takes subject to a security interest created by the seller when notice has been given by one of three specified notice procedures. Two of the notice procedures apply where states have established central filing systems to provide notice to registered farm product buyers.

Minnesota created such a central filing system in 1992. Under Minnesota's system, a lender is authorized to register the security interest with the Secretary of State by filing an "effective financing statement." *Minn. Stat.§336A.04, subd. 1* (2004). The Secretary of State compiles a list of debtors whose farm products are subject to security interests and makes this list available to registered farm products dealers and to others on request. Before purchasing farm products, a buyer is expected to check the list.

At the time of the transactions at issue here, Minnesota's version of *UCC section 9-307* had been modified from the uniform provision. Between 1986 and 2001, Minnesota's version of that section eliminated the exclusion for buyers of farm products from the buyer in the ordinary course exception, meaning that a buyer of farm products could take free of a security interest "created by his seller" if he qualified as a "buyer in the ordinary course of business." *See* Act of March 14, 1986, ch. 322,§2, 1986 Minn. Laws 20, 21 (codified as *Minn. Stat.§336.9-307* (1998)); Act of April 11, 2000, ch. 399, art. I,§40, 2000 Minn. Laws 569, 610 (codified as *Minn. Stat.§336.9-320* (2004)).

To summarize, under *7 U.S.C.§1631* a buyer of farm products in the ordinary course of business (1) takes free of security interests created by the seller, unless notice of the seller-created security interest has been given by one of three specific notice procedures, which include the Minnesota central filing system provided under *chapter 336A*; but (2) takes subject to security interests created by someone other than the seller. Similarly, under Minnesota's version of the UCC applicable at the time of the subject transactions, a buyer of farm products in the ordinary course of business (1) takes free of security interests created by the seller, but (2) takes subject to a security interest created by someone other than the seller.

B. THE SUMMARY JUDGMENT RECORD

With this legal framework in mind, we turn to the undisputed facts in this record. In 1999, Fin Ag made an operating loan of $249,995 to Buck. As collateral for this loan, Buck granted Fin Ag a security interest in Buck's corn crops for 1999. Fin Ag filed UCC financing statements in Hubbard and Wadena Counties (where the crops were grown), but not in Itasca County (where the Bucks resided). Fin Ag also filed an "effective financing statement" with the Minnesota Secretary of State, which caused the security interest to be listed in Minnesota's central filing system. *See Minn. Stat.§336A.04* (2004).

Meschke purchased several loads of corn that were produced by Buck. Because Meschke is a registered farm products dealer, he received an electronic copy of Minnesota's listing from the central filing system of sellers whose grain is subject to security interests. *See Minn. Stat.§336A.11* (2004). Meschke learned from the central filing system that Buck's corn was subject to a security interest held by Fin Ag. When Meschke bought corn directly from Buck, he generally included Fin Ag's name on the check. But twice Meschke bought corn directly from Buck without making the check payable to both

Buck and Fin Ag; the amount of these sales was $7,129.24. Meschke does not dispute Fin Ag's claims with regard to these two payments.

Meschke was also offered corn by persons who claimed that the sellers were, variously, Mark Tooker, Mickey Buck, Paul Zuk, and Ryan Buck (collectively the Tookers).[5] The Tookers were not listed in the central filing as having corn that was subject to any security interest. Meschke made payment for this corn solely in the names of the Tookers. Meschke bought corn from the Tookers on seven separate occasions and paid a total of $38,443.85. Each of the checks to the Tookers was subsequently deposited into Buck's bank account but was not applied to Buck's debt to Fin Ag.

Mark Tooker and Paul Zuk were employees of the Bucks. The parties agree that Mickey and Ryan Buck were Ronda and Larry Buck's minor children.

When Buck failed to repay the Fin Ag loan, Fin Ag sued Meschke for conversion of Fin Ag's collateral in the corn that was involved in the Tooker sales and the two Buck sales. Fin Ag moved for summary judgment against Meschke. Meschke opposed the motion, arguing that he was entitled to take the corn free of Fin Ag's security interest under *7 U.S.C. §1631* because he did not receive notice of Fin Ag's security interest when he checked the central filing system for the names of the Tookers. The district court granted summary judgment in favor of Fin Ag, awarding damages for the seven Tooker sales and two Buck sales in the amount of $45,573.09, plus costs and interest. The court of appeals affirmed, and we granted Meschke's petition for review.

* * *

Fin Ag's argument requires us to consider how *section 1631* works in the situation of "fronting" sales. The parties describe "fronting" as being where a seller of farm products that are subject to a security interest has a third party sell them under the third party's name. Here, Meschke bought the corn from the Tookers and, when Meschke checked the central filing system, he found no security interests listed in the Tookers' names. As a result, both Meschke and Fin Ag can be viewed as innocent parties in the sense that they each did everything they were required or expected to do under the FSA.

Meschke advances several policy-based arguments that emphasize how difficult it is for a buyer of farm products to discover a security interest in a fronting situation. We recognize that difficulty, but we are constrained to apply the plain language of the statutes, as enacted by Congress and the Minnesota Legislature, and to follow where they lead. The difficulty with those statutes, as highlighted earlier, is that the protection for the buyer is narrowly limited by the clause "created by the seller."

The presence of this limitation in *UCC section 9-307* has received much criticism, both from the courts and scholars. *See* William H. Lawrence, *The "Created by His Seller" Limitation of Section 9-309(1) of the UCC: A Provision in Need of an Articulated Policy, 60 Ind. L.J. 73, 73-74 (1984-85).* Yet, all efforts to eliminate or amend this clause have failed since the UCC was rewritten in 1957. *See* Richard H. Nowka, *Section 9-302(a) of Reviewed Article 9 and The Buyer in the Ordinary Course of Pre-Encumbered Goods: Something Old and Something New, 38 Brandeis L.J. 9, 23-24 (1999-2000).* And, as noted, Congress essentially incorporated this clause in *section 1631* when it attempted to correct some of the other shortcomings, from the perspective of buyers, of *UCC section 9-307.*

Neither Congress nor the Commissioners on Uniform State Laws have enunciated a policy reason for this clause.[4] *See Nowka, supra, at 23.* But the Official Comment to *section 9-320*, when revised and renumbered in 2000, makes it clear that the "created by the buyer's seller" clause is a serious limitation on the rights of buyers in the ordinary course of business, citing this example:

> Manufacturer, who is in the business of manufacturing appliances, owns manufacturing equipment subject to the perfected security interest in favor of Lender. Manufacturer sells the equipment to Dealer, who is in the business of buying and selling used equipment. Buyer buys the equipment from Dealer. Even if Buyer qualifies as a buyer in the ordinary course of business, Buyer does not take free of Lender's security interest under *subsection (a) [of section 9-320]*, because Dealer did not create the security interest; Manufacturer did.
>
> U.C.C.§*9-320*, official cmt. 3 (2000), 3 U.L.A. 219-20 (2002).

The inclusion of the "created by the seller" clause in *section 1631* means that the statute does not provide protection for buyers in a fronting situation where the security interest from which protection is sought was not created by the fronting parties. Under the facts of this case, no matter what factual assumptions we make, there are none under which Meschke could take the corn free of Fin Ag's security interest. This is because if we view Buck as the

---

4   One commentator suggests the following:

Thus, the policy underlying the "created by his seller" language is to limit the exception to security interest validity codified in section 9-307(1) to cases in which the secured party has clothed the debtor with the indicia of apparent authority to sell the goods. Nonpossessory inventory financing establishes apparent authority in dealer-debtors to sell to buyers in ordinary course because (1) the intended result of inventory financing is sale of the collateral to third persons, (2) the sale is facilitated by entrusting the collateral to dealer-debtors in the business of selling goods of the kind compromising the collateral, and (3) most of these sales are made pursuant to actual secured party authorization. Debtor sales of consumer goods and equipment are distinguishable. Improper sales of these categories of collateral generally do not occur, nor are they expected to occur; therefore, secured parties have been relieved of the burden of policing such sales. The absence of apparent authority to sell is the justification for continuing the validity of the security interest in such situations even against a buyer in ordinary course of business.

Lawrence, supra, at 87.

seller, we must conclude that Meschke's rights are subject to Fin Ag's security interest under *section 1631* because Fin Ag filed an "effective financing statement" that put Meschke on notice of Fin Ag's security interest in Buck's products. And, if we view the Tookers as the sellers, we must conclude that Meschke's rights are subject to Fin Ag's security interest, under either *section 1631* or Minnesota's UCC, because both statutes only protect a buyer from a security interest created by the seller and not from a security interest created by an undisclosed owner, which continues in the product despite the sale.

---

2. AMATEUR TRANSACTIONS

The buyer in the ordinary course exception does not protect the purchaser of second hand consumer goods—consumers are not in the business of selling goods. But consumer goods are often subject to a secret lien—recall that a purchase money security interest in consumer goods is automatically perfected—there is no need to file a financing statement to perfect it. Thus, the absence of a financing statement in the Article 9 filing system does not necessarily mean that consumer goods are not subject to a perfected security interest. Article 9 protects the amateur buyer—the consumer buying second hand goods from another consumer—by allowing the amateur to take free of a security interest as long as she gives value and is without knowledge of the security interest. 9-320(b).

The following problems explore the protection given to the buyers in these so-called amateur transactions by what others have labeled the "garage sale exception."

PROBLEM 6–5

Ray sold a stacked washer-dryer unit to a young couple that had recently moved into his neighborhood. He retained a security interest in the unit to secure the couple's promise to pay for it. Twelve months later, as the couple prepared to move into their new custom-built home, they held a moving sale to get rid of the many things they would not need in their new home. Since the new home came with all new appliances, the washer-dryer unit was one of the items they sold at their sale. They did not tell the buyer about Ray's security interest. The couple stopped making payments to Ray and he wants to repossess the washer-dryer unit. Will Ray be able to enforce his security interest against the new buyer? Does it matter whether Ray filed a financing statement? Why might Ray have not filed a financing statement for this transaction? See 9-320(b) and 9-309(1).

PROBLEM 6–6

REVIEW!

If the couple in the last Problem had instead sold the washer-dryer unit to Discount Appliances (the used appliance dealer), would Ray be able to enforce the security interest against Discount if he had not filed a financing statement to perfect his security interest? See 9-320(b).

B. PURCHASERS OF CHATTEL PAPER

Most of Ray's customers will be unable (or unwilling) to pay cash for the appliances he sells them—they will need to buy on credit. Many of these customers will use some variation of an "installment plan" provided by Ray as the means for obtaining credit. The installment plan most likely will require the customer to sign a note in an amount that reflects both the price of the appliance and the cost of financing the purchase, as well as a security agreement giving Ray a security interest in the appliance purchased. As we've previously discussed, the note and the security agreement together constitute chattel paper. The more sales Ray makes on the installment plan, the more chattel paper he collects.

To Ray, the chattel paper represents a stream of income—the monthly payments by his customers—over an extended period of time, often years. A steady stream of income for his business is a good thing as long as it is sufficient to cover his costs of operating the shop—which include paying the vendors that supply him with the appliances he sells. Most likely his obligations to the vendors are of a shorter term than the obligations of his customers to pay for their purchases. In other words, Ray's obligations to his vendors will mature long before he has collected enough from his customers to pay off the vendors.

So, although the chattel paper looks good in the long term, it can create a problem—a cash flow problem—in the short term. One way Ray can solve this cash flow problem is by selling the chattel paper or using the chattel paper as collateral for a loan. And believe it or not, there are companies whose principal business is purchasing debt instruments like notes and chattel paper. These companies will pay cash today for the long term stream of income represented by debt instruments—they expect to buy at a discount (for example, 80% of the face value of the notes), but are willing to wait out the payment term in return for the profit they make on the discounted price they pay for the notes. Ray gets the cash he needs today—not as much as he would have gotten had he been able to wait out the payment terms of the notes—but he has the opportunity to do more business and generate additional income from that business.

There is, however, a potential glitch in Ray's plan. Ray's vendors most likely took security interests in the appliances they sold him on credit. Because Ray got the chattel paper in exchange for the vendors' collateral, the chattel paper is proceeds of the vendors' security interest—which means the vendors now have a security interest in the chattel paper itself. And under the general priority rules, if that security interest has been perfected, the vendors will have priority over a subsequent purchaser of or lender against the chattel paper. So, why would anyone buy it—or lend against it—if it's already subject to the claim of Ray's vendors?

Anticipating that Ray might have this problem if he tries to sell his chattel paper (or use it as collateral), Article 9 protects a qualifying purchaser of Ray's chattel paper by giving the purchaser priority over the security interests of his vendors. 9-330. The purchaser can acquire Ray's chattel paper without the risk of losing it later to Ray's vendors if Ray should fail to pay them back.

The problems that follow develop the 9-330 priority exception in more detail.

PROBLEM 6-7

About half of Ray's sales each month are on an installment plan under which the customer signs (1) a promissory in the amount of the purchase price plus finance charge and (2) a security agreement giving Ray a security interest in the appliance purchased. At the end of each month, Ray bundles the installment plan papers together for the local finance company which purchases them for 80% of the face value of the notes. The finance company knows that all of Ray's inventory is subject to the bank's perfected security interest and that the paper is proceeds of that security interest, but it takes the paper anyway. If Ray stops paying the bank, can the bank get the paper back from the finance company? On what basis will the bank claim to have priority over the finance company? Would your answer be different if Ray's security agreement with the bank required him to turn over to the bank all installment loan paperwork as soon as it was created in connection with a sale out of inventory? See 9-330.

PROBLEM 6-8

Would your answer to the last Problem be different if the bank's security agreement with Ray also provided that in each installment plan transaction, Ray would use paper provided by the bank that at the top of each page stated "THIS PAPER IS SUBJECT TO A SECURITY INTEREST CREATED ~~STARRED~~ FOR THE BENEFIT OF LOCAL BANK"? Would the outcome be affected if Ray did not use the paper provided by the bank? What if Ray used the bank's paper for some of, but not all of, the installment plan transactions? See 9-330.

PROBLEM 6-9

A bank officer usually stopped by Ray's store every Friday afternoon to pick up the installment plan paperwork generated during the week by appliance sales. The finance company knows about the bank's weekly pick up when it agrees to purchase the paper from Ray, so it makes arrangements to pick up the paper it purchases every Friday morning. Will the finance company have priority over the bank if the bank claims the chattel paper? See 9-330.

PROBLEM 6–10

Instead of a security interest in Ray's inventory, the bank takes a security interest in the installment plan paper created when Ray sells appliances. The security agreement prohibits Ray from selling or otherwise encumbering the installment plan paper. The bank perfects its security interest by filing a financing statement. At the end of each month, the finance company purchases Ray's paper at a discount of 80% of face value. The finance company knows that Ray's bank has a security interest in the installment plan paperwork but takes it anyway. If Ray stops paying the bank, can the bank get the paperwork back from the finance company? See 9-330.

PROBLEM 6–11

Sometimes Ray sells appliances on credit but does not retain a security interest in the appliances. In many of these transactions Ray will have the customer sign a promissory note in the amount of the purchase price plus finance charge. Ray also sells these notes to the finance company at a discount on a regular basis. The finance company knows that Ray's bank has a security interest in Ray's inventory and that the notes are proceeds of the bank's security interest, but it takes the notes anyway. If Ray stops paying the bank, can the bank get the notes back from the finance company? See 9-330.

C. STATUTORY LIENS

In most states, certain persons who service or repair personal property are entitled by either statute or local common law to assert a lien against the property serviced or repaired for the cost of the services or repairs. Although statutory liens are not subject to Article 9's requirements for creation and perfection of security interests in personal property, they do exist, and when a statutory lien is asserted against property that is also subject to a perfected Article 9 security interest, we will have a priority dispute that requires resolution. Article 9 resolves the dispute in favor of the statutory lien creditor if the lien satisfies the requirements of 9-333. The threshold requirement under 9-333 is that the lien be possessory—that the lien is effective under state law only if the lien creditor has possession of the property against which the lien is asserted.

The *Borden* case examines the requirements for priority of a statutory lien under 9-333.

IN RE: BORDEN

United States Bankruptcy Appellate Panel for the Eighth Circuit
361 B.R. 489 (B.A.P. 8th Cir. 2007)

SCHERMER, *Bankruptcy Judge.*

Bellamy's Inc. ("Artisan") appeals the bankruptcy court's order determining that the lien of Genoa National Bank ("Lender") in certain farm equipment owned by Michael R. Borden ("Debtor") takes priority over the Artisan's lien in the same equipment. For the reasons set forth below, we reverse.

ISSUE

This case involves a priority dispute between two lienholders: the Lender who asserts a first priority blanket lien on all of the personal property of the Debtor and his wife, and the Artisan who asserts an artisan's lien on certain equipment by virtue of repairs to the equipment. After filing bankruptcy, the Debtor took the equipment from the Artisan without authority, used it in his farming operations, and later returned the equipment to the Artisan's possession. The question on appeal is whether the Artisan has a lien which takes priority over the Lender's lien. In order to answer this question, we must determine if the Artisan lost its lien when the Debtor removed the equipment from the Artisan's possession and what impact, if any, the Debtor's post-petition return of the equipment to the Artisan had on its lien. We conclude that the Artisan did not lose its lien when the Debtor took the equipment from its possession, that the Debtor's return of the equipment was not necessary for the Artisan to have a lien, and that the Artisan's lien has priority over the Lender's blanket lien.

BACKGROUND

On June 25, 2002, the Debtor and his wife granted the Lender a blanket security interest on all of their personal property, including machinery and equipment then owned and thereafter acquired. The Lender perfected its security interest by filing a UCC financing statement with the Nebraska Secretary of State on June 26, 2002.

On separate occasions in late 2004, the Debtor took a certain cornhead and a certain tractor (collectively the "Equipment") to the Artisan for repairs. The Artisan performed the repairs and in February 2005 sent the Debtor a bill in the amount of $3,811.46 for the work performed on the cornhead and in March 2005 sent a bill in the amount of $1,281.34 for the work performed on the tractor. The Debtor did not have the money to pay for the repairs and the Artisan refused to release the Equipment to the Debtor without payment, so the Equipment remained in the Artisan's possession.

On April 1, 2005 ("Petition Date"), the Debtor and his wife filed a joint voluntary petition for relief under Chapter 12 of the Bankruptcy Code. The Equipment was in the Artisan's possession on the Petition Date. In June 2005, the Debtor took the tractor from the Artisan's lot without permission, drove it to his farm, and used it in connection with his farming operations. The Artisan discovered the tractor was missing and contacted the Debtor to inquire if he had it in his possession. The Debtor admitted that he had taken the tractor, explained that he needed it for his farming operations, and agreed to return it to the Artisan as soon as he was finished using it. The tractor broke down while the Debtor was using it. Nevertheless, the Debtor returned the tractor to the Artisan in the fall of 2005.

In September 2005, the Debtor took the cornhead from the Artisan's lot without permission. The Artisan became aware that the cornhead was missing and contacted the Debtor regarding its whereabouts. The Debtor admitted that he had taken the cornhead, explained that he was using it to harvest corn, and agreed to return it as soon as he completed harvesting the crop. The Debtor returned the cornhead to the Artisan in November 2005.

In April 2006, the Lender filed a motion to determine the priority of the respective liens asserted by the Lender and the Artisan in the Equipment. The bankruptcy court determined that no controlling law existed in Nebraska governing the situation of competing liens where an artisan loses possession of the personal property through action of the property owner. The bankruptcy court looked to other jurisdictions for guidance and found that other courts faced with the issue had reached conflicting results. The bankruptcy court decided that the Lender's lien had priority over the lien asserted by the Artisan. In reaching its decision, the bankruptcy court concluded that continuous possession is required to maintain an artisan's lien. Therefore the Artisan could not have had a possessory artisan's lien. The Artisan filed a motion to reconsider which was denied by the bankruptcy court. The Artisan appealed.

* * *

DISCUSSION

Nebraska law provides a lien to any person who repairs a vehicle, machinery, or a farm implement while in such person's possession for the reasonable or agreed charges for the work done or materials furnished on or to such vehicle, machinery, or farm implement and authorizes the artisan to retain possession of the property until the charges are paid. Such a lien is referred to as an artisan's lien. Nebraska law also recognizes a possessory lien as an interest, other than a security interest or an agricultural lien, which secures payment or performance of an obligation for services or materials furnished with respect to goods by a person in the ordinary course of such person's business which is created by statute or rule in favor of the person and whose effectiveness depends on the person's possession of the goods. *Neb. Rev. Stat. U.C.C.§9-333(a)*. An artisan's lien falls within this definition of possessory lien under Nebraska law. A possessory lien on goods, such as an artisan's lien, has priority over a security interest in the goods unless the possessory lien is created by a statute that expressly provides otherwise. *Neb. Rev. Stat. U.C.C.*

§9-333(b). The artisan's lien statute does not provide otherwise; accordingly, an artisan's lien has priority over a previously perfected security interest in the same goods.

In order to determine the respective rights of the Lender and the Artisan in the Equipment, we must determine if the Artisan has an artisan's lien in the Equipment under Nebraska law. If the Artisan does, its lien has priority over the Lender's security interest in the Equipment. In making this determination, we must answer the difficult question of whether the Artisan has a possessory lien where it involuntarily lost and later regained possession of the Equipment without court authority following the Debtor's bankruptcy filing. The statute is silent on this situation and no Nebraska court has addressed this situation other than the trial court below.

Courts from other jurisdictions have addressed various situations where artisans have lost possession of the personal property to which they provided services yet asserted a lien thereon either without possession or after regaining possession. Some general rules can be gleaned from the case law. First, possession is generally required for a possessory lien. *Mack Fin. Corp. v. Peterbilt of Chattanooga, Inc. (In re Glenn), 20 B.R. 98, 99-100 (Bankr. E.D. Tenn. 1982); Gen. Motors Acceptance Corp. v. Colwell Diesel Serv. & Garage, Inc., 302 A.2d 595, 597 (Me. 1973); Yellow Mfg. Acceptance Corp. v. Bristol, 193 Ore. 24, 236 P.2d 939, 946 (Or. 1951).* If an artisan surrenders possession, the artisan no longer has a possessory lien with priority over pre-existing security interests. *Yellow Mfg. Acceptance Corp. v. Bristol, 236 P.2d at 946.* Some courts recognize a continuing lien as between the artisan and the owner after return of possession to the owner; however, such lien lacks priority over pre-existing security interests. *Forrest Cate Ford, Inc. v. Fryar, 62 Tenn. App. 572, 465 S.W.2d 882, 883-84 (Tenn. Ct. App. 1971); Yellow Mfg. Acceptance Corp. v. Bristol, 236 P.2d at 946-47.* Other courts relegate the lien to a state of suspended animation upon release of the goods to the owner; the artisan cannot enforce the lien while it is in a state of suspended animation. *Gordon v. Sullivan, 88 U.S. App. D.C. 144, 188 F.2d 980, 981-82 (D.C. Cir. 1951).* In this situation, if the artisan regains possession lawfully, the ability to enforce the artisan's lien is once again available to the artisan. *Id. at 982.*

Where the artisan loses possession involuntarily, the artisan does not necessarily lose the artisan's lien. *Smith v. Cooper Chevrolet, Inc., 404 So. 2d 49, 51 (Ala. 1981); Finch v. Miller, 271 Ore. 271, 531 P.2d 892, 893 (Or. 1975)*(en banc); *Gen. Motors Acceptance Corp. v. Colwell Diesel Serv. & Garage, Inc., 302 A.2d at 597; Yellow Mfg. Acceptance Corp. v. Bristol, 236 P.2d at 947.* Likewise, a conditional release of goods does not necessarily defeat the artisan's lien. *Smith v. Cooper Chevrolet, Inc., 404 So. 2d at 51.* This result follows at least with respect to holders of prior security interests who are not impaired by the conditional release. *M & I W. State Bank v. Wilson, 172 Wis. 2d 357, 493 N.W.2d 387, 390 (Wis. Ct. App. 1992).* Some courts hold that an artisan's lien lost when possession is lost is revived upon resumption of possession. Such a lien retains its priority as before the release except that the lien is subordinate to the interests of a bona fide purchaser or a creditor who attached or levied on the property while it was in the possession of the owner. *M & I W. State Bank v. Wilson, 493 N.W.2d at 390.* The *M & I Western State Bank v. Wilson* court expressly held that continuous or retained possession is not required. *Id. at 392.* See also *Thorp Commercial Corp. v. Mississippi Road Supply Co., 348 So. 2d 1016 (Miss. 1977),* holding that where there was no change in the status or rights of the parties between the date personal property was delivered to the owner and the date it was returned to the artisan, the prior lender was not prejudiced by the restoration of the artisan's lien which had priority over the pre-existing security interest.

We conclude that the Artisan did not lose its artisan's lien in the Equipment when the Debtor took the Equipment without the Artisan's knowledge or consent. Such involuntary loss of possession does not defeat the Artisan's lien. Furthermore, even if the Artisan's failure to take action to regain possession of the Equipment can be deemed consent to the Debtor's prior wrongful taking of the Equipment, such after-the-fact consent could not have been more than a conditional consent to the Debtor's temporary use of the Equipment with an agreement to return it to the Artisan. A conditional consent to a prior wrongful taking likewise does not defeat the Artisan's lien.

This result is consistent with the policy underlying the creation and priority of security interests. A lien or security interest must be perfected. The purpose of perfection is to give the world notice of the lien or security interest. Notice is generally accomplished in one of three ways: by registering the lien with an agency (usually a local government entity or a secretary of state's office), by noting the lien on the title, or by possession. Third parties can learn of any liens or security interests in any particular property by searching the records of the appropriate authority or by viewing the title. If no lien or security interest is disclosed, the third party may rely on the assumption that the property is owned free and clear of any liens if the property is in the owner's possession.

An artisan's lien does not require registration with any entity. Therefore, in order to give notice of the lien, the artisan is permitted to retain the property until receiving payment for the services provided to the property. Upon payment the lien is satisfied and the artisan releases the property. A third party interested in the property can easily learn that the property is not in the owner's possession and is then put on inquiry notice to determine why the owner does not have possession of the property. If the owner cannot produce the property, the third party has notice that another entity, including an artisan, may assert an interest in such property. A third party who continues to deal with the property owner after learning the owner lacks possession of the property does so at his or her peril.

With respect to competing holders of liens or security interests in the same property, notice of the various liens and security interests allows each interested party to know where he or she falls in the pecking order. With respect to recorded interests, the general rule is that first in time has priority. However, artisan's liens are not recorded and invariably are created after security interests have been granted. Courts and legislatures generally recognize that a party who provides labor and materials to property enhances the value of the property. Therefore, the principles of natural justice and commercial necessity dictate that the entity who enhances the value of property should be entitled to payment for such services and may retain the property until receipt of payment therefor. Indeed, the Nebraska statute at issue in this case provides exactly that. Artisan's lien laws are to be liberally construed to accomplish their equitable purpose of aiding materialmen and laborers to obtain compensation for materials used and services bestowed upon property of another which thereby enhances the value of such property.

A lender who advances funds to acquire certain property or who loans money secured by existing property does so on the basis of the property at the time of the loan. The lender generally assumes the owner will maintain the property after the loan is made and often mandates such maintenance in the loan documentation. If the property later breaks or is in need of maintenance, the owner takes the property to an artisan for repair or maintenance. Such repair or maintenance enhances the value of the property, thus enhancing the value of the lender's collateral. The lender thus benefits from the repair. This was the case with the Equipment. The Lender took the security interest in the Equipment long before the Artisan performed the repairs to it. Immediately prior to the repairs, the Equipment was not working properly and therefore its value was diminished. By performing the repairs, the Artisan enhanced the value of the Equipment, thus benefitting the Lender by increasing the value of its collateral. Recognizing the superiority of the Artisan's lien over the Lender's security interest is consistent with the policy underlying artisan lien law.

The bankruptcy court was troubled by the lack of certainty where an artisan is permitted to retain a lien without maintaining possession of the property. By requiring continuous possession in order to maintain an artisan's lien, the court limited uncertainty. While certainty is a valid goal in statutory interpretation, it should not come at the expense of the purpose behind the statute. Artisan's liens are designed to be equitable in nature and to protect the rights of artisans. If the artisan voluntarily surrenders possession, the artisan loses its lien. However, if the artisan loses possession through no action of his or her own, the artisan should not be punished. This is especially true where the Lender benefitted from the repairs to its collateral and its interests in the Equipment were in no way impaired when the Debtor took the Equipment from the Artisan nor when he later returned the Equipment to the Artisan.

The bankruptcy court relied on the *Glenn* decision in reaching its conclusion that continuous possession is required for an artisan's lien. In *Glenn*, the artisan returned the property to the owner upon receipt of a check for payment of the services. When the check was dishonored, the artisan requested the owner to return the property to the artisan, which the owner did. The *Glenn* court concluded that once the artisan relinquishes possession, the artisan's lien is lost and cannot be re-established by regaining possession. *Mack Fin. Corp. v. Peterbilt of Chattanooga, Inc. (In re Glenn), 20 B.R. at 100*. However, the *Glenn* court expressly acknowledged that wrongfully obtaining possession of the property subject to the lien dispute might change the result. *Id. at 101*. The present situation, where the Debtor took the Equipment without permission, is such a situation. In *Glenn*, the artisan could have protected itself by demanding payment in collectible funds prior to release of the property. In the present case, the Debtor took the Equipment from the Artisan without permission. The Artisan could not have prevented such wrongful action on the part of the Debtor.

The bankruptcy court was also concerned that allowing an artisan to regain its lien by regaining possession of property would give the Debtor control over the respective priorities between the Artisan and the Lender. The bankruptcy court cited the *Glenn* decision which in turn quoted from the dissent in *Thorp Commercial Corp. v. Mississippi Road Supply Co.* to support this policy argument. See *Mack Fin. Corp. v. Peterbilt of Chattanooga, Inc. (In re Glenn), 20 B.R. at 100-101*, quoting *Thorp Commercial Corp. v. Mississippi Road Supply Co., 348 So. 2d at 1018* (Patterson, C.J., dissenting). We hold that the Artisan did not lose its lien when the Debtor took the Equipment without the Artisan's permission. Therefore, this policy argument does not impact our holding. Furthermore, the bankruptcy court's decision accomplished the very thing it set out to avoid—it allowed the Debtor to dictate the respective priorities between the Artisan and the Lender by permitting the Debtor's wrongful taking of the Equipment to determine the outcome of the priority dispute at the trial level.

Finally, the bankruptcy court determined that even if an artisan's lien does not require continuous possession and that such a lien can be revived when possession is regained, the automatic stay of *Section 362 of the Bankruptcy Code* prevented the Artisan from gaining possession of the Equipment or from perfecting a lien postpetition. See *11 U.S.C.§362*. Therefore, according to the bankruptcy court, without relief from the automatic stay the Artisan should not have been able to regain possession of the Equipment. While technically true, this statement is incomplete and ignores the entire picture.

On the Petition Date, the Artisan was in possession of the Equipment and thus had an artisan's lien with priority over the Lender's security interest. The petition date controls the allowance of claims in bankruptcy. See *11 U.S.C.§502(b)*. Therefore, with respect to the Debtor's bankruptcy case, the Artisan has a claim secured by an artisan's lien. Such a claim has priority over the Lender's secured claim under Nebraska law. *Neb. Rev. Stat. U.C.C.§9-333(b)*. Nothing in the Bankruptcy Code alters this result. Therefore, the Artisan's lien in the Equipment has priority over the Lender's security interest therein.

Furthermore, if all parties had played by the rules, the result would be the same as that reached in this opinion. As of the Petition Date, the Artisan had possession of the Equipment. If the Debtor wanted possession of the Equipment, he should have sought its turnover pursuant to *Section 542 of the Bankruptcy Code.* See *11 U.S.C. §542.* The Artisan, in turn, would no doubt have demanded adequate protection of its artisan's lien under *Section 363 of the Bankruptcy Code* prior to releasing possession of the Equipment. See *11 U.S.C. §363(e).* At such point in time, the parties might have agreed upon a resolution or the court would have fashioned a remedy that protected the Artisan's lien interest while allowing the Debtor to use the Equipment. It is fundamentally unfair to punish the Artisan for a technical violation of the automatic stay which occurred as a result of the Debtor's actions, not the Artisan's actions. This is especially true where the Lender was not harmed by the Debtor's taking of the Equipment and its subsequent return to the Artisan, and may, in fact, have benefitted from the Debtor's use of the Equipment to plant and harvest a crop which may have produced funds to pay the Lender's claim.

CONCLUSION

The Artisan had an artisan's lien in the Equipment on the date the Debtor filed bankruptcy which had priority over the Lender's security interest under Nebraska law. The Artisan did not lose its artisan's lien nor its priority over the Lender's security interest when the Debtor took the Equipment from the Artisan's possession postpetition without authority. Accordingly, under these circumstances we REVERSE the bankruptcy court's order determining that the Lender's security interest in the Equipment takes priority over the Artisan's lien therein.

PROBLEM 6–12

Ray's customers often have old appliances they want to trade in as part of the consideration they pay for the new appliances he sells them. Most of these trade-ins need repairs and/or refurbishing. Ray sends them to the local appliance-repair shop which restores them to saleable condition, and Ray puts them on display in the used appliances section of his store. Recent cash-flow problems have prevented Ray from paying for the repairs to the last load of appliances he left with the repair shop. A state statute gives the repair shop a lien on the appliances it services until the owner pays for the repairs. The lien has priority over other claims to the appliances as long as the repair shop has possession. Ray can't sell the appliances if they are at the repair shop—so he talks the owner of the shop into letting him load the repaired appliance onto a truck, which he parks at his store when it's open but then drives back and parks at the repair shop each night when he closes his store. In a dispute with the bank claiming a security interest in the inventory of Ray's store, will the repair shop have priority over the bank as to the appliances that are subject to its statutory lien for the repairs it made? See 9-333.

D. Waiver

Under 9-315(a)(1), if the secured party authorizes the debtor to sell or transfer its collateral, the general rule that the security interest follows the collateral does not apply. When the secured party actually authorizes the debtor's disposition of the collateral, courts have refused to allow the secured party to enforce its security interest against the debtor's transferee under 9-315(a)(1) and its predecessor, 9-306(2). But under old Article 9, courts sometimes refused to enforce a security interest against a debtor's transferee who could not qualify as a buyer in the ordinary course, where there was no actual authorization by the secured party, or where there was a clause in the security agreement that prohibited a transfer of the collateral without a prior written authorization by the secured party. In these cases the courts usually relied on some concept of "waiver" to hold that the secured party could not enforce the security interest against the transferee. As the next case explains, the wording of the authorized disposition clause in 9-315(a)(1) of Revised Article 9 is different from the wording of that clause under old Article 9. Does the difference in wording strengthen or weaken the basis for holding that a secured party has waived its right to enforce the security interest against a transferee of the debtor?

IN RE: JERSEY TRACTOR TRAILER TRAINING INC.

United States Court of Appeals for the Third Circuit
580 F.3d 147 (3rd Cir. 2009)

BARRY, *Circuit Judge*.

This case arises out of the competing claims of Wawel Savings Bank ("Wawel") and Yale Factors LLC ("Yale") to the accounts receivable of debtor Jersey Tractor Trailer Training, Inc. ("JTTT"). Wawel entered into a loan agreement with JTTT and its president, William B. Oliver, for the principal amount of $315,000. In the corresponding security agreement, JTTT pledged all capital equipment and assets of the company as collateral, and Wawel perfected its security interest by filing Uniform Commercial Code Financing Statements ("UCC-1s") with the New Jersey Department of the Treasury and the Bergen County Clerk's Office. Approximately one year later, JTTT entered into a factoring agreement with Yale whereby JTTT agreed to sell the rights to its accounts receivable in return for, inter alia, a 61.5 percent up-front payment of the amount due on the particular account receivable. Yale subsequently filed a UCC-1 statement describing its lien on all present and after-acquired accounts receivable of JTTT.

On April 4, 2006, JTTT filed a voluntary petition for bankruptcy under Chapter 11 of the United States Bankruptcy Code, *see 11 U.S.C. §1101, et seq.*, and on June 29, 2006, Wawel brought this action seeking declaratory relief that its lien on JTTT's accounts receivable had priority over Yale's lien; that it was entitled to the proceeds of JTTT's accounts receivable that had been held in escrow following a state action filed by Yale; and that it was entitled to JTTT's outstanding accounts receivable until its lien was satisfied. Because the parties did not dispute that Wawel had a "first in time" lien against JTTT's accounts receivable—and thus a senior security interest—the central issue was whether Yale could establish that it maintained a priority position as a matter of law. *See N.J.S.A §12A:9-322(a)(1); U.C.C. §9-322(a)(1)* ("Except as otherwise provided … [c]onflicting perfected security interests … rank according to priority in time of filing or perfection."). More specifically, unless Yale could establish (a) that Wawel consented to the sale of JTTT's accounts receivable free of its security interest, *see U.C.C. §9-315(a)(1)*, … then Wawel was entitled to the relief it sought.

Following a two-day bench trial, the Bankruptcy Court found in favor of Wawel, stating that it was "entitled … to a judgment granting it … all [accounts] receivable proceeds presently held in escrow, as well as the proceeds of all outstanding accounts receivable." The Bankruptcy Court found, as a matter of fact, that Wawel did not authorize JTTT's factoring agreement with Yale, … Yale appealed to the District Court pursuant to *28 U.S.C. §158(a)*, and the District Court affirmed.

We will affirm in part because the Bankruptcy Court properly concluded that Wawel had not authorized the sale of JTTT's accounts receivable free of its security interest. The Bankruptcy Court's analysis of whether Yale should be considered a purchaser of instruments or a holder in due course, however, is undermined by its legal conclusion that a lien search is commercially unreasonable if it does not include the debtor's full corporate name. We will, therefore, vacate the judgment of the District Court affirming the order of the Bankruptcy Court, and remand to the District Court with the direction that the case be remanded to the Bankruptcy Court to determine whether Yale qualifies as a holder in due course or as a purchaser of instruments.

* * *

III. DISCUSSION

Generally, "[c]onflicting perfected security interests … rank according to priority in time of filing or perfection." *U.C.C. §9-322(a)(1)*. There are, however, exceptions—three of which Yale argues apply here. First, a senior secured creditor may waive its security interest, *see id.* at *§9-315(a)(1)*, and Yale asserts that Wawel did precisely that …

New Jersey has adopted revised Article 9 of the U.C.C., *see N.J.S.A 12A:9-101, et sec.*, and its decisions interpreting the U.C.C. are binding on us. *See Adams v. Madison Realty & Devel., 853 F.2d 163, 166 (3d Cir. 1988)*. Where, as here, such case law is lacking, we look to other courts' interpretation of the same language. *See id.*

A. CONSENT TO SALE & U.C.C. §9-315(A)(1)

Yale's argument that Wawel waived its security interest in JTTT's accounts receivable relies on *U.C.C. §9-315(a)(1)*, which states that "a security interest ... continues in collateral notwithstanding sale ... or other disposition thereof *unless the secured party authorized the disposition free of the security interest.* ..." (Emphasis added). The general rule, as the commentary notes, is "that a security interest survives the disposition of the collateral," and Yale must establish that JTTT's sale of its accounts receivable fits within the exception for "authorized disposition 'free of' the security interest." *Id.* at cmt. 2. The question we must answer is whether the Bankruptcy Court clearly erred in concluding that it did not do so.

Yale argues, first, that because the security agreement accompanying Wawel's loan to JTTT did not expressly prohibit the sale of collateral, Wawel waived its security interest. That argument is without merit, especially given that in its agreement with Wawel, JTTT represented that it "w[ould] not settle any account for less than its full value without your written permission," and that it would "collect all accounts until [told] otherwise." (App. at 837.) JTTT's sale of its accounts receivable, therefore, ran afoul of the security agreement.

Alternatively, Yale argues that Wawel, in its course of dealing, implicitly waived its security interest. That argument has two components: first, that the Bankruptcy Court clearly erred in finding that Wawel lacked knowledge of the factoring agreement until December 9, 2005; and, second, that Wawel approved of the agreement to the extent that it surrendered its security interest in JTTT's accounts receivable. We are receptive to Yale's position regarding knowledge. At least one of four officers at Wawel—each of whom, according to Ranzinger's testimony, had the authority to bind the bank—received notification (via phone, facsimile, or mail) of each of the 199 wire transfers from "Yale Factors NJ LLC" to JTTT. *Cf. NCP Litig. Trust v. KPMG LLP, 901 A.2d 871, 879, 187 N.J. 353 (N.J. 2006)* ("The imputation doctrine is derived from common law rules of agency ... [and p]ursuant to those common law rules, a principal is deemed to know facts that are known to its agent"). We assume, therefore, for purposes of our analysis (and contrary to the Bankruptcy Court's factual determination), that Wawel was aware that JTTT was involved with a factor—and thus was selling its accounts receivable.

Even assuming that knowledge, however, there is a substantial difference between Wawel knowing of the sale of JTTT's accounts receivable, and Wawel authorizing the sale "free of its security interest." *See U.C.C. §9-315(a)(1)*. Yale argues to the contrary, but relies exclusively on cases interpreting former *U.C.C. §9-306(2)*, which was replaced by revised *U.C.C. §9-315(a)(1)* in New Jersey, effective July 1, 2001. *See U.C.C. §9-315* cmt. 2 (stating that "*Subsection (a)(1) ... derives from former Section 9-306(2)*"). The two sections differ in one material respect. Former *§9-306(2)* stated that "a security interest continues in collateral notwithstanding sale, exchange or other disposition thereof, *unless the disposition was authorized* by the secured party in the security agreement or otherwise ..." (emphasis added), while revised *§9-315(a)(1)* states: "a security interest ... continues in collateral notwithstanding sale, lease, license, exchange, or other disposition thereof *unless the secured party authorized the disposition free of the security interest.* ..." (emphasis added).[5]

The question of whether a creditor's tacit approval of the sale of collateral was enough to waive that creditor's security interest was also addressed by the American Law Institute's Permanent Editorial Board ("PEB") for the U.C.C. in 1990. *See* U.C.C. P.E.B. Commentary No. 3 (1990). The PEB analyzed whether there was a "conflict between [former] *U.C.C. §9-306(2)*, which terminate[d] a security interest upon any disposition of collateral that ha[d] been authorized by the secured party, and ... [former] *U.C.C. §9-402(7)*, which continue[d] the effectiveness of a financing statement with respect to collateral that ha[d] been transferred even though the secured party kn[ew] of and consent[ed] to the transfer[.]" *Id.* The PEB found no conflict because the "intent underlying [*§9-306(2)* was] to permit a disposition of the collateral free and clear of the security interest when the secured party has authorized the disposition free and clear of its security interest . ..." *Id.* The PEB continued: *§9-306(2)*, which set forth an "exception to the rule of survivability," applied only if the secured party specifically "authorized the disposition, by agreement or otherwise, *free and clear of the security interest.*" *Id.* (emphasis in original). The PEB Commentary was expressly adopted by revised *U.C.C. §9-315(a)(1)*. *See U.C.C. §9-315* cmt. 2.

Consistent with revised *U.C.C. §9-315(a)(1)*, we must determine whether there is any evidence to support Yale's contention that Wawel impliedly authorized the sale of JTTT's accounts receivable free and clear of its security interest. In so doing, we keep in mind that the theory underlying *U.C.C. §9-315(a) (1)* "is that a security interest would be meaningless if the secured party could not reach the collateral in the hands of a third party ... when the debtor disposes of it without authorization." William D. Hawkland, Frederick H. Miller & Neil B. Cohen, 9B *Hawkland U.C.C. Series* §9-315:1 [Rev] (2008). Because *§9-315(a)(1)* does not require a secured party to take action to preserve its

---

5   Former U.C.C. §9-306(2) was, at times, interpreted to state that a creditor who knew of but did not prevent the sale of its collateral had waived its security interest. See, e.g., LifeWise Master Funding v. Telebank, 374 F.3d 917, 923 (10th Cir. 2004) ("It is well settled ... that under [U.C.C.] §9-306(2), a lienholder who authorizes the sale of property in which he has a security interest waives the lien on the collateral ... [and] courts have even terminated security interests simply by implying authorization from a party's conduct") (citations omitted); Neu Cheese, 825 F.2d at 1273 (where bank failed to object to debtor's repeated sales of collateral its "conduct warrant[ed] an inference of the relinquishment of the bank's right in the collateral"). That interpretation was not unanimous. In J.I. Case Credit Corp., for example, the Tenth Circuit (interpreting Oklahoma law) held that, even assuming a creditor knew of the sale of its collateral, it did not waive its security interest where there was no suggestion in the record that the creditor "intended to ratify the prior sale and free the [collateral] from its security interest." 851 F.2d at 313 (emphasis in original).

security interest, inaction alone may not lead to a finding of implied authorization. Inaction, however, is all Yale can demonstrate—specifically that Wawel failed to stop the ongoing sales of JTTT's accounts receivable. Acts of "[i] mplied authorization ... must unequivocally demonstrate an intent to waive the security interest," Lary Lawrence, 11 *Anderson U.C.C.* §9-315:9 [Rev] at 439 (2007), and evidence of such unequivocal intent is absent here.

* * *

III. CONCLUSION

For the foregoing reasons, we will affirm the District Court's decision to the extent it affirms the Bankruptcy Court's determination that Wawel did not waive its security interest in JTTT's accounts receivable.

E. LEASES

Article 9, as we've seen, prevents the enforcement of a security interest against certain buyers of collateral from the debtor. But what if, instead of selling the secured party's collateral, the debtor leases the collateral to another? Since Article 9 does not apply to lease transactions—at least not when the lease is a "true" lease—does the security interest follow the collateral in the absence of 9-315(a)(1)? If it does, can a lessee qualify somehow as a buyer in the ordinary course under 9-320 and take free of the security interest?

Consider the following problems:

PROBLEM 6–13

When Ray leases appliances to his customers, do the customers take the appliances they lease subject to the security interest of Ray's bank in the inventory of his store? Would your answer be different if the customers know that the appliances they lease are subject to the bank's security interest? See 9-321.

PROBLEM 6–14

Ray sold a commercial grade range to one of the upscale eateries in town. The sale was on credit, and Ray retained a security interest in the range. Earlier this year, the buyer agreed to lease the refrigerator to the 24-hour coffee shop next door for two years. If the buyer stops making payments to Ray, can Ray repossess the range from the buyer's lessee if the lessee is not in default under the lease? See 2A-307. Is there anything the lessee could have done to protect his interest in the range from repossession by Ray? See 2A-311.

F. Subordination

In Chapter 5, we looked at how purchase money priority allowed a later secured party to avoid subordination of its security interest under the general first in time rule. Another possible way to modify the first in time rule is through a subordination agreement. A secured party entitled to priority under 9-322 can agree to relinquish its priority to another creditor under 9-339. Seems simple enough, but beyond recognizing the right to subordinate, Article 9 does not address the construction or interpretation of subordination agreements. Construction and interpretation are left to the courts, and, as the following case shows, there may be more to a subordination agreement than the actual agreement itself.

ITT DIVERSIFIED CREDIT CORP., ET AL. v. FIRST CITY CAPITAL CORP.

Supreme Court of Texas
737 S.W.2d 803 (Tex. 1987)

GONZALEZ, *Judge.*

This is a case of first impression concerning the effect of a subordination agreement made between the first and third lienholders on the priority status of a second lienholder. The trial court gave the second lienholder priority over the first and third lienholders. The court of appeals affirmed the judgment of the trial court. *717 S.W.2d 419.* We reverse and remand.

First City National Bank (the Bank) acquired a first lien security interest on personal property owned by Sisco Enterprises. First City Capital Corporation (FCCC) obtained a second lien and ITT Diversified Corporation (ITT) obtained a third lien on the same assets.

In order for ITT to lend money to Sisco Enterprises, the Bank executed a subordination agreement to ITT, in which the Bank subordinated its interest in certain assets of the debtor to the interest of ITT. Thereafter, ITT foreclosed on these same assets. FCCC claimed the proceeds of the sale and when it was not paid, filed suit alleging that its security interest was superior to ITT's interest. The trial court held that the subordination agreement between the Bank and ITT did not give ITT priority over the interest possessed by FCCC. The trial court rendered judgment that FCCC recover from ITT the proceeds from the sale of the assets in question, plus interest and costs, and the court of appeals affirmed. ITT asserts that the trial court and the court of appeals erred in holding that the subordination agreement did not allow ITT to succeed to the interest of the Bank.

The Texas Business & Commerce Code provides that nothing in article 9 prevents subordination by agreement by any person entitled to priority. *Tex. Bus. & Com. Code Ann. §9.316* [Now 9-339] (Vernon Supp. 1987). *Section 1.102* of the Code specifically allows provisions of the Code to be varied by agreement. *Tex. Bus. & Com. Code Ann. §1.102(c)* (Vernon 1968). Moreover, a subordination agreement is nothing more than a contractual modification of lien priorities and must be construed according to the expressed intention of the parties and its terms. *Vahlsing Christina Corp. v. First Nat'l Bank of Hobbs, 491 S.W.2d 954* (Tex. Civ. App.—El Paso 1973, writ ref'd n.r.e.).

The court of appeals relied on *McConnell v. Mortgage Inv. Co. of El Paso, 292 S.W.2d 636, 638* (Tex. Civ. App.—El Paso 1955), *aff'd*, 157 Tex. 572, 305 S.W.2d 280 (1957). *McConnell* is inapplicable because it dealt exclusively with the priorities between a deed of trust, a vendor's lien, and a mechanic's and a materialman's lien. In *McConnell*, we specifically noted that the litigation involved the priority of liens arising from a real estate transaction. In a non-real property situation, the third lienholder should be able to succeed to that part of the interest that was subordinated by the first lienholder, so long as the second lienholder is neither burdened nor benefitted by the subordination agreement. For example, A, B and C have claims against the debtor which are entitled to priority in alphabetical order. "A" subordinates his claim to "C." After foreclosure of the secured interest, the resulting fund is insufficient to satisfy all three claims. The proper distribution of the fund is as follows.

1. Set aside from the fund the amount of "A"'s claim.

2. Out of the money set aside, pay "C" the amount of its claim, pay "A" to the extent of any balance remaining after "C"'s claim is satisfied.

3. Pay "B" the amount of the fund remaining after "A"'s claim has been set aside.

4. If any balance remains in the fund after "A"'s claim has been set aside and "B"'s claim has been satisfied, distribute the balance to "C" and "A".

Thus, "C", by virtue of the subordination agreement, is paid first, but only to the amount of "A"'s claim, to which "B" was in any event junior. "B" receives what it had expected to receive, the fund less "A"'s prior claim. If "A"'s claim is smaller than "C"'s, "C" will collect the balance of its claim, in its own right, only after "B" has been paid in full. "A", the subordinator, receives nothing until "B" and "C" have been paid except to the extent that its claim, entitled to first priority, exceeds the amount of "C"'s claim, which, under its agreement, is to be first paid.

The trial court should set aside from the fund the amount of the Bank's claim and out of this amount, pay ITT the amount of its claim. Then, the trial court should allocate to the Bank any balance remaining after ITT's claim is satisfied, and then allocate to FCCC the amount of the fund remaining after the Bank's claim has been set aside. If any balance remains in the fund after the Bank's claim has been set aside and FCCC's claim has been satisfied, the court should distribute the balance to ITT and then to the Bank. Thus, ITT, by virtue of the subordination agreement, is paid first but only to the amount of the Bank's claim, to which FCCC was in any event junior. FCCC will receive what it expected to receive, the fund less the Bank's prior claim. The judgment of the court of appeals is reversed and this cause is remanded to the trial court for rendition of judgment consistent with this opinion.

CHAPTER 7

FIXTURES

Long before the Code, real property law laid claim to personal property that had in some way become connected to specific real estate. Once the personal property became subject to real property law, anyone claiming an interest in the real property acquired an interest in the personal property—now called a fixture. Fixtures were subject to the local real estate recording system, and anyone claiming an interest in the fixture as personal property would have to record that interest in the real property records to protect it against claims to the real property.

A. FIXTURES UNDER ARTICLE 9: 9–334

Article 9 does not change this pre-Code law regarding fixtures. Instead, 9-334 anticipates conflicting claims to fixtures between someone claiming an interest in the fixture as personal property and another claiming an interest in the fixture as real property, and provides rules for resolving such conflicts. It leaves almost everything else to non-Code law—including the determination of when personal property becomes a fixture:

> "Fixtures" means goods that have become so connected to particular real property that an interest in them arises under real property law.

9-102(41). Because real property law is anything but uniform from state to state—or as Gilmore described it "inconsistent, crotchety and unpredictable,"[1] Article 9 provides no further guidance on what constitutes a fixture. Parties must consult the law of the jurisdiction where the potential fixture will be located for a definitive answer in each transaction.

---

1   Gilmore, Security Interests in Personal Property, 819.

In re Moore and *In Re Jarvis* introduce a three-factor test that many courts have used or adapted for use to determine whether particular personal property has become a fixture. For our purposes, the three factors provide a working definition we can use to at least identify a potential fixture issue.

IN RE MOORE

United States Bankruptcy Court for the District of Kansas
2011 Bankr. LEXIS 1069 (D. Kan. March 23, 2011)

NUGENT, *Judge*.

This matter came before the Court on December 14, 2010, for evidentiary hearing on Trustee's Complaint to avoid, pursuant to *11 U.S.C. ß 544(a)*, the defendant Dickinson County Bank's lien on a 2000 16x76 foot single wide manufactured home, which is part of the Debtors' homestead.

FINDINGS OF FACT

The Court makes the following findings of fact, based upon the stipulations in the Pretrial Order, the testimony of the witnesses, and the exhibits admitted by stipulation.

Debtors Ivan C. Moore and Brandy L. Moore (hereafter collectively "Debtors") filed a voluntary petition for relief under Chapter 7 on April 15, 2009. Their schedules include as real property a residence located near Abilene, Kansas with a value of $74,000, subject to a lien of $80,000 held by Dickinson County Bank (hereafter "Bank"). Debtors claim the residence as their exempt homestead. J. Michael Morris was appointed Chapter 7 Trustee.

The homestead property is comprised of approximately 10.4 acres in a rural area on which there is a 2000 Bonn 16 x 80 foot manufactured home, VIN 8115, which is a manufactured home within the definition of the Kansas Manufactured Housing Act (hereafter the "Act"), *Kan. Stat. Ann. 58-4201, et seq*. Debtors purchased the property under a Real Estate Lease to Own Contract dated January 14, 2004 from Jesse and Dolly Vincent. As purchased, the property included the manufactured home which was already located on the real estate. The contract describes the interest purchased as a parcel of ground, without separate descriptions of the residence or other improvements. Monthly payments were due the sellers beginning July 15, 2004 and continuing until June 15, 2006, at which time a balloon payment of the amount owed to Solomon Sate Bank (which held a lien form [sic] the Vincents) was due. Since their purchase, Debtors have resided in the home.

In July, 2005, Debtors completed the purchase by borrowing $68,000 from the Bank. Debtors executed a promissory note, due on July 8, 2005, and a mortgage granting a lien of $68,000 on the property. The Vincents signed over the title to the manufactured home to Debtors, Solomon Bank released its lien, and Debtors delivered the title certificate to the Bank. The Bank knew that the residence was a manufactured home. The Bank's July 6, 2005 appraisal identifies the improvements as including a ranch style manufactured home. In addition, the Bank and Debtors signed an affidavit of Permanently Affixed Manufactured/Mobile Home and Application to Eliminate Title in which they each represented that the Bonn was indeed a manufactured home. For reasons unknown, the affidavit was never filed with the Department of Revenue. The Bank renewed the loan on November 27, 2007. Debtors made a renewal note for $84,475.44 that had a maturity date of November 1, 2010 and executed a second real estate mortgage for $17,000. The two mortgages were recorded, but the Bank took no other steps to perfect the Bank's interest in the residence.

The manufactured home has been affixed to the land as demonstrated by the following facts. The wheels have been removed from the manufactured home, which sits on cement block piers behind skirting. Tie down straps secure the manufactured home to the ground. The evidence establishes that this is the method often used to affix mobile homes to the land when they are situated on property not owned by the owner of the home, such as in mobile home parks, although the witnesses also testified that some manufactured homes are set on more permanent foundations. An enclosed mud room has been added to the rear of the manufactured home. The mud room is attached to the manufactured home with screws or nails, has a roof line that is a continuation of the roof of the manufactured home, and is permanently attached to a cement slab. The mud room is accessed by what would otherwise be the back door of the residence. The exit from the mud room is to a cement patio. The residence is permanently connected to electric service, a water line supplied with well water, a propane tank at the rear of the home, and a septic system. Debtors use an adjacent garage. Although Debtor Ivan Moore testified that the garage is owned by a relative of the Vincents, not by Debtors, the garage is included in the appraisal prepared for the Bank in July 2005 and is appraised as part of the property for tax purposes.

* * *

ANALYSIS AND CONCLUSIONS OF LAW

The Plaintiff Trustee asserts that the manufactured home is a fixture.

* * *

A. DEBTORS' MANUFACTURED HOME IS A FIXTURE

"A fixture is an article in the nature of personalty, which, has been so annexed or affixed to realty that it is regarded for legal purposes as part of the realty …" Kansas common law follows the widely used three part test to define fixtures. Under this test, whether personal property affixed to real estate is a fixture depends: "(1) whether it is actually annexed to the real estate; (2) whether it is adapted to the use of the land; and (3) whether the parties to the transaction intended the personalty to be permanently annexed." This common law test is consistent with *Article 9 of the UCC* "which adds a fourth dimension to the test: would the average buyer of the real estate reasonably expect the goods to be sold as part of the real estate?"[2] The Kansas Court of Appeals has recognized that a mobile home may become a fixture when affixed to real property.

By applying the common-law fixture elements, the Court can easily conclude that this manufactured home is a fixture. The wheels have been removed, the chassis sits on concrete block piers, and straps secure the home to the ground. It is not set on a permanent foundation, but this fact is not determinative. Many other factors support a finding that the home is a fixture. The home is permanently attached to electricity, water, propane, and a septic system. A mud room has been constructed. It is attached to a permanent concrete slab and either nailed or screwed to the manufactured home. The mud room, which is an integral part of the home, would have to be removed before the manufactured home could be detached from the real property.

The home has been adapted to use as real property. The real property is approximately 10 acres in a rural area and is suitable for residential use. The home was placed on the property before the home and the real property were purchased as a unit by the Debtors. The home and land were purchased by Debtors for use as their home, and they have lived there since the purchase. There is common ownership of the land and the home. A septic system has been installed and connected to the home. There is a concrete patio. The real property is served by utilities which are connected to the home.

The most important element is intent. There is no evidence that Debtors regarded the home other than as a permanent residence and as a part of the real property. The Bank financed Debtors' purchase of the land and the home as a single unit. Indeed, the Bank executed a document (the elimination certificate) in which it *agreed* the home was part of the reality. It just did not get the job done. As will be more fully examined below, the Bank intended, and did, acquire a lien in the land and the home by the real estate mortgages. The Bank paid the premiums for insurance on the home and the real property, since regulators regarded the home as part of the Bank's collateral.

---

2   *Peoples State Bank of Cherryvale v. Clayton, 2 Kan. App.2d at 439, 580 P.2d at 1377.* Although the UCC statutory definition of fixture has been amended since the *Clayton* decision, the substance of definition has not changed. *Kan. Stat. Ann. ß 84-9-102* (2009 Supp.), Official UCC Comment, [para.] 18. Under the prior version of *Article 9*, "goods are 'fixtures' when affixing them to the real estate so associates them with the real estate that, in the absence of any agreement of understanding with his vendor as to the goods, a purchaser of the real estate with knowledge of interests of others of record, or in possession, would reasonably consider the goods to have been purchased as part of the real estate." *Kan. Stat. Ann. ß 84-9-313(1)(a)* (Furse 1996). Revised *Article 9* provides, fixtures are "goods that have become so related to particular real property that an interest in them arises under real property law." *Kan. Stat. Ann. ß 84-9-102(a) (41)* (2009 Supp.).

The Court finds that an average buyer of the real property would assume that a purchase of the real property would include the manufactured home. As shown by the appraisal evidence, there are similar properties in the area where manufactured homes are affixed to rural land.

B. THE MORTGAGES EXECUTED BY DEBTORS GRANTED THE BANK A LIEN IN THE MANUFACTURED HOME.

The Bank initially contended that the mortgages granted by Debtors did not convey a lien in the manufactured home, but this argument is met by the plain language of the mortgages. The granting clauses of the mortgages state, "For valuable consideration, Grantor mortgages and warrants to Lender the following described real property, together with all existing or subsequently erected or *affixed* buildings, improvements and fixtures." The mortgages also grant "a Uniform Commercial Code security interest in the Personal Property and Rents" and define Personal Property as meaning "all equipment, *fixtures*, and other articles of personal property now or hereafter owned by Grantor, and now or hereafter attached or *affixed* to the Real Property ..." The security agreement portion of the mortgages states, "This instrument shall constitute a Security Agreement to the extent any of the Property constitutes *fixtures* ..." There can be no question that Debtors granted the Bank a lien in the described real property, fixtures attached to the real property, and other personal property attached to the real property and that the lien attached.

IN RE JARVIS
United States Bankruptcy Court for the Northern District of Ohio
310 B.R. 330 (N.D. Ohio 2004)

SPEER, *Judge*.

FACTS

With respect to the matter raised in the Parties' pleadings, these facts are not in dispute. The Debtors operate a hog raising business. As a part of their business operations, the Debtors own a parcel of real property, approximately three acres in size. On September 20, 2000, the Debtors executed in favor of Pandora Bank, two open-end mortgages on their real property as security for Pandora Bank making, under two separate promissory notes, loans totaling $242,800.00. On October 12, 2000, these mortgages were duly recorded under Ohio law so as to make them effective against any subsequent bona fide purchaser.

As a part of their hog operation, the Debtors formed a Limited Liability Company known as Jarvis Swine. The sole members of Jarvis Swine were the Debtors, and the Debtors' daughter, Allison Hiser. Jarvis Swine, however, had no interest in the real property the Debtors utilized in their hog operation.

However, the Debtors, in order to expand their hog operation, caused Jarvis Swine to enter a lease agreement with Telmark, the basis of which was to have Telmark finance the construction of two primary structures: (1) a 20-crate farrowing building; and (2) a 60' x 32' addition to a hog gestation building which included reroofing the existing building whose original dimension was 150' x 32'. Construction on these structures began on or around May 1, 2001, and continued for some time thereafter, with a "sales agreement" concerning construction on the structures being issued as late as December 20, 2001. The structures themselves are one full story in height, are set in a sturdy concrete foundation, and are hooked up to utilities.

The terms of this lease provided that, commencing May 1, 2002, Jarvis Swine would make 143 consecutive monthly payments to Telmark in the amount of $1,191.00. Notably lacking in the lease, was any provision allowing Jarvis Swine or the Debtors to buy the structures at the end of the lease term for a nominal amount. Instead, the lease provided three options at its termination: (1) renewal; (2) purchase of the buildings at a fair market value; or (3) repossession of the structures by the lessor. As it regards the latter, the testimony elicited at the Trial revealed that, as with other leases issued by Telmark of a similar nature, this option is exercised with some regularity.

To protect its lease interest, Telmark filed a UCC financing statement which set forth both the farrowing and gestation buildings as security for the lease; also, set forth therein was a short description of the Debtors' realty. This financing statement, which was filed on October 24, 2001, named as the debtors both Jarvis Swine and the Debtors in their personal capacity. Also, as additional security for the lease, the Debtors, in their individual capacity, granted to Telmark a mortgage interest in the improvements financed by Telemark; this mortgage was dated October 10, 2001, and then recorded on October 15, 2001. Later, this mortgage was assigned to Wells Fargo, who is the real party defending in the present action, with the notice of the assignment being recorded on March 27, 2003.

On December 31, 2002, the Debtors filed a petition in this Court for relief, as family farmers, under Chapter 12 of the United States Bankruptcy Code. Prior to filing, Pandora Bank had, through the filing of certificates of judgment, obtained separate liens against the Debtors' property: a lien for $153,029.52 dated December 23, 2002; a lien for $69,569.27 dated December 23, 2002; and a lien solely against Mr. Jarvis' interest in the property for $79,530.74 dated December 10, 2002. On June 30, 2003, the Debtors initiated the instant action seeking a determination as to the status of the respective Defendants' interest in their real property so as to enable them to properly put forth a plan of reorganization.

DISCUSSION

Based upon the above facts, Wells Fargo seeks to be treated as a lessor for purposes of *11 U.S.C. §365*. It is Pandora Bank's position, however, that, by virtue of the mortgage liens it holds against the Debtors' real property, its interest in the hog and farrowing structures constructed on this property is superior to that of Wells Fargo, as assignee of Telmark's financing lease. Based thereon, Pandora Bank seeks to be treated, to the detriment of Wells Fargo, as a secured creditor for the value of these structures, thereby entitling it to the benefits afforded by *11 U.S.C. §1225(a)(5)*.

In arguing for the superiority of its mortgage interests, Pandora Bank relies upon a single supposition: both the hog and farrowing structures constructed by Jarvis Swine, and financed by Telmark, are "fixtures" by virtue of their attachment to the Debtors' realty. As with other interests in property, whether an item of property is a fixture and the effect thereof, is determined by reference to applicable state law. *Butner v. United States, 440 U.S. 48, 54, 99 S.Ct. 914, 59 L.Ed.2d 136 (1979)*; *In re Shelton, 35 B.R. 505, 508 (Bankr. E.D.Va.1983)*. In this case, therefore, since Ohio is the situs of all the property at issue, Ohio's law on fixtures is controlling.

Under Ohio law a "fixture" is defined as an "article which was a chattel, but which by being physically annexed or affixed to the realty, became accessory to it and part and parcel of it." *Holland Furnace Co. v. Trumbull S. & L. Co., 135 Ohio St. 48, 52,13 O.O. 325, 19 N.E.2d 273, 275 (1939)*. In line with this definition of a fixture and also in line with Pandora Bank's position, Ohio law generally provides that an item of personalty that subsequently becomes a fixture takes subject to any previously recorded mortgage covering the realty, even though the mortgaging instrument makes no reference to the fixture. *Id.* In opposition to the applicability of this legal principle, Wells Fargo raised a number of different arguments, the most elemental of which, and the one that will be addressed first, is simply that the farrowing and gestation structures are not actually "fixtures" for purposes of Ohio law.

In *Teaff v. Hewitt*, the Supreme Court of Ohio set forth the following three-part test to determine whether an item [sic] personalty has become a fixture:

> (1) Actual annexation to the realty, or something appurtenant thereto;

> (2) Appropriation to the use or purpose of that part of the realty with which it is connected;

> (3) The intention of the party making the annexation, to make the article a permanent accession to the freehold.

1 Ohio St. 511, 527 (1853). As it pertains to these requirements, much of the evidence presented at the Trial centered on the first element: annexation. At the conclusion of the Trial, however, Wells Fargo, given the clear overwhelming weight of the evidence, conceded to the applicability of this element, thus leaving just the second and third elements of the "*Teaff*" test for this Court to decide.

As between the second and third requirements of the *Teaff* test, the Supreme Court of Ohio has held that "the intention of the annexing party is of primary importance." *Masheter v. Boehm, 37 Ohio St.2d 68, 73-74, 66 O.O.2d 183, 185, 307 N.E.2d 533, 538-39 (1974)*. With respect to the issue of intent, Ohio law looks not simply at the intent to affix a chattel to a parcel of reality, but beyond, asking whether the affixor, in fact, intended to "devote the chattel to the use and service of the land or structure already a part of the land, in such manner to enhance the serviceability of the whole as a permanent unit of property to whatever use it may be devoted." *Zangerle v. Standard Oil Co. of Ohio, 144 Ohio St. 506, 519, 60 N.E.2d 52 (1945)*. Telling in this regard, is any express agreement created between the parties.

As applied to this case, the evidence presented shows that the lease agreement between Telmark and Jarvis Swine specifically set forth that the farrowing and gestation structures were personal property. In doing so, the lease provided that at its expiration, Telmark, as the lesseer, was entitled to remove the buildings, at the expense of Jarvis Swine, if one of these two conditions was not met: (1) the lease was either not renewed; or (2) the buildings were not purchased for a fair market value. Additional enabling clauses of this lease provided the means by which Telmark could repossess its collateral. For example, Telmark was entitled to detach the hog and farrowing structures from any connected utilities. Thus, based upon these provisions of Telmark's lease, the intent of the Parties, at least from a contractual standpoint, was undoubtably to keep the farrowing and gestation structures personal property subject to Telmark's lease.

Nevertheless, while an agreement between the parties is relevant as to the issue of intent, it is not necessarily dispositive of the issue. Rather, an intent to create a fixture also has an objective component in that for a chattel to be found to be a fixture, it must be affixed to the realty in such a manner that it will indicate to all persons dealing with the realty that it was the intention and purpose of the owner of the chattel to make it a permanent attribute of the realty. *Holland Furnace Co. v. Trumbull Sav. & Loan Co., 135 Ohio St. 48, 13 Ohio Op. 325, 19 N.E.2d 273 (1939)*. Many different considerations are useful in this regard—for example, the permanent or impermanent nature of the property, the mode of attachment, and the relationship between the parties.

Of such objective considerations, particular attention is paid to the relationship between the parties—e.g., mortgagor/mortgagee; vendor/vendee; landlord/tenant. In the words of the Ohio Supreme Court, "the same article may be a fixture under certain circumstances and a chattel under others, and that there could be such a difference in the same article as between vendor and vendee, landlord and tenant, heir and executor, or a tenant for life and remainderman." *Roseville Pottery, Inc. v. County Bd. of Revision of Muskingum Cty., 149 Ohio St. 89, 95, 77 N.E.2d 608, 612 (1948)*. What is particularly important here is whether credit was extended based upon the assumption that the chattel was a fixture.

Looking now at this case, very little concerning the relationship among all of the Parties would suggest that there existed any intent to make the hog farrowing and gestation structures permanent attributes of the Debtors' realty. Of particular importance, Pandora Bank, having lent money to the Debtors prior to the time the farrowing and gestation buildings were constructed, did not extend credit based upon any enhancement in value such structures conferred upon the Debtors' realty. Also relevant in this regard, the evidence presented shows that, while no specific understanding was reached between the Parties, Pandora Bank was aware that the Debtors were contracting to have structures built on their property; however, Pandora Bank never sought nor obtained any sort of subordination agreement.

Additional objective considerations also do not support the conclusion that the hog and farrowing structures were intended to be permanent attributes of the Debtors' realty. Of particular noteworthiness, the evidence presented shows that, while being firmly attached to the realty, the structures at issue were constructed of light weight materials, similar to that of a mobile home. Also similar to a mobile home, the hog and farrowing structures, while longer, were similar in height and width to a standard mobile home, and the structures were connected to utilities. This is very telling given that mobile homes may or may not be fixture depending upon the individual circumstances. Along this same line, the testimony presented at the Trial revealed that it is the regular practice of Telmark/Wells Fargo to exercise its right of repossession in situations involving similar structures.

Based, therefore, on the above objective considerations, in conjuncture with the express terms of Telmark's lease agreement, it is this Court's conclusion that the greater weight of the evidence supports a finding that no intent existed, as it applies to the test set forth by the Ohio Supreme Court in *Teaff*, to create a fixture. Similarly, the greater weight of the evidence, as will now be explained, also supports a finding that the structures constructed on the Debtors' property are not fixtures for purposes of the second element of the *Teaff* test.

The second element of the *Teaff* test looks to the chattel's adaptability and/or applicability to the use and purpose of the realty to which it is attached. In the context of property used in the operation of a business, the Ohio Supreme Court, in *Zangerle v. Republic Steel Corp.*, addressed the issue of appropriation under the second element of the *Teaff v. Hewitt* test, holding, in paragraph seven of its syllabus:

> The general principle to be kept in view in determining whether what was once a chattel has become a fixture is the distinction between the business which is carried on in or upon the premises, and the premises. The former is personal in its nature, and articles that are merely accessory to the business, and have been put on the premises for this purpose, and not as accessions to the real estate, retain the personal character of the principal to which they belong and are subservient. But articles which have been annexed to the premises as accessory to it, whatever business may be carried on

upon it, and not peculiarly for the benefit of a present business which may be of temporary duration, become subservient to the realty and acquire and retain its legal character.

144 Ohio St. 529, 530, 30 Ohio Op. 160, 60 N.E.2d 170 171-72 (1945).

Based upon the application of this legal holding, the Court in *Zangerle v. Republic Steel Corp.*, found that steel processing machinery and equipment was personal property, rather than real property, stating, in paragraph eight of its syllabus, that, "the business of manufacturing is a pursuit personal in its character and not strictly subservient to real estate or essential to the enjoyment of the freehold or inheritance in land." *Id.*

Thus, when business property is at issue, the essence of the second element of *Teaff* test is whether the chattel is specific to the type of business conducted on the realty? If so, then it will retain its character as personal property; this, as noted in *McGowan v. McGowan*, is what is commonly referred to as a "trade fixture." *18 N.E.2d 419, 420, 59 Ohio App. 397, 399, 27 Ohio Law Abs. 212 (1938).* On the other hand, if the personalty is of the type that would generally be found on the realty, just the opposite is true, and the property (assuming, of course, that the other conditions of the *Teaff* test are met) may be deemed to be a fixture.

As for how this rule of law has been subsequently applied, a review of Ohio's case law shows that courts have looked primarily to the utility of the chattel with respect to a hypothetical purchaser (or even a simple occupier) of the underlying realty. For example, the following types of property have all been found to be particularly suited to the underlying business, and thus an accessory to the business rather than the underlying realty: … an oxygen furnace used for the manufacture of steel; a caging system for an egg production facility, a hydraulic boat lift that rests on the floor of a harbor channel; and a radio transmission tower.

By comparison, when an attached chattel may be more easily utilized by a subsequent buyer or occupier of the realty, courts are more apt to find that the chattel is a fixture based upon its improvement of the underlying realty.

As applied to this case, this Court is presented with a very close call. On the one side, the hog farrowing and gestations structures are unique to the Debtors' business of hog breeding. On the other hand, similar types of structures—i.e., storage structures for animals and/or equipment—are typically found on property utilized in the agricultural business.

On the whole, however, the latter statement has a clear weakness over the former. Specifically, the latter statement presumes that the Debtors' property would be utilized by a subsequent buyer for agricultural use, not in a residential or industrial capacity where the value of farrowing and gestation structures would be, at best, dubious. Although not an unreasonable assumption with many rural properties, such an assumption is too questionable in this case given the relatively small physical size of the Debtors' property—i.e., approximately three acres. Thus, in following the principle that doubts should be resolved in favor of finding that an item of property retains its characteristics as a chattel, this consideration, in this Court's judgment, tips the balance in favor of finding that the hog and farrowing structures do not, as is required to be a fixture under the second part of the *Teaff* test, conform to the typical use of structures utilized with that type of property.

In summation, the Court is not persuaded that either the farrowing and/or gestation structures constructed on the Debtors' property have the attributes so as to meet either the second or third elements of the *Teaff* test. As such, these structures cannot be deemed to be fixtures for purposes of Ohio law. In turn, this means that since the hog farrowing and gestation structures are personal property, Pandora Bank's mortgage interests in the Debtors' realty do not attach to the structures.

———————————————

The determination of whether goods are fixtures or personal property also determines under Article 9 which filing system controls the transaction. Fixtures require a fixture filing which is to be made in the "office designated for the filing or recording of a record of a mortgage on the related [real] property, ..." 9-501(a)(1)(B). A fixture filing must include the minimum 9-502(a) requirements for a financing statement (name of the debtor, name of the secured party, and indication of collateral) and (1) indicate that it covers fixtures, (2) indicate it's to be filed in the real property records, (3) provide a description of the real property, and (4) provide the name of the owner of the property if the debtor is not the owner. 9-502(b). Filing a financing statement in the personal property filing system will not, subject to the limited exceptions in 9-334(e)(2) and (3), protect a security interest in a fixture against competing claims to that fixture made by parties with rights in the real property.

PROBLEM 7–1

Ray obtained a loan from his bank to finance the construction of a new building for his appliance store. Part of the loan was used to acquire the land on which the new store would be built. To secure the loan, Ray gave the bank a mortgage on the land as well as "any and all real and personal property, including fixtures, presently part of or otherwise connected to said real estate or which shall in the future become part of or otherwise connected to said real estate." The bank properly recorded its mortgage in the real property recording system.

Ray has contracted with several vendors to supply products for the new store but each is concerned about a possible conflict with the bank's interest in the property under its mortgage. In each of the following transactions, determine whether there will be a conflict between the vendor and the bank.

If you identify a conflict, determine whether the bank or the vendor will have priority under 9–334.

Transaction 1:   Ray has contracted with Ace Elevators for the purchase and installation of a freight elevator at the loading dock of the new building. The elevator will be installed within a special shaft constructed for it in the new building. The shaft will include a concrete subterranean pit where the hydraulic plunger that moves the elevator car will be torque bolted to the slab. Ace will retain a security interest in the elevator to secure Ray's promise to pay for it. Ace recorded its security interest in the real property records before the elevator was installed.

Transaction 2:   Ray purchased the HVAC system for the new store from A-1 Heating & Air Conditioning. The furnace will be installed in a corner of the storage room and connected to the air changer located along with the condenser unit on the roof of the building. All vents will be ceiling mounted and connected to the main components by way of a soft duct system. A-1 will retain a security interest in the HVAC system to secure Ray's promise to pay for it. A-1 recorded its security interest in the real property records 15 days after the HVAC system was installed.

Transaction 3:   Store Fixtures, Inc. ("SFI") has agreed to build the custom display shelving Ray has designed to show off the appliances he sells. The shelving is made from laminated plywood and uses steel girders for the structural support required to hold heavy items like washers, dryers, and ranges. Each shelving unit is 10 feet long by 5 feet wide by 8 feet high and weighs 500 pounds. SFI will retain a security interest in the shelves it supplies to secure Ray's promise to pay for the shelves. SFI filed a financing statement before the shelves were delivered. Would your analysis change if the shelving was installed after all work on the new building itself had been completed?

Transaction 4:   Ray purchased on credit a photocopy machine and a desktop computer from Royal Copier. Although the copier is commercial grade, its built-in wheels allow it to be easily moved around the store as required. It does require a 220 volts connection, and there is only one such outlet in the work room where the copier will be located. Royal will retain a security interest in the copier. Royal filed a financing statement 30 days after the copier and computer were delivered.

PROBLEM 7–2

Could the vendors whose security interests you determined were subordinate to the interest of the bank in Problem 7–1 have done anything to avoid subordination? See 9-334(f).

PROBLEM 7–3

After the new store opened, one of Ray's customers obtained a judgment against Ray on a breach of warranty claim. The customer recorded the judgment in the real estate records. Would the judgment creditor prevail over any of the vendors from Problem 7–1 who did not record their security interests in the real property records?

PROBLEM 7–4

Ray sold a refrigerator on credit to a customer who bought it to replace the refrigerator that was in her apartment when she rented it. Ray retained a security interest in the refrigerator but did not file a financing statement. When Ray tried to repossess the refrigerator after the customer defaulted, the bank with a mortgage on the apartment building asserted that Ray's security interest in the refrigerator was subordinate to its fixture interest in the refrigerator. Is the bank right? See 9-334(2).

B. REPOSSESSING FIXTURES

Section 9-604(c) allows a secured party to enforce its security interest against a fixture by removing the fixture from the real property to which it has become connected. The right to remove is, however, burdened by an obligation imposed on the removing secured party to reimburse the owner of the real property for any physical injury to that property caused by removing the fixture. As the next case illustrates, when the damage done by removal of the fixture is such that the obligation to reimburse exceeds the value of the removed fixture, the secured party is unlikely to exercise its right to remove the fixture. Does (should) the secured party have an alternative means to enforce its security interest in such a situation? Cases decided under Old Article 9 ruled that removal was the exclusive remedy for the secured party. Does Revised Article 9 require a different result?

MAPLEWOOD BANK AND TRUST V. SEARS, ROEBUCK AND CO.
Superior Court of New Jersey, Appellate Division 1993
625 A.2d 537

This appeal requires us to decide whether a first mortgage lender or a fixture financier is entitled to priority in the funds realized from a foreclosure sale of the mortgaged premises. We hold that a first mortgagee is entitled to priority in such funds.

Plaintiff Maplewood Bank and Trust is the holder of a first purchase money mortgage dated September 20, 1988 and recorded on October 5, 1988 on premises owned by defendants Edward and Terre Capers. The original mortgage debt was for $ 121,000. On May 31, 1989, Sears, Roebuck and Company (Sears) filed a Financing Statement covering a completely new kitchen, consisting of "new countertops, cabinets, sinks, disposal unit, dishwasher, oven, cooktop and hood," installed in the mortgaged premises at the request of the Capers after they executed a Security Agreement. The Financing Statement, known as the UCC-1 form, filed by Sears gave notice that Sears had a security interest in the new kitchen installed in the mortgaged premises in the sum of $ 33,320.40.

On August 18, 1989 the Capers executed a second mortgage on the previously mortgaged premises to defendant New Jersey Savings Bank for the sum of $ 34,000. That mortgage was recorded on August 23, 1989.

When the Capers eventually defaulted in the payments due plaintiff and Sears, plaintiff declared the entire unpaid balance on the mortgage was due. Nonpayment of the entire balance plus interest prompted plaintiff to file its complaint for foreclosure on November 5, 1990 and an amended complaint on or about December 6, 1990. Sears filed an answer and a counterclaim. Sears sought a declaration that its debt was "prior to the mortgage of the plaintiff" and, among other things, to compel plaintiff to "pay [Sears] the amount due on its Agreement." The essence of the counterclaim was that under *N.J.S.A.* 12A:9-313, Sears was entitled to priority over the plaintiff in the funds realized from the anticipated foreclosure sale. Sears' answer and counterclaim were stricken on July 26, 1991, and the matter proceeded as an uncontested foreclosure action. A final judgment in foreclosure was entered on February 28, 1992.

Sears has appealed the dismissal of its counterclaim. It argues that the priority given Sears as a purchase money security interest holder under the Uniform Commercial Code "applies to the proceeds of a judicial sale instituted" by a purchase money mortgagee. This is the same issue Sears raised in *Orange Savings Bank v. Todd*, 48 *N.J.* 428, 430, 226 *A.*2d 178 (1967), wherein Sears asserted that it was entitled to priority over the purchase money mortgagee "in the funds realized on foreclosure." *Ibid.* The Supreme Court concluded that although the briefs raised "interesting and important questions under the secured transactions provisions of the Uniform Commercial Code (*N.J.S.A.* 12A:9-101 *et seq.*), we find no present occasion to deal with any of them in view of the position now taken by the parties." *Ibid.* In the present case, we have considered the contention raised by Sears and conclude that it is unsound and must be rejected.

It is undisputed that the new kitchen Sears installed and financed satisfies the definition of a fixture under *N.J.S.A.* 12A:9-313(1)(a). It is also undisputed that Sears obtained a purchase money security interest in the fixture to secure full payment. *See N.J.S.A.* 12A:9-107(a). Sears perfected its security interest by filing a financing statement (UCC-1) covering the fixtures in the Hunterdon County Clerk's Office where the first mortgage held by plaintiff was recorded. *N.J.S.A.* 12A:9-313(1)(b) and *N.J.S.A.* 12A:9-402(5).

The purchase money security interest of Sears attached to the goods or chattels before they became affixed to the realty as fixtures. *N.J.S.A.*

12A:9-313(4)(a). By perfecting the security interest, Sears was able to make its security interest in the fixtures permanent, or until paid or discharged. The point to be made is that Sears' security interest is limited to the fixtures and does not extend to the realty otherwise.

By statute, Sears' purchase money security interest, when perfected, "has priority over the conflicting interest of an encumbrancer or owner of the real estate ... ." *N.J.S.A.* 12A:9-313(4). This concept was expressed more clearly in the version of the statute which predated the 1981 amendments. The prior version of *N.J.S.A.* 12A:9-313(2) provided "A security interest which attaches to goods before they become fixtures *takes priority as to the goods* over the claims of all persons who have an interest in the real estate except as stated in subsection (4)." This means the purchase money security interest of Sears in the goods or chattels which became fixtures gives it a "super priority" as to those goods or chattels which became fixtures.

Next we must focus upon the remedies available to a purchase money security interest lienholder upon default by the debtor. Sears contends it should be entitled to receive from the proceeds obtained at the foreclosure sale, the difference between the value of the realty with the new kitchen and the value of the realty after the new kitchen has been removed. We reject this entire approach as an inappropriate remedy absent authorization by statute.

The Uniform Commercial Code, as adopted in New Jersey, provides at *N.J.S.A.* 12A:9-313(8) that:

> When the secured party has priority over all owners and encumbrancers of the real estate, *he may*, on default, subject to the provisions of subchapter 5, *remove his collateral from the real estate* but he must reimburse any encumbrancer or owner of the real estate who is not the debtor and who has not otherwise agreed for the cost of repair of any physical injury, but not for any diminution in value of the real estate caused by the absence of the goods removed or by any necessity of replacing them ... . (Emphasis added).

Thus based on the plain language of § 9-313(8), Sears has two options: removal of the fixtures or foregoing removal of the fixtures.

New York, the only other jurisdiction which has addressed the issue, rejected Sears' argument. In *Dry Dock Savings Bank v. DeGeorgio*, 61 *Misc.*2d 224, 305 *N.Y.S.*2d 73 (1969) the defense asserted a lien superior to the mortgage by reason of a properly filed fixture financial statement covering aluminum siding on a house which was the subject of a foreclosure action. The mortgage was recorded prior to the time the fixture financial statement was filed.

The court held that under § 9-313 the purchase money security interest holder may remove his fixtures from the real estate, but must reimburse any owner or encumbrancer for the cost of repair. *Id.* 305 *N.Y.S.*2d at 75. The court observed:

He merely has the right to remove the goods after posting security to repair any damage. This may turn out to be a somewhat Pyrrhic victory, giving the lienor a pile of dubious scrap not worth the labor of getting it off the house, repairing nail holes, etc. ... [Removal] may hurt the mortgagee without doing the lienor any corresponding good. However, that is something for the parties to consider and beyond the control of the court.

Ibid.

In *Nu-Way Distributing Corp. v. Schoikert*, 44 *A.D.*2d 840, 355 *N.Y.S.*2d 475, 14 UCC Rep.Serv. 1058 (N.Y.App.Div.1974), plaintiff instituted an action to recover the price of fixtures (kitchen cabinets, etc.) sold by plaintiff, after the goods or chattels had been installed in the realty as fixtures. The Appellate Division construed § 9-313 "as merely providing the creditor with the statutory right of repossession, provided that he first comply with the security provision of the statute." *Id.* 355 *N.Y.S.*2d at 476.

The Appellate Division opined that even if the purchase money security interest holder failed or did not desire to repossess the fixtures upon default, that lienholder was not entitled to maintain an action for the purchase price against a subsequent purchaser of the real property. *Ibid.* The court further held that the same rule would apply even in cases where the fixtures are custom-made and would be of no use or value should they be repossessed. The underlying rationale for the rule was that such a lienholder as the one involved in *Nu-Way* must be assumed to have known and understood the risk he was taking.

Sears' approach has been adopted only in Louisiana and there it was based on the legislature's definitive modification of § 9-313(8) by adding the following language:

A secured party may also demand separate appraisal of the fixtures to fix his interest in the receipts of the sale thereof in any proceedings in which the real estate is sold pursuant to execution upon it by a mortgagee or other encumbrancer. [Uniform Commercial Code § 9-313, 3 *U.L.A.* 332 to 23 (1992)] (Action in Adopting Jurisdictions)].

The most compelling authority supportive of Sears' position is an article "An Integrated Financing System for Purchase Money Collateral: A Proposed Solution to the Fixture Problem Under Section 9-313 of the Uniform Commercial Code" by Morris G. Shanker. 73 Yale L.J. 795 (1964). In this article, Professor Shanker states "[w]here the fixture secured debt is not paid, removal of the fixture seems to be the favorite means of foreclosing on the fixture security interest." *Id.* at 804.

The article goes on to cite certain instances where the fixture secured party may prefer not to exercise his removal rights. For example, if an elevator was designed for a specific building, it would have little or no value apart from that building. *Ibid.* Other cited examples include situations where a fixture secured party should be *required* to use judicial foreclosure proceedings even though he has the right of removal. For example a secured party should not be free to remove a heating system in a large apartment building in the dead of winter, even where the debtor defaulted.

Shanker opines that "the Code, as it now stands, *probably* authorizes the fixture secured party to employ judicial foreclosure proceedings to enforce his security interest" *in lieu of removal of the fixtures. Ibid.* He states that limiting the remedy to the right to remove or choosing not to remove, in no way detracts from the fixture secured party's paramount security interest in his collateral; it merely requires him to enforce his security interest in a sensible and equitable fashion. *Id.* 805.

We decline to adopt the creative approach articulated by Professor Shanker. Such action, in our view, would be legislating. We prefer the approach followed in Louisiana where the legislature, upon its preference and initiative, provided the innovative remedy sought by Sears. To adopt Sears' argument in the absence of legislation, would mean that a mortgagee's security interest could be impaired substantially without the Legislature pronouncing an intention to do so. Any modification of long established fundamental property rights of purchase money mortgagees, must be done in some straight forward manner and may not be implied from the existing statute. The fact that fixtures may be custom made does not require any different result.

We are also persuaded that Sears is not entitled to any remedy, other than removal of the fixtures, based on equitable principles. Sears knew its remedy was limited to removal upon default. Indeed, the Retail Installment Contract and Security Agreement prepared by Sears and signed by the Capers provided that the Capers were giving Sears a "security interest under the Uniform Commercial Code in all merchandise purchased under this contract … [and] *the security interest allows Sears to repossess the merchandise*" in the event the Capers did not make payments as agreed. (Emphasis added).

Summary judgment in favor of plaintiff is affirmed.

The problem secured parties like Sears face when a fixture debtor defaults is that the secured party's obligation to reimburse other parties for the damage done by removing its fixture that is imposed by 9-604(d) often will exceed the value of the removed fixture. So exercising its right to remove the fixture on default actually puts the secured party in a worse position than doing nothing. So fixture creditors like Sears have asserted their claims against the value of the real property as a whole, but without much success, as the Maplewood Court noted.

Revised Article 9 added a provision to Chapter 6 intended to address the issue presented in the Maplewood Bank case. New section 9-604(a)(2) provides that when a security agreement covers both real and personal property that a "secured party may proceed … as to both the personal property and the in which case the other provisions of this part do not apply." Comment 3 explains that the new provision "makes clear that a security interest in fixtures may be enforced either under real-property law or under any of the applicable provisions of Part 6." The Comment goes on to state that this provision "also serves to overrule cases holding that a secured party's only remedy after default is the removal of fixtures from the real property. See, e.g., Maplewood Bank & Trust v. Sears, Roebuck & Co."

But as the next case demonstrates, 9-604(a)(2) does address the underlying problem with the position that parties like Sears Roebuck advocated in these cases, and suggests that outside of Louisiana, the result under Revised Article 9 ultimately will be the same as under old Article 9.

Carmel Fin. Corp. v. Castro
Court of Appeals of Texas, Fourteenth District, Houston 2016
514 S.W.3d 291

This dispute focuses on the reach of a Texas Uniform Commercial Code (UCC) fixture filing and subsequent efforts to foreclose on a lien arising from Carmel's financing of a water treatment system installed in a house. Carmel contends that its security interest and the accompanying lien extended to the real property. According to Carmel, it has "a super-priority lien on the Property" that became "superior to the existing mortgage on the property and was not extinguished" by a subsequent foreclosure. According to HUD and Dickson, Carmel's fixture filing did not create a lien on real property; they contend the fixture filing only entitled Carmel to repossess the water treatment system.

Because we agree with HUD and Dickson that Carmel's fixture filing did not create a lien on real property under the circumstances presented here, we affirm the trial court's summary judgment orders.

BACKGROUND

Carmel financed the purchase and installation of a $5,990 water treatment system in April 2008, for a house in Katy, Harris County, Texas. The governing contract is a consumer credit document with a revolving charge agreement. This agreement provides as follows:

> 13. Security Agreement: This agreement is a Security Agreement covering the purchased products and/or services and title thereto shall not pass to you until all payments hereunder, including collection charges, and attorney's fees, if any, are fully paid. You further agree that all purchased products shall be kept and or installed on the premises described herein and shall not be removed therefrom without our written consent or our assignee's written consent and that you shall not make any material change therein without our consent.

The "product" is identified as "New Water Treatment System, Aqua Tech USA."

Carmel perfected its purchase money security interest in the water treatment system through an April 2008 fixture filing recorded in the real property records in Harris County. *See* Tex. Bus. & Com. Code Ann. § 9.502 (Vernon Supp. 2016). The fixture filing states as follows: "This Financing Statement covers the following collateral — New Whole House Water Treatment System Model: Aqua Tech USA Serial # 280023." Carmel recorded no other lien to secure payment for the water treatment system. At the time Carmel recorded its fixture filing, Bank of America held a first-mortgage lien on the house.

The homeowner subsequently defaulted on payment for the water treatment system. He also defaulted on his mortgage. Bank of America foreclosed in September 2010 and transferred its rights in the property to HUD in May 2013.

HUD notified Carmel in September 2013 that it would not pay the full amount owed to Carmel for the water treatment system; instead, HUD offered $1,000. Carmel declined the offer. HUD then removed the water treatment system from the house. Carmel refused to accept delivery when HUD attempted to return the system. HUD sold the house to Dickson in January 2014; at that time, the water treatment system no longer was attached to the house.

Carmel sued HUD in December 2013, seeking judicial foreclosure and a declaratory judgment; Carmel added Dickson as a defendant in 2014, after she bought the house from HUD. Carmel alleged that its fixture filing lien attached to the real property and so allowed Carmel to judicially foreclose on the real property to obtain payment for the water treatment system. Carmel asserted that Dickson took possession of the property subject to Carmel's lien. Carmel also maintained that HUD's removal of the water treatment system did not eliminate the lien because Carmel's lien already had attached by the time HUD removed the system.

The parties filed cross-motions for traditional summary judgment. The trial court decided all issues in favor of Dickson and HUD and dismissed Carmel's claim against HUD. The trial court further ordered that Carmel take nothing on its claims against Dickson, and denied Carmel's request for a declaration that Carmel is "authorized to foreclose on the subject property." Additionally, the trial court awarded Dickson attorney's fees. This appeal timely followed.

ANALYSIS

In a single issue on appeal, Carmel argues that the trial court erred in granting summary judgment because (1) the fixture filing perfected Carmel's security interest and created a super-priority lien; (2) the fixture filing extended to the real property; (3) removing the fixture did not extinguish the lien; (4) Carmel's remedies are not limited to repossession of the fixture; and (5) homestead protection may not be asserted against a prior lien holder.

Dickson and HUD argue that Carmel's fixture security interest applies only to the water treatment system itself as collateral.

Article 9 of the Texas Uniform Commercial Code (UCC) establishes a "comprehensive scheme for the regulation of security interests in personal property and fixtures." *See* Tex. Bus. & Com. Code Ann. § 9.101 cmt. 1 (Vernon 2011). It applies to transactions creating a "security interest in personal property or fixtures by contract." *Id.* § 9.109(a) (Vernon Supp. 2016).[3]

A "security agreement" is "an agreement that creates or provides for a security interest." *Id.* § 9.102(a)(74) (Vernon Supp. 2016). "Security interest means an interest in personal property or fixtures which secures payment or performance of an obligation." *Id.* § 1.201(b)(35) (Vernon Supp. 2016). "Collateral" is "the property subject to a security interest … ." *Id.* § 9.102(a)(12). "Fixtures" are "goods that have become so related to particular real property that an interest in them arises under the real property law of the state in which the real property is situated." *Id.* § 9.102(a)(41). "Goods" are "all things that are movable when a security interest attaches. The term includes … fixtures." *Id.* § 9.102(a)(44).

The parties do not dispute that the water treatment system at issue here is a fixture under section 9.102(a)(41).

Carmel looks to sections 9.334(d) and 9.604(b) in arguing that its fixture filing securing payment for the water treatment system created a "super-priority lien" that attached not just to the fixture itself but also to the real property to which the fixture was attached.

Section 9.334 is entitled "Priority of Security Interests in Fixtures and Crops." Section 9.334(d) provides:

[A] perfected security interest in fixtures has priority over the conflicting interest of an encumbrancer or owner of the real property if the debtor has an interest of record in or is in possession of the real property and:

(1) the security interest is a purchase-money security interest;

(2) the interest of the encumbrancer or owner arises before the goods become fixtures; and

(3) the security interest is perfected by a fixture filing before the goods become fixtures or within 20 days thereafter.

See Tex. Bus. & Com. Code Ann. § 9.334(d) (Vernon 2011). Carmel cites section 9.334(d)(1) for the proposition that "the fixture filing attached to the real property and obtained priority."

---

3 Article 9 does not apply to the "creation or transfer of an interest in or lien on real property" except in limited situations. The exceptions are as follows: "(A) liens on real property in Sections 9.203 and 9.308; (B) fixtures in Section 9.334; (C) fixture filings in Sections 9.501, 9.502, 9.512, 9.516, and 9.519; and (D) security agreements covering personal and real property in Section 9.604." *See* Tex. Bus. & Com. Code Ann. § 9.109(c)(11)(A-D) (Vernon Supp. 2016).

Section 9.604 is entitled "Procedure if Security Agreement Covers Real Property or Fixtures." Section 9.604(b) provides:

> (b) Subject to Subsection (c), if a security agreement covers goods that are or become fixtures, a secured party may proceed:
>
> (1) under this subchapter; or
>
> (2) in accordance with the rights with respect to real property, in which case the other provisions of this subchapter do not apply.
>
> (c) Subject to the other provisions of this subchapter, if a secured party holding a security interest in fixtures has priority over all owners and encumbrancers of the real property, the secured party, after default, may remove the collateral from the real [**9] property.

Tex. Bus. & Com. Code Ann. § 9.604(b) (Vernon 2011). Section 9.604(b) was added in 2001. According to the official UCC comment, "Subsection (b) … serves to overrule cases holding that a secured party's only remedy after default is the removal of the fixtures from the real property." *See id.* § 9.604(b) cmt. 3 (citing *Maplewood Bank & Trust v. Sears, Roebuck & Co.*, 265 N.J. Super. 25, 625 A.2d 537 (N.J. Super. Ct. App. Div. 1993)).

According to Carmel, section 9.604(b)(2) means its fixture filing allows it to enforce its interest under real property law against third parties. Carmel further asserts that "[s]uch real property remedy can only be judicial fore-closure because to hold otherwise would be to assume that there is no real property remedy."

Carmel's contentions bypass a threshold issue: What was the nature of the security interest established by Carmel's security agreement with the homeowner for the purchase and installation of the water treatment system?

"The security agreement defines the collateral to enable the debtor and other interested persons to identify the property that the creditor may claim as security." Accordingly, the security agreement must describe the collateral." [See]Tex. Bus. & Com. Code Ann. § 9.203 (Vernon 2011). "The financing statement is the instrument designed to notify third parties … that there may be an enforceable security interest in the property of the debtor." *Villa v. Alvarado State Bank*, 611 S.W.2d 483, 486-87 (Tex. Civ. App.—Waco 1981, no writ). "A proper security agreement is a requisite for attachment of the security interest … and a proper financing statement is a requisite for perfection of the security interest; both attachment and perfection are necessary for the enforcement of the … security interest against a third party … ." *Id.* Carmel did not contract with the homeowner to create a security interest in real property in connection with the water treatment system; instead, Carmel contracted to create a security interest in the system itself. Carmel contends that its security agreement with the homeowner "merely references the [water treatment system] for contractual purposes" and does not limit Carmel's security interest "to only the [water treatment system]." This contention fails because the underlying security agreement contained no authorization to give the fixture lien holder a security interest in real property. Paragraph 13 states: "This agreement is a Security Agreement covering the purchased products and/or services and title thereto shall not pass to you until all payments hereunder, including collection charges, and attorney's fees, if any, are fully paid." The "purchased product[]" is the water treatment system.

Neither section 9.334(d) nor section 9.604(b)(2) operates independently to create a security interest in real property that the underlying security agreement did not authorize. These provisions address mechanisms for pursuing the security interest that the creditor and debtor agreed to create.

Section 9.334(d) addresses the priority of fixture liens when encumbrancers of real property have conflicting liens. Moreover, section 9.334(d) references a security interest in "fixtures," which, in turn, contemplates a financing statement that sets forth the requirements for goods that are to become fixtures. *See, e.g.*, Tex. Bus. & Com. Code Ann. § 9.502(a), (b) (A financing statement for goods that are to become fixtures must provide, among other information, "a description of the real property to which the collateral is related sufficient to give constructive notice of a mortgage under the law of this state if the description were contained in a record of the mortgage of the real property.") (Vernon Supp. 2016).

Carmel also misplaces its reliance on section 9.604(b)(2). This provision addresses the right of a holder of a fixture lien to utilize appropriate remedies, if any, available under state real property law to obtain payment. *See* Tex. Bus. & Com. Code Ann. § 9.604(b) cmt. 3 (Subsection (b) "makes clear that [**12] a security interest in fixtures may be enforced either under real-property law or under any of the applicable provisions of Part 6, including sale or other disposition either before or after removal of the fixtures … .). Section 9.604(b)(2) does not operate independently to expand the collateral covered by a Texas UCC fixture lien to include the whole of the real property to which the fixture is attached, and it does not itself create a security interest in the real property. *Cf. Lankhorst v. Indep. Sav. Plan Co.*, 787 F.3d 1100, 1103 (11th Cir. 2015) ("Lankhorst has cited no authority to support the assertion that a security interest in a fixture constitutes a security interest in the real property on which the fixture is installed. Nor has our research uncovered any such case … . The security interest in a fixture does not give the party a security interest in the realty on which it is installed.") (applying Florida law).

We overrule Carmel's issue insofar as it challenges the propriety of the trial court's grant of Dickson's summary judgment motion.

PROBLEM 7-5

Several years after the store opened, the HVAC system failed, and Ray had to replace it. He purchased the new system from Acme Heating & Cooling.

Acme retained a security interest in the system to secure Ray's promise to pay for it and recorded its interest in the real property records. Shortly thereafter, Ray defaulted on his obligation to Acme. When Acme repossessed the HVAC system, it did severe damage to the roof of the store, and removal of the HVAC left the store sprinkler system inoperative. Shortly after the HVAC was removed, a fire broke out in the store that would have been contained had the sprinkler system worked. Instead, the store, along with everything in it, was destroyed. Can Ray recover his losses caused by the fire from Acme under 9-604(d)?

PROBLEM 7-6

If, in Problem 7-5, Acme had not removed the HVAC system after Ray's default, would it be entitled to assert its claim against the proceeds of a foreclosure sale held by the bank after Ray defaulted on his obligation to the bank? See 9-604.

CHAPTER 8

PROCEEDS

What happens to a security interest if the debtor sells the collateral to another person? Unless the collateral is inventory, the security agreement will likely prohibit the debtor from selling or disposing of the collateral in any manner. But debtors sometimes disregard such prohibitions. We've already seen that, unless the secured party authorizes a disposition of the collateral free of the security interest, the security interest follows the collateral and is enforceable against most transferees. Article 9 also provides that a security interest automatically attaches to "proceeds" of collateral, regardless of whether the security agreement so provides. 9-315(a)(2) and 9-203(f). Proceeds, in their simplest form, are "whatever the debtor acquires upon the sale, lease, license, exchange, or other disposition of the collateral." 9-102(64)(A). Thus, when the debtor sells or disposes of collateral, whatever the debtor gets in exchange for the collateral itself becomes collateral.

But when has there actually been a "disposition" of the collateral? Is the milk produced by the debtor's cows proceeds of the credit company's security interest in the cows? Are the lambs birthed by the debtor's sheep proceeds of the farm credit bureau's security interest in the debtor's flock? Are the rental payments Hertz collects from its customers proceeds of the bank's security interest in the fleet of cars Hertz rents on a daily basis? Is the debtor's breach of warranty claim against Ford proceeds of finance company's security interest in the debtor's auto? Is an actual "disposition" necessary to create proceeds? The cases and problems that follow explore the contours of Article 9's concept of proceeds.

IN RE WIERSMA
United States Bankruptcy Court, D. Idaho
283 B.R. 294 (Bankr. D. Idaho 2002)

PAPPAS, *Chief Judge.*

I. INTRODUCTION

Debtors Jim Wiersma and Patty Wiersma (hereinafter "Debtors") filed a petition for relief under Chapter 11 of the Bankruptcy Code on October 1, 2001. A significant factor leading to Debtors' financial problems stems from the electrical work performed by Gietzen Electric, Inc. (hereinafter "Gietzen") at the Debtors' dairy. Apparently, as a result of Gietzen's alleged negligence in completing the job, Debtors' dairy cows were subjected to varying degrees of electric shocks. This ultimately caused the cows to produce a lower quantity and quality of milk, to become sick, and in some cases, to die. Debtors sued Gietzen in state court for their losses. Negotiations for settlement of that action have taken place, and Debtors received an offer from Gietzen to resolve their claim. Debtors have now filed a motion with the Court to approve the settlement.

* * *

On June 26, 2002, Debtors filed a Motion to Determine Secured Status (hereinafter "Motion") to establish the relative rights of Debtors and two of their creditors in any settlement proceeds generated by the Gietzen lawsuit. Those creditors are United California Bank (hereinafter "UCB") and O.H. Kruse Grain & Milling (hereinafter "O.H. Kruse"), both of whom assert an interest in Debtors' claim against, and in any recovery from, Gietzen.

* * *

FACTS

In addition to those recited above, the Court finds the following to be the facts.

In April, 1998, Debtors borrowed funds from UCB. In connection with that loan, Debtors signed a security agreement in favor of UCB, in which Debtors granted UCB a security interest in Debtors' "Inventory ... Accounts and Contract Rights ... General Intangibles ... Livestock ... Milk Products Quota ... [and] Monies, Deposits or Accounts in Possession." ... In addition, the security agreement provided that UCB's "interest in the collateral shall be a continuing lien and shall include all proceeds and products of the collateral including, but not limited to, the proceeds of any insurance thereon." ... UCB filed a UCC–1 financing statement to perfect its security interest. ... The balance due on the UCB loan is over $2.2 million. ...

In January, 2001, Debtors executed a promissory note in favor of O.H. Kruse in the amount of $550,000.00. This note represented amounts due from Debtors on their livestock feed account with O.H. Kruse. ... In addition to the note, the Debtors signed another document which provided:

> We, JIM WIERSMA and PATTY WIERSMA ... in order to secure the payment of that certain Promissory Note executed by us ... hereby assign, transfer and convey to O.H. KRUSE ... all our right, title and interest in and to any and all proceeds received by the undersigned from the lawsuit entitled *Jim Wiersma and Patty Wiersma v. Gietzen Electric.* ...

Gietzen's insurer has apparently offered Debtors $2.5 million to settle their claim against Gietzen. Debtors intend to accept this offer and, subject to Court approval, must pay their state court attorneys fees and costs. After doing so, Debtors would expect to receive approximately $1.5 million from the settlement. ...

II. DISCUSSION AND DISPOSITION OF THE ISSUES

A. UCB's SECURED STATUS

The parties do not dispute that UCB holds a valid, perfected secured interest. Rather, the current dispute centers on the extent of the UCB security interest, and whether any settlement funds Debtors may receive as a result of their claims against Gietzen fall within the scope of the collateral in which UCB has an interest. Before resolving that dispute, a discussion of applicable law is necessary.

Security interests in Idaho are governed by the Uniform Commercial Code–Secured Transactions. Idaho Code §28–9–101 et seq. Revised Article 9 instructs that "except as otherwise provided in this part, this act applies to a transaction or lien within its scope, even if the transaction or lien was entered into or created before this act takes effect." Idaho Code §28–9–702.

* * *

1. DEBTORS' CLAIM AGAINST GIETZEN AS PROCEEDS OF UCB's COLLATERAL

UCB also argues that Debtors' claim against Gietzen represents proceeds of encumbered cows and milk. Proceeds are defined as:

> (A) whatever is acquired upon the sale, lease, license, exchange or other disposition of collateral;
>
> (B) whatever is collected on, or distributed on account of, collateral;
>
> (C) rights arising out of collateral;

(D) to the extent of the value of collateral, claims arising out of the loss, nonconformity, or interference with the use of, defects or infringement of rights in, or damage to, the collateral; or

(E) to the extent of the value of collateral and to the extent payable to the debtor or the secured party, insurance payable by reason of the loss or nonconformity of, defects or infringement of rights in, or damage to, the collateral.

Idaho Code §28–9–102(64).

A security interest attaches to any identifiable proceeds of collateral. Idaho Code §28–9–315(a)(2). Further, a security interest in proceeds is a perfected security interest if the security interest in the original collateral was perfected. Idaho Code §28–9–315(c).

Debtors' complaint requests unspecified amounts of damages for lost milk production, the cost of additional replacements to the herd, milk quality loss, diminished herd size, and for miscellaneous costs, future losses, and extra labor. ... According to a report prepared by Debtors' economic expert, absent any present value adjustment, these damages likely exceed $5.82 million. ...

To some extent, UCB's argument that any settlement payment represents proceeds of collateral suffers from the same problems seen in characterizing Debtors' claims as arising in tort or contract. Debtors argue that some of the components of their damages do not represent proceeds of cows and milk serving as collateral and should not, therefore, be subject to UCB's security interest. For example, their complaint includes a reservation of a right to amend the complaint to request punitive damages. Because Gietzens' insurer is offering to settle all claims, including potential punitive damage claims which are not attributable to any particular item of UCB's collateral, Debtors contend the settlement represents some damages not directly related to the loss of collateral.

In this instance, though, the legislature has spoken. The UCC definition of "proceeds" includes within its scope whatever is acquired upon disposition of collateral, all *rights* arising out of collateral, and includes all claims arising out of the loss of, or damage to, collateral. Idaho Code §28–9–102(64) (emphasis added). All of the categories listed in Debtors' damage analysis stem from either damage to Debtors' cows or from the loss of milk and cows. ... Even the "miscellaneous" and "labor" categories arise from damage to or loss of cows and milk because they represent expenses such as veterinarian bills and the Debtors' extra labor costs associated with dealing with the electrical problem affecting the cows. The same is true with respect to Debtors' claim for punitive damages. Thus, given these facts, the Court concludes Debtors' claims against Gietzen arose out of the loss of, and damage to, UCB's collateral, the cows and milk.

Under the language employed in Idaho Code §28–9–102(64), any Gietzen settlement payment represents compensation to Debtors for the loss of and damage to UCB's collateral and must be considered proceeds. In *Fifteenth RMA Partners, L.P. v. Pacific/West Communications Group, Inc. (In re Pacific/West Communications Group, Inc.), 301 F.3d 1150, 1151–52 (9th Cir.2002)*, the court held that provisions of California's UCC, which are substantially similar to those in Idaho, allowed a security interest to continue in lawsuit settlement funds as proceeds of collateral. *See also McGonigle v. Combs, 968 F.2d 810, 828 (9th Cir.1992)* (defining a recovery on a lawsuit to be proceeds under Article 9); *Figueroa v. Acropolis, 192 Ariz. 563, 968 P.2d 1048, 1050 (Ct. App.1997)* (holding settlement funds to be proceeds under Article 9). Thus, UCB's security interest attaches to the Gietzen lawsuit as proceeds, pursuant to Idaho Code §28–9–315(a)(2).

UCB's interest in the Gietzen lawsuit, as proceeds of collateral, is also a perfected interest. Idaho Code §28–9–315(c) provides that a security interest in proceeds is perfected if the security interest in the original collateral was perfected. The Official Comment to this section reiterates this rule and elaborates on it by noting that a continuing security interest in proceeds of collateral only remains perfected if a filed financing statement covered the original collateral, the proceeds are collateral in which a security interest may be perfected by filing in the office where the financing statement has been filed, and the proceeds have not been acquired with cash proceeds. Idaho Code §28–9–315(d)(1); Official Comment at 4. In applying the Former Article 9 provision that corresponds to Idaho Code §28–9–315, a court held that a secured party's interest in proceeds remained perfected because the secured party perfected its interest in the original collateral by filing in the same place necessary to perfect an interest in the proceeds. *Cassel v. Kolb, 72 Cal.App.4th 568, 84 Cal.Rptr.2d 878, 883–84 (1999)*.

* * *

UCB perfected its security interest in the original collateral by filing a financing statement with the Idaho Secretary of State. Because that is the same place where a creditor would file to perfect an interest in the proceeds (i.e., the Gietzen lawsuit in this instance), and because there is no issue regarding the proceeds being acquired with cash proceeds, UCB is a perfected secured creditor in the proceeds of the original collateral. Idaho Code §28–9–315(c), (d).

* * *

B. DEBTORS' STATUS

In addition to arguing that neither UCB nor O.H. Kruse has an enforceable security interest in the Gietzen lawsuit, Debtors alternatively argue that this Court should, through use of its inherent equitable powers, order an appropriate allocation of any lawsuit recovery among Debtors and the creditors.

While this argument is creative, Debtors have made no factual showing to justify such a result. Such an order would also run afoul of the dictates of the Idaho State Legislature, as expressed in Revised Article 9, and of Congress, as expressed in the Bankruptcy Code. These legislative bodies have made the relevant policy decisions regarding how Debtors' and the creditors' property interests must be treated in a bankruptcy case. This Court is not free to disregard these laws. Since Debtors offer no factual or legal basis for their proposal for an equitable allocation, it must be rejected.

Swope v. Commer. Sav. Bank (In re Gamma Ctr.)
U. S. Bankruptcy Court N. D. Ohio, Western Division 2013
489 B.R. 688

MEMORANDUM AND ORDER REGARDING CROSS-MOTIONS FOR SUMMARY JUDGMENT

This adversary proceeding is before the court on cross-motions for summary judgment filed by Plaintiff, and Defendants Commercial Savings Bank ("the Bank") and Sudesh Reddy, M.D. ("Reddy")'

Plaintiff is the Trustee in Debtor Gamma Center, Inc.'s underlying Chapter 7 case. In his complaint, Plaintiff seeks a declaratory judgment that the Bank does not have a perfected security interest in Debtor's accounts receivable and funds collected thereon and that those accounts and funds collected on the accounts are assets of Debtor's Chapter 7 case to be administered for the benefit of Debtor's unsecured creditors. ...

Having considered the parties' motions and briefs in support of their respective positions, for the reasons that follow, the court will grant Plaintiff's motion for summary judgment and will deny the motions for summary judgment filed by Reddy and the Bank.

FACTUAL BACKGROUND

Unless indicated otherwise, the following are facts to which Plaintiff and the Bank have stipulated and on which Reddy relies in support of his motion or facts gleaned from the Promissory Note and UCC Financing Statement attached to Plaintiff's and the Bank's motions for summary judgment, which Reddy and Indi Singh rely on or refer to in arguments in support of their respective positions.

On November 26, 2004, Debtor executed a Universal Note and Security Agreement ("Note" or "Security Agreement") in favor of the Bank. Pursuant to the Note, the Bank loaned Debtor $300,000.00, which funds were used for the purchase of a piece of equipment, namely, a Millennium Myosight Integrated Systems—Xelesis [**5] Nuclear Stress Test Camera ("Camera") and other related equipment. The introductory paragraph of the Security Agreement includes boilerplate language that provides that "a security interest in all of the Property described below ... and all proceeds and products of the Property" is granted. [Doc. # 19, Ex. A, p.2, unnumbered ¶ 1].

Following the introductory paragraph of the Security Agreement is a list of ten asset categories to be checked to the extent they describe "Property" in which a security interest is being granted. Included in that list is "Accounts and Other Rights to Payment" described as "[a]ll rights to payment, whether or not earned by performance, including, but not limited to, payment for property or services sold, leased, rented, licensed, or assigned." In addition to the asset categories listed is property identified under "Specific Property Description." Only "Specific Property Description" is checked, and it is followed by a description that the "Property includes, but is not limited by, the following: MILLENNIUM MYOSIGHT INTEGRATED SYSTEMS - XELERIS NUCLEAR STRESS TEST CAMERA INCLUDING ANY AND ALL RELATED EQUIPMENT. THIS NOTE IS FURTHER EVIDENCED AND PERFECTED BY A UCC FINANCING STATEMENT DATED NOVEMBER 26, 2004. The Note was also personally guaranteed by several individuals, including Reddy and Defendants Sanjeev Verna and Parminder Singh.

On December 30, 2004, the Bank filed with the Ohio Secretary of State a UCC-1 Financing Statement. In the Financing Statement, the Bank claimed as collateral the Camera and related equipment as well as both "Proceeds of Collateral" and "Products of Collateral." The Bank filed a continuation statement with the Ohio Secretary of State on December 22, 2009.

The nature of the medical practice conducted by Debtor was nuclear heart stress testing. The Camera and related equipment securing the obligation owed to the Bank was used exclusively in that medical practice. It is undisputed that the Camera and related equipment do not create or manufacture a tangible product.

On January 15, 2010, Debtor filed its Chapter 7 bankruptcy petition. Debtor includes accounts receivable in the amount of $325,653.33 as an asset in its bankruptcy schedules. Debtor states in bankruptcy Schedule B that the scheduled value of its accounts receivable "is the billed amount to patients" but that "[t]he actual expected payment from insurance and patients is much less that this amount." The net amount of Debtor's accounts receivable that has been collected by Plaintiff totals $91,353.90.

LAW AND ANALYSIS

* * *

II. THE SECURITY AGREEMENT

Plaintiff asks the court to find that the Bank does not have a perfected security interest in Debtor's accounts receivable or in the funds collected thereon and that the accounts and funds collected on the accounts are assets available to be distributed to unsecured creditors in the underlying Chapter 7 case... . It is the Bank's and Reddy's position that identifying "proceeds and products" of the Camera as collateral reasonably identifies Debtor's accounts receivable as collateral. ... Indi Singh, for his part, argues that Debtor's failure to check the box indicating that the property in which a security interest was being granted includes "Accounts" defeats any claim that accounts receivable were collateralized. The burden of proving that an item of property is subject to a security interest is on the party asserting the interest.

Although Plaintiff initially argues that the Security Agreement evidences no security interest in proceeds and products of the Camera, the court disagrees. Albeit in boilerplate, the Security Agreement clearly states that a security interest is being granted in "all of the Property described below" and in "all proceeds and products of the Property." As the only "Property" identified in the Security Agreement is the Camera and related equipment, the issue is whether "proceeds and products of the Property" sufficiently describes Debtor's accounts receivable and funds collected on the accounts.

A. Proceeds of Collateral

The term "Proceeds" is defined in the UCC to mean the following:

> (a) Whatever is acquired upon the sale, lease, license, exchange, or other disposition of collateral;
>
> (b) Whatever is collected on, or distributed on account of, collateral;
>
> (c) Rights arising out of collateral;
>
> (d) To the extent of the value of collateral, claims arising out of the loss, nonconformity, or interference with the use of, defects or infringement of rights in, or damage to the collateral; or
>
> (e) To the extent of the value of collateral and to the extent payable to the debtor or the secured party, insurance payable by reason of the loss or nonconformity of, defects or infringement of rights in, or damage to the collateral.

Ohio Rev. Code § 1309.102(A)(64). The Security Agreement also defines "proceeds" in language mirroring the statutory definition. In addition, proceeds of proceeds are themselves proceeds. *See* Ohio Rev. Code § 1309.102(A)(12) (defining "collateral" as "the property subject to a security interest or agricultural lien, including: (a) Proceeds to which a security interest attaches ... .") and Official Comment 13(c) ("[t]hat idea is expressed in the revised definition of "collateral").

In arguing that Debtor's accounts receivable are proceeds of the Camera, the Bank relies on the part of the definition that "[w]hatever is collected on, or distributed on account of, collateral" is proceeds. The Bank reasons that use of the Camera by Debtor resulted in a right to payment, or the accounts receivable, and that right to payment is proceeds of the Camera "since payment was certainly collected *on account of* the Camera." The court finds the Bank's argument flawed in several respects.

First, the Bank reasons that because the nature of Debtor's medical practice was nuclear heart stress testing and because its collateral is the nuclear stress test Camera, then "it only stands to reason that the collateral was the primary, if not exclusive, generator of accounts receivable. ..." This contention, however, assumes facts not in evidence. The record is silent with respect to how Debtor's accounts receivable were generated. For example, the record is silent as to whether the accounts receivable were generated simply by use of the Camera or whether there was another ingredient in the generation of the accounts, such as the expertise and services of physicians comprising Debtor's medical practice. The record is silent as to whether the Camera produced an image that was then interpreted by the physicians. To the extent that the accounts receivable include the value of services rendered by the physicians, and are from an indistinguishable mixture of services and other assets of the business operation, they were not exclusively generated by the Camera. The record is also silent as to whether the Camera was the only camera or equipment that was used by Debtor's medical practice. This lack of evidence alone precludes a finding on summary judgment that the Bank has a security interest in all of Debtor's accounts receivable and funds collected thereon.

Nevertheless, the court also finds the Banks reasoning faulty in other respects. Even if Debtor's accounts receivable were generated solely by use of the Camera, the funds collected by Plaintiff were "collected on" the accounts receivable, not "collected on" the Camera. While those funds are proceeds of the accounts receivable, they are proceeds of the collateral only if the accounts receivable are themselves proceeds of the Camera. Because the accounts receivable represent debt owed to Debtor or a right to payment, it strains the statutory language to conclude that Debtor's accounts receivable constitute something that is "collected on" the Camera. Unlike, for instance, a right to payment under a contract where the contract is collateral securing an obligation, there is no right to payment that is generated by, or arises out of, the Camera itself.

In addition, according to the Bank, the accounts receivable were generated by *use* of the Camera. The Bank argues that the words "on account of, collateral" in § 1309.102(A)(64)(b) includes money collected from the use of the collateral. However, the entire provision states "[w]hatever is collected on, or distributed on account of, collateral." Ohio Rev. Code § 1309.102(A)(64) (b). As shown by the comma after the word "on," the phrase "on account of" modifies "distributed," not "collected." There was no distribution on account of the Camera, there was only funds collected on Debtor's accounts receivable. The Bank cites no authority that supports its position, and the court is not persuaded, that accounts receivable or funds collected thereon as the result of *using* equipment collateral constitute proceeds under the UCC.

The court finds support for its determination that Debtor's accounts receivable do not constitute proceeds in the report of the Permanent Editorial

Board for the UCC (PEB Report) prior to Article 9 being amended to provide the expanded definition of "proceeds" found in § 1309.102(A)(64). While the PEB Report recommended expanding the definition of "proceeds," it attempts to define the logical limit of the term, a limit the Bank's argument obliterates:

At some point, the acquisition of assets by a debtor, in part as a result of a diminution in value of collateral, will be too attenuated for those assets to be considered proceeds. For example, accounts generated by a construction contractor should not be considered proceeds of the contractor's construction equipment, even though the equipment depreciates as a result of its use in generating the accounts. Nor should inventory fabricated by a debtor's factory equipment be considered proceeds of that equipment. Cash earned from music or video machines presents a case closer to the margin. Has the equipment merely provided a service, or is the better analogy that of a short-term rental? The Committee is inclined to leave such marginal cases to the courts.

R. Wilson Freyermuth, *Rethinking Proceeds: The History, Misinterpretation and Revision of U.C.C. Section 9-306*, 69 Tul. L. Rev. 645, 698 (1995) (quoting Permanent Editorial Bd. for the U.C.C., PEB Study Group U.C.C. Article 9 at 111, n.16 (1992)); *see also 1st Source Bank v. Wilson Bank & Trust*, 2012 U.S. Dist. LEXIS 143024, *8-9, 2012 WL 4711989, *3, (M.D. Tenn. Oct. 3, 2012) (finding that "accounts receivable" relating to the use of collateral do not fall within the definition of "proceeds"); *cf. In re S & J Holding Corp.*, 42 B.R. 249 (Bankr. S.D. Fla. 1984)(security interest in video game equipment collateral does not attach to cash generated from use of game machines). The court likewise concludes that accounts receivable generated from use of equipment do not constitute proceeds of the equipment.

B. Products of Collateral

Reddy and the Bank also argue that Debtor's accounts receivable are a product of the Camera. The term "product" is not defined in the UCC. The parties rely on a definition of "product" as "yield, income, receipts, [or] return." Black's Law Dictionary 1209 (6th ed. 1990). Those terms are further defined as follows: "Yield" is defined as "[c]urrent return from an investment or expenditure as a percentage of price of investment or expenditure." *Id.* at 1616. "Income" is defined as "[t]he return in money from one's business, labor, or capital invested." *Id.* at 763. "Receipt" is defined as "[t]hat which comes in, in distinction from what is expended. . . ." *Id.* at 1268. "Return" is defined as "[p]rofit on sale, or income from investments." *Id.* at 1318.

As discussed above, however, the accounts receivable consist of debt that is owed to Debtor. As such, it does not constitute yield, income, receipts or return. Debtor has obtained no yield, income, receipt or return on the Camera until payment is received. As stated in Debtor's Schedule B, the listed value of its accounts receivable "is the billed amount to patients. The actual expected payment from insurance and patients is much less than this amount."

Although the Security Agreement clearly provides for a security interest in proceeds and products of the Camera, the court finds that those terms do not reasonably describe Debtor's accounts receivable or the funds collected thereon. Neither the term "proceeds" nor the term "products" of the collateral, described only as the Camera and related equipment, constitute a sufficient description of accounts receivable. Furthermore, any person reviewing the Security Agreement and observing the unchecked box next to "Accounts and Other Rights to Payment" would unambiguously conclude that the accounts receivable were *not* collateralized. Especially since the box for "Accounts and Other Rights to Payment" is not checked, it is not objectively determinable from the Security Agreement that it creates a security interest in Debtor's accounts receivable. The Security Agreement's description does not "do the job assigned to it," which the Bank asserts is to create a security interest in Debtor's accounts receivable. That is, it does not "[m]ake possible the identification of the collateral described." Ohio Rev. Code § 1309.108, Official Comment 2. As such, the Security Agreement does not create a security interest in favor of the Bank in the accounts receivable or the funds collected on those accounts.

CONCLUSION

Having found, based upon the undisputed facts, that the Security Agreement does not provide the Bank a security interest in Debtor's accounts receivable or the funds collected thereon, the court will grant Plaintiff's motion for summary judgment and will deny both the Bank's and Reddy's motions for summary judgment. The court will enter a separate judgment in accordance with this memorandum of decision and order.

PROBLEM 8–1

Maytag has a security interest in all of the Maytag appliances in Ray's inventory. What, if anything, can Maytag claim as proceeds of its collateral in the following transactions:

Transaction 1: Ray sells a Maytag dryer to a customer who pays the $500 purchase price in cash. *$500*

Transaction 2: Ray sells a Maytag cook top to a customer who pays the purchase price with a personal check. *CHECK*

Transaction 3: Ray sells a Maytag refrigerator to a customer who signs a promissory note for the purchase price and trades in her old refrigerator. *FRIDGE ⟶ OLD FRIDGE + PN*

Transaction 4: Ray sells a Maytag washer to the local laundromat on credit, payment due in 60 days. *PMSI ⟶ A/R*

Transaction 5: Ray leases a Maytag range to the local burger shop for one year, rent at $100 a month. *LEASE = CHATTEL PAPER*

Even if the court in Swope had determined that the accounts receivable were proceeds of the bank's camera collateral, would the bankruptcy trustee have still prevailed if the bank had not identified "proceeds" as part of its collateral in the financing statement it filed? We've learned that an unperfected security interest loses to a lien creditor like the bankruptcy trustee. 9-317. The bank's security interest in the proceeds would have been protected from the bankruptcy trustee under 9-315(c) which provides that a security interest in proceeds is automatically perfected if the security interest in the original collateral was perfected. So in Swope, the bank's security interest in proceeds of its collateral would have been perfected when the security interest attached to the accounts receivable because the bank had filed a financing statement perfecting its security interest in the camera. And the bank would have the same priority to the proceeds as it had in the camera.

Section 9-315(c) is not the end of the proceeds perfection story. Automatic perfection of a security interest in proceeds expires on the twenty-first day after it attaches to the proceeds unless one of the conditions in 9-315(d) is satisfied. If the proceeds are first generation proceeds and are not in the form of cash, then perfection of the proceeds security interest continues beyond twenty days only if you would file a financing statement to perfect a security interest in the proceeds collateral in the same place you filed the financing statement to perfect the security interest in your original collateral. For example, if the debtor traded the drill press subject to your security interest, which you perfected by filing a financing statement with the secretary of state, for a photocopier, your security interest in the photocopier as proceeds of the drill press would continue to be perfected on day 21 and beyond because you would file a financing statement to perfect a security interest in the photocopier with the secretary of state.

If the debtor had sold the drill press for $500 and used the money to buy the photocopier, a different condition applies. Here we have proceeds of proceeds—multiple generations of proceeds—the photocopier is proceeds of the $500 which was proceeds of the drill press. The security interest jumps from each generation of proceeds to the next. When one of those generations of proceeds happens to be cash, then the security interest in the next generation of proceeds would continue to be perfected on day 21 and beyond only if the collateral description in the financing statement on file would cover the proceeds. If the financing statement identified the collateral as equipment, it would cover the photocopier. But if the financing statement identified the collateral as a drill press, it would not cover the photocopier, so perfection of the security interest would expire on day 21. The following problems illustrate the basic proceeds perfection rules.

PROBLEM 8–2

Ray's day-to-day operations are funded in part by a revolving credit facility provided by the local bank. In return for the credit facility, the bank took, and perfected, a security interest in "all office equipment" owned by the store. In which of the following cases will the bank need to act in order to prevent its security interest in proceeds from losing its perfection after 20 days:

> Case 1: Ray traded the microwave in the break room for a printer that he connected to the store's computer.

[handwritten: SAME PLACE = AUTO PERF.]

> Case 2: Ray traded the store's document shredder for a painting he hung in the customer lounge.

[handwritten: SHREDDER → PAINTING = AUTO PERF.]

> Case 3: Ray traded the multi-color photocopier for a motorcycle.

[handwritten: → DIFF (COT)]

> Case 4: Ray sold several file cabinets for $400 and deposited the money in the store's bank account. Would your answer be different if he put the $400 in the offering plate at church the next Sunday?

> Case 5: Ray sold the store's forklift and used the money as the down payment on a hobby farm he purchased for his family.

[handwritten: FL → $ → HF]

> Case 6: Ray sold the espresso machine in the customer lounge for $200 and bought 10 sheep for the hobby farm.

[handwritten: EM → $ → 10 SHEEP]

> Case 7: Ray traded the store's laptop computer to the farm supply store for a three-month supply of sheep feed which he fed to his sheep.

[handwritten: COMP → SHEEP FEED]

Cash proceeds, as the following case illustrates, create a different kind of proceeds problem. Because cash from the sale of collateral is routinely commingled by the debtor with other funds, we can no longer identify the actual dollars she received for the collateral. We have more than just a perfection issue—what, if anything, remains to be perfected if the secured party can no longer distinguish the proceeds collateral from the rest of the debtor's funds?

McCOURT v. TRIPLETT
Court of Appeals of Arkansas, Division Two
2010 Ark. App. 567 (Ark. Cir. Ct. 2010)

GLOVER, *Judge*.

Appellants, Charles and Julia McCourt, and appellee, Jacqueline Triplett, are creditors of McCourt Manufacturing Company (MMC). In circuit court, they asserted competing claims to $57,099.76 held in MMC's two bank accounts. The circuit judge awarded $37,099.76 to Triplett, as a judgment creditor, and $20,000 to the McCourts, as secured creditors, after attempting to apply a tracing method known as the lowest-intermediate-balance rule. Both sides appeal, each seeking all of the money in both accounts. For the reasons explained below, we reverse the court's order and remand with instructions to award the entire $57,099.76 to Triplett.

On May 11, 2006, Triplett obtained a judgment against MMC in the state of Iowa for more than $500,000. She registered the judgment in Arkansas on March 4, 2008. Approximately one year later, she served a writ of garnishment on First National Bank of Fort Smith, where MMC had a checking account containing $51,454.76, and a savings account containing $5,645.00, for a combined total of $57,099.76. On June 2, 2009, the circuit court ordered First National to pay Triplett the $57,099.76 from both accounts.

The following day, the McCourts moved to quash the court's order, claiming a prior lien on MMC's bank accounts. Attached to their motion was a promissory note from MMC that was secured by various collateral, including the proceeds of MMC's inventory and accounts receivable. The McCourts asserted that the entire $57,099.76 on deposit at First National represented the proceeds of MMC's accounts receivable and inventory sales and therefore belonged to them as secured creditors.

The circuit court held a hearing on the McCourts' motion to quash on August 6, 2009. Mark McCourt, the son of appellant Charles McCourt, testified that he succeeded his father as president of MMC in January 2009. Mark stated that, prior to assuming the office of president, he was a shareholder in MMC with no office duties or involvement in the day-to-day affairs of the company. He said, however, that he had personal knowledge of the money deposited into MMC's bank accounts. According to him, the money in both the checking account and the savings account came from sales of inventory and accounts receivable. He further testified that the money his father loaned MMC was also deposited into the bank accounts; however, he did not say when those deposits occurred.

Charles McCourt testified that he and his wife had loaned money to MMC over the years and that, upon their retirement, wanted to document and safeguard the loans. As a result, MMC executed a $366,000 promissory note to the McCourts on January 3, 2008, and the McCourts perfected a security interest in, among other things, the company's accounts receivable, inventory, and the proceeds therefrom. According to Charles, MMC had only one checking account, and the money from the small savings account came from the checking account. He also stated that he had a "sweep" account so that when the checking account contained more than $20,000, it was swept into an investment account. With regard to the history of the checking account, Charles stated that the checking balance had dropped to as little as $1000, but probably not in the last couple of years. He said that, since January 2008, the account's lowest balance would probably have been "20 some thousand." However, he could not say so with certainty because the balance "fluctuates." Charles also testified that "almost all" of the money in the checking account came from MMC's accounts receivable, although the account may also have contained some interest from a tax return and some money from the loans that he had made to the company. Neither Charles nor Mark produced any deposit slips, bank statements, or other documentary evidence regarding the account balances.

The circuit court attempted to determine, on the testimonial evidence, what portion of the $57,099.76 on deposit at First National Bank constituted proceeds from MMC's accounts receivable and inventory sales, which would belong to the McCourts as secured creditors, and what portion was derived from other sources, which would belong to Triplett. In post-hearing briefs, Triplett cited the lowest-intermediate-balance rule as a means of tracing and identifying the source of the accounts' funds but stated that the McCourts had not produced sufficient evidence to apply the rule. The court apparently disagreed and attempted to utilize the rule as follows:

[U]nder the intermediate balance rule, the McCourts were entitled to the $57,099.76 unless the balance of the account was lower than $57,099.76. If there was a lower balance, the McCourts were entitled only to an amount equal to the lower balance. Here, by his own testimony, Mr. McCourt stated the lowest it got was twenty some thousand. Without any specificity being obtained from either direct or cross examination, the Court finds that the lowest the account got was $20,000.00. The McCourts would be entitled to that sum of money and [Triplett] would be entitled to $37,099.76.

The McCourts and Triplett filed timely notices of appeal from the court's order.

A secured creditor may retain an interest in the proceeds of collateral when those proceeds are deposited into the debtor's bank account. However, the proceeds must be "identifiable" as coming from the sale of collateral. *See* Ark.Code Ann. §4–9–315(a) (Repl.2001). Difficulties may arise in segregating collateral proceeds from other funds in a bank account when the debtor intermingles the proceeds with other types of deposits and draws on the account for operating expenses. In such instances, the Uniform Commercial Code (UCC) permits a secured creditor to identify the collateral proceeds by employing a tracing method. *See* Ark.Code Ann. §4–9–315(b)(2) (Repl.2001). It is the secured creditor's burden to trace and identify the funds as proceeds from the sale of secured collateral. ... Thus, in this case, the McCourts, as secured creditors, had the burden to trace and identify the funds in which they had a security interest.

The favored tracing method in instances such as this one appears to be the lowest-intermediate-balance rule. Under this rule, a presumption exists that the proceeds from the sale of collateral remain in the debtor's bank account so long as the balance equals or exceeds the amount of the proceeds. *Metropolitan,* supra. When the balance drops below the amount of the proceeds, the creditor's security interest in the account abates accordingly. *Id.* For example, if the debtor deposits $50,000 from the sale of collateral, the creditor has a security interest in that amount; however, if the debtor spends from the account and reduces the balance to $45,000, the creditor retains a security interest only to the extent of $45,000. When additional collateral proceeds are deposited, the creditor's security interest in the account increases correspondingly. But if the debtor again spends the account down below the new amount, a revised lowest intermediate balance is created. ... Subsequent deposits of proceeds will again increase the creditor's security interest in the account, but subsequent deposits of non-proceeds will not. ... The lowest intermediate balance is therefore a variable figure depending upon the nature and amount of the debtor's deposits and expenditures over time.

In the case at bar, the circuit court essentially treated the checking and savings accounts as one account containing $57,099.76. The court attempted to establish the lowest intermediate balance in the accounts by using Charles McCourt's estimate of the lowest balance that had occurred in the checking account in the preceding few years. However, application of the lowest-intermediate-balance rule requires more than simply pinpointing an account's lowest historical balance; the court must view the debtor's deposits and expenditures over time to arrive at the lowest intermediate balance on the date that the competing claims arise. Because the court did not do so, we agree with both parties that reversal is in order.

The fighting point in this case is how to apportion the money in the checking and savings accounts upon reversal. The McCourts argue that they are entitled to the entire $57,099.76 contained in both accounts, citing Mark McCourt's testimony that both MMC accounts contained proceeds from its sales of inventory and accounts receivable. This testimony, however, does not meet the McCourts' burden, as secured creditors, to identify the account proceeds as originating from the sale of collateral. If the burden could be met that easily—by a simple, verbal identification of collateral proceeds without the support of any bank records whatsoever—it would be virtually meaningless. The McCourts cite *Metropolitan*, supra, in which our court held that a secured creditor was not required to produce invoices to "conclusively establish" that account funds were identifiable as collateral proceeds. However, the secured creditor in *Metropolitan* produced at least some bank records and explained the inability to produce further documentation. There, the person who handled the debtor's accounts identified, from first-hand knowledge, several bank deposit slips as either containing proceeds from the sale of collateral or money from other sources. She also explained that she was unable to produce corroborating invoices because the debtor had been locked out of its offices at some point. These circumstances distinguish *Metropolitan* from the case at bar.

We therefore conclude that the McCourts did not meet their burden of identifying the money in MMC's accounts as proceeds from the sale of collateral. The money should be awarded on remand to MMC's judgment creditor, cross-appellant Jacqueline Triplett. Our resolution of this issue in Triplett's favor makes it unnecessary for us to address her argument regarding the McCourts' standing.

Problem 8–3

Last month, Ray sold 10 washers subject to Maytag's security interest for cash—his customers writing him checks for the full amount of each purchase. Ray deposited all the checks together at the end of the month in his personal checking account at the bank. This was the first time he had deposited proceeds from the sale of Maytag's collateral in his personal account. The

$7000 deposit brought the balance in the account to $9000. Several days later he withdrew $3000 to make his monthly mortgage payment. The next day he deposited $5000 of the commissions he had received from GEICO in the account. The following week he withdrew $10,000 to pay his daughter's college tuition. Are there any of Maytag's proceeds left in the account? See 9-315(b). Would your answer be different if, after withdrawing the funds to pay tuition, he deposited another $3000 of Maytag's proceeds in the account?

PROBLEM 8–4

Ray has been depositing the cash proceeds from the sale of Whirlpool's collateral in the store's bank account for years. Last month, in return for a cash advance from the bank, Ray gave the bank a security interest in the store's bank account. Does the bank have a claim to Whirlpool's proceeds that Ray has deposited in the account? As between Whirlpool and the bank, which would have priority to the funds in the account? See 9-327. If Ray writes a check on the account to pay his son's college tuition, does the college take the funds subject to the bank's security interest? See 9-332(b).

[handwritten annotations:]

BANK —DIRECT→ ACCOUNT

DEP $7K = TOTAL $9K

WD $3K = TOTAL $6K

DEP. $5K = TOTAL $11K

WD $10K = TOTAL $1K ——→ CAP ON PROCEEDS CLAIM

DEP $3K = TOTAL $4K

WHIRLPOOL ——→ PROCEEDS ↓ BANK

CONTROL > FILING

CHAPTER 9

ENFORCEMENT

Creditors taking security interests in personal property expect that payment of the obligations secured will come from their debtors—not from their collateral. The collateral is intended as a safety net, available to absorb the loss—at least part of it—that may occur if the debtor is unable to make its expected payments. Debtors, on their part, expect to make their payments and, in the end, retain the personal property that serves as collateral. But, as we've seen, expectations are not always fulfilled—economies falter, unanticipated catastrophic events undermine careful financial planning, individual debtors lose jobs, and businesses fail.

When debtors stop making their payments secured creditors start looking to their collateral as an alternative source of payment. In most cases, however, the secured party will not be in possession of the collateral, and therefore it will need to obtain possession before it can turn the collateral into cash and apply it to the debtor's obligation. Part 6 of Article 9 empowers the secured party to take possession of its collateral and then to sell that collateral, using the proceeds from the sale to pay down the debtor's obligation, without initiating any form of legal proceeding against the debtor. As we will see in the materials that follow, this right of "self help" is not without limits, and the courts are frequently called upon in later actions to assess the propriety of a creditor's conduct in repossessing and reselling collateral under the standards imposed by Article 9. Enforcement of a security interest against the collateral does not always result in full satisfaction of the debtor's obligation—sometimes as a result of depreciation, but other times as a result of the manner in which it was disposed of by the secured party. Because the debtor remains obligated to pay any amount of her obligation not paid off with the proceeds from the collateral, debtors have a powerful incentive to challenge everything the secured party does in connection with enforcing its security interest if the secured party subsequently sues to recover a deficiency.

A. ELECTION OF REMEDIES

Before Article 9, a secured party might be forced, upon the debtor's default, to choose—elect—between suing on the debt and repossessing its collateral. If the secured party repossessed its collateral, it lost the right to sue on the debt and, consequently, the right to recover for any deficiency if the proceeds from the collateral were not sufficient to satisfy the debtor's obligation in full. If, instead, the secured party brought suit on the debt, it lost its claim to the specific property that was subject to its security interest. As the *GEC Corporation* case makes clear, Article 9 rejects the election of remedies doctrine. A secured party that repossesses its collateral no longer waives any claim for a deficiency against the debtor simply because it has repossessed the collateral.

GEC v. JOHN CARLO, INC.
United States District Court, E.D. Michigan, Southern Division
2010 U.S. Dist. LEXIS 106133 (E.D. Mich. Oct. 5, 2010)

O'Meara, *Judge.*

BACKGROUND FACTS

General Electric Capital Corporation ("GE Capital") loaned Defendant John Carlo, Inc., money to purchase construction equipment on several occasions from 2004 to 2006. GE Capital perfected a security interest in that equipment. The parties entered into a Forbearance Agreement on June 29, 2009, which consolidated the loans into one promissory note. Defendants Joseph Catenacci and Carlo Catenacci executed guarantees of the loan.

Defendant John Carlo, Inc. has defaulted on the loan and owes Plaintiff approximately $1,000,000. The court has already granted a preliminary injunction allowing Plaintiff to repossess the collateral equipment. Plaintiff now requests that the court reduce its claim to a judgment. Although they do not dispute liability, Defendants object for two primary reasons: (1) they claim that the parties contractually agreed to bring any suit for legal (as opposed to equitable) relief in Connecticut and New York; and (2) they claim that it is premature to allow Plaintiff to obtain a judgment when it has not yet disposed of the collateral.

LAW AND ANALYSIS

* * *

III. ENTRY OF JUDGMENT BEFORE COLLATERAL IS SOLD

Defendants argue that the entry of judgment is premature, because GE Capital has recovered the collateral, but not yet sold it. Defendants suggest that entering a judgment before GE Capital has disposed of the collateral in a commercially reasonable manner would amount to a double recovery. GE Capital contends that the Uniform Commercial Code and the Security

Agreement provide that it may reduce its claim to judgment and foreclose upon the equipment simultaneously.

The Security Agreement provides that "[a]fter default, Secured Party [GE Capital] shall have all of the rights and remedies of a Secured Party under the Uniform Commercial Code, and under any other applicable law." The Security Agreement further provides that, upon default, GE Capital has the right to sell, lease, or otherwise dispose of the collateral. The Agreement also expressly states that GE Capital's "rights and remedies under this Agreement or otherwise arising are cumulative and may be exercise [sic] singularly or *concurrently*." (emphasis added).

The UCC contains similar language. Section 9-601 provides a secured party's remedies in the event of a default. Under section 9-601(a), a "secured party: (1) May reduce a claim to judgment, foreclose or otherwise enforce the claim [or] security interest … by any available judicial procedure. …" *Conn. Gen. Stat. §42a-9-601(a)*. Section 9-601(c) provides that "[t]he rights under subsections (a) and (b) are *cumulative* and, except as may otherwise be prohibited under other law in a consumer transaction, *may be exercised simultaneously*." *Conn. Gen. Stat. §42a-9-601(c)* (emphasis added); *see also id. at cmt. 5*.

The statutory and contractual language is clear. Plaintiff may foreclose upon the collateral (which it has) and seek a judgment simultaneously, as long as it is acting in good faith. *See, e.g., Highland Capital Corp. v. Western Foot & Ankle Center, Inc., 2009 U.S. Dist. LEXIS 129613, 2009 WL 315727 (D. N.J. Feb. 9, 2009); General Elec. Cap. Corp. v. JLT Aircraft Holding Corp., 2009 U.S. Dist. LEXIS 118543, 2009 WL 5169532 (D. Minn. Dec. 18, 2009)*. When Plaintiff disposes of the collateral, it must credit the amount received against the amount of the judgment. Defendants are further protected in that the UCC requires the collateral to be disposed of in a "commercially reasonable" manner. *Conn. Gen. Stat. §42a-9-610(b)*. Should Defendants wish to contest whether the collateral was sold in a commercially reasonable manner, they may seek relief from judgment pursuant to Fed. R. Civ. P. 60(b) at the appropriate time.

B. DEFAULT

The secured party's right to enforce its security interest against the collateral under Article 9 is triggered by the debtor's default. Article 9 does not define "default," so the parties will have to do so themselves in the security agreement. Although the security agreement can make just about anything a default—re-locating the collateral, giving another creditor a security interest in it, failing to insure it against loss, selling it to another, using it for other than its intended purposes, the list is endless—the most likely ground on which default will be based is non-payment by the debtor. A secured party who doesn't want to wait until a final meltdown by the debtor to enforce its security interest can give itself the right to declare a default anytime the secured party becomes concerned about the debtor's ability to keep making payments. As the *Richards Engineering* case explains, the Code sanctions the inclusion of such "insecurity clauses" in a security agreement but it also expects that courts will review the propriety of a secured party's invocation of the clause if challenged by the debtor.

RICHARDS ENGINEERS, INC. v. SPANEL
Court of Appeals of Colorado, Division One
745 P.2d 1031 (Colo. Ct. App. 1987)

Pierce, *Judge*.

Defendants, Charles and Frances Spanel, d/b/a Inter-Mountain Engineering, Ltd., appeal the trial court judgment entered in favor of plaintiffs, Carol, Kenneth, and David Richards, Janice A. Nottingham, Patricia A. Loder, Sandy and John H. Schwartze, d/b/a Richards Engineers.

* * *

This dispute arises from a purchase agreement between the parties, whereby defendants acquired plaintiffs' businesses, Richards Engineers, Inc., and Carol's Secretarial and Printing Service. The contract provided that a portion of the purchase price would be in the form of a $91,000 promissory note, which was payable in bi-annual installments over a ten-year period. The contract further provided that at the end of five years, defendants were to use their best efforts to obtain refinancing of the principal balance in order to pay off the plaintiffs.

The note was secured by a security agreement containing an "insecurity" clause. This clause allowed defendants' obligations to be accelerated under the note "if [plaintiffs] deemed itself insecure."

Timely payments were made by defendants in accordance with the ten-year amortization schedule incorporated into the note. At the end of five years, plaintiffs sought to obtain payment of the entire balance of the note; however, defendants were unable to obtain refinancing. Plaintiffs then deemed themselves insecure pursuant to the insecurity clause.

Defendants refused immediate payment of the balance, and plaintiffs brought this action. The trial was to the court, and judgment was entered in favor of plaintiffs. The trial court found that although the parties had agreed to a ten-year payment schedule, plaintiffs actually expected full payment at the end of five years. The trial court further found that plaintiffs' insecurity arose when defendants refused to pay the entire balance at the end of five years. Using a subjective test, the trial court determined that plaintiffs were insecure. The court further ordered defendants to pay plaintiffs' attorney fees as a cost of collection.

I.

Defendants first contend that the trial court erred when it applied a purely subjective test in determining whether plaintiffs' declaration of insecurity was in good faith. We agree.

Section 4-1-208 [Rev. 1-309], C.R.S., provides that:

> "A term providing that one party or his successor in interest may accelerate payment or performance or require collateral or additional collateral 'at will' or 'when he deems himself insecure' or in words of similar import shall be construed to mean that he shall have power to do so only if he in good faith believes that the prospect of payment or performance is impaired. The burden of establishing lack of good faith is on the party against whom the power has been exercised."

Section 4-1-201(19) [Rev. 1-201(20), C.R.S. defines "good faith" as:

> "[H]onesty in fact in the conduct or transaction concerned."

We are aware that, in the context of a holder in due course who must take an instrument in good faith, this definition has been construed as requiring a purely subjective inquiry. *Money Mart Check Cashing Center, Inc. v. Epicycle Corp., 667 P.2d 1372 (Colo.1983)*. However, §4-1-201, C.R.S. specifies that the code definitions are applicable "unless the context otherwise requires." Thus, we must determine whether "good faith" in the context of an insecurity clause otherwise requires the use of an objective rather than a subjective standard.

Although we find no Colorado case law governing this particular issue, we are guided by persuasive authority from other jurisdictions. Many jurisdictions have determined that "good faith" in this context is to be measured by wholly subjective standards. *See Ginn v. Citizens & Southern National Bank, 145 Ga.App. 175, 243 S.E.2d 528 (1978); Farmers Cooperative Elevator, Inc. v. State Bank, 236 N.W.2d 674 (Iowa 1975); Fort Knox National Bank v. Gustafson, 385 S.W.2d 196 (Ky.1964); Van Horn v. Van De Wol, Inc., 6 Wash.App. 959, 497 P.2d 252 (Ct.App.1972)*. Thus, in these jurisdictions, the state of mind of the creditor is the measure of good faith, regardless of the reasonableness of such mental state.

Other jurisdictions have chosen an objective standard reasoning that a purely subjective test is susceptible to arbitrary abuse by the creditor. *See Black v. Peoples Bank & Trust Co., 437 So.2d 26 (Miss.1983); Universal C.I.T. Credit Corp. v. Shepler, 164 Ind.App. 516, 329 N.E.2d 620 (1975); see also Blaine v. GMAC, 82 Misc.2d 653, 370 N.Y.S.2d 323 (N.Y.Co.Ct.1975)*. These latter authorities have further opined that a subjective standard would allow a creditor to place his debtor in an unjust position, since the creditor might at any time call the entire debt and require the debtor to prove the unfathomable state of mind of the creditor. *See Universal C.I.T. Credit Corp. v. Shepler, supra (J. Garrard, concurring)*.

In determining the appropriate standard, we are also guided by pre-code Colorado case law governing similar transactions. Under such rulings, when a mortgagee sought to foreclose upon a mortgagor because of insecurity, such a determination had to be founded upon good faith, and the decision had to be based on reasonable grounds and probable cause. *Thomas v. Beirne, 94 Colo. 429, 30 P.2d 863 (1934); see also Ramstetter v. MacGinnis, 100 Colo. 494, 68 P.2d 454 (1937).* Further guidance is obtained from Professor Gilmore, a drafter of the Uniform Commercial Code. He writes that:

"The creditor has the right to accelerate if, under all the circumstances, a reasonable man, motivated by good faith, would have done so. ... The Code adopts such a rule in §1-208. ..." *2 G. Gilmore, Security Interests in Personal Property, §43.4 at 1197 (1965).*

We are of the opinion that an objective standard of reasonableness is the better rule of law and hereby adopt it in the context of an insecurity clause such as the one before us. A declaration of insecurity is a unilateral decision made by the creditor which places a severe hardship upon the debtor. This hardship is unjust if the creditor's decision is unreasonable or based upon mistaken facts which the creditor may honestly believe to be true. Thus, we conclude that the appropriate determination in the context of an insecurity clause is whether a reasonable person, under all the circumstances of the transaction, and motivated by good faith, would have accelerated the debt. *See 2 G. Gilmore, supra.*

Further support for the adoption of a reasonableness test in the context of an insecurity clause is found by analysis of other code provisions. Section 4-2-609, C.R.S., provides that:

"When reasonable grounds for insecurity arise with respect to the performance of either party, the other may in writing demand adequate assurance of due performance. ..."

It would be highly inequitable to require less than reasonable grounds in order to accelerate an entire debt based on insecurity, especially in light of the more onerous burden placed on the debtor by acceleration.

The facts of the present case make clear the inequity of a purely subjective standard. Defendants made all payments in accordance with the ten-year payment schedule that had been agreed to by the parties. These payments were all timely made in full compliance with the agreement. The fact that plaintiffs mistakenly believed they would receive complete payment of the entire debt after five years could not operate to place such an onerous burden upon defendants. Thus, a subjective test of insecurity would be wholly unjust. Plaintiffs contend that even if an objective standard is applied, adequate facts are present to sustain the trial court's holding. We disagree.

Although there was testimony that defendants had violated certain terms of the contract, there were no findings of fact sufficient alone to demonstrate the existence of reasonable grounds for plaintiffs to have deemed themselves insecure. Accordingly, this case must be remanded for further findings of fact and conclusions of law applying an objective reasonableness test.

PROBLEM 9–1

The security agreements that Ray has his customers sign always provide that:

> The parties agree that if at any time the secured party deems itself insecure because it believes that the prospect of payment or performance is impaired, the secured party shall have the right to declare a default and to accelerate payment of all unpaid sums or performance.

In each of the following cases, determine whether Ray has grounds for declaring a default under the insecurity clause:

Case 1: The store's third-quarter sales were way below Ray's expectations, and he's worried about whether he'll be able to keep the store open much longer if things don't improve soon.

Case 2: Midway through a severe recession in the U.S. economy, Ray is depressed by his firm conviction that things are only going to get worse, and that a deep depression like that of the 1930s is a certainty.

Case 3: One of Ray's customers who bought a washer-dryer combo on credit stops by the store to purchase vacuum-cleaner bags. When he tries to pay for the bags with his VISA card, VISA rejects the card and instructs Ray to confiscate the card.

Case 4: During a meeting over lunch with his neighbor who owns the building leased by the local yogurt shop, Ray learns that the shop has not made its lease payments for the last two months. Ray sold a freezer to the yogurt shop on credit earlier this year.

Case 5: A representative from a collection agency stops by Ray's store to inquire whether Ray has seen the owner of the burger shop across the street recently. Ray has sold several appliances to the shop on credit.

Case 6: Ray opens his morning newspaper and sees an ad for a "Going Out of Business Sale" placed by the local grocery store. Ray sold the grocery all of its freezer cases on credit last year.

Case 7: Ray receives by mail a notice from the United States Bankruptcy Trustee for his district that one of his customers has filed for relief under Chapter 7 of the Bankruptcy Code. The customer purchased replacements for all of his kitchen appliances from Ray recently.

As the next case illustrates, a secured party that refrains from declaring a default when one has occurred in the hope of saving the transaction and thereby avoiding the expense and inconvenience of repossession and suit on a deficiency could later be found to have waived the default, making any subsequent enforcement of its security interest improper. Usually, the security agreement will attempt to provide cover for the secured party who refrains from declaring a default, when one has technically occurred, by including a no waiver clause. But as Gilmore has noted:

> [T]he courts pay little attention to clauses that appear to say that meaningful acts are meaningless and that the secured party can blow hot or cold as he chooses.

Gilmore, at 1214.

MOSE MINOR v. CHASE AUTO
Supreme Court of Arkansas
2010 Ark. 246 (2010)

Sheffield, *Justice*.

The Arkansas Court of Appeals certified this case to us pursuant to Arkansas Supreme Court Rule 1–2(b)(1), (4), and (5) (2009), as a case involving an issue of first impression, having a substantial public interest and needing clarification or development of the law. We have been asked to determine whether nonwaiver and no-unwritten-modifications clauses in a financing agreement preclude a creditor from waiving future strict compliance with the agreement by accepting late payments. *In Mercedes–Benz Credit Corp. v. Morgan, 312 Ark. 225, 850 S.W.2d 297 (1993)*, this court explicitly reserved ruling on this question until it had been properly raised and argued in an appropriate case. The question is now ripe for our review.

On March 15, 2003, Appellant, Mose Minor (Minor), entered into a Simple Interest Motor Vehicle Contract and Security Agreement with Appellee, Chase Auto Finance Corporation (Chase), to finance the purchase of a 2003 Toyota Tundra. By the terms of the agreement, Minor was to make sixty-six payments of $456.99 on the fourteenth of each month. The payments would start on April 14, 2003, and end on September 14, 2008. The agreement also included the following relevant provisions:

> G. Default: If you breach any warranty or default in the performance of any promise you make in this contract or any other contract you have with us, including, but not limited to, failing to make any payments when due, or become insolvent, or file any proceeding under the U.S. Bankruptcy Code, ... we may at our option and without notice or demand (1) declare all unpaid sums

immediately due and payable subject to any right of reinstatement as required by law (2) file suit against you for all unpaid sums (3) take immediate possession of the vehicle (4) exercise any other legal or equitable remedy. ... Our remedies are cumulative and taking of any action shall not be a waiver or prohibit us from pursuing any other remedy. ...

J. Other Agreements of Buyer: ... (2) You agree that if we accept moneys in sums less than those due or make extensions of due dates of payments under this contract, doing so will not be a waiver of any later right to enforce the contract terms as written. ... (12) All of the agreements between us and you are set forth in this contract and no modification of this contract shall be valid unless it is made in writing and signed by you and us. ...

K. Delay in Enforcement: We can delay or waive enforcement of any of our rights under this contract without losing them.

Minor's first payment was late, as were several subsequent payments. At times he failed to make any payment for months. Chase charged a late fee for each late payment, and sent several letters requesting payment and offering to assist Minor with his account. Chase also warned Minor that continued failure to make payments would result in Chase exercising its legal options available under the agreement, including repossession of the vehicle. Minor claims he never received these letters. At one point, Minor fell so far behind in his payments that Chase was on the verge of repossessing the vehicle. However, on October 19, 2004, the parties agreed to a two-month extension of the agreement, such that the final installment would be due on November 14, 2008. The extension agreement indicated that all other terms and conditions of the original contract would remain the same.

On November 2, 2004, Minor filed for Chapter 7 bankruptcy in the Eastern District of Arkansas. In his petition, Minor stated that the value of the vehicle was $5000.00.[1] On February 24, 2005, Chase sent Minor a letter acknowledging that Minor's debt to Chase had been discharged in bankruptcy. The letter further stated that Chase still had a valid lien on the vehicle, and if Minor wished to keep the vehicle, he would have to continue to make payments to Chase. Otherwise, Chase would repossess the vehicle. Chase sent a similar letter to Minor on May 22, 2006, and to Minor's bankruptcy attorney on November 16, 2004. Minor claimed he never received any of these letters.

* * *

Minor filed a complaint against Chase in the Johnson County Circuit Court. In the complaint, Minor alleged that, during the course of the contract,

---

1 [Chase, through its repossession agent, repossessed the vehicle in September 2006]

the parties had altered the provisions of the contract regarding Chase's right to repossess the vehicle and Chase had waived the right to strictly enforce the repossession clause. ... Also, Minor asserted that he was not in default on his payments, pursuant to the repayment schedule, at the time Chase authorized repossession. ...

A jury trial was held on February 19, 2009. At the close of Minor's case, Chase moved for a directed verdict. ... Chase further maintained that, by Minor's own admission when he testified before the circuit court, he was at least three payments past due at the time of the repossession. Therefore, under the terms of the contract, Chase asserted that it had a right to repossess the vehicle peacefully, and Minor's argument that he should have received notice that Chase would require strict compliance with the contract failed because the contract included nonwaiver and no-unwritten modification clauses. Chase argued that the case upon which *Minor relied, Mercedes–Benz Credit Corp. v. Morgan, 312 Ark. 225, 850 S.W.2d 297 (1993)*, was distinguishable, and instead the holding of *Westlund v. Melson, 7 Ark.App. 268, 647 S.W.2d 488 (1983)*, indicated that Chase's acceptance of late payments had not effected a waiver of its right to demand future strict compliance.

* * *

In response, Minor argued that ... he had presented sufficient evidence that he had a right to possess the vehicle, and that, by continually accepting late payments, Chase had established a course of dealing that modified the contract and waived Chase's right to repossess the vehicle without notice to Minor that Chase would require strict compliance in the future. Minor cited *Mercedes–Benz Credit Corp. v. Morgan, 312 Ark. 225, 850 S.W.2d 297 (1993)*, and *Ford Motor Credit Co. v. Ellison, 334 Ark. 357, 974 S.W.2d 464 (1998)*, as support for this position. ...

After hearing these arguments, the circuit court ruled ... that by the express terms of the contract Chase's acceptance of late payments did not effect a waiver of its rights in the future; that at the time of repossession, Minor was behind in his payments and in breach of the contract; that Chase had the right under the contract to repossess the vehicle and did not commit conversion. ... Therefore, the court granted Chase's motion for a directed verdict on all grounds. On March 27, 2009, the circuit court entered an order reflecting this ruling and dismissed the complaint with prejudice. Minor filed a timely notice of appeal on April 23, 2009.

We have accepted certification of this case from the court of appeals in order to determine the effect of nonwaiver and no-unwritten-modification clauses in a contract when a secured creditor has routinely accepted delinquent payments from a debtor. While we have never considered this specific issue, Arkansas courts have held that, when the contract does not contain the provisions at issue before us now, the creditor's previous acceptance of late payments in the past from the debtor waives the creditor's right to demand strict compliance from the debtor in the future. *See, e.g., Ford Motor Credit Co. v. Ellison, 334 Ark. 357, 974 S.W.2d 464 (1998); Am. Law Book Co. v. Hurst, 168 Ark. 28, 268 S.W. 605 (1925).* This waiver remains in effect until the creditor notifies the debtor that it will no longer accept late payments, and instead will require strict compliance. *Ellison, 334 Ark. at 367, 974 S.W.2d at 470.* The majority of jurisdictions around the country have adopted this same general rule. *See, e.g., Ford Motor Credit Co. v. Waters, 273 So.2d 96, 100 (Fla.Dist.Ct.App.1973); Dunn v. Gen. Equities of Iowa, Ltd., 319 N.W.2d 515 (Iowa 1982); Nev. Nat'l Bank v. Huff, 94 Nev. 506, 582 P.2d 364 (1978); Slusser v. Wyrick, 28 Ohio App.3d 96, 502 N.E.2d 259 (1986); Lee v. Wood Prods. Credit Union, 275 Or. 445, 551 P.2d 446 (1976); Ford Motor Credit Co. v. Washington, 573 S.W.2d 616 (Tex.Civ.App.1978).*

The existence of nonwaiver and no-unwritten-modification provisions in the contract changes the situation, however. As previously mentioned, this court in *Mercedes–Benz Credit Corp. v. Morgan, 312 Ark. 225, 850 S.W.2d 297 (1993),* reserved considering the effect of such clauses. In *Morgan,* Morgan purchased a Porsche with an installment contract assigned to Mercedes–Benz Credit Corporation (MBCC). Morgan made many late payments, and about a year into the forty-eight month contract, MBCC decided to exercise its right to repossess the vehicle under the contract. Morgan then brought his account current, and MBCC offered to return the Porsche, but Morgan refused and filed an action for conversion. On appeal, this court considered Morgan's argument that the fact that MBCC had routinely accepted Morgan's late payments constituted a waiver of strict compliance, and, at the very least, MBCC had to provide notice to Morgan before it repossessed the vehicle. This court noted that its prior decisions in *Commercial Credit Co. v. Ragland, 189 Ark. 349, 72 S.W.2d 226 (1934),* and *General Motors Acceptance Corp. v. Hicks, 189 Ark. 62, 70 S.W.2d 509 (1934),* decided before the adoption of the Uniform Commercial Code, required a creditor, who had accepted late payments in the past, to notify a debtor that the practice would no longer be continued before the creditor could take appropriate action to declare a default. The court then quoted a long passage from *Steve H. Nickles's Rethinking Some U.C.C. Article 9 Problems, 34 Ark. Law Rev. 1, 136–37 (1980–1981),* that indicated that this rule did not change with the adoption of the Uniform Commercial Code. This court concluded that, given this authority, the jury could have found that MBCC had waived its right to repossession by its course of dealing in accepting late payments, and that MBCC would need to provide Morgan with notice in order to reinstate its right to strict compliance.

However, this court noted that MBCC relied on the holding in *Westlund v. Melson, 7 Ark.App. 268, 647 S.W.2d 488 (1983),* that acceptance of a late payment precludes acceleration of the due date of the note because of the lateness of that payment, but is not a waiver for the right to accelerate when default occurs in a subsequent installment. While this court rejected MBCC's argument because MBCC had brought it up for the first time on appeal, the court did not reject the holding in Westlund outright. Further, the court sua sponte acknowledged that the contract at issue in the case before it contained nonwaiver and no-unwritten-modification clauses, and seemed to imply that if MBCC had addressed these clauses in its argument, the outcome of the case might have been different. Accordingly, we affirm our previous decisions that when a contract does not contain a nonwaiver and a no-unwritten-modification provision and the creditor has established a course of dealing in accepting late payments from the debtor, the creditor waives its right to insist on strict compliance with the contract and must give notice to the debtor that it will no longer accept late payments before it can declare default of the debt. However, we announce today that, if a contract includes nonwaiver and no-unwritten-modification clauses, the creditor, in accepting late payments, does not waive its right under the contract to declare default of the debt, and need not give notice that it will enforce that right in the event of future late payments. In arriving at this conclusion, we adhere to the principle that "a security agreement is effective according to its terms between the parties." *Ark.Code Ann. §4–9–201 (Repl.2001); Fordyce Bank & Trust Co. v. Bean Timberland, Inc., 369 Ark. 90, 97, 251 S.W.3d 267, 273 (2007)*. We have long held that nonwaiver clauses are legal and valid. *See Philmon v. Mid–State Homes, Inc., 245 Ark. 680, 684, 434 S.W.2d 84, 87 (1968) (citing Johnson v. Guar. Bank & Trust Co., 177 Ark. 770, 9 S.W.2d 3 (1928))*. Also, section 4–2–209(2) (Repl.2001) of the Arkansas Code declares that no-unwritten-modification provisions are binding.

We acknowledge that there is a difference of opinion among the courts in other jurisdictions over the effect of nonwaiver and no-unwritten-modification clauses. The United States District Court for the District of Connecticut described this split of authority best:

> There are three schools of thought on the anti-waiver provision and its effect on the general rule. One line of cases has construed the anti-waiver provision as giving the secured party the right to take possession of the collateral without notice upon default. *Virgil Van Bibber, et al, v. Norris [275 Ind. 555], 419 N.E.2d 115 (Ind.1981); Hale v. Ford Motor Credit Co., 374 So.2d 849 (Ala.1979); Wade v. Ford Motor Credit Co., 455 F.Supp. 147 (D.C.E.D.Mo.1978)*. In contrast, a second line of cases holds that the anti-waiver clause is irrelevant because acceptance of late payments does not constitute a waiver of the secured party's right to demand prompt payments. These jurisdictions have decided that waiver is not the issue to be determined, but rather "the issue is the right of the [debtor] … to be notified of a modification of such conduct on part of the [creditor]." *Waters, 273 So.2d at 100*. In reaching a determination of this issue, the courts essentially reverted to the general rule concluding that the debtor has the right to be notified of the secured party's demand of prompt payments. "The basis for imposing this duty on the secured party is that the secured party is estopped from asserting his contract rights because his conduct had induced the justified reliance of the debtor in believing that late payments were acceptable." *Cobb, 295 N.W.2d at 236*.

In *Westinghouse* [*Credit Corporation v. Shelton, 645 F.2d 869 (10th Cir.1981)*], supra, the United States Court of Appeals for the Tenth Circuit expressed a third view with respect to the anti-waiver provision. The court concluded that it was possible for the creditor to waive the anti-waiver provision pursuant to basic contract principles as illustrated in Article 2 of the Uniform Commercial Code. *Id. at 871–74.* Arriving at this conclusion, the court reasoned that an Article 9 security agreement may also be a contract for a sale and, therefore, Article 2 principles are applicable. *Id. at 872 n. 3.* The court went on to state that U.C.C. §2–208 permitted the creditor to waive its right to strictly enforce the contract's terms. *Id. at 872–73. Tillquist v. Ford Motor Credit Co., 714 F.Supp. 607, 611 (D.Conn.1989); see also Smith v. Gen. Fin. Corp. of Ga., 243 Ga. 500, 255 S.E.2d 14, 14 (1979)* ("[E]vidence of the buyer's repeated, late, irregular payments, which are accepted by the seller, does create a factual dispute as to whether a quasi new agreement was created under Code §20–116, and a jury question is also raised as to whether the anti-waiver provision in the loan contract was itself waived."); *Battista v. Sav. Bank of Balt., 67 Md.App. 257, 507 A.2d 203, 209 (1986)* ("We hold, therefore, that a waiver of a contractual right to prompt payment or a waiver of a contractual right to repossess … may be effected by conduct, and the same is true as to the provisions of a non-waiver clause. When such a waiver has occurred, the creditor, before it can insist on future performance in strict compliance with the contract, must give plain and reasonable notice to the debtor that it intends to do so."); *Moe v. John Deere Co., 516 N.W.2d 332, 338 (S.D.1994)* ("We hold that the repeated acceptance of late payments by a creditor who has the contractual right to repossess the property imposes a duty on the creditor to notify the debtor that strict compliance with the contract terms will be required before the creditor can lawfully repossess the collateral.").

By our holding, we have adopted the reasoning of the first line of cases. We concur with the Supreme Court of Indiana's decision in *Van Bibber v. Norris, 275 Ind. 555, 419 N.E.2d 115 (1981)*, that a rule providing that nonwaiver clauses could themselves be waived by the acceptance of late payments is "illogical, since the very conduct which the [non-waiver] clause is designed to permit[,] acceptance of late payment[,] is turned around to constitute waiver of the clause permitting the conduct." *Id. at 121.* We also agree that the approach of jurisdictions that require creditors who have accepted late payments in the past to notify debtors that they expect strict compliance in the future, despite the existence of a nonwaiver provision in the contract, is not "sound." *Id. at 121.* Such a rule, we recognize, "begs the question of validity of the non-waiver clause." *Id. at 121.* Finally, our holding is in line with the Indiana Supreme Court's ruling that it would enforce the provisions of the contract, since the parties had agreed to them, and that it would not require the creditor to give notice, because the nonwaiver clause placed the secured party in the same position as one who had never accepted a late payment. *Id. at 122; see also Hale v. Ford Motor Credit Co., 374 So.2d 849 (Ala.1979); Gen. Grocer Co. of Ill.*

v. Bachar, 51 Ill.App.3d 907, 8 Ill.Dec. 720, 365 N.E.2d 1106 (1977); First Nat'l Bank of Cincinnati v. Cianelli, 73 Ohio App.3d 781, 598 N.E.2d 789 (1991).

In holding that nonwaiver and no-unwritten-modification clauses in a contract preclude waiver of a secured creditor's right to demand strict compliance with the contract in the future, even where the creditor's past acceptance of late payments has established a course of dealing, we address only the question certified to us by the court of appeals. We remand this case to the court of appeals for a determination on the merits.

Certified question answered; remanded to court of appeals.

Default will often trigger other rights of the secured party under the security agreement. For example, most security agreements include an acceleration clause—a clause that gives the secured party, upon the debtor's default, the right to declare the entire unpaid balance of the debtor's obligation due.

PROBLEM 9–2

When Ray's customer failed to make her monthly payment for two consecutive months, Ray declared a default under the security agreement she signed and, on the basis of the acceleration clause in the security agreement, declared the remaining balance on the note she signed due immediately. She had made 15 of the 24 monthly payments of $200 when she defaulted. When she showed up at the shop with $400 cash in hand to make the payments she had missed, Ray refused to accept the money, telling her that as a result of her default, she had to pay $1800 if she wanted to keep the appliances she bought from Ray. Can Ray repossess the appliances if she doesn't pay the $1800? See 1-309.

If the debtor fails to make the sixteenth and seventeenth payments out of the twenty-four she promised to make, the secured party can sue to recover the entire amount of the debtor's obligation—payments 16 through 24—even though under the terms of the agreement, the time for making payments 17 through 24 has not passed. Once the secured party exercises its right to accelerate, the debtor cannot cure the default by simply tendering the missed payments. To prevent repossession of the collateral by the secured party after acceleration, the debtor will have to pay off the balance of her obligation in full (unless the secured party is willing to accept less).

C. REPOSSESSION

Default by the debtor triggers the secured party's right to take possession of the collateral. Under Article 9, as we've previously noted, the secured party is not required to use judicial process to repossess its collateral. 9-609. This "self-help" repossession must, however, be accomplished "without breach of the peace." 9-609(b)(2). Article 9 leaves it to the courts to define "breach of the peace," and as a result, courts have become the referees in what Gilmore called the "underworld" of secured financing where "repossession is a knock-down, drag-out battle waged on both sides with cunning guile and complete disregard for the rules of fair play." Gilmore at 1212.2

As it turns out, refereeing breaches of the peace in repossessions is no less subjective then calling pass interference in football or traveling in basketball, so the reported decisions are somewhat inconsistent and without predictive value except where the secured party's conduct is so extreme as to make it objectively indefensible. But, as the following case demonstrates, even conduct that many would intuitively consider to be extreme and outside the pale of reasonable, still might not cross the vague line demarcated by the "without breach of the peace" standard.

CHAPA v. TRACIERS & ASSOCIATES
Court of Appeals of Texas, Houston (14th Dist.)
267 S.W.3d 386 (Tex. App. Houston 14th Dist. 2008)

Guzman, *Justice*.

In this appeal, we must determine whether appellants, the parents of two young children, have legally cognizable claims for mental anguish allegedly sustained when a repossession agent towed their vehicle out of sight before he realized their children were inside. The parents filed suit against the financing company, the repossession company it hired, and the repossession agent who towed the vehicle. They asserted claims for mental anguish and its physical manifestations under (a) section 9.609 of the Business and Commerce Code, … The trial court granted summary judgment for the defendants on the parents' claims. Neither parent witnessed the vehicle being towed from the street, and the repossession agent discovered the children and returned them and the vehicle within minutes. On these facts, we conclude that, as a matter of law, appellants Carlos and Maria Chapa do not have a viable claim for breach of the peace under section 9.609 of the Business and Commerce Code. …

I. FACTUAL AND PROCEDURAL BACKGROUND

Ford Motor Credit Corp. ("FMCC") hired Traciers & Associates ("Traciers") to repossess a white 2002 Ford Expedition owned by Marissa Chapa, who was in default on the associated promissory note. Traciers assigned the job to its field manager, Paul Chambers, and gave him an address where the vehicle could be found. FMCC, Traciers, and Chambers were unaware that the address was that of Marissa's brother, Carlos Chapa. Coincidentally, Carlos and his wife Maria Chapa also had purchased a white Ford Expedition financed by FMCC. Their vehicle, however, was a 2003 model, and the Chapas were not in default.

---

2   Although Gilmore confined his characterization to consumer transactions, in my experience commercial transactions were a part of the same "underworld."

On the night of February 6, 2003, Chambers went to the address and observed a white Ford Expedition. The license number of the vehicle did not match that of the vehicle he was told to repossess, and he did not see the vehicle's vehicle identification number ("VIN"), which was obscured. Chambers returned early the next morning and still could not see the Expedition's VIN. He returned to his own vehicle, which was parked two houses away.

Unseen by Chambers, Maria Chapa left the house and helped her two sons, ages ten and six, into the Expedition for the trip to school. Her mother-in-law's vehicle was parked behind her, so Maria backed her mother-in-law's vehicle into the street, then backed her Expedition out of the driveway and parked on the street. She left the keys to her truck in the ignition with the motor running while she parked her mother-in-law's car back in the driveway and reentered the house to return her mother-in-law's keys.

After Chambers saw Maria park the Expedition on the street and return to the house, it took him only thirty seconds to back his tow truck to the Expedition, hook it to his truck, and drive away. Chambers did not leave his own vehicle to perform this operation, and it is undisputed that he did not know the Chapa children were inside.[3] When Maria emerged from the house, the Expedition, with her children, was gone. Maria began screaming, telephoned 911, and called her husband at work to tell him the children were gone.

Meanwhile, on an adjacent street, Chambers noticed that the Expedition's wheels were turning, indicating to him that the vehicle's engine was running. He stopped the tow truck and heard a sound from the Expedition. Looking inside, he discovered the two Chapa children. After he persuaded one of the boys to unlock the vehicle, Chambers drove the Expedition back to the Chapas' house. He returned the keys to Maria, who was outside her house, crying. By the time emergency personnel and Carlos Chapa arrived, the children were back home and Chambers had left the scene.

Maria testified that the incident caused her to have an anxiety attack, including chest pain and numbness in her arm. She states she has continued to experience panic attacks and has been diagnosed with an anxiety disorder. In addition, both Carlos and Maria have been diagnosed with post-traumatic stress disorder. Acting individually and on behalf of their children, Carlos and Maria Chapa sued Traciers, Chambers, and FMCC. Appellees settled the children's claims but contested the individual claims of Carlos and Maria. The trial court granted summary judgment on the parents' claims in favor of Traciers, Chambers, and FMCC, and this appeal ensued.

* * *

---

3   Chambers did not see the children in the back seat through the tinted windows of the Expedition.

IV. ANALYSIS

A. SECTION 9.609 OF THE TEXAS BUSINESS AND COMMERCE CODE

The Chapas first argue that the trial court erred in granting summary judgment against them on their claim that appellees are liable under section 9.609 of the Business and Commerce Code. This statute provides in pertinent part:

(a) After default, a secured party:

(1) may take possession of the collateral; ...

(b) A secured party may proceed under Subsection (a):

...

(2) without judicial process, if it proceeds without breach of the peace.

Tex. Bus. & Com.Code Ann. §9.609 (Vernon 2002). The Chapas correctly point out that this statute imposes a duty on secured creditors to take precautions for public safety when repossessing property. *See MBank El Paso, N.A. v. Sanchez, 836 S.W.2d 151, 153 (Tex.1992)* (interpreting predecessor statute). Thus, the creditor who elects to pursue nonjudicial repossession assumes the risk that a breach of the peace might occur. *Id. at 154*. A secured creditor "remains liable for breaches of the peace committed by its independent contractor." *Id. (citing Restatement (Second) of Torts, Precautions Required by Statute or Regulation, §424 (1965))*. Thus, a creditor cannot escape liability by hiring an independent contractor to repossess secured property.

* * *

In their arguments concerning breach of the peace and its associated liability, the Chapas rely most heavily on authorities addressing breaches of the peace under Texas criminal law and cases from other jurisdictions discussing breaches of the peace under the Uniform Commercial Code. Because a breach of the peace under the criminal code would also constitute a breach of the peace under the Uniform Commercial Code, we address both sources of authority.

1. BREACH OF THE PEACE UNDER CRIMINAL LAW.

In support of their argument that Chambers breached the peace, the Chapas rely on the following language from Corpus Juris, adopted by the Texas Court of Criminal Appeals in 1936:

The term 'breach of the peace' is generic, and includes all violations of the public peace or order, or decorum; in other words, it signifies the offense of disturbing the public peace or tranquility enjoyed by the citizens of a community; a disturbance of the public tranquillity by any act or conduct inciting to violence or tending to provoke or excite others to break the peace; a disturbance of public order by an act of violence, or by any act likely to produce violence, or which, by causing consternation and alarm disturbs the peace and quiet of the community. By 'peace,' as used in this connection, is meant the tranquillity enjoyed by the citizens of a municipality or a community where good order reigns among its members. ...

The offense may consist of acts of public turbulence or indecorum in violation of the common peace and quiet, of an invasion of the security and protection which the laws afford to every citizen, or of acts such as tend to excite violent resentment or to provoke or excite others to break the peace. Actual or threatened violence is an essential element of a breach of the peace. Either one is sufficient to constitute the offense. Accordingly, where means which cause disquiet and disorder, and which threaten danger and disaster to the community, are used, it amounts to a breach of the peace, although no actual personal violence is employed. Where the incitement of terror or fear of personal violence is a necessary element, the conduct or language of the wrongdoer must be of a character to induce such a condition in a person of ordinary firmness.

*Head v. State, 131 Tex.Crim. 96, 99, 96 S.W.2d 981, 982–83 (1936)
(on mot. for reh'g).*

As further explained in Corpus Juris Secundum, "[t]he acts involved, to constitute a breach of the peace, must also be voluntary, unnecessary, and contrary to ordinary human conduct." *11 C.J.S. Breach of the Peace §4 (1995).* The Chapas argue that Chambers's conduct is of the type that has been found to constitute a breach of peace under Texas criminal law. Without further explanation, the Chapas assert that "[t]he act of taking children from the possession of their mother which leaves her in a hysterical crying state, is clearly a breach of peace."

2. CRIMINAL BREACH OF THE PEACE DISTINGUISHED

Whether a specific act constitutes a breach of the peace depends on the surrounding facts and circumstances in the particular case. *Miles v. State, 241 S.W.3d 28, 40 (Tex.Crim.App.2007) (citing Woods v. State, 152 Tex.Crim. 338, 341, 213 S.W.2d 685, 687 (1948)).* But in each of the cases on which the Chapas rely, the described conduct falls within the proscription adopted in *Head v. State.* Conduct such as driving while intoxicated, or publicly assaulting someone without provocation, with or without a weapon, poses an immediate threat of violent physical injury. Fleeing the scene of an accident or attempting concealment on private property during a manhunt are acts that invade "the security and protection which the laws afford to every citizen." *See id.* The public use of verbally abusive language that is "calculated to disturb" others is an act of "public indecorum" that is intended to disrupt the public peace or tranquility. Finally, all of these acts are "voluntary, unnecessary, and contrary to ordinary human conduct." *See 11 C.J.S. Breach of the Peace §4 (1995).*

In contrast, here the parties do not assert that Chambers behaved violently or threatened physical injury to anyone. *Cf. id.* ("[A]ctual or threatened violence is an essential element of a breach of the peace. ..."). Further, it is undisputed that Chambers did not know the children were in the vehicle when he moved it; thus, his actions cannot be appropriately characterized as "contrary to ordinary human conduct." *Cf. id.* When Chambers learned of the children's presence, he immediately ceased any attempt to repossess the vehicle and instead drove the children home. He did not communicate by word or gesture with Carlos or Maria Chapa before or during the attempted repossession. *Cf. Coggin v. State, 123 S.W.3d 82, 92 (Tex.App.–Austin 2003)* (suggesting that conduct that would "incite an immediate breach of the peace contemplates a face-to-face encounter").

In sum, the Chapas do not argue that Chambers's words or behavior toward the children or anyone else were intimidating, indecorous, or calculated to have a disturbing effect. *Cf. Heath v. Boyd, 141 Tex. 569, 573, 175 S.W.2d 214, 216 (1943)* (concluding that appellant who did not exhibit a weapon, "yell, shriek, curse, abuse or threaten anybody, or commit any other act denounced as a breach of the peace" by statute did not breach peace). On these facts, we cannot say that Chambers's conduct constitutes a "breach of the peace" as that phrase ordinarily is used in criminal or common law.

3. BREACH OF THE PEACE UNDER THE UNIFORM COMMERCIAL CODE.

The Chapas also rely on cases from other jurisdictions specifically addressing breaches of the peace as described in the Uniform Commercial Code concerning repossession of property. They cite *Robinson v. Citicorp National Services, Inc.*, a Missouri case in which Clarence Robinson defaulted on his automobile payments. *921 S.W.2d 52, 53 (Mo.Ct.App.1996).* Agents of the financing company's assignee attempted to repossess the car from property owned by Marie Robinson. *Id.* Marie's husband, Odell Robinson, Sr., "told [a repossession agent] to get off the property numerous times to no avail. The alleged trespass and breach of peace ensued, and Odell suffered a heart attack and died." *Id.* (emphasis added). This case stands for the proposition that the duty to avoid a breach of peace is non-delegable, but the conduct constituting a breach of the peace is not described. We can determine only that there was a confrontation on the appellant's property between repossession agents and a person objecting to the repossession. Here, however, Chambers removed the vehicle without confrontation and without trespassing on the Chapas' premises.

The Chapas also point to *Nixon v. Halpin. 620 So.2d 796 (Fla.Dist. Ct.App.1993).* In that case, Halpin, a repossession agent, was seen by the vehicle's owner and mistaken for a car thief. *Id.* at 797. The car's owner summoned his office mate, Nixon, and the two men attempted to detain

Halpin. *Id.* While driving away, Halpin struck Nixon. *Id.* The Nixon court concluded that the vehicle owner had a right to object to the attempted repossession. *Id.* at 798. It further held that if the creditor "had not already peaceably removed the vehicle when the owner objected, it's [sic] continuation with the attempt at repossession was no longer 'peaceable and without a breach of the peace.'" *Id.* In this case, however, the repossession agent had "already peaceably removed the vehicle" and did not continue to attempt repossession after he learned of the Chapa children's presence. Thus, the reasoning in Nixon supports the conclusion that Chambers did not breach the peace.[4]

4. UCC USAGE DISTINGUISHED

Most frequently, the expression "breach of the peace" as used in the Uniform Commercial Code "connotes conduct that incites or is likely to incite immediate public turbulence, or that leads to or is likely to lead to an immediate loss of public order and tranquility." *Johnson v. Grossinger Motorcorp, Inc.*, 324 Ill.App.3d 354, 257 Ill.Dec. 236, 753 N.E.2d 431, 440 (2001); *see also Madden v. Deere Credit Servs., Inc.*, 598 So.2d 860, 865 (Ala.1992) ("[S]ecured creditor, in exercising privilege to enter upon premises of another to repossess collateral, may not perpetrate '[a]ny act or action manifesting force or violence, or naturally calculated to provide a breach of peace' (quoting *Crews & Green v. Parker*, 192 Ala. 383, 68 So. 287, 288 (1915))"); *Salisbury Livestock Co. v. Colo. Cent. Credit Union*, 793 P.2d 470, 474 n. 3 (Wyo.1990) ("[A]lthough actual violence is not required to find 'breach of the peace,' within meaning of self-help repossession statute, disturbance or violence must be reasonably likely, and not merely a remote possibility."); *cf. Ash v. Peoples Bank of Greensboro*, 500 So.2d 5, 6–7 (Ala.1986) (no breach of peace when vehicle repossessed from public street while debtor inside house). In addition, "[b]reach of the peace … refers to conduct at or near and/or incident to seizure of property." *Jordan v. Citizens & S. Nat'l Bank of South Carolina*, 278 S.C. 449, 298 S.E.2d 213, 214 (1982); *see also Census Fed. Credit Union v. Wann*, 403 N.E.2d 348, 351–52 (Ind.Ct.App.1980) ("[E]ven in attempted repossession of a chattel off a street, parking lot or unenclosed space, if repossession is verbally or otherwise contested at actual time of and in immediate vicinity of attempted repossession by defaulting party or other person in control of chattel, secured party must desist and pursue his remedy in court.").

---

4 In addition, the Chapas rely on *Griffith v. Valley of the Sun Recovery & Adjustment Bureau, Inc.*, another case in which the repossession agent was mistaken for a car thief. 613 P.2d 1283, 1284 (1980). The agent set off the car's burglar alarm, and one of the car owner's neighbors responded to the scene with a shotgun. *Id.* The owner shouted for the gun, and as the neighbor passed the gun to the vehicle owner, it accidently discharged and severely injured a bystander. *Id.* As with the previous cases, this case is readily distinguishable from the present case, in which the repossession agent was unseen and no confrontation occurred.

Here, there is no evidence that Chambers proceeded with the attempted repossession over an objection communicated to him at, near, or incident to the seizure of the property. To the contrary, Chambers immediately "desisted" repossession efforts and peaceably returned the vehicle and the children when he learned of their presence. Moreover, Chambers actively avoided confrontation. By removing an apparently unoccupied vehicle from a public street when the driver was not present, he reduced the likelihood of violence or other public disturbance.

In sum, the Chapas have not identified and we have not found any case in which the repossession of a vehicle from a public street, without objection or confrontation, has been held to constitute a breach of the peace. *Cf. Wallace v. Chrysler Credit Corp.*, 743 F.Supp. 1228, 1231–33 (W.D.Va.1990) (deputy sheriff did not breach the peace when he repossessed debtor's truck because, even if he violated traffic regulation when he drove away, he did so before debtor had an opportunity to confront him); *Wann*, 403 N.E.2d at 351–52 (no breach of the peace occurred when repossession from parking lot was not verbally or otherwise contested). We therefore conclude that Chambers's conduct did not violate a duty imposed by section 9.609 of the Texas Business and Commerce Code.

PROBLEM 9–3

In each of the following cases, Ray's customer defaulted under the terms of Ray's security agreement, and Ray sent Repo Man to pick up the collateral. Determine, in each case, whether Repo Man went too far in his quest to recover Ray's collateral—did he breach the peace in violation of Article 9:

Case 1: The customer's eleven-year-old daughter answered the door when Repo Man knocked and let Repo Man into the house after he explained to her that her parents had called and asked him to come get the refrigerator. Repo Man then removed the refrigerator that was subject to Ray's security interest.

Case 2: When the customer drove away from his home leaving the garage door open, Repo Man, who had been watching the house from his car parked down the street, walked into the garage, picked up the shop vac that was subject to Ray's security interest, took it back to his car, and drove it to Ray's store.

Case 3: The customer had installed the range he bought from Ray in the RV trailer his family used for vacations. The trailer was parked to the side of the customer's driveway on a pod the customer had built for it. In the early morning hours one night, while the family was asleep, Repo Man entered the trailer though its unlocked door to remove the range. Once inside, he realized that he would need special tools to remove the range without severely damaging the trailer. Instead of leaving and returning with the proper tools, Repo Man hitched the trailer up to his pick-up truck and brought it back to Ray's shop.

Case 4:   Repo Man shows up at the customer's home dressed in a police officer uniform and tells the customer to let him into the house to pick up the dishwasher on which the customer had stopped making payments. The customer lets Repo Man enter and remove the dishwasher.

Case 5:   Repo Man sneaks onto the customer's patio through the back gate in the fence surrounding the property one night to pick up the gas grill subject to Ray's security interest. The customer hears Repo Man and confronts him on the patio—ordering Repo Man to leave. Repo Man leaves, but then comes back several hours later and successfully removes the grill.

Case 6:   Customer has moved all of her appliances into her garage while her kitchen is being remodeled. While the customer is at work one day, Repo Man shows up with a locksmith who picks the lock on the side door to the garage allowing Repo Man access. Repo Man backs his truck up to the garage and loads all of the appliances subject to Ray's security interest onto the truck. The locksmith did no damage to the lock—there was no physical evidence that it had been picked.

PROBLEM 9–4

Would any of your answers in the last Problem be different if Ray's security agreement had provided:

> The parties agree that upon default, and without notice, the secured party shall have the right to enter any premises and to retake possession of the property described herein.

PROBLEM 9–5

Is Ray personally liable for any trespass and damages caused by Repo Man while repossessing Ray's collateral? Would it matter if Ray could establish that Repo Man was working as an independent contractor when repossessing Ray's collateral?

D. DISPOSITION OF COLLATERAL

Repossession is the first step in converting the collateral into cash that is applied to pay down the debtor's obligation. To complete the collateral-to-cash conversion, the secured party will need to dispose of the collateral. In most cases, the secured party will resell the collateral and apply the proceeds from the sale to the debtor's unpaid obligation. But the secured party is not limited to reselling the collateral, and under certain circumstances the secured party can even keep the collateral in full or partial satisfaction of the debtor's obligation. Regardless of how the secured party disposes of the collateral, Article 9 requires that all aspects of that disposition be "commercially reasonable." 9-609.

Article 9 does not define commercially reasonable—leaving it instead to the courts to give content to the standard. Gilmore believed that "commercially reasonable" incorporated pre-Code sentiment that foreclosing creditors had an obligation to use best efforts to maximize the price received on resale of collateral, and the references to the effect of price on commercial reasonableness scattered among the comments to part 6 of Article 9, at the very least, recognize a connection between price and how the secured party goes about disposing of collateral. The concern with the price the secured party receives when it disposes of the collateral is not surprising in light of the fact that the debtor is liable for any deficiency that results when the proceeds from the sale of collateral are not sufficient to pay the entire amount of the debt owed by the debtor. And even though Article 9 proclaims that a low price by itself does not establish that a disposition was commercially unreasonable, 9-627, it's not necessary to wade very deeply into the pool of cases where the commercial reasonableness of a secured party's sale of collateral is at issue to discern that the "factors" developed by the courts to test commercial reasonableness "are almost entirely proxies for price." White & Summers, 1343. As White and Summers explain:

> Reasoning backward from a low price to a conclusion of commercial unreasonableness is not fair to the secured creditor. On the other hand, we suspect that low price (lower than the court thinks right) is in fact the single most important fact in most of these cases—even in cases where it is not identified as the basis for the court's finding of noncompliance with former 9-504. So, price is the eminence grise. Even though the court may not mention price, a high price will save the creditor and a low price is likely to put the creditor in trouble.

White & Summers at 1345 (footnotes omitted).

The following sections explore the major issues associated with the secured party's disposition of collateral after repossession.

1. NOTICE

One of the few specific requirements that Article 9 imposes on the foreclosing secured party is that the secured party provide notice of a disposition to interested parties. 9-611. The debtor, guarantors, and other secured parties with claims against the collateral each have an interest in making sure the disposition is conducted in a way that yields the best price for the collateral. Notice allows them to monitor the foreclosing secured party's conduct in disposing of the collateral for compliance with Article 9, and in the case of the debtor, the notice will also indicate when the debtor's right to redeem the collateral will terminate.

PROBLEM 9–6

DEBTOR = SHOP
OWNER + SPOUSE

Ray sold the local gourmet coffee shop all of the appliances—refrigerators, freezers, latte machines, dishwashers—it used in the operation of its business. He retained a security interest in all of the appliances he sold to secure the shop's promise to make monthly payments on the appliances. Ray also took a security interest in the personal checking account the owner shared with her spouse, which he perfected by letter agreement. The owner later obtained a line of credit from the local loan company to fund the shop's day-to-day operations. The loan company took a security interest in all of the shop's equipment, including the appliances Ray had sold it.

A year after it opened, the coffee shop began having financial problems. A customer severely burned by an excessively hot coffee he purchased successfully sued the shop and executed his judgment against the shop's personal property. That finally forced the owner to close the coffee shop and to default on his obligation to Ray. Ray repossessed of his collateral and has scheduled a foreclosure sale to dispose of the collateral. Which of these parties is entitled to notice of Ray's foreclosure sale? If any of the notices are returned undelivered, has Ray's obligation to provide commercially reasonable notice been satisfied? See 9-611.

PROBLEM 9–7

If Ray sells the collateral at a public auction, should he also provide notice to the public at large? Will his notice be commercially reasonable if he does not?

PROBLEM 9–8

If Ray's collateral had included the restaurant's inventory—meats, vegetables, fruits, etc.,—would he have to provide at least 10 days advance notice of its sale to meet the commercially reasonable safe harbor provided by 9-612?

Revised Article 9 creates safe harbors intended to eliminate many of the disputes regarding the timing and content of the required notice that accounted for much of the litigation over commercial reasonableness under Old Article 9. See 9-612 (timing), 9-613 and 614 (content). But as the following case demonstrates, creating safe harbors only benefits those who actually take advantage of them.

STATES RESOURCES CORP. v. GREGORY
Missouri Court of Appeals, Southern District, Division Two
339 S.W.3d 591 (Mo. Ct. App. 2011)

Francis, Jr., *Judge.*

Jeff Gregory ("Appellant") appeals the trial court's grant of summary judgment in favor of States Resources Corp. ("Respondent") for the deficiency amount on a promissory note. Because Respondent failed to establish it met the statutory notice requirements for a deficiency judgment, we reverse and remand this matter to the trial court.

FACTUAL AND PROCEDURAL HISTORY

On November 15, 2006, Appellant executed, for the purchase of a 2001 Ford F–250 truck (the "truck"), a consumer promissory note (the "Note") in the principal amount of $19,669.51, plus interest, and delivered it to Hume Bank. Repayment of the Note was secured by a security interest in the truck and a 1998 Chevrolet Lumina. The Federal Deposit Insurance Corporation ("FDIC") was subsequently appointed receiver of Hume Bank and in that capacity, became the owner and holder of the Note. FDIC then assigned the Note to Respondent. Appellant failed to make the required payments and defaulted on payment of the Note.

On September 24, 2008, Respondent sent Appellant a "RIGHT TO CURE" letter (the "September 24 Letter"), "VIA CERTIFIED & REGULAR MAIL," that notified Appellant he was in default under the terms of the Note and permitted him twenty-one days to cure the default. The letter advised Appellant:

> Allow this letter to serve as formal notice that your account is in default! You now have twenty-one (21) days to bring your account current.
>
> The amount needed to cure this default is $4,606.50. You must remit this amount either by cashier's check, money order, or Western Union Quick Collect within the next twenty-one (21) days.
>
> Please be advised that if the amount due is not paid within the next twenty-one (21) days. [sic] I will be left with no other alternative but to proceed with all remedies available to collect the total amount due on your account.
>
> If you voluntarily surrender possession of the vehicle, you could still owe additional money, money received from the sale of the collateral is deducted from the total amount you owe.
>
> I can be reached at either number below. If I am unavailable[,] please leave me a voice message and I will return your call as soon as possible.
>
> Your prompt attention to resolving this default is appreciated.

Notice of the September 24 Letter was delivered to Appellant's address on September 26, 2008, and again on October 1, 2008. However, Appellant failed to claim the September 24 Letter and it was returned to Respondent on October 11, 2008. Respondent conceded in its brief "it was premature to discuss the truck's disposition as of the date the September 24 Letter was sent."

Respondent repossessed the truck on October 19, 2008. On October 20, 2008, Respondent sent Appellant a second letter (the "October 20 Letter") by "CERTIFIED MAIL RETURN RECEIPT REQUESTED "and advised him the truck had been repossessed and the time period Appellant had to redeem the truck. This letter explained:

> Please be advised that the 2001 Ford F–250 truck, VIN No.: 1FTNX21L01EC71912 has been repossessed by States Resources Corp.
>
> You have ten (10) days to bring this account current and pay the repossession fees to redeem the vehicle. After the ten days or after October 30, 2008 the vehicle will be sold at public auction. The proceeds from the sale will be applied to your loan.
>
> If you would like to redeem the vehicle, please call me at 800–279–8295, extension 108 for the amount needed to redeem the vehicle.

The October 20 Letter was delivered to Appellant, and Appellant signed the certified receipt acknowledging receipt of that letter.

Sometime after October 20, 2008, the truck was sold by Manheim Auction ("Manheim")[5] at a "private 'dealer-only' [auction]." The sale of the truck brought a net sale price of $6,890.00. Appellant applied the net proceeds from the truck's sale to Appellant's debt. As of November 9, 2009, the principal amount remaining due on the Note was $10,259.37, together with accrued interest in the amount of $2,482.41 and late charges in the amount of $332.00, or a total owed by Appellant of $13,073.78. Interest accrued on the Note, after that date, in the amount of $2.59998 per day.

On January 4, 2010, Respondent filed its "Petition for Deficiency on Promissory Note" against Appellant. Appellant filed his answer on February 9, 2010. On April 16, 2010, Respondent filed its "Motion for Summary Judgment," along with its suggestions, statement of uncontroverted facts, and supporting exhibits. Respondent argued, in part:

> There are no genuine issues of material fact. [Appellant] defaulted on the Note, and pursuant to the term of the Note and after notice of the right to redeem, the collateral securing payment of the Note was sold at a commercially reasonable sale and the proceeds were applied to the balance due under the Note. [Respondent] is entitled to the deficiency still due and owing on the Note along with its costs in collection including reasonable attorney fees, all as a matter of law.

Respondent's statement of uncontroverted material facts included the following: "On or about October 19, 2008, [Respondent] repossessed the

---

5   December 4, 2008, is the date on the sale invoice from Manheim Auction.

[truck] from [Appellant], and on October 20, 2008, [Respondent] notified [Appellant] of his right to redeem the [truck], and of its intent to dispose of the [truck] at a public auction." In support, Respondent attached a copy of the October 20 Letter. Respondent's statement of uncontroverted facts also recited: "Thereafter, at a commercially reasonable sale, the [truck] was sold and the proceeds applied to the balance due under the Note." Respondent referenced as support the affidavit of Cory Butler ("Butler"), "account manager" for Respondent, and "a true and correct copy of the Manheim Auction Sale Invoice." Butler's affidavit stated in relevant part: "Thereafter, at a commercially reasonable sale, the [truck] was sold and the proceeds applied to the balance due under the Note." Respondent admits it "erroneously argued in its Motion for Summary Judgment that the truck had been sold at a 'public' auction."

Appellant filed his response to the Motion for Summary Judgment on May 25, 2010. Appellant admitted in part many of Respondent's facts. Specifically, he admitted "payments have not been made on the [truck] in question." Appellant objected throughout his response "to the use of any unauthenticated documents for purposes of sustaining [Respondent']s motion for summary judgment." Appellant denied "the [truck] was sold in a commercially reasonable manner," and specifically objected to the admissibility of Butler's affidavit as to the commercial reasonableness of the sale of the truck "as such testimony amounts to nothing more than a legal conclusion unsupported by underlying facts" and "is void of any foundation or statements of qualification of [Butler] to act as an expert for the purpose of testifying to the standard of a 'commercially reasonable' sale of the [truck] in question. ..." Appellant also argued Respondent "failed to authenticate the auction sale invoice."

Appellant attached his affidavit stating he did not "recall" receiving the September 24 Letter or the October 20 Letter. He also stated:

> I do not believe that the repossession and sale of the [truck] in question was handled in a commercially reasonable manner. Although I cannot speak to the legal definition of 'commercially reasonable,' I do not believe that I received all required notices and I do not believe that the [truck] in question was sold for its value.

On August 12, 2010, the trial court concluded Appellant failed "to controvert [Respondent]'s allegations or create a dispute as to material facts" and considered Respondent's statement of uncontroverted material facts "as either admitted or proven and not in dispute." Summary judgment was entered against Appellant and in favor of Respondent. This appeal followed.

Appellant alleges the trial court erred in granting Respondent's summary judgment because: (1) Respondent failed to prove as a matter of law it complied with statutorily mandated notice requirements for disposition of collateral; (2) Respondent's petition failed to plead facts or provide supporting documents showing Respondent met the statutory preconditions of a commercially reasonable sale ...

FAILURE TO PROVE COMPLIANCE WITH NOTICE REQUIREMENT

Appellant claims the notice sent to him did not comply with section 400.9–614 and, therefore, precludes a deficiency judgment against him. Respondent submits its notice substantially complied with the notice requirements and thus, is entitled to summary judgment as a matter of law. The determinative issue is whether Respondent established it met the statutory notice requirements for a deficiency judgment as a matter of law.

Section 400.9–611(b) requires a secured party to provide the debtor with reasonable notice of its intent to sell the collateral. The content and form of the notice required for consumer transactions are dictated by section 400.9–614. Subsection (1) of that statute sets out what must be included in the notice:

> (1) A notification of disposition must provide the following information:
>
> (A) The information specified in section 400.9–613(1);
>
> (B) A description of any liability for a deficiency of the person to which the notification is sent;
>
> (C) A telephone number from which the amount that must be paid to the secured party to redeem the collateral under section 400.9–623 is available; and
>
> (D) A telephone number or mailing address from which additional information concerning the disposition and the obligation secured is available[.]

§400.9–614(1). Section 400.9–614(1)(A), with reference to section 400.9–613(1), requires the notification also:

> (A) Describe the debtor and the secured party;
>
> (B) Describe the collateral that is the subject of the intended disposition;
>
> (C) State the method of intended disposition;
>
> (D) State that the debtor is entitled to an accounting of the unpaid indebtedness and state the charge, if any, for an accounting; and
>
> (E) State the time and place of a public disposition or the time after which any other disposition is to be made.

The statute does not require a "particular phrasing" of the notification. *§400.9–614(2).*

"The purpose of statutory notice is to apprise a debtor of the details of a sale so that the debtor may take whatever action he deems necessary to protect his interest." *Chrysler Capital Corp. v. Cotlar, 762 S.W.2d 859, 861 (Mo.App. E.D.1989).* Proper notice provides the debtor the opportunity to: (1) discharge the debt and reclaim the collateral, (2) find another purchaser, or (3) verify that the sale is conducted in a commercially reasonable manner. *Mancuso v. Long Beach Acceptance Corp., 254 S.W.3d 88, 95 (Mo.App. W.D.2008).*

"The right to a deficiency judgment accrues only when there is strict compliance with statutory requirements." *Chrysler Capital Corp., 762 S.W.2d at 861*. Any doubt as to whether there has been compliance is to be resolved in favor of the debtor. *Mancuso, 254 S.W.3d at 92*. A creditor's failure to give proper notice, waives the creditor's entitlement to pursue a deficiency judgment. *Chrysler Capital Corp., 762 S.W.2d at 861*.

Here, the September 24 Letter and October 20 Letter are the only evidence of notification to Appellant of disposition of the truck. As such, we first determine whether the September 24 Letter constitutes a notification or part of Respondent's notification of disposition.

Section 400.9–611(b) requires a secured party that disposes of collateral to send a "reasonable authenticated notification of disposition." … Here, Respondent is essentially arguing that because the September 24 Letter contained some of the information also required under section 400.9–614, it was in fact part of their notification of disposition to Appellant. We decline to apply Respondent's reasoning. A letter that does not inform the debtor of the creditor's intent to sell the collateral—even if it contains some of the information required in a notification of disposition—cannot provide reasonable notification of disposition.

The September 24 Letter did not inform Appellant of Respondent's intent to sell his truck. In fact, Respondent admits in its brief this was because, at that point, it was premature to discuss the truck's disposition:

> [A]t the time the September 24 Letter was sent, Appellant's truck was still in [Appellant's] possession and had not been repossessed. It [was] clear from [the] September 24 Letter that Respondent was still hoping that Appellant would voluntarily pay his debt or at least surrender the truck … *it was premature to discuss the truck's disposition as of the date the September 24 Letter was sent.*

(Emphasis added). Thus, it would have been impossible to provide reasonable notification of disposition when there was in fact no impending disposition of the truck of which to inform Appellant. In addition to Appellant's admission that this letter was not sent to discuss the disposition of the truck, the content of the letter also does not inform Appellant his truck will be sold.[6] The only reference to a possible sale of the truck is noted in the limited case of Appellant's voluntary surrender of the truck.

Adhering to Respondent's reasoning would permit almost any correspondence to be considered part of the requisite notification of disposition if it happened to contain some of the information required by section 400.9–614. For obvious reasons, this would defeat the purpose of the statutory notice requirement of apprising a debtor of the details of a sale so that the debtor could take whatever action he deemed necessary to protect his interest and would create significant uncertainty as to what actually constituted proper notice.

---

6   The September 24 Letter begins: "Allow this letter to serve as formal notice that your account is in default!"

Thus, the September 24 Letter should not be considered part of Respondent's notification of disposition. Accordingly, we look to the October 20 Letter to determine whether it establishes Respondent fulfilled the statutory notice requirements as a matter of law.

First, we note Respondent is misguided in arguing substantial compliance with the notice requirements entitled Respondent to a deficiency judgment. In support of this argument, Respondent erroneously cites to section 400.9–613(2)–(3), which sets forth a more relaxed notification provision that is applicable "[e]xcept in consumer-goods transactions." Section 400.9–614 provides the rules for consumer-goods transactions, such as this transaction, and by reference only incorporates the requirements contained in section 400.9–613(1). Contrary to Respondent's contention, in consumer-goods transactions, strict compliance is required. *Chrysler Capital Corp., 762 S.W.2d at 861.* While we acknowledge the statute does not require a "particular phrasing of the notification," a notification that lacks any of the information set forth in section 400.9–614(1) is insufficient as a matter of law.[7] *Uniform Commercial Code Comment 2 to section 400.9–614.*

The October 20 Letter failed to meet the statutory notification requirements in the following respects: (1) it did not state Appellant is entitled to an accounting of the unpaid indebtedness; (2) it failed to provide a description of any liability for a deficiency; and (3) it incorrectly stated the nature of the sale.

An "accounting" is a record that: (1) is authenticated by the secured party, (2) indicates the aggregate unpaid secured obligations within thirty-five days of the record, and (3) identifies the components of the obligations in reasonable detail. *§400.9–102(a)(4)(A)–(C).* Here, the October 20 Letter neither provided Appellant with an accounting, nor did it inform Appellant he was entitled to an accounting as required by section 400.9–613(1)(D).

Furthermore, the October 20 Letter failed to provide a "description of any liability for a deficiency" as required by section 400.9–614(1)(B). The letter merely states, "The proceeds from the sale will be applied to your loan."

Finally, the October 20 Letter stated the truck would be sold at "public auction" without including the time and place of a public disposition as required for a public disposition by section 400.9–614(1)(E) with reference to section 400.9–613(1)(A). We additionally note this information was incorrect as it was actually sold at a "private dealer-only auction." Any doubt as to whether there has been compliance is to be resolved in favor of the debtor. *Mancuso, 254 S.W.3d at 92.*

Respondent has not proven strict compliance with these notice provisions and, therefore, is not entitled to a deficiency judgment as a matter of law based

---

7 Although this strict compliance requirement can result in harsh consequences for creditors who fail to provide proper notification, the legislature provided clear requirements for consumer-goods transactions to ensure consumer protection, and the statute provides clear instructions and a "Safe–Harbor Form of Notification" to assist creditors in complying with the notification requirement.

upon the record before us. *See Chrysler Capital Corp., 762 S.W.2d at 861.* Point I is granted. We reverse and remand to the trial court for further proceedings not inconsistent with this opinion.

RAHMEYER, P.J., and BATES, J., concur.

PROBLEM 9–9

If those parties entitled to notice of Ray's foreclosure sale in Problem 9–6 receive it one week before the sale is to take place, is the notice commercially reasonable under Article 9? See 9-612. What must be included in a commercially reasonable notice? See 9-613.

PROBLEM 9–10

Would your answer in Problem 9–9 be different if the debtor had used the appliance he bought from Ray in his home kitchen? See 9-612. Could Ray use the same notice he sent to the parties in Problem 9–9? See 9-614.

2. SALE OF COLLATERAL

Most secured parties are not interested in keeping the collateral after repossession—the bank that loaned the debtor the money to buy industrial equipment doesn't have room in its lobby to store that equipment after repossession. The goal of the repossessing secured party is to convert the collateral to cash and use that cash to pay down the debtor's obligation. Although Article 9 does not dictate how the secured party accomplishes this conversion, it assumes that in most cases, the secured party will convert the collateral to cash by selling it. Traditionally, collateral was converted to cash by way of a public sale—the collateral was auctioned off to the highest bidder at a sale open to the public in general, and often held on the steps of the local courthouse. These auctions on the steps of the courthouse were believed to provide the best prospects for obtaining the highest price—with everyone interested in the goods up for auction present and competitively bidding against one another, the price ultimately paid would fairly reflect the actual market value of the collateral. In reality, however, these sales on the steps of the courthouse seldom lived up to their billing:

> At a "public sale," it may be hoped, there will be that lively concourse of bidders which will … drive the price up to those Himalayan peaks of fair value and true worth. It may be hoped but the hope will almost certainly be disappointed. The concourse of bidders at the typical foreclosure sale, be it ever so "public," is apt to be about as lively as a group of mourners at a funeral.
>
> Gilmore, at 1242.

Article 9 retains the public sale as an option for disposing of collateral but also provides that collateral may be sold through a private sale.

PROBLEM 9–11

On the 15th of each month, Ray holds a public auction for all of the appliances he repossessed the previous month. Notice goes out to those entitled to notice on the 1st of the month informing them that their appliances will be sold "on the 15th of this month at the store." Ads announcing the auctions are placed in the local newspaper the first and second weeks of the month. All repossessed appliances that are not sold the day of the auction are sold the next day to Discount Appliances, the local second-hand appliance store. No additional notice goes out before the sale to Discount. Discount is owned by Ray's son and seldom pays more than garage sale prices for the repossessed appliances it buys from Ray. Are the sales Ray makes to Discount commercially reasonable under Article 9? See 9-611, 9-615, and 9-610 Comment 10.

PROBLEM 9–12

Last month, on the day Ray had scheduled the public auction for repossessed appliances, the National Weather Service had issued a hurricane warning for his area, and although no hurricane hit, the severe storms that day produced 10 inches of rain and wind gusts during the day of 50 mph. No one showed up for the auction, so Ray sold everything to Discount. Was Ray's disposition of the repossessed appliances commercially reasonable? See 9-610.

PROBLEM 9–13

Ray has a policy of not making repairs or servicing any of the appliances he repossesses before he disposes of them. He offers them for sale in whatever condition they happen to be in when Repo Man brings them into the shop. He doesn't even bother to wipe them down or clean them in any way. Does the requirement that "every aspect of a disposition of collateral, including the method, manner, time, place, and other terms, must be commercially reasonable," require more than just selling the stuff in whatever condition it's in when he repossesses it? See 9-610 and Comment 4.

3. RETENTION OF COLLATERAL BY SECURED PARTY: STRICT FORECLOSURE

Occasionally, the secured party may want to keep the collateral after it has been repossessed. If the secured party believes the value of the collateral exceeds the amount owed by the debtor, or that disposing of the collateral would be inconvenient and/or expensive, or that a suit on any deficiency would be fruitless, the secured party might be willing to waive all or part of its claim against the debtor in exchange for being able to keep the collateral. The common law had long recognized a creditor's right to "strictly foreclose"—to keep its collateral—and Old Article 9 included it as an alternative to disposition of the collateral by the secured party. Revised Article 9 continues strict foreclosure as an alternative to resale within a revised framework intended to clarify strict foreclosure procedures. 9-620-9-622.

The following problems introduce and develop the basic requirements for strict foreclosure.

PROBLEM 9–14

Ray repossessed a Sub-Zero refrigerator from a customer last year and finally sold it at the last monthly auction, nearly 18 months after it had been repossessed. Ray initially held it out of the monthly auctions because his nephew had expressed an interest in buying it. But the nephew never came up with the money, and the refrigerator was left in a seldom visited area in the store's large storeroom. The market value of the refrigerator had dropped significantly during the 18 months Ray had it because Sub-Zero had introduced all new models and no longer made the model Ray had repossessed. As a result, Ray is seeking a large deficiency judgment against the customer. The customer has asserted that by holding the refrigerator for 18 months, Ray should be deemed to have strictly foreclosed his security interest and waived any deficiency. Is the customer right? See 9-620.

PROBLEM 9–15

Does the secured party have an absolute right to strictly foreclose on repossessed collateral? See 9-620(a). In the last Problem, could Ray have kept the refrigerator and sold it to his nephew if the customer had paid 70% of what she owed on the refrigerator prior to its repossession? See 9-620(e).

4. RECOVERY OF DEFICIENCY

More often than not, the proceeds received on the secured party's disposition of the collateral will be insufficient to pay off the debtor's obligation in its entirety. This is really not surprising—collateral depreciates in value over time, repossessed goods may not have been properly maintained by a debtor struggling to avoid default—there are any number of legitimate explanations for why the value of collateral is less than the amount owed by the debtor by the time it has been repossessed and sold.

But debtors are usually disappointed when this happens and are quick to find fault with the conduct of the secured party. As a result, when the secured party subsequently brings suit to recover the deficiency—the amount of the debtor's obligation that remains after the proceeds from the sale of the collateral have been applied to the debt—debtors frequently challenge the reasonableness of the secured party's conduct in repossessing and disposing of the collateral. As the *Southern Developers* case illustrates, debtors have a powerful incentive for making such challenges: if the challenge succeeds, the court can deny the secured party's deficiency claim in whole or in part.

SOUTHERN DEVELOPERS & EARTHMOVING, INC. V. CATERPILLAR FIN. SERVICES CORP.
Court of Appeal of Florida, Second District
56 So.3d 56 (Fla. Dist. Ct. App. 2d Dist. 2011)

Villanti, *Judge.*

A.

Southern Developers [and Ronald Gill], Appeal the final summary judgment entered in favor of Caterpillar Financial Services Corporation (CAT) in its action for a deficiency judgment under a promissory note and security agreement covering industrial earthmoving equipment that CAT sold to Southern and subsequently repossessed. Because CAT failed to prove the amount of the deficiency judgment to which it was entitled, summary judgment was improperly granted in its favor. Therefore, we reverse the final summary judgment and remand for further proceedings. This ruling requires us also to reverse the subsequent final judgment for attorney's fees entered in favor of CAT.

In 2003, Southern purchased five pieces of industrial earthmoving equipment from CAT. Southern executed a promissory note and security agreement as part of the purchase, and Gill signed a personal guaranty of the note. The following year, Southern allegedly breached the terms of the note by failing to make the payments as required. Based on the terms of the security agreement, CAT retook possession of the equipment. CAT subsequently sold four pieces of the equipment through a private sale and the remaining piece of equipment through an Internet auction.[8] When those sales did not produce funds sufficient to cover the amount due under the note, CAT sued Southern for its alleged breach of the note, and it sued Gill for his alleged breach of the personal guaranty.

CAT's amended complaint alleged that it had sold the repossessed equipment in a commercially reasonable manner but had recovered less than the amount of the debt owed by Southern. CAT therefore sought a deficiency judgment from Southern. In its answer, Southern specifically denied that the

---

8   CAT originally noticed the sale of all five pieces of equipment through private sales. The first notice, dated September 30, 2004, scheduled a private sale of four pieces of the equipment for October 11, 2004. The second notice, dated December 8, 2004, scheduled the private sale of the remaining piece of equipment, a "Caterpillar D6MLGP track-type tractor," for December 20, 2004. For reasons undisclosed by the record, the December 20 private sale was not completed. Instead, on March 28, 2005, CAT sent a new "notice of public sale" for that tractor, indicating that the new notice "took precedence over the previous notice" and indicating that the tractor would be sold at an Internet auction on April 7, 2005. Apparently this tractor was sold at this Internet auction.

sale of the repossessed equipment had been done in a commercially reasonable manner, and it also raised this claim as an affirmative defense.

CAT subsequently filed a motion for summary judgment, in which it again asserted that it had sold the repossessed equipment in a commercially reasonable manner. In support of its motion, CAT filed the affidavit of a "Special Accounts Representative," who alleged that proper notice was given to Southern and Gill of both of the intended private sales and the subsequent Internet auction. The affidavit also authenticated the various sale notices that were sent to both Southern and Gill and alleged again that the sales were all commercially reasonable. However, neither the affidavit nor the motion provided any details of the sales transactions themselves. CAT did not file any of the contracts or purchase orders relating to the sales, and it submitted nothing to establish what amount it obtained for each piece of repossessed equipment. Further, neither CAT's motion nor its affidavit included any facts concerning the general practices and methodology of selling used equipment in the industrial earthmoving equipment industry.

In response to CAT's motion for summary judgment, Southern filed Gill's affidavit in which he alleged that, based on his experience in owning and using industrial earthmoving equipment, sale of the repossessed equipment through private sales or Internet auctions was not a commercially reasonable practice in the industrial earthmoving equipment industry. Gill alleged that this type of equipment was more usually sold through public auctions specifically held for this purpose. Attached to Gill's affidavit was a letter from Richie Brothers Auctioneers, which indicated that Richie Brothers would have purchased the equipment for $730,000—an amount $22,589.40 more than what CAT had obtained through its private sale and Internet auction. This unsigned letter from Richie Brothers was not sworn or certified, nor was it otherwise authenticated in Gill's affidavit. Further, Gill alleged in his affidavit that the $730,000 figure from Richie Brothers was not a firm price for the equipment but rather was a "floor" below which the auction price for the equipment would not go.

Despite this apparent factual dispute concerning whether the sale of the repossessed equipment was commercially reasonable and despite the lack of any documentation from CAT concerning the details of the sales it conducted, the trial court granted final summary judgment in favor of CAT in the amount of $140,812. This figure is the amount of the debt less the amount recovered by CAT through its private sale and Internet auction less the $22,589.40 difference between CAT's recovery and the amount listed in the Richie Brothers' letter. Notably, the judgment contains no finding of fact as to whether either sale of the repossessed equipment was conducted in a commercially reasonable manner. Southern and Gill now seek review of this final judgment.

Under Article 9 of the Uniform Commercial Code, as codified in section 679.609(1), Florida Statutes (2006), a secured party, such as CAT, may take possession of collateral after a default by the debtor. The secured party then "may sell, lease, license, or otherwise dispose of any or all of the collateral in its present condition or following any commercially reasonable preparation or processing." *§679.610(1)*. However, if the secured party wishes to preserve its right to seek a deficiency judgment, the secured party is not at liberty to dispose of the repossessed collateral in any manner it wants. Instead, "[e]very aspect of a disposition of collateral, including the method, manner, time, place, and other terms, must be commercially reasonable." *§679.610(2)*. This rule is in place "'to protect the debtor, because [it] help[s] prevent the creditor from acquiring the collateral at less than its true value or unfairly understating its value so as to obtain an excessive deficiency judgment.'" *Burley v. Gelco Corp.*, 976 So.2d 97, 100 (Fla. 5th DCA 2008) (quoting *Allen v. Coates*, 661 So.2d 879, 884 (Fla. 1st DCA 1995)).

If a secured party elects to repossess and resell its collateral, the debtor is liable for any deficiency remaining after the sale as a matter of law. *See §679.608(1)(d); see also Weiner v. Am. Petrofina Mktg., Inc.*, 482 So.2d 1362, 1364 (Fla.1986). However, the amount of the deficiency judgment to which the secured party is entitled is a matter of fact, not law. To establish entitlement to a deficiency judgment in a certain amount, the secured party must show that its disposition of the collateral was commercially reasonable but nevertheless resulted in the recovery of an amount less than the amount of the secured debt. *Burley*, 976 So.2d at 101. Accordingly, if the debtor places the commercial reasonableness of the disposition of collateral "in issue," the secured party has the burden to establish that every aspect of that disposition was commercially reasonable. *See §679.626(2); see also Weiner*, 482 So.2d at 1364–65; *Burley*, 976 So.2d at 100. Alternatively, the secured party may concede that its disposition of the collateral was commercially unreasonable, introduce evidence to prove the fair market value of the collateral at the time of repossession, and allow the debtor an additional credit for the difference between the fair market value and the amount obtained by the secured party at the commercially unreasonable sale. *See Weiner*, 482 So.2d at 1364. As applicable to this case, "commercial reasonableness" is defined as a disposition "in conformity with reasonable commercial practices among dealers in the type of property that was the subject of the disposition." *§679.627(2)(c)*.

Here, CAT's pleadings and its affidavit in support of its motion for summary judgment specifically alleged that its sales of the repossessed equipment were commercially reasonable. Southern disputed the commercial reasonableness of the sales in its pleadings. Thus at the summary judgment hearing, the commercial reasonableness of the sales was in issue and, to be entitled to summary judgment in its favor, CAT was required to establish that it sold the repossessed equipment "in conformity with reasonable commercial practices among dealers" of industrial earthmoving equipment. However, CAT submitted absolutely no evidence to satisfy its burden on this issue.

The only evidence offered by CAT in support of its motion for summary judgment was the affidavit of its "Special Accounts Representative" with the attached notices of sale. While this evidence shows that CAT complied with the procedural requirements of section 679.611, it does not bear on the question of whether the sales themselves were conducted in conformity with the reasonable commercial practices among dealers in the industrial earth-moving equipment industry. On the issue of commercial reasonableness, CAT failed to submit the purchase contracts for any of the pieces of repossessed equipment or any information to establish the sale price it obtained for any single piece of the repossessed equipment. Nor did CAT submit any evidence to support its implied assertion that the prices it obtained through the private sale and Internet auction were higher than those it could have obtained by selling the repossessed equipment through other means. CAT also presented no evidence concerning how contracts for the sale of used industrial earth-moving equipment are customarily reached within the industry and whether private sales and Internet auctions are commonly used. Thus, there was simply no evidentiary basis upon which the trial court could have found that CAT's sale of the repossessed equipment was commercially reasonable, and because CAT failed to carry its evidentiary burden to establish commercial reasonableness, it was not entitled to final summary judgment in its favor.

In this appeal, CAT contends that the issue of damages is moot because it established the amount of the deficiency judgment through the alternative method of proving that the amount it recovered through its sales was less than the fair market value of the repossessed equipment. We first note that CAT never alleged or asserted this alternative measure of damages in any pleading. Instead, CAT's position until the very start of the hearing on the motion for summary judgment was that its sales were commercially reasonable and that it was entitled to a deficiency judgment measured by the difference between the amount of the debt and the amount obtained through its sales of the equipment. Southern had no notice that CAT would concede commercial unreasonableness at the hearing and then attempt to obtain a deficiency judgment based on an alternative measure of damages. Thus, we question whether the trial court properly granted CAT's motion based on a measure of damages raised for the first time at the hearing on the motion for summary judgment.

However, even if this measure of damages was properly considered by the court, CAT failed to meet its burden of proof. When a sale of collateral is commercially unreasonable, a presumption arises that "the fair market value of the collateral at the time of repossession was equal to the amount of the total debt that it secured." *Weiner, 482 So.2d at 1365.* To overcome this presumption, the secured party must offer evidence to prove that the fair market value of the collateral was less than the amount of the debt. *Id.* Until CAT offered such evidence, it was not entitled to a deficiency judgment at all.

Here, CAT offered no evidence to establish the fair market value of the equipment at the time of repossession. Instead, it "conceded" to the amount included in the Richie Brothers' letter. But when Southern attempted to use the Richie Brothers' letter to prove commercial unreasonableness, the trial court specifically declined to accept the letter as evidence. The court properly noted that the letter was not sworn to or otherwise authenticated so as to make it admissible into evidence. Having rejected the letter as inadmissible when offered by Southern, the court could not then allow CAT to rely on the same inadmissible letter as proof of fair market value because a summary judgment may not be predicated on inadmissible evidence. *See Fla. R. Civ. P. 1.510(c), (e)* (providing that a motion for summary judgment must be based on the "affidavits, answers to interrogatories, admissions, depositions, and other materials as would be admissible in evidence" and that "[s]worn or certified copies of all papers or parts thereof referred to in an affidavit shall be attached thereto"). Thus, CAT failed to rebut the presumption that the fair market value was equal to the amount of the debt and so was not entitled to a deficiency judgment in its favor.

As the court explained in *Southern Developers*, the debtor is "liable, for any deficiency remaining after the sale [of the collateral] as a matter of law." Article 9 presumes the secured party is entitled to recover the deficiency—the secured party is not required to prove, as part of its case in chief, that its repossession and disposition of the collateral were commercially reasonable in order to recover a deficiency. But the debtor in a non-consumer transaction can contest the secured party's right to recover a deficiency by "putting in issue" the commercial reasonableness of the secured party's actions. Once the debtor has raised the issue, the secured party has the burden of proving that its repossession and disposition of the collateral were commercially reasonable. If the secured party is unable to prove that its conduct was commercially reasonable, a presumption arises under Article 9 that the proceeds from the sale of the collateral would have been sufficient to satisfy the debtor's obligation in its entirety. In which case, there would be no claim for a deficiency. The secured party, however, can rebut the presumption by proving that even if its conduct had been commercially reasonable, the proceeds from the sale of the collateral would still not have been sufficient to satisfy the debtor's obligation in full. The secured party would then be entitled to recover the difference between the amount the debtor owed and the amount of proceeds that a commercially reasonable disposition of the collateral would have produced.

PROBLEM 9–16

Ray has sued several of the customer-debtors whose collateral was sold under the circumstances in Problem 9–12 for the deficiency that remained after he applied the proceeds from the sale of their appliances to discount to their outstanding balances. Each of the customers has challenged the commercial reasonableness of Ray's disposition of their appliances. Three of the customers were consumer buyers. How will the court calculate Ray's deficiency against the non-consumer buyers if Ray is unable to convince the court that the disposition was commercially reasonable? How will it calculate Ray's deficiency against the consumer buyers if the resale was commercially unreasonable? See 9-626.

CPSIA information can be obtained
at www.ICGtesting.com
Printed in the USA
LVHW020251210723
752936LV00011B/39